Apache Adaptation to Hispanic Rule

As a definitive study of the poorly understood *Apaches de paz*, this book explains how war-weary, mutually suspicious Apaches and Spaniards negotiated an ambivalent compromise after 1786 that produced over four decades of uneasy peace across the Southwest. In response to drought and military pressure, thousands of Apaches settled near Spanish presidios in a system of reservation-like *establecimientos*, or settlements, stretching from Laredo to Tucson. Far more significant than previously assumed, the establecimientos constituted the earliest and most extensive set of military-run reservations in the Americas and served as an important precedent for Indian reservations in the United States. As a case study of indigenous adaptation to imperial power on colonial frontiers and borderlands, this book reveals the importance of Apache–Hispanic diplomacy in reducing cross-cultural violence and the limits of indigenous acculturation and assimilation into empires and states.

Matthew Babcock earned his Ph.D. from Southern Methodist University, his M.A. from the University of New Mexico, and his B.A. from Dartmouth College. He is currently Assistant Professor of History at the University of North Texas at Dallas and is a recipient of a prestigious Dornsife Long-Term Research Fellowship at the Huntington Library. He has written numerous journal articles and book chapters, which have been published in Spain, Canada (Quebec), and the United States. He is a member of the American Historical Association, American Society for Ethnohistory, Western History Association, and Texas and East Texas State Historical Associations.

Studies in North American Indian History

Editors

Frederick Hoxie, *University of Illinois, Urbana-Champaign*

Neal Salisbury, *Smith College, Massachusetts*

Tiya Miles, *University of Michigan, Ann Arbor*

Ned Blackhawk, *Yale University*

This series is designed to exemplify new approaches to the Native American past. In recent years scholars have begun to appreciate the extent to which Indians, whose cultural roots extended back for thousands of years, shaped the North American landscape as encountered by successive waves of immigrants. In addition, because Native Americans continually adapted their cultural traditions to the realities of the Euro-American presence, their history adds a thread of non-Western experience to the tapestry of American culture. Cambridge Studies in North American Indian History brings outstanding examples of this new scholarship to a broad audience. Books in the series link Native Americans to broad themes in American history and place the Indian experience in the context of social and economic change over time.

Also in the series

Kiara Vigil *Indigenous Intellectuals: Sovereignty, Citizenship, and the American Imagination, 1880–1930*

Lucy Murphy *Great Lakes Creoles: A French-Indian Community on the Northern Borderlands, Prairie du Chien, 1750–1860*

Richard White *The Middle Ground, 2nd. ed.: Indians, Empires, and Republics in the Great Lakes Region, 1650–1815*

Gary Warrick *A Population History of the Huron-Petun, A.D. 500–1650*

John Bowes *Exiles and Pioneers: Indians in the Trans-Mississippi West*

David J. Silverman *Faith and Boundaries: Colonists, Christianity, and the Community among the Wampanoag Indians of Martha's Vineyard, 1600–1871*

Jeffrey Ostler *The Plains Sioux and U.S. Colonialism from Lewis and Clark to Wounded Knee*

Claudio Saunt *A New Order of Things: Property, Power, and the Transformation of the Creek Indians, 1733–1816*

Jean M. O'Brien *Dispossession by Degrees: Indian Land and Identity in Natick, Massachusetts, 1650–1790*

Frederick E. Hoxie *Parading through History: The Making of the Crow Nation in America, 1805–1935*

Colin G. Calloway *The American Revolution in Indian Country: Crisis and Diversity in Native American Communities*

Sidney L. Harring *Crow Dog's Case: American Indian Sovereignty, Tribal Law, and United States Law in the Nineteenth Century*

Apache Adaptation to Hispanic Rule

MATTHEW BABCOCK

University of North Texas, Dallas

CAMBRIDGE
UNIVERSITY PRESS

CAMBRIDGE
UNIVERSITY PRESS

University Printing House, Cambridge CB2 8BS, United Kingdom

One Liberty Plaza, 20th Floor, New York, NY 10006, USA

477 Williamstown Road, Port Melbourne, VIC 3207, Australia

314-321, 3rd Floor, Plot 3, Splendor Forum, Jasola District Centre, New Delhi - 110025, India

79 Anson Road, #06-04/06, Singapore 079906

Cambridge University Press is part of the University of Cambridge.

It furthers the University's mission by disseminating knowledge in the pursuit of education, learning and research at the highest international levels of excellence.

www.cambridge.org
Information on this title: www.cambridge.org/9781107547322

© Matthew Babcock 2016

This publication is in copyright. Subject to statutory exception and to the provisions of relevant collective licensing agreements, no reproduction of any part may take place without the written permission of Cambridge University Press.

First published 2016
First paperback edition 2018

A catalogue record for this publication is available from the British Library

Library of Congress Cataloging in Publication data
NAMES: Babcock, Matthew, author.
TITLE: Apache adaptation to Hispanic rule / Matthew Babcock.
DESCRIPTION: Dallas : University of North Texas, 2016. | Series: Studies in North American Indian history | Includes bibliographical references and index.
IDENTIFIERS: LCCN 2016019202 | ISBN 9781107121386 (Hardback : alk. paper)
SUBJECTS: LCSH: Apache Indians–Government relations. | Apache Indians–History.
CLASSIFICATION: LCC E99.A6 B125 2016 | DDC 979.004/9725–dc23 LC record available at https://lccn.loc.gov/2016019202

ISBN 978-1-107-12138-6 Hardback
ISBN 978-1-107-54732-2 Paperback

Cambridge University Press has no responsibility for the persistence or accuracy of URLs for external or third-party internet websites referred to in this publication, and does not guarantee that any content on such websites is, or will remain, accurate or appropriate.

Contents

List of Figures	*page* vii
List of Maps	ix
List of Tables	xi
Acknowledgments	xiii
A Note on Terminology	xvii
Introduction	1
1 Peace and War	19
2 Precedents	61
3 Ambivalent Compromise	105
4 Acculturation and Adaptation	141
5 Collapse and Independence	172
6 Resilience and Survival	213
Epilogue	250
Appendix	261
Bibliography	265
Index	287

Figures

1.1 A Ndé painted deerskin by Naiche, ca. 1909. *page* 22
1.2 Detail of map depicting the Ndé homeland as 'Terra Apachorum,' or 'Apache Country,' ca. 1705. 37
2.1 Detail of Nicolas de Lafora's 1771 Map depicting the outcome of the Marqués de Rubí's 1768 policy recommendations, with eastern Apache groups confined to the margins of the southern plains and Comanches north of the Red River. 75
4.1 Detail of Alexander von Humboldt's 1804 Map of the Kingdom of New Spain, showing Apache groups west of the Rio Grande. 152
4.2 Ndé playing cards for the game Monte. 157

Maps

I.1 Ndé resettlement, 1786–1798	page 3
I.2 The Apache–Spanish frontier, ca. 1800	4
1.1 The Ndé and their neighbors, ca. 1630	20
1.2 The expanding Ndé homeland, 1670–1718	34
2.1 Eastern Apache movements and resettlement in missions, 1715–1766	67
2.2 Ndé movements, peace pacts, and resettlement near Presidios, 1732–1783	78
3.1 Spanish–Indian military campaigns into the Apachería, 1786–1798	109
3.2 The Ndé homeland and raiding and trading routes, 1766–1846	124
5.1 The Apache–Mexican frontier, 1821–1832	198
6.1 The Apache–Mexican frontier and revived *establecimientos*, 1842–1845	214

Tables

3.1 Summary of Apache and Spanish Hostilities in the Interior
Provinces of New Spain, 1778–95 (Selected Years)   *page* 130
5.1 Janos Presidio Average Garrison Strength, 1791–1834
(Selected Years)   188
5.2 Annual Expenditures for the *Apaches de paz* at Janos
Presidio, 1791–1843 (Selected Years)   190

Acknowledgments

Numerous people from six nations on three continents contributed to this book, which began as a dissertation at Southern Methodist University (SMU). I owe an enormous debt to my advisor, David Weber, whom I sorely miss and whose wise counsel, helpful comments, and generous sharing of research materials helped make this a strong and compelling project from its inception. Special thanks as well to the other members of my dissertation committee: Sherry Smith and Peter Bakewell from the Clements Department of History and James Brooks at the School of American Research. SMU's History Department, the Clements Center for Southwest Studies, and the Jonsson Foundation provided me with fellowships and grants that enabled me to complete the research and writing of the dissertation, and the members of the history faculty, particularly Ed Countryman and Sherry Smith, have been enormously supportive of the manuscript in the years since graduation.

The scope and emphasis of this project changed significantly in the summer of 2013, when I received an unsolicited email from Manuel P. Sanchez, Chairman of the Chihene Nde Nation of New Mexico, telling me, "Our people are living proof of your dissertation at SMU." Startled and excited, I learned that the Chihenes were descendants of many of the late eighteenth- and early nineteenth-century Mimbres, Gila, and Mogollon leaders I had been reading about in the archives. Over time, I also discovered that although their history is closely related to that of the neighboring Chokonen or Chiricahua, they were a distinct people whose story is centered in the area of modern New Mexico and Chihuahua, not the Chiricahua Mountains of modern Arizona. Mistakenly, based on the claims of various anthropologists, I had assumed that Ndé or Apache collective historical memory only went as far back as about 1850. I am extremely grateful to Manny for contacting me and his help in connecting me with Ndé people from San Antonio to the Pacific Coast. Thanks as well to Lorraine Garcia and Michael Paul Hill, whose contributions are acknowledged in the footnotes herein.

A long-term Dana and David Dornsife Fellowship at the Huntington Library in San Marino, California, in 2013–2014 enabled me to revise the manuscript and expand its timeframe. Steve Hindle, Fred Hoxie, Roy Ritchie, James Simpson, and Joan Waugh were especially helpful in offering intellectual support. I also wish to thank Eric Ash, William Deverell, Alicia Dewey, Alison Games, Sarah Grossman, Paul Hammer, Steve Hackel, Rob Harper, Aurelio Hinarejos, Theresa Kelley, Kathleen Murphy, Lindsay O'Neill, Julie Orlemanski, Sandra Rebok, Francois Rigolot, Stephanie Sobelle, Isaac Stevens, and Valerie Traub for helping me balance productivity and pleasure during a memorable year that I wish never ended.

I am also grateful for financial support from the University of North Texas at Dallas, where I completed the book, and for the encouragement and support of colleagues and administrators.

I feel extremely fortunate to publish my first book with Cambridge University Press, and I wish to thank Ned Blackhawk, Kristina Deusch, Debbie Gershenowitz, Fred Hoxie, and Robert Judkins for offering such valuable advice, insights, and help in producing it. For their assistance with digital images and maps, I thank Anne Blecksmith at Huntington Reader Services; Manuel Flores at Huntington Imaging Services; Lorraine Garcia; Richard La Motte; Liza Posas at Braun Research Library at the Southwest Museum of the American Indian; Marilyn Van Winkle at the Autry National Center of the American West; and Tom Willcockson.

To tell this story I consulted Spanish archival collections from repositories in three nations: the United States, Mexico, and Spain. At the University of Oklahoma's Western History Collections, Kristina Southwell was especially helpful. Michael Hironymous, Adan Benavides, and Christian Kelleher helped make my many trips to the Benson Latin American Collection at the University of Texas at Austin enjoyable ones, and thanks to Joaquín Rivaya-Martinez and his family for hosting me during several return visits. Claudia Rivers at the University of Texas at El Paso's Special Collections Library and Nancy Brown-Martínez at the University of New Mexico's Center for Southwest Research graciously answered my questions about their microfilm collections. More recently, archivists Peter Blodgett and the late Bill Frank took time to guide me through the most pertinent materials from the Huntington Library's vast Western and Hispanic manuscript and microfilm collections, and Nayiri Partamian and Damon Russell were wonderful hosts in Pasadena. Brian DeLay was kind enough to loan me several rolls of microfilm from the Archivo General de la Nacíon (AGN) in Mexico City, and Karl Jacoby generously shared copies of Apache documents from the Archivo General del Estado de Sonora (AGES) in Hermosillo and his *Shadows at Dawn*. In Spain I am grateful to Isabel Simó Rodríguez and her staff at the Archivo General de Indias (AGI) in Sevilla, and José María Burrieza Mateos and the staff at the Archivo General de Simancas (AGS). Special thanks to David Rex Galindo and his family for housing me in Madrid and Valladolid.

Numerous colleagues have generously commented on the manuscript as it progressed from dissertation to book. Brian DeLay provided insightful guidance at a critical early stage. At the New Mexico Historical Review, Durwood Ball and Sonia Dickey helped me improve a portion of the manuscript, and I am grateful for the editorial advice of Salvador Bernabeú Albert at the Consejo Superior de Investigaciones Científicas in Sevilla and Eric Chalifoux at *Recherches Amérindiennes au Québec*. At the invitation of Ron Hoffman, I also had the good fortune of presenting material at an Omohundro Institute of Early American History and Culture colloquium, where I received thoughtful commentary from Mark Hanna, Paul Mapp, and Brett Rushforth. I am especially thankful for Ed Countryman's invitation to participate in the Contested Spaces of Early America Symposium in David Weber's honor, where I benefited from extensive feedback from Juliana Barr, Daniel Richter, and Ed himself. Ned Blackhawk, Chantal Cramaussel, Brian DeLay, Pekka Hamalainen, Michael Jarvis, Cynthia Radding, and Sam Truett also helped me improve my work. Thanks as well to Chantal Cramaussel for the opportunity to take part in the Semanario Permanente sobre el Norte de Mexico y el Sur de los Estados Unidos at El Colegio de Michoacán in Michoacán, Mexico, where I received helpful commentary from Clementina Campos, Susan Deeds, Martín González de la Vara, Cynthia Radding, and Joaquín Rivaya-Martínez.

For offering intellectual stimulation, support, and encouragement, I would like to thank George Avery, Mark Barringer, Andrea Boardman, Jennifer Beisel, Tom Britten, Robert Caldwell, Court Carney, John Chávez, Paul Conrad, Troy Davis, George Díaz, Ruth Ann Elmore, Francis Galán, Alan Gallay, Luis García, Morris Jackson, Ben Johnson, Gabriel

Martínez-Serna, John Mears, Sara Ortelli, Mildred Pinkston, David Rex Galindo, Florencia Roulet, Joaquín Rivaya-Martinez, Jeff Shepherd, Scott Sosebee, Margo Tamez, and Blair Woodard.

Finally, I would like to thank my family and friends, especially Dawn and the Dallas running community, for helping me find the strength and endurance to see this project through.

A Note on Terminology

This book is written from multiple perspectives and reflects American Indian, Spanish, Mexican, and Anglo American viewpoints. Therefore the terminology I utilize derives from each of those cultures. Since members of the Chihene Nde Nation of New Mexico contacted me and expressed interest in my work, I have employed their preferred Athapaskan terms for their people instead of Spanish or American terms. That means that I use "Ndé" for "Apache" and "Chihene" for Gileños, Mimbreños, Warm Springs, and Copper Mine Apaches. At their request, I have also used "Southern Apaches" in place of the cover term "Chiricahuas." Although employing the term "Southern Apaches" for people whose homeland lies between Ndé groups commonly called Eastern and Western Apaches is potentially confusing from a geographical standpoint, U.S. Indian Agent Michael Steck and anthropologist William B. Griffen also followed this practice. In an effort to minimize the usage of all three of those larger geographical groupings, I have tried to identify Ndé people, especially Southern Apaches, by their specific bands whenever possible. Since headmen tended to marry women in multiple bands and followed a pattern of matrilocal residence, that decision has proven enormously challenging.

Rooted in Spanish archival research, this book also reflects a Hispanic perspective. Since the Athapaskan-speaking people I write about were in close contact with Spaniards and Mexicans who called them "Apaches" and "Apaches de paz," I also employ those terms, when writing from a Hispanic perspective, for broader clarity (such as in the title), variety of terminology, or when it is impossible to determine the precise band affiliations of individuals or groups. I encourage all readers to consult the Appendix for further clarification of the terminology used for the Athapaskan-speaking groups described in this book.

Introduction

In the spring of 1794 five hundred Apaches lived peacefully on a Spanish-run reservation surrounding Janos presidio in northwestern Nueva Vizcaya. Led by fifty-two-year-old *nantan* (leader) El Compá, these Indians called themselves Ndé ("The People") and consisted of nine Chihene ("Red Paint People") and two Chokonen ("Juniper People") bands. Spaniards named them Mimbreños ("people of the willows") and Chiricaguis (Ópata for "mountains of the wild turkey") after the principal mountain ranges that they inhabited, the Sierras de las Mimbres and Chiricagui.[1] Today they are better known as the Black Range of southwestern New Mexico and the Chiricahua Mountains of southeastern Arizona.

After initially making peace at Janos in late 1789, Ndé numbers rose steadily, reportedly reaching 312 in March of 1792 and 406 a year later. Rather than risk being killed, captured, imprisoned, or enslaved by Spanish troops and their Indian allies, these Apaches opted to receive rations and gifts in exchange for their men serving as scouts and auxiliary troops with Spanish soldiers. Apache families received weekly rations of beef, *pinole* (meal made of ground corn and mesquite beans), salt, maize, and cigars and periodic gifts of horses and sheep. Ten of the eleven Ndé bands lived close to the presidio and included such well-known leaders as Vívora, Tetsegoslán, and Nac-cogé (El Güero or "the light-haired one"). Most prominent of all was the Chokonen El Compá, whom Spaniards had named "principal chief of the peaceful Apaches" three years earlier. Favored over the other headmen, El Compá resided inside the walls of Janos presidio with more than fifty of his people, including his two well-known sons, the future Chihene leaders Juan José and Juan Diego Compá (Nayulchi).[2]

The Ndé at Janos were not alone. A prolonged regional drought and coordinated attacks from Spanish troops and their Indian allies influenced thousands of Apaches to relocate and resettle in a group of reservation-like *establecimientos* (establishments or settlements) near Spanish presidios beginning in 1786. Stretching across more than nine hundred miles of arid desert and temperate mountains at its height in the late 1790s – from Laredo, in the east, to Tucson, in the west – this little-known Spanish experiment constituted the earliest and most extensive system of military-run reservations in the Americas. By 1793 approximately 2,000 of an estimated 11,500 Mescaleros, Southern Apaches, and Western Apaches had settled on eight reservations across the American Southwest (see Map I.1).[3] More precisely, along the northern presidial line in Nueva Vizcaya (modern Chihuahua and Durango), from east to west, at least 800 Mescaleros settled at El Norte; 63 Mescaleros, whom Spaniards called Faraons, at San Elizario; 254 Chihenes at Carrizal; and 408 Chihenes and Chokonens (Chiricahuas) at Janos. Farther west in Sonora 77 Chokonens and Chihenes lived at Fronteras; 81 Chokonens at Bacoachi; and 86 Tsézhinés ("Black Rocks People"), or Aravaipas, at Tucson (see Map I.2). Finally, more than 200 miles north of El Paso, 226 Chihenes resided near the village of Sabinal, New Mexico. In September 1798, three Lipan bands camped along the banks of the Salado River in Coahuila near Laredo presidio briefly joined these groups.[4] At the system's height in this decade, these Apaches probably comprised at least 50 percent of all Mescaleros and Southern Apaches and less than 10 percent of all Lipans and Western Apaches.[5]

A simple question frames this study. How did so many Ndé, who were the primary object of Hispanic military might for more than a century, avoid full-scale incorporation into the Spanish empire and Mexican nation? Carrying out the enlightened Indian policies of Spanish officials, presidial commanders hoped to resettle semisedentary equestrian Apaches on fertile plots of land and transform them into productive town-dwelling farmers subject to crown authority. But, in practice, so-called peaceful Apaches (*Apaches de paz*), largely shaped the system. Subverting Spanish efforts to make them wholly sedentary, the Ndé adapted to reservation life by remaining semisedentary and using Spanish rations, gifts, and military protection to sustain and preserve their families. A minority of Apaches de paz worked together with Spaniards and Mexicans to reduce violence in the region by serving as scouts and auxiliaries, while the majority relied on what they always had to ensure their survival – movement, economic exchange, and small-scale livestock raiding. Although

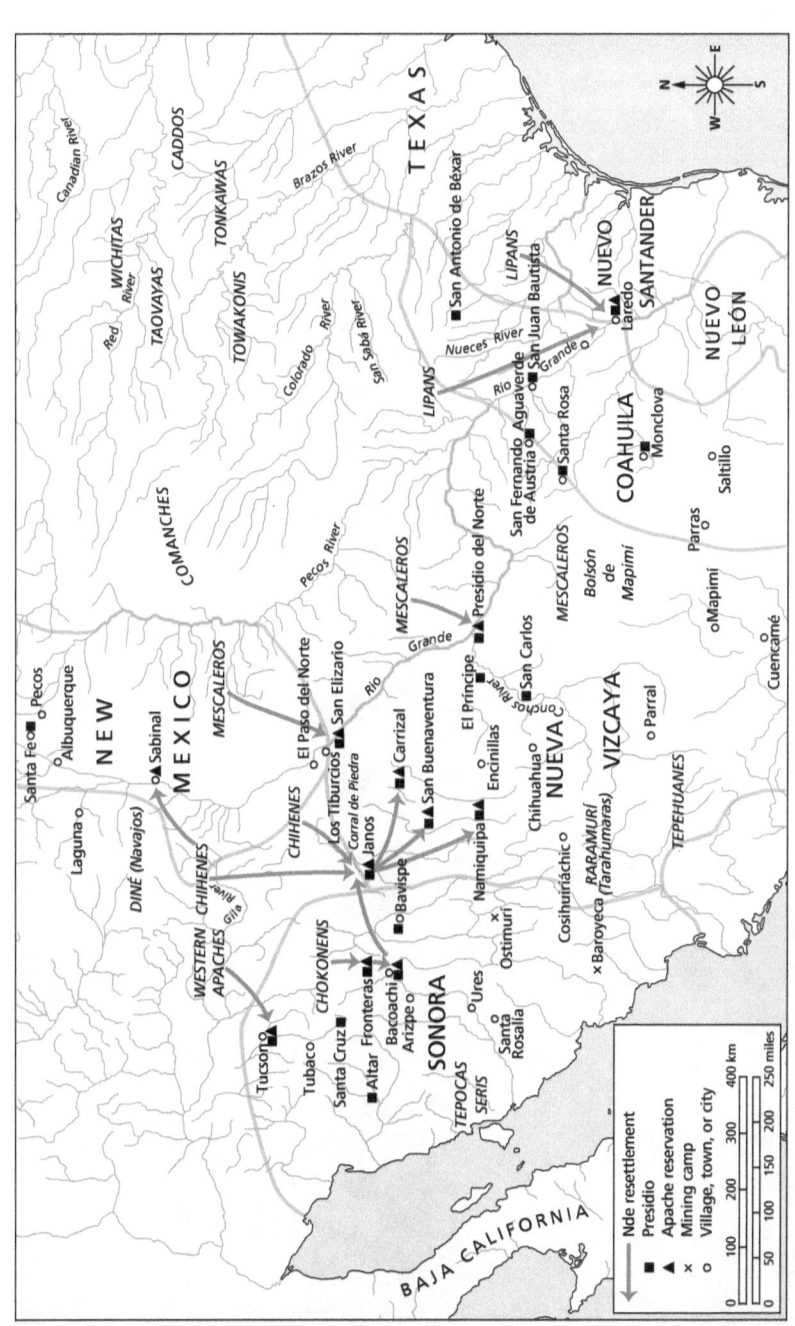

MAP 1.1 Ndé resettlement, 1786–1798.

Source: AGI; AGS; AGN; Janos Presidio Archives; Max L. Moorhead, *The Presidio: Bastion of the Spanish Borderlands*, 28, 62–63; Max L. Moorhead, *The Apache Frontier: Jacobo Ugarte and Spanish-Indian Relations in Northern New Spain, 1769–1791* (Norman: University of Oklahoma, 1968), 88–90n3, 171, 201; Peter Gerhard, *The North Frontier of New Spain* (Princeton, NJ: Princeton University Press, 1982; reprint, Norman: University of Oklahoma Press, 1993) 162, 246, 280, 315, 326, 337.

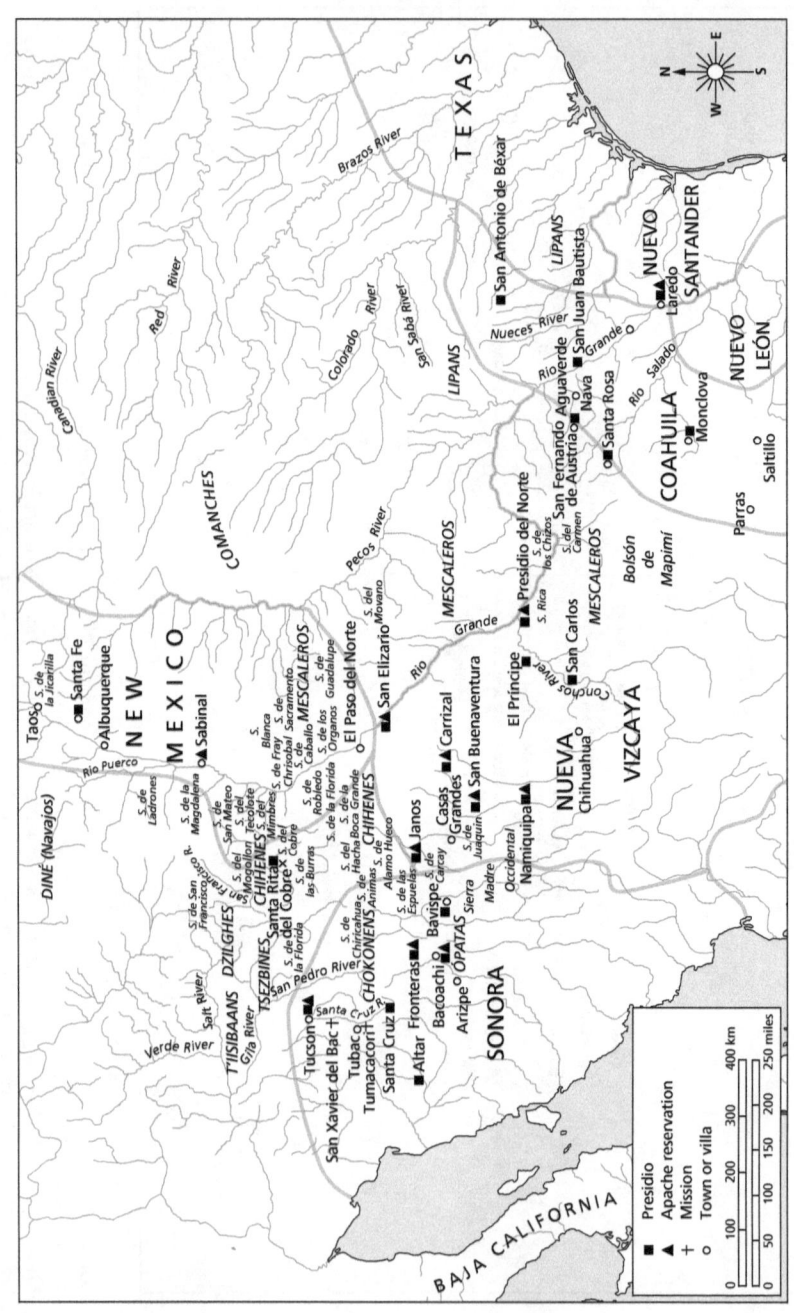

MAP 1.2 The Apache–Spanish frontier, ca. 1800.

Source: Adapted from Moorhead, *The Apache Frontier,* 171, 201; Moorhead, *Presidio,* 28; Forbes, *Apache, Navaho, and Spaniard,* 77; Griffen, *Apaches at War and Peace,* 20; Gerhard, *North Frontier of New Spain,* 315, 326; Robert S. Weddle, *San Juan Bautista: Gateway to Spanish Texas* (1968; reprint, Austin: University of Texas Press, 1991), page not listed.

these dual strategies caused confusion, periodic disruptions, and results that Spanish policy makers never anticipated, that does not mean that the establecimientos were a failure. Instead, they enabled the system to endure and function largely on Ndé terms and the Ndé to reassert their political and territorial sovereignty by 1832.[6]

Ndé adaptations offer deeper insight into the various ways indigenous peoples and colonized groups of all sorts negotiated cultural conquest on frontiers and borderlands across North America and around the world. Those who regard equestrian raiders as backward and barbaric people ripe for conquest by advanced and prosperous empires and states have their facts backwards. The Ndé who chose to relocate to reservations made a strategic decision to do so, fully recognizing that they could continue to move in and out of Spanish zones of control, depending on their needs. Like other upland indigenous peoples, their subsistence routine, social organization, and physical dispersal were purposeful adaptations undertaken to maintain political autonomy and avoid state incorporation. Much more than relentless warriors and savvy traders, Ndé men and women also played important and underexamined roles as diplomats, interpreters, scouts, and auxiliary soldiers. Most importantly, all four groups who settled on Spanish-run reservations practiced at least some agriculture prior to doing so, which meant they never needed Spaniards to teach them how to become "civilized."[7]

This work also aims to improve scholarly understanding of the balance of power between indigenous peoples and colonizing powers in the Southwest. The recent focus on Comanche ethnogenesis and economic and territorial expansion southward from the southern plains, while important and highly instructive, has shifted attention away from Spaniards' primary goal in the late eighteenth century: pacifying the Apaches. Facing west and south of the Rio Grande reminds us that the rise of the so-called Comanche empire was not the central compelling historical process transpiring in the eighteenth- and early-nineteenth-century lower midcontinent. Apaches had a vast territory of their own, Kónitsąąhįį gokíyaa (Big Water Peoples' Country), which Spaniards called the Gran Apachería (Great Apache Country). Comprising most of modern Texas, New Mexico, eastern Arizona, and upland and arid portions of Coahuila, Nueva Vizcaya, and Sonora in the mid-eighteenth century, this well-established elastic space overlapped the emerging Comanchería (Comanche Country), extending more than 700 miles from the Colorado River in the east to the middle Gila River in the west, and more than 350 miles from the Mogollon Mountains and Texas Hill Country in the north to the

Sierra Madre ranges and Bolsón de Mapimí in the south. Although independent Apaches and Comanches helped make much of the Southwest what one scholar has called "an Indian land during the age of European empire," my book shows that from the late eighteenth century onward Spanish soldiers and their Indian allies regularly penetrated the Apachería and influenced – but never forced – Apaches to settle peacefully near Spanish presidios in the region.[8] Apaches used their reservations for their own purposes and culturally reinvented themselves while in contact with Spaniards, not in isolation.

A third goal of this study is to resolve the long-standing scholarly debate over when, why, and how the establecimiento system ended. Indeed, a whole host of borderlands historians have mistakenly argued that it collapsed at the outbreak of the Mexican War of Independence in 1810, when Apache raiding allegedly increased in response to a drastic decline in military defense and gifts to Indians across northern New Spain.[9] Other writers have recognized the uneven decline of the establecimientos and the region's economy, maintaining that prosperity continued longer in Chihuahua and Sonora than in Coahuila and Texas, but they disagree on whether decline began in 1820–1821 or 1831 and whether it was because "Apaches grew restless" or Mexicans stopped issuing them rations.[10] Relying primarily on the observations of Ignacio Zúñiga, historian Cynthia Radding has challenged these interpretations, arguing that the "peace encampments" from Janos to Tucson "collapsed by the mid 1820s" because of dwindling supplies stemming from a "lack of fiscal resources (and political will) to maintain them." As presidial defense and diplomacy broke down at this time, Radding holds that Indian raiding increased and the frontier began receding, a process that would continue through the 1840s.[11]

So how do we reconcile this cacophony of arguments? First, some scholars pinpointed the beginning of the deterioration, while others have identified the point of total collapse. That said, the contention that the system completely broke down in 1810 is simply incorrect and has misled two generations of historians. All that happened in the 1810s was a temporary reduction in money and military defense. With the exception of the Lipans, who spent less time in establecimientos than Mescaleros and Apache groups west of the Rio Grande, there is no evidence that Apaches increased their raids in the last decade of Spanish rule. Second, despite the disagreement over the precise timing of the breakdown, scholars generally agree on the overall pattern of decline. As historian David J. Weber has aptly noted, the unraveling of peace with Apaches and other independent Indians "was specific to individual bands and tribes" and the collapse of Mexican presidial defenses probably preceded Apaches' recognition that they could raid again successfully.[12] Indeed, scholars concur that Southern and Western Apache bands remained at peace longer than Mescaleros. Finally, it is important to distinguish peaceful Apaches' responses to the weakening of Mexico's military defenses from independent Apaches' reactions. Increased raiding by independent Apaches alone, for instance, would not necessarily signal the collapse of the establecimientos, especially if Apaches at peace were helping Spaniards attack them.

This picture of Apache–Hispanic relations is quite different from the one presented by most writers or envisioned by the general public. When most people think of Apaches, they conjure up images of peerless nomadic warriors of the desert Southwest, such as Geronimo and Cochise, who struggled relentlessly to defend their freedom against the U.S. Army in the late nineteenth century. As one early-twentieth-century scholar put it, "The Apache was the original 'bad man' of the Southwest." Hollywood films such as *Geronimo* (1993), *The Missing* (2003), and *The 3:10 to Yuma* (2007) have simply reinforced this stereotype in American popular culture. Some of the most respected English, Spanish, and French language dictionaries are also part of the problem. They continue to offer antiquated definitions for the word Apache, such as "bandit," "highway robber," and "ruffian or thug," which derive from the ethnocentric observations of nineteenth-century European observers.[13]

The portrayal of Apaches as relentless warriors is at best superficial. It fails to address cultural change over time and varieties among tribal groups. Specialists understand, of course, that Apaches have a long history of contact with Euro-Americans, which dates back at least to Francisco Coronado's expedition in 1540.[14] Few historians of the nineteenth-century American West, however, are aware that thousands of Apaches, including the relatives of well-known future leaders such as Juan José Compá, Mangas Coloradas, and Cochise, settled on Spanish-run reservations fifty years prior to the U.S.–Mexican War. Frequently these same scholars mistakenly assume that the Spanish and Mexican military only minimally impacted Apache culture, their soldiers "could do next to nothing to control the Apaches," and Apaches' first significant contact with outsiders began when Anglo Americans entered the region in significant numbers during the 1840s.[15] Mexican scholars, on the other hand, are much better versed in Apache history prior to 1846. They, too, however, regard Apaches as *indios bárbaros*, or savages, owing to the escalation of Apache raiding in northern Mexico during the 1830s.[16] Even most regional specialists concur that Apaches never made lasting peace agreements with Spaniards. These historians view the mission, not the presidio, as the primary institution for "civilizing" Apaches in the region and ignore the presidio's role as a reservation agency.[17]

Challenging these assumptions, this book offers a new interpretation of Apache–Hispanic relations that examines both cultures from multiple perspectives in a global context. Borderlands specialists may be surprised to learn that Spaniards and Mexicans did not call garrisoned Apache settlements *establecimientos de paz*. This phrase and its various English equivalents – peace establishments or peace settlements – have been concocted by Mexican and American scholars. Although "reservation" is not a literal translation of "establecimiento" either, this term more accurately reflects the degree of control the Spanish military sought to exercise over peaceful Apache communities and places the system in a broader comparative context.[18] The fact that the most knowledgeable Spanish officers learned the Athapaskan names and culture patterns of the nine Apache groups they recognized in the late eighteenth century may prove equally startling.[19]

Several intriguing parallels also exist between Spanish and United States Indian policy in the late eighteenth and early nineteenth centuries. First, in the same way that enlightened Spanish Indian policy makers such as Bernardo de Gálvez and Pedro de Nava inaccurately argued that Apaches were primitive nomadic hunters who needed to become farmers to become civilized, so too Thomas Jefferson and his intellectual progeny advocated that Native peoples of the eastern woodlands, such as the Iroquois and Cherokees, needed to become agricultural even though they had farmed for centuries. Second, Gálvez and Jefferson made these grave policy errors at the same time that Spanish and U.S. troops were destroying Apache and Iroquois croplands. Third, Spaniards and Anglo Americans shared a similar desire to rationalize conquest, colonization, and Indian land dispossession and a preference for negotiating with Indian men who sought to protect their hunting grounds rather than with women who assumed "ownership of the land as its principal cultivators."[20]

"Reserved areas for indigenous populations," then, were not simply a product of the nineteenth-century United States. They began on Spanish and British colonial frontiers in Europe, North Africa, and North America, where the establecimientos constituted one of the most extensive systems on the continent.[21] That I focus more on peace than violent warfare does not mean I am in any way adopting a romanticized Boltonian or "White Legend" viewpoint on the region's history. Apache–Spanish relations, like those between the Iroquois and the British in the mid-eighteenth century, were characterized as much by mutual suspicion as by mutual need. Violent warfare predominated between Apaches and Spaniards for most of the late seventeenth and eighteenth centuries and between Apaches and Mexicans from the 1830s onward.[22] One of the lessons we can learn from the Apache experience at the establecimientos, however, is that even the most war-ravaged and violent indigenous cultures at the periphery of colonial empires and emerging nations pursued peaceful diplomacy as a political strategy when it was in their best interest to do so. What is significant about the period from 1786 to 1832 is the extent that reservation-dwelling Apaches and Spaniards across the colonial Southwest worked together to reduce reciprocal treachery and violence and overcome deep-seated mutual distrust, even though those practices never entirely disappeared. To gain a fuller appreciation of the enormously complex history of North America's early frontiers and borderlands, it is just as important to understand Native and European motivations for making peace as it is for making war.[23]

To that end, the ensuing six chapters explore the following questions: How did the Ndé adapt to their environment prior to Spanish contact, and what cultural transformations did they make while in contact with Spaniards prior to 1700? Why did Spanish officials resort to resettling Apaches on reservations, and what precedents influenced their decision? Why did so many Ndé, who had dominated the Spanish militarily for nearly two centuries, agree to stop raiding Spanish livestock and farm on the margins of Spanish colonial society? How did the establecimiento system function in practice, and when, why, and how did it break down? Finally, how did Ndé relations with Mexicans and Americans change after the collapse of the reservations, and what were their most important legacies?

Chapter 1 begins by showing that the majority of Ndé groups initially embraced Catholicism in the late 1620s and got along with Spanish missionaries and their native neighbors. Adopting a "deep history" approach, it briefly examines Ndé cultural origins and environmental adaptations prior to Spanish contact in 1540 before focusing more thoroughly on their major cultural adaptations after contact. A central argument of the chapter is that Apache violence toward Spaniards and their indigenous enemies increased after 1667, as Apaches adapted to Spanish colonialism and environmental change by becoming equestrians and actively participating in the Pueblo and Great Southwestern Revolts.

Chapter 2 argues that although the reservation system had transcontinental origins, centralized Spanish policy was a less important influence than face-to-face negotiations between Apaches and Spaniards. Chichimeca "peace camps" in central New Spain in the 1590s and the seldom-recognized *moros de paz* (peaceful Moors) program in North Africa from 1739 to 1803 served as potential precedents, as well as prior Spanish experiments to resettle Apaches in missions, pueblos, and trade with them at presidios. The first Ndé reservation at Presidio del Norte, however, resulted from Mescalero-Spanish agreements at the local level and preceded Viceroy Bernardo de Gálvez's well-known 1786 policy.

Chapter 3 maintains that external military pressure from Spaniards and other Indians, opportunities for economic and cultural exchange, and the ability of Ndé leaders to work the treaty terms in their favor influenced Ndé groups to relocate to reservations after 1786. Although Spanish military officers offered Apaches the opportunity to receive protection and material benefits, the fact that they killed, captured, exiled, and enslaved those who refused angered all Ndé people and created inherent instability within the program.

Chapter 4 examines the pros and cons of the Spanish resettlement program at its height from Ndé and Spanish perspectives. Three beneficial results of the Apache peace from a Spanish perspective were Hispanicization and demographic and economic expansion. The reservation system was also cheaper than the combined cost of waging an all-out war and paying for lost resources from retaliatory raids. Although a small number of Ndé and Spaniards reached an enduring accommodation, the majority of Ndé who settled on Spanish reservations did so only to fulfill temporary needs. Demonstrating minimal signs of acculturation and incorporation, they circumvented the overambitious incorporation efforts of Spanish officials by spreading unsettling rumors, recovering captives, gambling away their rations and gifts, forging interband and intertribal alliances, and continuing to hunt, gather, and raid.

Seeking to resolve the scholarly debate on the establecimiento system's collapse, I argue in Chapter 5 that it transpired unevenly, breaking down more quickly in eastern Nueva Vizcaya and Coahuila than in western Nueva Vizcaya and Sonora because of Comanches' ongoing wars with Mescaleros and Lipans. In tracing the decline I look at several interrelated factors: increased desertion of Apaches de paz, intensified Apache and Comanche raiding, reduced rations and Mexican military manpower, disease outbreaks, and land dispossession.

Chapter 6 opens with the treacherous Johnson Massacre of 1837, using it to symbolize a new era of Ndé relations with Mexicans and Americans in which violent mercenary warfare trumped trading and diplomacy.

It demonstrates that Mexican presidios and towns, which were previously zones for reciprocal diplomacy and exchange, disintegrated into arenas of treacherous violence. Desperate to curtail Apache raiding and killing, officials in underfunded and undermanned northern Mexican states implemented an Apache scalp bounty, and money-hungry soldiers, citizens, and contact killers gunned down unsuspecting and unarmed Ndé men, women, and children, which simply escalated the reciprocal violence.

Violence would remain the dominant trend for the rest of the nineteenth century, but former Apaches de paz continued to seek compromises with Mexican and American military officers, traders, miners, and settlers at the local level. During the 1830s and 1840s, former Apaches de paz worked together with independent Ndé groups to reassert control of their homeland and, together with Navajos and Comanches, dominate the Southwest. Yet, they never forgot their experience on Hispanic-run reservations, which served as a precedent for their descendants, enabling them to negotiate conquest more shrewdly and adapt to life on U.S. reservations before and after the Civil War.

Notes

1 [Lt. Dionisio Valle], "Padrón que manifiesta la Apachería que se halla de paz en este presidio," Janos, March 2 and April 2, 1794, roll 10, microfilm, Janos Historical Archives, Special Collections, University of Texas at El Paso Library (hereafter JHA-UTEP). For "nantan," see Eve Ball, *In the Days of Victorio: Recollections of a Warm Springs Apache* (Tucson: University of Arizona Press, 1970), 8; Morris E. Opler, "Chiricahua Apache," in *Handbook of North American Indians: Southwest*, Vol. 10, ed. Alfonso Ortiz (Washington, DC: Smithsonian Institution, 1983), 411. For "Ndé" (pronounced in-dé) and its various equivalents as a synonym for "the People," see Frederick Webb Hodge, ed., *Handbook of American Indians North of Mexico*, Smithsonian Institution, Bureau of American Ethnology, Bulletin 30 (Washington: Government Printing Office: 1907), 63, 67; Daniel S. Matson and Albert H. Schroeder, eds. and trans., "Cordero's Description of the Apache – 1796," *New Mexico Historical Review* 32 (October 1957): 336n3. For "Chihene," see Morris E. Opler, *An Apache Life-Way: The Economic, Social, and Religious Institutions of the Chiricahua Indians* (1941; reprint, New York: Cooper Square Publishers, 1965), 1. For "Chokonen," see John G. Bourke, "Notes Upon the Gentile Organization of the Apaches of Arizona," *Journal of American Folklore* 3 no. 9 (April–June 1890): 115. For the inaccurate claim that Chokonen "does not yield to linguistic analysis," see Opler, *An Apache Life-Way*, 2. For the meanings of 'Mimbreños" and "Chiricaguis," see Juan Nentvig, S.J., *Rudo Ensayo: A Description of Sonora and Arizona in 1764*, ed. Alberto Francisco Pradeau and Robert R. Rasmussen (Tucson: University of Arizona Press, 1980), 21n3; Albert H. Schroeder, *A Study of the Apache Indians: Parts*

IV and V, American Indian Ethnohistory: Indians of the Southwest Series, vol. 4 (New York: Garland, 1974), 117.

2 For Ndé population figures, see Capt. Manuel de Casanova, "Padrón que manifiesta la Apachería que se halla de paz en este presidio," Janos, March 1, 1792 and 1793, roll 10, JHA-UTEP. For rations, see Ensign Miguel Díaz de Luna, "Subministración de Apaches," April 10, 20, May 7, 16, 25, June 2, 12, 20, 1794, roll 10, JHA-UTEP. For El Compá as "Chiricagui" (Chokonen), see William B. Griffen, *Apaches at War and Peace: The Janos Presidio, 1750–1858* (1988; reprint, Norman: University of Oklahoma Press, 1998), 62; Commander-in-Chief Jacobo Ugarte to Gov. Juan Bautista de Anza, Hacienda de San Salvador de Orta, December 2, 1788, Archivo General de la Nación, Provincias Internas, 128, f. 522, Max Leon Moorhead Collection, Western History Collections, University of Oklahoma, Norman (hereafter AGI, Guadalajara, Legajo number, MLMC); "Padrón que manifiesta la Apachería que se halla de paz en este presidio," roll 10, Janos, March 1, 1794, JHA-UTEP; Lt. Col. Antonio Cordero to the Janos commander, El Paso, August 12, 1791, Folder 7, Section 1, Janos Presidio Records, Benson Latin American Collection, University of Texas at Austin (hereafter, F number, S number, JPR-UTA). The quotation is from the last document. For a closer look at the Compá family, see William B. Griffen, "The Compás: A Chiricahua Family of the late 18th and Early 19th Centuries," *American Indian Quarterly* 7 (1983): 21–49.

3 For "Southern Apache" as an equivalent for the broader grouping "Chiricahua," which was not recognized by colonial Spaniards, nineteenth-century Mexicans, nor modern Chihene people, see Griffen, *Apaches at War and Peace*, xiv, 3, 5. For more on the origins and meanings of Spanish names for Apache groups, see Willem J. de Reuse, "Synonymy" in Morris E. Opler, "The Apachean Culture Pattern and Its Origins," in Handbook of North American Indians: *Southwest*, Vol. 10, ed. Alfonso Ortiz (Washington, DC: Smithsonian Institution, 1983), 385-392. For an estimate of 5,000 Apache warriors, which would correspond to 20,000 Apaches, including the Navajos, see Lt. and Sec. Manuel Merino y Moreno, "Report of the Council of Monclova," Monclova, December 11, 1777, in Herbert Eugene Bolton, ed. and trans., *Athanase de Mézières and the Louisiana-Texas Frontier, 1768–1780*, vol. 2 (Cleveland, OH: Arthur H. Clark, 1914), 153. For an estimate of at least 11,500 Mescaleros, Southern Apaches, and Western Apaches in c. 1850, which roughly corresponds with the 1777 estimate, see Opler, "Mescalero Apache," 428; Opler, "Chiricahua Apache," 411; Grenville Goodwin, "The Social Divisions and Economic Life of the Western Apache," *American Anthropologist* 37 (1935): 55.

4 Commander-in-Chief Pedro de Nava, "Estado que manifiesta el número de rancherías Apaches existentes de paz," Chihuahua, May 2, 1793, Audiencia de Guadalajara, Legajo 289, Archivo General de Indias, Seville, Spain (hereafter AGI, Legajo number, Seville); Max L. Moorhead, *The Presidio: Bastion of the Spanish Borderlands* (Norman: University of Oklahoma Press, 1975), 260–261; Griffen, *Apaches at War and Peace*, 267–268. Naming of all Chihene groups is in accordance with former Chihene Ndé Nation of New Mexico Historical Record Keeper Lorraine Garcia (email, 7/14/14). For "Tséҳhiné," see Karl Jacoby, *Shadows at Dawn: A Borderlands Massacre and the Violence of*

History (New York: Penguin, 2008), 158, 290; Willem J. de Reuse, *A Practical Grammar of the San Carlos Apache Language* (Munich: Lincom Europa, 2006), 195. For Lipans, see Viceroy Miguel Joseph de Azanza to Minister of War Juan Manuel de Alvarez, no. 95, México, September 26, 1798, Archivo General de Simancas, Guerra Moderna, Legajo 7029, Expediente 2, Simancas, Spain (hereafter AGS, GM, Legajo number, Exp. number, Simancas); Sherry Robinson, *I Fought a Good Fight: The History of the Lipan Apaches* (Denton: University of North Texas Press, 2013), 164; Thomas A. Britten, *The Lipan Apaches: People of Wind and Lightning* (Albuquerque: University of New Mexico Press, 2009), 164.

5 For the Mescalero and Southern Apache estimates, see William B. Griffen, "Apache Indians and the Northern Mexican Peace Establishments," in *Southwestern Culture History: Collected Papers in Honor of Albert H. Schroeder* (Santa Fe, NM: Ancient City Press, 1985), 189; William B. Griffen, "The Chiricahua Apache Population Resident at the Janos Presidio, 1792 to 1858," *Journal of the Southwest* 33 (Summer 1991): 155, 180–181. The Lipan and Western Apache estimates are my own. For an estimate of 3,000 Lipans in 1779, see Fray Juan Agustín Morfi, *History of Texas, 1673–1779*, ed. and trans. Carlos Eduardo Castañeda, Quivira Sociery Publications (Albuquerque, NM: Quivira Society, 1935), 372.

6 For the respective arguments that Spanish efforts to turn Apaches, Navajos, and Comanches into farmers were failures because they never became self-sufficient farmers as authorities hoped, see Rick Hendricks and W. H. Timmons, *San Elizario: Spanish Presidio to Texas County Seat* (El Paso: Texas Western Press, 1998); David J. Weber, *Bárbaros: Spaniards and Their Savages in the Age of Enlightenment* (New Haven, CT: Yale University Press, 2005), 194. Weber withholds final judgment on Apache reservations.

7 On the incorporation of indigenous peoples into the world system, see, for example, Thomas D. Hall, "Incorporation in the World System: Toward a Critique," *American Sociological Review* 51 (1986): 393–395, 397–399; Thomas D. Hall, *Social Change in the Southwest, 1350–1880* (Lawrence: University Press of Kansas, 1989), 10, 18, 24, 29, 112–114, 243–245. Although more recent theoretical revisions acknowledge "reversibility," the overall theory is still inherently teleological, emphasizing the difficulties peripheral peoples have in "weakening" their "degree of incorporation" into the nation state. See Thomas D. Hall, "Frontiers, Ethnogenesis, and World-Systems: Rethinking the Theories," in *A World-Systems Reader: New Perspectives on Gender, Urbanism, Cultures, Indigenous Peoples, and Ecology*, ed. Thomas D. Hall (Lanham, MD: Rowman and Littlefield, 2000), 243. For notable critiques of this viewpoint, see Pierre Clastres, "Society against the State," in *Society against the State: Essays in Political Anthropology*, ed. Pierre Clastres (1977; reprint, New York: Zone Books, 1987), 189–190; Benjamin H. Johnson and Andrew R. Graybill, "Introduction: Borders and Their Historians in North America," in *Bridging National Borders in North America: Transnational and Comparative Histories*, ed. Benjamin H. Johnson and Andrew R. Graybill (Durham, NC: Duke University Press, 2010), 2; Pekka Hämäläinen and Samuel Truett, "On Borderlands," *Journal of American History* 98 no. 2 (September 2011): 340; Juliana Barr and Edward Countryman, "Introduction:

Maps and Spaces, Paths to Connect, and Lines to Divide," in *Contested Spaces of Early America*, ed. Juliana Barr and Edward Countryman (Philadelphia: University of Pennsylvania Press, 2014), 22–23. On the strategies of indigenous peoples to preserve their political autonomy, see James C. Scott, *The Art of Not Being Governed: An Anarchist History of Upland Southeast Asia*, Yale Agrarian Studies Series (New Haven, CT: Yale University Press, 2009), 8–9; Clastres, "Society Against the State," 218. On Apache agriculture, see Morris E. Opler, "Cause and Effect in Apachean Agriculture, Division of Labor, Residence Patterns, and Girls' Puberty Rites," *American Anthropologist* 74 (October 1972): 1133–1146.

8 On Comanche imperialism, see Pekka Hämäläinen, *The Comanche Empire*, Lamar Series in Western History (New Haven, CT: Yale University Press, 2008), 3, 353–356. For "Kónitsąąhįį gokíyaa," see India Reed Bowers et al., "Apache-Ndé-Nneé Working Group Shadow Report," United Nations CERD Committee, 88th Session, Review of the Holy See (November 2015), 17, 50; Margo Tamez, "The Texas-Mexico Border Wall and Ndé Memory," in *Beyond Walls and Cages: Prisons, Borders, and Global Crisis*, ed. Jenna M. Loyd, Matt Mitchelson, and Andrew Burridge (Athens: University of Georgia Press, 2012), 58. For the Gran Apachería, see Max L. Moorhead, *The Apache Frontier: Jacobo Ugarte and Spanish-Indian Relations in Northern New Spain, 1769–1791*, Civilization of the American Indian Series (Norman: University of Oklahoma Press, 1968), 3; Enrique Gilbert-Michael Maestas, "Culture and History of Native American Peoples of South Texas" (Ph.D. diss., University of Texas at Austin, 2003), 40. For the quotation, see Gary Clayton Anderson, *The Indian Southwest, 1580–1830: Ethnogenesis and Reinvention* (Norman: University of Oklahoma Press, 1999), 109.

9 Historians arguing the establecimientos collapsed in 1810 include Joseph F. Park, "Spanish Indian Policy in Northern Mexico, 1765–1810," *Arizona and the West* 4 (Winter 1962): 343; Joseph F. Park, "Spanish Indian Policy in Northern Mexico, 1765–1810," in *New Spain's Northern Frontier: Essays on Spain in the American West, 1540–1821*, ed. David J. Weber (Albuquerque: University of New Mexico Press, 1979), 231; Sidney B. Brinckerhoff and Odie B. Faulk, eds. and trans., *Lancers for the King: A Study of the Frontier Military System of Northern New Spain, with a Translation of the Royal Regulations of 1772* (Phoenix: Arizona Historical Foundation, 1965), 92; Moorhead, *Apache Frontier*, 289; Moorhead, *Presidio*, 265.

10 Writers noting the uneven decline of the establecimientos and the region's economy include Hubert Howe Bancroft, *History of Arizona and New Mexico, 1530–1888* (San Francisco, CA: The History Company, 1889), 402; Hubert Howe Bancroft, *History of the North Mexican States and Texas*, vol. 2 (San Francisco, CA: The History Company, 1889), 750–751; Sidney B. Brinckerhoff, "The Last Years of Spanish Arizona, 1786–1821," *Arizona and the West* 9 (Spring 1967): 18–19. The quotation is from p. 19. For the decline of the presidio system after 1821, see David J. Weber, *The Mexican Frontier, 1821–1846: The American Southwest under Mexico* (Albuquerque: University of New Mexico Press, 1982), 107–120. For the endurance of the

establecimiento system in Chihuahua until 1831, see William B. Griffen, *Utmost Good Faith: Patterns of Apache-Mexican Hostilities in Northern Chihuahua Border Warfare, 1821–1848* (Albuquerque: University of New Mexico Press, 1988), 11.

11 Cynthia Radding, *Landscapes of Power and Identity: Comparative Histories in the Sonoran Desert and the Forests of Amazonia from Colony to Republic* (Durham, NC: Duke University Press, 2005), 260–262. The first quotation is from p. 260 and the others are from p. 261.

12 Weber, *Bárbaros*, 378n60.

13 For the first quotation, see Frank C. Lockwood, *The Apache Indians* (New York: Macmillan, 1938), 5. For examples of scholars who have identified this "Apache myth" and called for its correction, see Grenville Goodwin, *Western Apache Raiding and Warfare*, ed. Keith H. Basso (Tucson: University of Arizona Press, 1971), 9–11; Edward H. Spicer, *Cycles of Conquest: The Impact of Spain, Mexico, and the United States on the Indians of the South-West, 1533–1960* (1962, reprint; Tucson: University of Arizona Press, 1997), vii, 593–594; Kieran McCarty, ed. and trans., *Desert Documentary: The Spanish Years, 1767–1821* (Tucson: Arizona Historical Society, 1976), 1. For the three respective remaining quotations, see *Diccionario de la lengua española*, ([Madrid]: Real Academia Española, 2012), available online, accessed June 4, 2015, www.rae.es/recursos/diccionarios/drae; Fernando Corripio, *Gran diccionario de sinónimos: voces afines e incorrecciones*. (Barcelona: Ediciones B, S.A., 2000); Paul Robert, *Le petit Robert 2: dictionnarie universel des noms propres alphabétique et analogique* (Paris: Le Robert, 1991); *The Oxford English Dictionary*, 2nd ed., 1989, available through *OED Online*, Oxford University Press, accessed June 4, 2015, www.oed.com.

14 For the most thorough treatment of Apache–Spanish relations in the sixteenth and seventeenth centuries, see Jack D. Forbes, *Apache, Navaho, and Spaniard*, 2nd ed. (1960; reprint, Norman: University of Oklahoma Press, 1994). For Apache–Spanish relations in the late eighteenth century, see Moorhead, *Apache Frontier*; Moorhead, *Presidio*. For an overview of Western Apache relations with Spaniards, Mexicans, and Americans, see Spicer, *Cycles of Conquest*. For the best syntheses of Spanish and Mexican–Indian relations, see David J. Weber, *The Spanish Frontier in North America* (New Haven, CT: Yale University Press, 1992); Weber, *Mexican Frontier*; Andrés Reséndez, *Changing National Identities at the Frontier: Texas and New Mexico, 1800–1850* (New York: Cambridge University Press, 2005); Brian DeLay, *War of a Thousand Deserts: Indian Raids and the U.S.–Mexican War* (New Haven, CT: Yale University Press, 2008).

15 Patricia Nelson Limerick, *The Legacy of Conquest: The Unbroken Past of the American West* (New York: W.W. Norton, 1987), 227; William T. Hagan, "How the West Was Lost," in *Indians in American History: An Introduction*, ed. Frederick E. Hoxie and Peter Iverson (Wheeling, IL: Harlan Davidson, 1998), 163. Quotation is from Limerick. For an example of an ethnohistorian making the same errors for the period from 1700 to 1848, see Forbes, *Apache, Navaho, and Spaniard*, 280–281. For works that devote one chapter or less to the Spanish and the Mexican period, see Lockwood, *The Apache Indians*;

C. L. Sonnichsen, *The Mescalero Apaches*, 2nd ed. (Norman: University of Oklahoma Press, 1973); Donald E. Worcester, *The Apaches: Eagles of the Southwest* (Norman: University of Oklahoma Press, 1979).

16 This historiographical trend began with northern Mexican observers in the 1830s. For example, see José Agustín de Escudero, ed., "De las naciones bárbaras que habitan las fronteras del estado de Chihuahua," in *Noticias estadísticas del estado de Chihuahua* (Mexico: Juan Ojeda, 1834); Ignacio Zúñiga, *Rápida ojeada al estado de Sonora: dirigida y dedicada al supremo gobierno de la nación* (Mexico: Juan Ojeda, 1835); José Agustín de Escudero, *Noticias estadísticas de Sonora y Sinaloa (1849)*, ed. Héctor Cuauhtémoc Hernández Silva (Hermosillo, Mexico: Universidad de Sonora, 1997). For more recent examples, see José Juan Izquierdo, "El problema de los indios bárbaros a la terminación de la guerra con los estados unidos," *Memorias de la academia mexicana de la historia* 7 (1948): 5–14; Isidro Vizcaya Canales, ed., *La invasión de los indios bárbaros al noreste de México en los años de 1840 y 1841* (Monterrey, Mexico: Publicaciones del Instituto Tecnológico y de Estudios Superiores de Monterrey, 1968); Isidro Vizcaya Canales, *Incursiones de indios al noreste en el México independiente (1821–1855)* (Monterrey, Mexico: Archivo General del Estado de Nuevo León, 1995). For a more balanced view, see Martha Rodríguez, *La guerra entre bárbaros y civilizados: El exterminio del nómada en Coahuila, 1840–1880* (Saltillo, Mexico: Centro de Estudios Sociales y Humanísticos, A.C., 1998).

17 Historians emphasizing Apache–Spanish conflict over cooperation and ignoring the establecimientos include Sonnichsen, *The Mescalero Apaches*, 35–64; Odie B. Faulk, "The Presidio: Fortress or Farce?," *Journal of the West* 8 (January 1969): 22–28. For further examples of scholars omitting the presidio's role as a reservation, see Judith A. Bense, "Introduction: Presidios of the North American Spanish Borderlands," *Historical Archaeology* 38 (2004): 4; Thomas Wm. Dunlay, "Indian Allies in the Armies of New Spain and the United States: A Comparative Study," *New Mexico Historical Review* 56 (July 1981): 239–258. In the following special issue devoted to presidios, only one author mentions in a single sentence that presidios were used "to attract Native Americans to live under reservation-like conditions near the presidios." See Jack S. Williams, "The Evolution of the Presidio in Northern New Spain," *Historical Archaeology* 38 (2004): 16. The mission emphasis began with Herbert Eugene Bolton, "The Mission as a Frontier Institution," *American Historical Review* 22 (1917): 42–61. Notable exceptions to this trend offering a collective perspective on the establecimientos include Moorhead, *Apache Frontier*, 170–290; Moorhead, *Presidio*, 243–266; Weber, *Spanish Frontier*, 232–234; Weber, *Bárbaros*, 193–194. For works treating individual reservations, see Henry F. Dobyns, *Spanish Colonial Tucson: A Demographic History* (Tucson: University of Arizona Press, 1976); Marc Simmons, *Coronado's Land: Essays on Daily Life in Colonial New Mexico* (Albuquerque: University of New Mexico Press, 1991); Hendricks and Timmons, *San Elizario*; Griffen, *Apaches at War and Peace*; Jacoby, *Shadows at Dawn*; Lance R. Blyth, *Chiricahua and Janos: Communities of Violence in the Southwestern*

Borderlands, 1680-1880 Borderlands and Transcultural Studies (Lincoln: University of Nebraska Press, 2012).

18 Moorhead, *Presidio*, 242–243; R. Douglas Hurt, *The Indian Frontier, 1763–1846*, Histories of the American Frontier Series. (Albuquerque: University of New Mexico Press, 2002), 49–51. Use of the term "establecimientos de paz" in the United States goes back at least to 1962. See Park, "Spanish Indian Policy," 341–342. U.S. scholars probably borrowed the expression from Mexican scholars. See Laureano Calvo Berber, *Nociones de Historia de Sonora* (Mexico: Librería de Manuel Porrúa, 1958), 48. Historian Joseph F. Park cites Berber in his 1962 article. For examples of how subsequent U.S. scholars, with the notable exception of Max L. Moorhead, have repeated Park's mistake, see Griffen, "Apache Indians," 183; Griffen, *Apaches at War and Peace*, 14; Weber, *Spanish Frontier*, 233; Weber, *Bárbaros*, 194; Hämäläinen, *Comanche Empire*, 129; Blyth, *Chiricahua and Janos*, 35. Max L. Moorhead uses "settlements," "villages," "camps," and "reservations" in his first book and strictly "reservations" in his second book. See Moorhead, *Apache Frontier*, 184, 186, 276, 289–290; Moorhead, *Presidio*, 243–266.

19 For evidence of Spanish knowledge of Athapaskan names and culture patterns, which is likely based on a detailed 1790 report voluntarily supplied by the Chihene leader Yagonglí (Ojos Colorados), see Antonio Cordero y Bustamante, "Noticias relativas a la nación apache, que en el año de 1796 extendió en el Paso del Norte, el Teniente Coronel D. Antonio Cordero, por encargo del Sr. Comandante general Mariscal de Campo D. Pedro Nava," in *Geografía de las lenguas y carta etnográfica de México*, ed. Manuel Orozco y Berra (Mexico: Impr. de J. M. Andrade y F. Escalante, 1864), 368–387; Moorhead, *Apache Frontier*, 199n62. For an English translation, see Matson and Schroeder, "Cordero's Description," 335–356. On the correlation between Cordero's ethnological data and much of the information gathered by John Bourke in the 1880s and twentieth-century anthropologists, see Edwin R. Sweeney, *Mangas Coloradas: Chief of the Chiricahua Apaches* (Norman: University of Oklahoma Press, 1998), 15.

20 Although the comparisons are my own, I draw from Daniel H. Usner, Jr., "Iroquois Livelihood and Jeffersonian Agrarianism: Reaching behind the Models and Metaphors," in *Native Americans in the Early Republic*, ed. Frederick E. Hoxie, Ronald Hoffman, and Peter J. Albert (Charlottesville: University Press of Virginia, 1999), 200–225. Quotation is on p. 215.

21 For the quotation, see Richard J. Perry, *Apache Reservation: Indigenous Peoples and the American State* (Austin: University of Texas Press, 1993), 4. On reservations for Chichimecas in New Spain, see Philip Wayne Powell, *Soldiers, Indians, and Silver: The Northward Advance of New Spain, 1550–1600* (Berkeley: University of California Press, 1952), 197–216; Philip Wayne Powell, *Mexico's Miguel Caldera: The Taming of America's First Frontier, 1548–1597* (Tucson: University of Arizona Press, 1977), 121–149, 277–280; Philip Wayne Powell, "Genesis of the Frontier Presidio in North America," *Western Historical Quarterly* 13 (April 1982): 121–141. On British-run reservations in the Scottish and Irish borderlands prior to 1607,

see Christine Bolt, *American Indian Policy and American Reform: Case Studies of the Campaign to Assimilate the American Indian* (London: Allen and Unwin, 1987), 29. On reservations in colonial British America, see Yasu Kawashima, "Legal Origins of the Indian Reservation in Colonial Massachusetts," *American Journal of Legal History* 13 (January 1969): 42–56; James H. Merrell, *The Indians' New World: Catawbas and Their Neighbors from European Contact through the Era of Removal* (Chapel Hill: University of North Carolina Press, 1989); Jean M. O'Brien, *Dispossession by Degrees: Indian Land and Identity in Natick, Massachusetts* (New York: Cambridge University Press, 1997); Frederic W. Gleach, *Powhatan's World and Colonial Virginia: A Conflict of Cultures* (Lincoln: University of Nebraska Press, 1997). On Spanish-run reservations for *moros de paz* (peaceful Moors) in eighteenth-century North Africa, see José Cortés, *Views from the Apache Frontier: Report on the Northern Provinces of New Spain by José Cortés, Lieutenant in the Royal Corps of Engineers, 1799*, ed. Elizabeth A. H. John and trans. John Wheat (Norman: University of Oklahoma Press, 1989), 7, 126; Enrique Arques and Narciso Gibert, *Los mogataces: los primitivos soldados moros de España en Africa* (Málaga, Spain: Editorial Algazara, 1992), 8–15, 45–57.

22 For a discussion of Hispanophobic and Hispanophilic interpretations of New Spain's northern frontier, see Weber, *Spanish Frontier*, 353–360. For the Iroquois–British comparison, see Alan Taylor, *The Divided Ground: Indians, Settlers, and the Northern Borderland of the American Revolution* (New York: Alfred A. Knopf, 2006), 6. On the importance of cycles of violence and indigenous trauma in North America prior to U.S. expansion, see Ned Blackhawk, *Violence over the Land: Indians and Empires in the Early American West* (Cambridge, MA: Harvard University Press, 2006).

23 On the importance and prevalence of peace among all societies, even the most "ethnocentric, mutually suspicious" and "bellicose" ones, see Lawrence H. Keeley, *War before Civilization* (New York: Oxford University Press, 1996), 157, 178. On the limits of violence in viceregal New Spain and negotiation as the preferred relationship between late eighteenth-century Native peoples and Spaniards in parts of the northern borderlands, see Brian Owensby, "Foreword," and Susan Kellogg, "Introduction – Back to the Future: Law, Politics, and Culture in Colonial Mexican Ethnohistorical Studies," in Ethelia Ruiz Medrano and Susan Kellogg, eds., *Negotiation within Domination: New Spain's Indian Pueblos Confront the Spanish State*, Mesoamerican Worlds Series (Boulder: University Press of Colorado, 2010), xii, 9. For a similar period of "relative peace" from 1785 to 1820 in Argentina, which reached its height during the same two decades as the Spanish–Apache peace from 1790 to 1810, see Raúl José Mandrini, "Transformations: The Rio de la Plata During the Bourbon Era," in *Contested Spaces of Early America*, ed. Juliana Barr and Edward Countryman (Philadelphia: University of Pennsylvania Press, 2014), 142–160.

I

Peace and War

More than a century and a half before Spanish officers tried to turn semisedentary Apaches into reservation-dwelling farmers, Franciscan missionaries conducted a similar experiment by attempting to convert them into town-dwelling Catholics. The deerskin-clad members of "the great Apache nation" live "in tents and villages (rancherías)" surrounding the Rio Grande pueblos of New Mexico "on all sides," reported Friar Alonso de Benavides in 1630. Like hundreds of other European observers, Benavides noted that Ndé men were "very valiant in battle" and frequently moved "from one mountain ridge to another, looking for game." But he also occasionally challenged this narrow vision. "Each main village has its own recognized territory in which they plant maize and other kinds of grain," he revealed, and "they take great pride in telling the truth." Since Ndé people already were self-sufficient and possessed strong moral values, taming the alleged belligerency of their young men was apparently the best justification Benavides could come up with for Catholicizing them.[1]

Contrary to popular belief, many Ndé groups responded favorably to Franciscan conversion efforts. The powerful Chihene nantan Sanaba, who governed "the province of the Xila Apaches," enthusiastically embraced the Catholic faith. From a pueblo situated fourteen leagues west of the Rio Grande Piro pueblo of San Antonio de Senecú, Sanaba reigned over the extensive Chi'laa ("land of the red paint people"), which encompassed modern southwestern New Mexico (see Map 1.1). A regular attendee at Benavides's weekly mass in Senecú, Sanaba also personally preached and converted his own people, making Benavides's job uncharacteristically easy. Before Benavides could visit Sanaba's

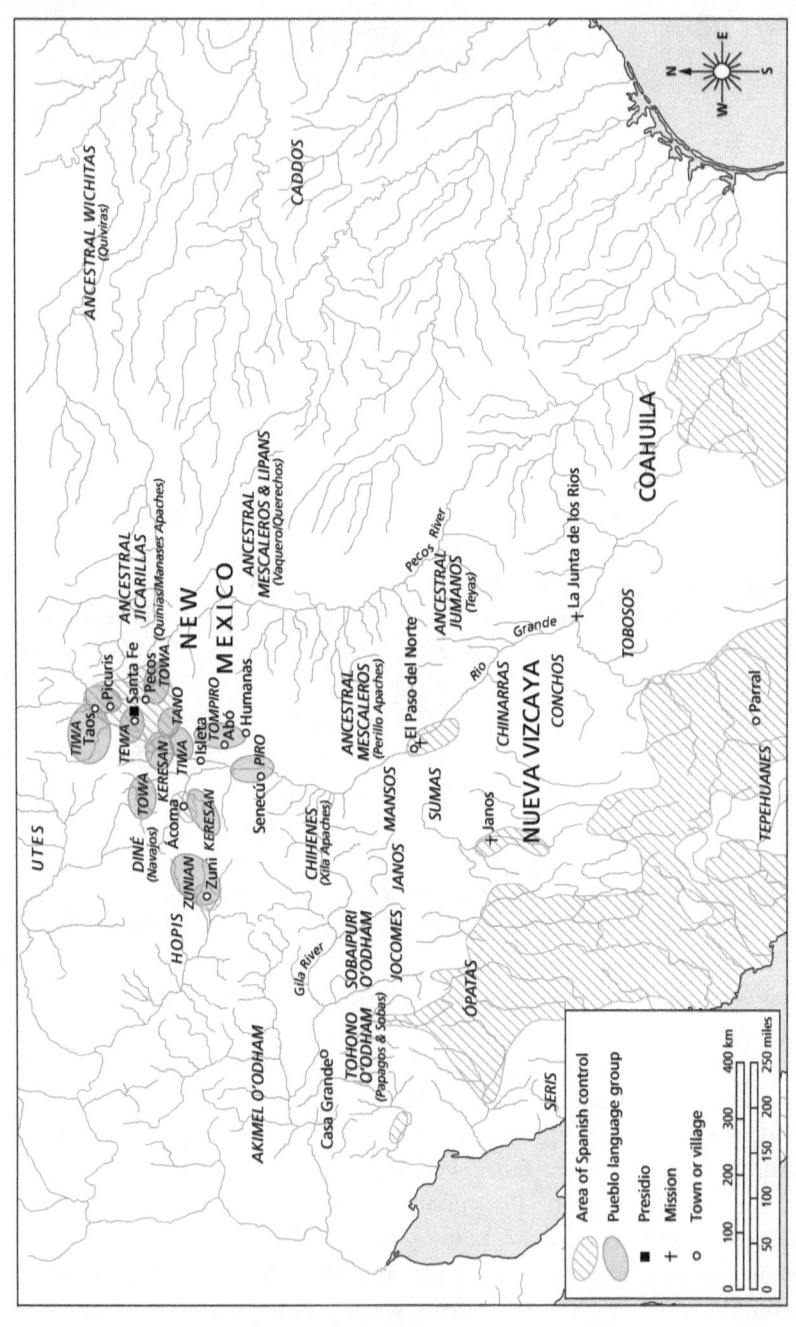

MAP 1.1 The Nde and their neighbors, ca. 1630.
Source: Adapted from Peter P. Forrestal, trans. and Cyprian J. Lynch, ed., *Benavides' Memorial of 1630* (Washington, D.C.: Academy of Franciscan History, 1954), 19; Edward H. Spicer, *Cycles of Conquest: The Impact of Spain, Mexico, and the United States in the Indians of the Southwest, 1533–1960* (1962; reprint, Tucson: University of Arizona Press, 1997), 154; John L. Kessell, *Spain in the Southwest: A Narrative History of Colonial New Mexico, Arizona, Texas, and California* (Norman: University of Oklahoma Press, 2002), 38; Sunday B. Eiselt, *Becoming White Clay: A History and Archaeology of Jicarilla Apache Enclavement* (Salt Lake City: University of Utah Press, 2012), 67, 71, 74.

people himself, the Chihene leader instead came to see Benavides and presented him with a rolled deerskin. After spreading it out, the priest observed a green sun above a dark gray moon, each surmounted by a cross (see Figure 1.1). Puzzled, Benavides asked Sanaba to explain the painting, and the Chihene headman stated, "I have ordered the cross painted over the sun and over the moon" to symbolize our understanding of your teaching "us that God is the Lord, and creator of the sun and moon and of all things."[2] Although Sanaba's explanation makes perfect sense, it is also important to remember that he and his people continued to revere the sun and moon, which the artist made the most prominent and brightly painted shapes on the deerskin, as important sources of spiritual power. This indicates the Chihenes were syncretically fusing Catholic elements with their own set of spiritual beliefs rather than replacing them. Yet, Benavides considered Sanaba's entire "pueblo of Xila" converted by 1628.[3]

The Ndé residing east of the Rio Grande were equally enamored with Catholicism. Following Sanaba's lead, the leader of an ancestral Mescalero group, whom Spaniards named Apaches del Perillo ("little dog") after a spring, also traveled to Senecú to hear Benavides preach and brought a hundred of his people to Sanaba's Xila pueblo to "be instructed and baptized."[4] Buffalo-hunting "Vaquero" Apaches east of the Rio Grande, who included ancestral Jicarillas, Mescaleros, and Lipans, also initially embraced Catholicism. Their leaders traveled to a Santa Fe chapel to visit *La Conquistadora*, a statue that Spanish priests claimed was an image of the Virgin Mary, and Friar Benavides had personally brought there. After the most influential Vaquero headman gave his word that he would become Catholic, the greed of Spanish civil authorities fractured the peace. New Mexico Governor Felipe de Sotelo Osorio ordered an enemy chief to bring him as many Vaquero captives as he could capture so that they could be sold into slavery in New Spain. The chief and several

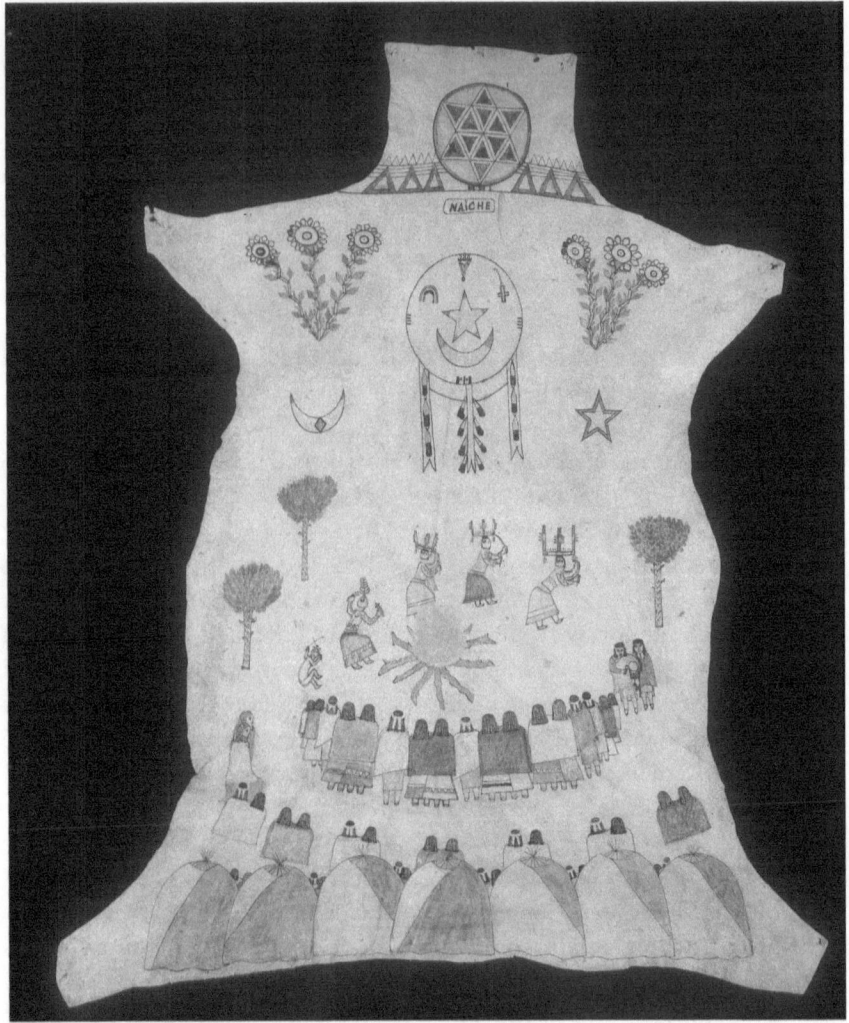

FIGURE 1.1 An Ndé painted deerskin by Naiche, ca. 1909.
Source: Courtesy of the Southwest Museum of the American Indian Collection, Autry National Center, Los Angeles, CA.

young men callously killed the Vaquero leader, despite the fact that he had held up a rosary from Benavides from around his neck.[5] And yet, several years later in 1629, after a brief uprising, Vaquero Apaches still wanted to become Christians. Within five years not only had many converted, but they were "all at peace" with Spaniards.[6]

Considering Governor Osorio's cruel and violent response, it is not surprising that most scholars have forgotten that Ndé leaders were once receptive to Catholic conversion and got along with Spaniards. Catholic conversion was just one of several major cultural adaptations the Ndé made to Spanish colonialism prior to residing on Spanish-run reservations in the late eighteenth century. Others included the adoption of the horse and gun, southward and westward territorial expansion, becoming a primarily mountain-dwelling people, and incorporating Spanish resources into their daily subsistence and raiding and trading networks. In the hundred and twenty years since Sanaba's Catholic conversion, Ndé men became so adept at plundering Spanish livestock and avoiding capture from presidial troops that officials in Nueva Vizcaya would declare an all-out war against Apaches in 1748.

This chapter examines Ndé cultural origins, environmental adaptations, and cultural transformations prior to 1700. It argues that, although the Ndé were fully capable of committing violent acts throughout their history, their relations with their indigenous neighbors and Spaniards remained predominately peaceful prior to the 1660s. The Ndé of the central and southern plains were engaged in a prolonged struggle with ancestral Wichitas and Jumanos for control of the regional political economy, and all Ndé groups retaliated against Spanish and Pueblo slaving expeditions. The available evidence suggests, however, with those notable exceptions, that Ndé violence in these years was confined to resource and captive raiding, and their northern relatives, the Diné ("the people"), or Navajos, and Spaniards were embroiled in the most intense warfare in the region. In a period of widespread drought-induced famine and disease from 1667 to 1672, the Ndé adapted to environmental stresses and Spanish colonialism by intensifying their resource raids on Spanish missions and villages, transforming themselves into mobile equestrians, and actively participating in the Pueblo and Great Southwestern Revolts.

NDÉ ORIGINS

Before discussing Ndé adaptations to Spanish colonialism, it is important to consider their cultural origins and transformations prior to Francisco Vásquez de Coronado's arrival in the region in 1540. Much like Christians, the Ndé themselves believe in a creator named Ussen, Giver of Life, who created the universe and the two other progenitors, White Painted Woman (*Ish son nah glash eh*) and Child of the Water (*Tu'ba scyne*), who created the earth. After warning White Painted Woman of a coming flood, Ussen had her take refuge in a large abalone shell, in which she floated on the surface of the water for several days, passing by the crest of White-Ringed Mountain, which stands south of modern Deming and was the only mountain visible from her shell. When the flood waters receded, she came to rest in the sandy area of today's San Agustin Plains. After emerging from the shell, Ussen told her to kneel down in the sand. The first three times she kneeled, nothing happened. But then Ussen told her to kneel a fourth time and let water drip from her. She did and gave birth to Child of the Water. Child of the Water, in turn, created the Ndé people.[7]

According to anthropologists, Southern Apacheans most likely arrived in the Southwest from subarctic Alaska and northwestern Canada via multiple routes between 950 and 1550 CE. In multistage, multipronged movements across a wide Rocky Mountain "corridor," these hunting, gathering, and farming groups began living in the river valleys of the southern plains by 1450 and the Rocky Mountain highlands of modern New Mexico and Arizona by 1550. Demonstrating a long-standing commitment to reciprocity, Eastern Apacheans intermarried, formed commercial alliances, and possibly established political confederacies with individual Pueblo villages prior to European contact. Although ancestral Southern and Western Apache interaction with neighboring ancestral Puebloans and Hopis appears limited, they likely had close contact with eastern Utes and Shoshones as they moved southward, based on shared elements in their origin stories; their ritual practices; and especially their dome-shaped, brush-covered dwellings.[8]

Although prominent nantans such as Sanaba could exercise authority over one or more named bands, the power of most Ndé headmen, especially among southern plains groups, was more limited and concentrated in networks of extended families known as a local group or in a clan. Local groups and clans were the basic cooperative social, political, economic, ceremonial, and military units, and each family resided seasonally in a separate dwelling in a large encampment, or *ranchería*, in the same named geographic area. Just as each band had specific names for their *goyas*, or sacred places, so each local group and clan laid claim to its seasonal places of residence by creating vivid names such as Be'iltson ("yellow valley of flowers") based on the plants they harvested, crops they planted, or the landscape's most distinctive features. The Ndé preference for matrilocal residence meant that the husband resided with his wife's extended family, and the wealthiest men, who were typically the most effective nantans, medicine men, and war leaders, often married multiple women. By marrying women from distinct bands, the most ambitious Ndé leaders effectively broadened their political power.[9]

Ndé men initially adapted to their new environments by become more efficient seasonal hunters of bison, elk, antelope, deer, and bighorn sheep. Having already adopted side-notched projectile points, and bows and arrows in the arctic, Apachean men further improved their hunting proficiency by stealth – disguising themselves as their prey or as native plants and slowly and silently approaching from upwind or firing arrows from behind brush blinds at water holes. Like other native peoples, they also improved their hunting efficiency by shaping the landscape – burning the woods to attract more game.[10]

Ndé men also refined and expanded their arsenal of weaponry for hunting, raiding, and warfare, by drawing on the abundant resources of the river valleys, mountains, and deserts in their southern plains and southwestern environments, which some scholars have mischaracterized as marginal. Apachean men fashioned their four-foot-long bows from seasoned hardwoods and softwoods such as mulberry or cedar. On the eve of Spanish contact, the Vaqueros of the plains had distinguished themselves from their western kinsmen by employing large Turkish-style bows. All Ndé groups constructed flint or bone-tipped arrows with distinctively colored and constructed shafts. Chokonens used desert broom, while Western Apaches relied on reeds or cane from the Gila River and other water sources. Over time, some groups learned how to drop a deer at a mere eighty yards by dipping their arrows in poison concocted from lichen or a deer's spleen, roots or stalk of nettles, and plants with a burning taste such as chili. Quivers came from deer, wolf, wildcat, or, best of all, mountain lion hides. Ndé men constructed their spear shafts from sotol stalks and whittled their blades from mountain mahogany, which were fastened with animal sinews, covered with buckskin, and often adorned with feathers. They fashioned their war clubs from hardwood branches and round rocks, which they covered with animal hide.[11]

At the same time, Ndé women became increasingly more adept at tanning hides; gathering wild plants, herbs, berries, and nuts; farming corn, melons, and pumpkins; and, of course, cooking. Ndé women and children harvested numerous edible wild plants including mescal, sotol, soapweed or palmilla, mesquite beans, and the fruits of several species of yucca and cacti, especially the tuna of the prickly pear. In the fall they also harvested wild potatoes; gathered acorns, walnuts, and piñon nuts; and picked grapes, strawberries, raspberries, mulberries, and gooseberries, among dozens of others. One of the most important new foods Ndé women and children obtained was mescal from the agave, or century plant, which they began harvesting annually on southward-facing arroyos and mountain slopes. Although mescal hearts typically ripen in April and May at the same time that the red agave flowers bloom, the Ndé learned to harvest a wide variety of the plants for food and fiber from November through early June. Selecting only those "woman" plants bearing a flower stalk, Ndé women and children efficiently dug out the white crowns of the plants by trimming the leaves with a broad stone knife and pounding a rock against a three-foot oak stick with a flattened tip. After roasting the crowns overnight in rectangular pit ovens lined with bear grass and heated flat stones, Ndé women either served them immediately as a sweet-tasting treat or pounded, dried, and stored them for future use. For a delicious and nutritious meal, Ndé women then soaked the desired amount in water and mixed them with ground piñon seeds, walnuts, or juniper berries. Of course, roasted mescal crowns could also be made into the alcoholic beverage mescal. After pounding the crowns into a pulp and placing it in a hide pouch, Ndé women buried the pouch underground for several days. They then squeezed the juice from the pulp into a container and fermented it for three days, at which point this extremely potent beverage was ready to drink.[12]

Ndé men and women also shaped the landscape to facilitate horticulture. Like their Navajo relatives, whose name means "large area of cultivated lands" in the Tewa Pueblo language, Chihenes of Chi'laa, Dzilgh'és ("On Top of the Mountain People") of the White Mountains, and T'iisibaans ("Cottonwood in Grey Wedge Shape People") of the Pinal Mountains and Tonto Basin burned to encourage small herbaceous plant habitats for seeds. Although experts disagree on whether Apacheans practiced agriculture prior to arriving in the region or learned it from Western Pueblos and Navajos, they concur that Apachean groups living in the higher elevations of today's western New Mexico and eastern Arizona, where there was adequate rainfall, probably cleared small fields in the forest, planted maize and other crops with digging sticks, and weeded them with wooden hoes. Western Apaches believe that they first obtained corn and learned to farm from their Hopi and Pueblo allies, who they called "People of the Rock," and their Piman-speaking O'odham ("the people") enemies. Like the Akimel O'odham ("river people") of the Salt and Gila River Valleys and San Juan Pueblos, these same Ndé groups learned to soak corn kernels in water prior to planting. Chihenes, Western Apaches, and Jicarillas also practiced canal irrigation, which they likely learned from Western Pueblos. Although Ndé groups were not able to farm extensively enough to rely solely on that activity for subsistence, the vast majority adapted to the ecological instability of their environment by combining farming with hunting and gathering. This means that prior to Spanish contact most Apaches were semisedentary rather than nomadic and had clearly defined home territories centered around their cultivated fields.[13]

That said, Ndé men and women clearly still traveled to hunt, gather, trade, visit relatives, and fight their enemies. They used dogs to carry their belongings and trade goods in small packs on a travois, and most Ndé women also used carrying baskets and baby carriers. On the eve of Spanish contact, Ndé groups generally got along well with neighboring native peoples, including their Diné kin to the north, eastern Utes and Shoshones from the Great Basin, Pueblo peoples along the Rio Grande, and Caddos on the southern plains. They exchanged origin stories, trade goods, and ideas about home-building, religious ceremonies, and agriculture with these groups. Their primary commercial competitors in the early 1500s were the Teyas or ancestral Jumanos, who, like eastern Ndé groups of the southern plains, traded bison meat and robes, deerskins, and tallow to Pueblos and Caddos. In addition, eastern Apacheans traded Alibates chert, finished tools, freshwater shell ornaments, and pottery to these groups in a trade network that extended at least as far northward as the Jemez Mountains and westward to the Pacific Coast.[14]

The Ndé and their neighbors also worked together to overcome environmental challenges to subsistence and quality of life before and after Coronado's arrival in the region. Two of the most serious were periodic widespread droughts and the extreme cold brought by the Little Ice Age beginning in 1350. The colder weather initially prompted Ndé groups to move southward in tandem with the game animals they hunted. The resulting wetter climate, however, also led to a rise in the bison population and increased trading of bison-related products across the region from 1450 to 1550.[15]

Although archaeologists have demonstrated that warfare was commonplace across precontact Native North America, thus far, they have uncovered minimal evidence of Ndé-initiated violence against their neighbors. O'odham oral tradition and archaeological evidence indicate they probably participated in the destruction of the Hohokam trade center of Casa Grande around 1400, but that is not certain. Given that the word "Apache" most likely derived from the Zuni word for the Navajos, *ápachu* ("enemy"), and that Apaches themselves regarded the O'odham and Jumanos as enemies, they must have committed some violent acts against these peoples prior to Spanish contact, but one should not assume they were inherently warlike or the most violent people in the region.[16]

NDÉ SPANISH POLICY: FROM AVOIDANCE TO RESISTANCE

In contrast to their embracement of Friar Benavides, the initial Ndé response to Spanish military exploration of their territory was avoidance. The Ndé likely first learned about Spanish slave-raiding expeditions from their conversations with native peoples in Sonora prior to the arrival of Francisco Vásquez de Coronado's expedition in 1540. The three encounters that Coronado eventually had with so-called Querecho or Vaquero Apacheans of the southern plains, however, were all peaceful. According to one Spanish member of the expedition, the Vaqueros were "a kind people and not violent" and "hold faithfully to friendship." Given that Coronado and his men noted their frequent exchanges of bison and deer products for Pueblo maize and blankets, the evidence suggests that Vaqueros also continued to get along well with neighboring Pueblos. As late as 1665, Chihenes were still "asking for baptism," and Franciscans were "settling and giving ecclesiastical ministers" to them. As one scholar convincingly argued more than fifty years ago, prior to 1667, the Diné were the Athapaskan-speaking group who demonstrated the most frequent and intense hostility toward Spaniards and Pueblos.[17]

Rather than resorting to raiding and warfare, the Ndé of the southern plains, who Spaniards called Querechos, Vaqueros, and Perillos, began acquiring Spanish horses indirectly through exchanges with Pueblos, and by the early 1640s they were obtaining them by direct trade with *nuevomexicanos*, including the Spanish governor. Eastern Ndé groups most frequently continued to travel westward to acquire horses from Pueblos along the Rio Grande villages of Pecos, Picuris, and Taos. On several occasions, however, Spanish hostilities compelled Pueblos to move eastward to live with Ndé groups on the plains of modern eastern Colorado and western Kansas, which meant that Pueblos sometimes brought horses, as well as architectural and agricultural expertise, to Apaches. In 1639, for example, Taos Pueblos rebelled against the aggressive policies of New Mexico Governor Luis de Rosas by moving in with their Plains Apache allies, constructing a pueblo that Spaniards called El Cuartelejo ("The Far Quarter"), and planting crops.[18] In October 1696, Santa Clara and Picuris Pueblos repeated the pattern, when in opposition to Governor Diego de Vargas's efforts to reconquer the region they, too, relocated to El Cuartelejo, where most remained for another decade.[19]

On at least one occasion in 1650 Pueblos also attempted to drive Spanish horses to Ndé living west of the Rio Grande. After uniting in an alleged pan-Pueblo and Athapaskan plot to overthrow the Spaniards on the night of Holy Thursday, Pueblos paid a heavy price for their efforts. Spaniards arrested as many Pueblo leaders as they could find, hanging nine and selling the rest into slavery. The principal goal of this intertribal alliance, however, was not to acquire horses in order to become more formidable Spanish adversaries, but instead to deprive Spaniards of their horse supply so that Apaches could live in peace. Given the propensity of New Mexico governors to authorize Spanish troops and Pueblo auxiliaries to conduct horse-mounted punitive expeditions into the Apachería, Ndé leaders understandably deemed the horse "the principal nerve of warfare" against them, and they simply wanted to "be left in freedom, like their ancestors, in ancient times."[20]

Of course, Ndé men were fully capable of raiding Spanish missions and settlements to retaliate against such offensives or to acquire horses for food and transportation. But the available evidence indicates that, prior to the late 1660s, they did so less frequently and intensely than some scholars have supposed. Bison-hunting Ndé groups of the central and southern plains, who were expanding southward after 1400, forged reciprocal political, economic, and kinship ties with surrounding sedentary and semisedentary agriculturalists and wintered with them. As of 1540 the Ndé held accords not only with northern Rio Grande Pueblos at Taos, Picuris, and Pecos but also with Caddoan-speaking ancestral Wichitas and Pawnees of Quivira and the Central Plains.

By the 1600s a central policy goal of these Ndé was to gain control of the regional political economy, which meant that they now tried to cut Wichitas and Jumanos out of Rio Grande Pueblo markets. The increased Ndé sale of Wichita slaves at Pecos during the 1620s suggests heightened conflicts with their former allies. By 1660 ancestral Jicarillas, Mescaleros, and Lipans had succeeded in pushing Wichitas eastward and Jumanos southward, gaining commercial access to Humanas Pueblo. The idea, however, that Spanish colonizers "proceeded from the beginning under the cloud of Apache terror" is a gross exaggeration.[21]

Ndé men began carrying out raids on horseback at least as early as 1671. In a period of food and resource scarcity, which began during the severe droughts of the late 1660s, mounted Ndé began targeting Piro horse herds in the Rio Abajo region. At high noon on August 1, 1671, a mixed group of equestrians consisting of ancestral Mescaleros from east of the Rio Grande whom Spaniards called Siete Rios and Nantan El

Chilmo's Chihenes successfully captured large numbers of horses at the Piro pueblo of Senecú, where the former Chihene leader Sanaba had regularly attended Friar Benavides's mass more than forty years earlier. They then struck the Tompiro villages east of the Manzano Mountains in 1672, most notably sacking and burning the convent at Abó and killing Fray Pedro de Ayala. Although the Ndé regarded Pueblos as intruders in their territory, this violent aggression, in combination with drought-induced famine, nevertheless caused the abandonment of all of these pueblos, a disruption in regional trade, and the relocation of more than 1,100 Pueblo families.[22]

Horses, however, were not nearly as revolutionary an acquisition as some scholars have supposed. The Ndé of the southern plains never struggled so much with their dogs as beasts of burden that they desperately begged Spaniards and Pueblos to trade them horses. Although the Ndé were initially curious about the new animals and recognized their value as a potential food source, it took them much longer to adopt them as a more efficient mode of transportation and begin revering them for spiritual power. Eastern Ndé groups were still using dogs to carry their trade goods nearly a century after Spanish contact in 1626, and they continued to rely on them until at least 1719.[23]

Like the dog and travois, the bow and arrow also persisted long after Spanish contact and continued to be the Ndé's preferred weapon for hunting and making war until well after 1800. Apaches and Spaniards alike recognized that bows and arrows were more effective weapons than harquebuses and muskets, and they were easier to maintain. Indeed, in the late eighteenth century, Ndé men could still fire four to ten times as many arrows as Spaniards could fire bullets.[24]

Southern Athapaskan military culture was not timeless, however. The Ndé acquired enough Spanish products through trading and raiding that they began modifying and improving many aspects of their material culture. The changes in weaponry alone illustrate this trend. Although arrows persisted, flint and bone points were gradually replaced by iron and steel ones. Mounted Ndé men also made excellent use of the fifteen-foot-long Spanish lance in hunting buffalo and in raiding and warfare, which Comanches soon imitated. Guiding their horses only with their knees, charging Ndé lancers held their weapons with both hands above their heads. Lipan Apaches began acquiring French guns, powder, hatchets, and sword blades through trade with the Bidais, and neighboring plains groups to the north began acquiring them more slowly by raiding their French-allied enemies. Bows, arrows, and lances, however, remained more important weapons than firearms for Apaches and every other Southwestern equestrian indigenous group in the colonial era.[25]

Contrary to Hollywood imagery, mounted Ndé men and women did not ride their horses bareback in any era. The closest they came to this was placing a robe over their horse's back when attempting to ride with the utmost speed. In general, however, the Ndé, like all other native North American equestrians, used European saddles. They first acquired these from Spaniards, along with iron stirrups and bridles with Spanish bits. Blending the best of native and European technological traditions, by at least 1694 Ndé young men were protecting their horses and themselves from enemy arrows with leather armor made from buffalo skins, and by the 1720s eastern Ndé groups were painting it red, blue, green, or white. Since pedestrian Ndé already wore leather armor prior to Spanish contact, they were not simply copying Spaniards in this case either. They were syncretically improving on their own native tradition.[26]

LOYAL ALLIES: THE NDÉ ROLE IN THE PUEBLO AND GREAT SOUTHWESTERN REVOLTS

Regardless of whether the Ndé initially embraced or despised Spanish horses, as Pueblo allies and active participants in the Pueblo Revolt of 1680 and reverberating Great Southwestern Revolt, they began increasing the frequency and intensity of their livestock raids. Although one scholar contends that "Gila Apaches took no part in the Pueblo Revolt, being far to the south," the reality is that they and other Ndé groups played a major role in both conflicts by welcoming fleeing mission Indians into their camps, assisting rebelling missionized indigenous groups, and attacking any missionized Indians who were serving as Spanish allies.[27]

The extent of Ndé-initiated destruction of Pueblo villages during the revolt, however, has been exaggerated both by Pueblos themselves in Spanish documents and by scholars who uncritically treat Pueblo testimony at face value. When a mixed Pueblo group of Piros and Tiwas apologized to Governor Antonio de Otermín in December 1681 for taking up arms against Spaniards because "they had believed themselves ambushed by Apaches," it should be taken with a very large grain of salt.[28] These informants were clearly only telling Spaniards what they wanted to hear.

Blaming acts of indigenous violence solely on Apaches in the presence of potentially hostile Spaniards was far less risky for Rio Grande Pueblo groups than implicating themselves or their kinsmen as traitorous rebels because Apaches were much harder for Spaniards to locate and punish. Pueblos were simply depicting Apaches as the malicious warriors that Spaniards believed they were. After retreating southward to El Paso (modern Ciudad Juárez, Chihuahua) in the fall of 1680, Spaniards had assumed that the bold and allegedly more numerous Apaches would wage relentless war on Pueblos, for they mistakenly believed that Apaches "have always oppressed them in this manner." And when Governor Otermín first returned, he expected to find the province in shambles. Instead, although Spaniards admittedly encountered some of the expected destruction, they were shocked to find Pueblos "allied and at peace with the Apaches."[29]

Only a small percentage of native participants were mounted during the early years of the Pueblo Revolt. According to a Spanish officer in December 1681, slightly more than ten percent of an estimated 1,000 rebel Indians they encountered were on horseback.[30] Those rebelling Indians who were mounted, however, still proved highly effective at intimidating Spanish troops and slowing their efforts to reoccupy the province. In late December 1681, for instance, a mixed equestrian force of more than fifty Pueblos and Apaches commanded by Picuris Pueblo leader Luis Tupatú appeared on a high bluff northeast of Isleta pueblo and caused Governor Otermín's force to retreat southward to the town to regroup.[31]

Although evidence is thin, it appears that by 1682 Chihenes had acquired a surplus of horses in part by raiding southward into northwestern Nueva Vizcaya. In March they made their first documented livestock raid in the province on a ranch near Casas Grandes, perhaps in conjunction with neighboring semi-nomadic Suma allies, whom Spaniards later found in their camp. In the same month, a recently escaped Jumano captive reported that "Apaches of the plains" traveled to the country of the "Apaches of the Sierra of Gila" in the Pinos Altos and Mogollon Mountains to acquire the horses they used to trade for at Pecos, which suggests that upland-dwelling Chihenes possessed more horses at this time than eastern Ndé groups on the southern plains. This makes sense, given that long-standing Rio Grande Pueblo trade networks had been disrupted by drought, disease, famine, and increased violence during the revolt and that the Ndé of the southern plains were at war with recently mounted Caddos within the year.[32] Here, then, during the early years of the Pueblo Revolt, is clear-cut evidence of intergroup cooperation between Chihenes, Sumas, and Ndé groups east of the Rio Grande. It also constitutes the first solid evidence of Ndé livestock raiding beyond the boundaries of their immediate territory in combination with expansion in any direction, which some historians have also mistakenly argued started much earlier.[33]

Although Chihenes were now engaged in at least some horse trading, the primary purpose of large-scale Ndé and Pueblo horse raids on Spaniards in the years preceding the Spanish reconquest was, quite obviously, to prevent Spaniards from reconquering native territory and reoccupying New Mexico.[34] Imperialistic empire-building was not part of the equation. Small-scale raids were often motivated by hunger. Again, these were drought- and disease-ridden years marked by violence. Since Isleta was the only Pueblo village that had an abundant harvest in fall 1681, these Indians subsequently sought Spanish aid because they feared that rebelling Pueblos and their Navajo and Apache allies would target their crops.[35]

The Pueblo, Diné, and Ndé war for independence in New Mexico spread southward, inspiring other oppressed native peoples around Parral and El Paso to war against Spaniards as well. In 1683, laboring mission Indians left the mines and farms in and around Parral and fled to the surrounding mountains, where they organized and launched attacks that "totally shut off" Nueva Vizcaya's interprovincial communications.[36] The fact that this spin-off revolt took place near Parral is potentially significant because it is the primary place where New Mexico governors and semisedentary Manso Indian allies had sold Apache captives into slavery to work in Spanish mines, homes, and fields from the 1630s through the 1670s.[37] Thus, Apache slaves in Parral may have participated in the uprising (see Map 1.2).

The following spring, Jano and Suma mission Indians at Janos (in northwestern Nueva Vizcaya) and El Paso boldly followed suit. Originally planned as a Manso revolt in El Paso on Easter, Spanish officials got wind of it and promptly arrested eight leaders, including Manso and Jano principal chief Luís and several Apaches living among them. On May 6, recently arrived Jano Indians and twenty-year resident Sumas at Janos mission proved more successful, burning the mission to the ground with the help of some of Chief Chiquito's independent Mansos and escaping with several Spanish captive women and children. A week later, missionized Sumas who had intermarried with Janos at Casas Grandes (seven miles southeast of Janos mission) left their mission as well. The revolution then spread quickly eastward to Sumas and Mansos in the Franciscan-run El Paso missions before reverberating southward again to the Conchos and other tribes living near Parral. Although it is clear that these groups

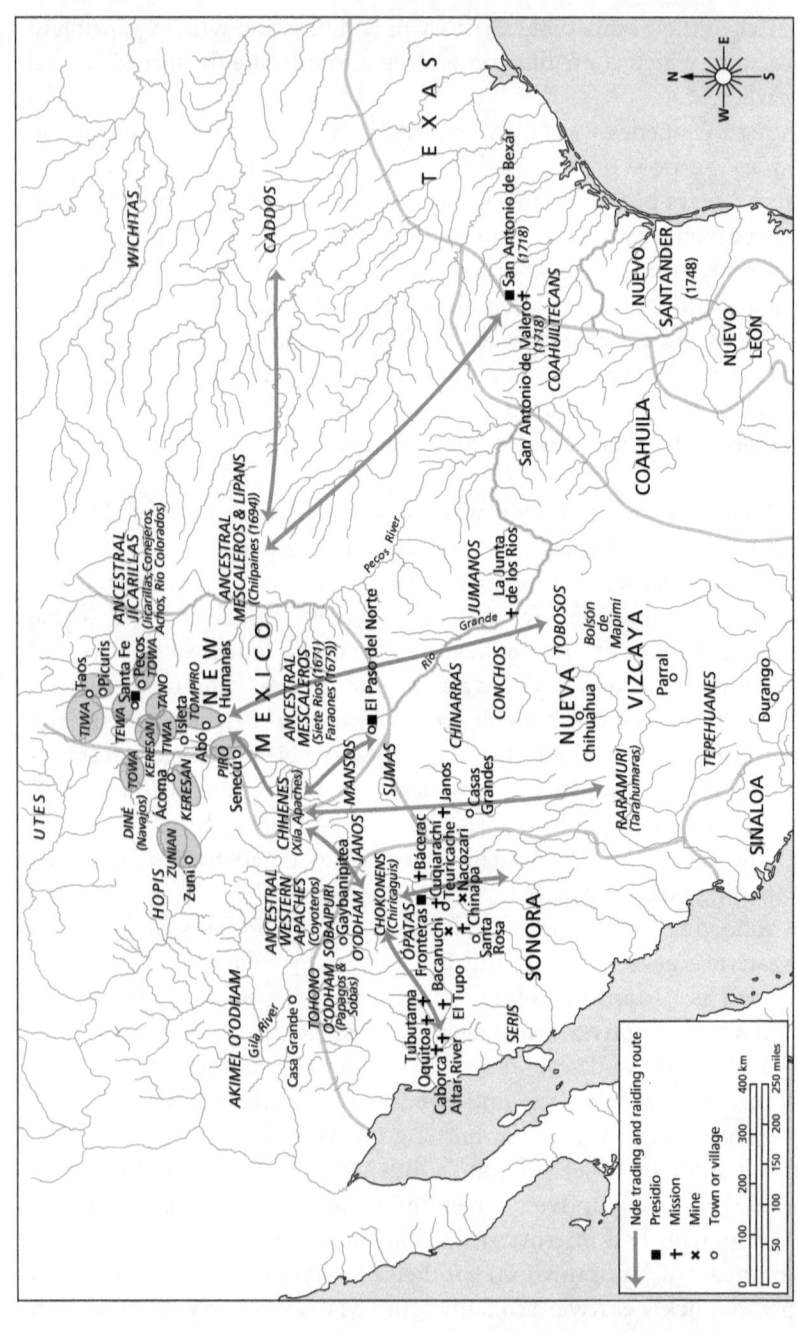

MAP 1.2 The expanding Ndé homeland, 1670–1718.
Source: Adapted from Spicer, Cycles of Conquest, 90, 122, 154, 237, 242; Gerhard, North Frontier of New Spain, 280, 315; Moorhead, Presidio, 28; Eiselt, Becoming White Clay, 73–74.

were not ethnic Athapaskans, many of them intermarried with Apaches, may have worked side by side with enslaved Apaches at Casas Grandes and Parral, and soon formed a pan-Indian alliance that included Apaches in what one astute scholar has called the Great Southwestern Revolt.[38]

In mid-September 1684, unnamed "enemy" Indians attacked the Franciscan-run mission and settlement at Casas Grandes, burning Spanish homes and supplies and running off the horse herd and a large number of livestock. The surviving residents were so "annihilated and destitute" that "everyone moved into the church," where they remained for at least the next nine months. In less than a year the rebelling Indians in Nueva Vizcaya had captured "more than 2,000 cattle and horses and almost another 2,000 smaller animals," which Captain Ramírez de Salazar believed they were doing simply because they "have nothing else to eat."[39] While hunger was a logical contributing factor, these native peoples were certainly resourceful enough to hunt and gather for food. A more likely primary goal was to weaken Spaniards' ability to wage offensive military campaigns against them and enslave their people, just like in New Mexico.

By the spring of 1685, it was clear to Spanish officials that, like Pueblos in New Mexico, revolting mission Indians in Nueva Vizcaya were destroying missions in that province and Sonora with Apache help in an apparent drive to reassert their sovereignty and independence. As Captain Ramírez de Salazar lamented in April, "The sacred vessels have been profaned, the holy vestments have been trampled, and Our Lord has been again crucified by a new breed of [savages]." In contrast to New Mexico, many of these sacked missions – the Jano mission of Soledad at Casas Grandes; the Suma missions of Santa Gertrudis, Torreón, and Carretas; and the Chinarra settlements – were never revived. Others, such as the Concho, Toboso, and Julime missions of San Pedro; San Francisco; Nombre de Dios; San Gerónimo; and San Antonio de Julimes, Spaniards would work to restore. The precise level of Ndé involvement in all of this violence prior to 1686 remains fuzzy, however. The only clearly documented Ndé-led raids in this region in 1685 were livestock raids conducted in the spring on the Tigua and Piro missions southeast of El Paso. With little left to destroy in Nueva Vizcaya, the revolting Indians turned to Sonora in the Spring of 1685, launching three attacks on the recently completed Ópata mission of Bácerac on the Bavispe River, which was the first Spanish mission established in that province in forty years.[40]

As Spaniards frantically began constructing five new presidios including Janos to contain this resurgent native revolution in 1686, Chihene groups west of the Rio Grande and so-called Siete Rios groups east of it retained their political alliances and family ties with Sumas, Mansos, Janos, and Jocomes. Fed up with Spaniards coercing them to work in surrounding silver mines and Spanish livestock trampling their crops, missionized Conchos, Tarahumaras, Sonoran O'odham, Tepehuanes, and numerous other Nueva Vizcayan bands joined the action in the spring of 1690, along with Piman-speaking Sobaipuris from the San Pedro River Valley and Seris in Sonora in 1691. In the southwestern corner of the Sierra Tarahumara these rebels deliberately killed Spanish horses and livestock and burned the missions, just as Pueblos did in New Mexico. As the Christianized Concho Indian Francisco clearly stated, "All we want to do is live like we used to."[41]

Some of the earliest evidence of coordinated southwestern expansion among Ndé groups west of the Rio Grande and their southern neighbors occurred in the spring of 1688. In May of that year and the following June, Chihenes, who "before this seemed to be contented" along the Gila River "and never invaded" Sonora, joined Jocomes, Sumas, and Janos and twice struck the Ópata pueblo of Santa Rosa north of Cuquiarachi. According to six Manso emissaries at Janos presidio, Chihenes, Janos, Jocomes, Sumas, O'odham, and Sobas together crossed into Sonora again in March 1691, targeting Bacachito pueblo near Chinapa. In August 1691 Spaniards discovered a multitribal confederation of Chihene Apaches, Chief Chiquito's Mansos, Janos, Sumas, Jocomes, and O'odham all residing together in the Florida Mountains north of Janos (south of today's Deming, NM, in Luna County), and Governor Vargas noted frequent communication between groups of two to six mountain-dwelling Apaches who visited Manso converts in El Paso and intermarriage between independent Apaches and rebelling Mansos and Sumas.[42]

In response to the perceived threat of this Chihene-led pan-Indian alliance, Spaniards launched one of their earliest punitive expeditions into the Chi'laa from Nueva Vizcaya in October 1691. This coordinated campaign, which departed from Janos presidio under the command of New Mexico Governor Vargas and Captain Juan Fernández de la Fuente, initially failed to engage any enemy Indians whatsoever. But after returning south to the Ópata pueblo of Teuricachi, Sonora, for provisions, and proceeding northward to the Gila River, "they came upon rancherías of Apaches" on both sides of the river and succeeded in capturing two of their men and twenty-three women and children. According to Fernández, they attacked the right group. He claimed these

FIGURE 1.2 Detail of map depicting the Ndé homeland as 'Terra Apachorum,' or 'Apache Country,' ca. 1705.
Source: Petrus Schenk, *Tabula Mexicae et Floridae*, ca. 1705. Courtesy of former Chihene Nde Nation of New Mexico Historical Record Keeper Lorraine Garcia.

Apaches "used to make war" on Spaniards settled in New Mexico and were the same ones "making a very raw war" around El Paso, Janos, and in Sonora. Despite this campaign's seeming "success," its main result was an escalation of Chihene-led indigenous violence around Janos in the ensuing months.[43]

On the heels of a bloody battle near Janos in February 1692, however, the Chihenes and their allies asked for peace, which Captain Fernández granted. The Janos commander issued Chihene leaders gifts of clothing and supplies, which resulted in a one-month cease fire. While a duplicitous Fernández prepared for a spring attack against the Chihenes in spite of the peace agreement, Chihenes and their allies responded with a deadly ruse of their own. After showing up at Janos under the guise of peace, they attacked and wounded several Spaniards, which one scholar has argued was an act of revenge for the prior October campaign.[44] But these were not typical Apache fighting tactics, and Chihenes had likely already avenged those deaths with their attacks on Janos from the previous November through February. What seems more likely is that they discovered that Fernández was treacherously preparing a spring punitive expedition against them, and they decided to respond proactively, just like Fernández, by employing the very same treacherous tactics that Spanish officers routinely used against them.

Throughout the late seventeenth century, Spanish officers in Nueva Vizcaya and Sonora generally understood the Apaches they fought to be Gila Apaches whose home base lay at the headwaters of the Gila River and extended southward across the region of modern New Mexico, not Chiricahuas based in the Sierra de Chiricagui (today's Chiricahua Mountains) or Western Apaches residing north of the Gila River in today's Arizona. That said, Spanish forces and their Indian allies periodically engaged confederated Chihenes, Janos, and Jocomes camped in the Chiricahua range during the 1690s, who were beginning to use these mountains as a stronghold and should be considered ancestral Chokonens (Chiricahuas).[45] One of the earliest references to "Apaches of the Sierra of Chiguacagui [Chiricagui]" (Ópata for "mountains of the wild turkey") is from November 1692, when Captain Francisco Ramírez traveled up the San Pedro River from Sonora to Aravaipa Canyon and convinced the Sobaipuris to sever their alliance with this Apache group and become Spanish allies through tactful diplomacy.[46]

In 1696 Spanish troops also attacked Janos, Jocomes, and Apaches, who may have included resident Chihenes, in the Pinaleño Mountains, which Spaniards called the Sierra Florida. In November 1697, as Sobaipuri O'odham scouts guided the Italian-born and German-educated Jesuit Father Eusebio Kino to Casa Grande, he identified the north bank of the Gila east of these ruins as part of "the very extensive Apachería," and in early March 1699 Piman-speaking guides told Captain Juan Mateo Manje that the Verde River "takes its rise in the land of the Apaches," suggesting Ndé lived at its headwaters. In November 1697, Captain Manje, who accompanied Father Kino to Casa Grande, identified the same "Sierra de Santa Rosa de la Florida" (Pinaleño Mountains) as a range "where many Apaches have their habitations," and he praised them as "the most resourceful and intelligent people found in these parts." These groups should be regarded as ancestral Western Apaches.[47]

Even in this violent era, Spaniards routinely exaggerated the extent of Apache-led hostilities in the region and underestimated their ability to remain self-sufficient in their home territory. Although Apaches sometimes targeted Spanish horses, mules, and cattle in New Mexico, Nueva Vizcaya, and Sonora, in many cases they were inaccurately blamed for the transgressions of their allies or of resident mission Indians themselves. In

July 1691, for example, after Governor Vargas initially received word that Apaches had stolen livestock from the relocated Piro and Tiwa (Tigua) villages of Socorro and Isleta del Sur near El Paso, he later learned that it was actually Sumas from Guadalupe mission. When Governor Vargas passed through the land of the alleged "enemy Apache" south of El Morro in early December 1692, he was surprised to discover through his Zuni guide Agustín, El Cabezón, that a maize-planting ranchería of Chihenes whom Spaniards called "Apaches Colorados" resided in the well-watered Sierra Peña Larga southwest of Acoma Pueblo, which lay near the headwaters of the Gila River and likely corresponded to the Mogollon Mountains.[48]

After reoccupying Santa Fe in December 1693, Spaniards worked to revive friendly relations with ancestral Jicarillas, Mescaleros, and Lipans of the southern plains. In March 1694 emissaries from "the far-flung rancherías of the Llanos Apache nation" traveled from Pecos to Santa Fe to resume peaceful relations with Vargas and the Spaniards in New Mexico. In the same month, a delegation from three of their tents proceeded to trade "buffalo meat and buckskins" to Spanish soldiers and settlers at Pecos and promised to return there in October to peacefully barter as they had in the decades preceding the devastating droughts of the late 1660s. Another Ndé headman, whom Governor Vargas called a Faraón during a May visit to Santa Fe, insisted that he be baptized, but Vargas and the priest refused, claiming that he "needed to know the prayers" first. In early July, Captain Antonio Jorge found another Apache ranchería friendly with Pecos Governor Juan de Ye camped along the road near Taos Pueblo, where they were waiting to trade. To symbolize their friendship with the Spaniards, the Ndé headman and his people all personally shook hands and embraced Captain Jorge and Governor Vargas, "surrendered their weapons," and "willingly took the holy cross that the captain was carrying ... to set up within sight of the sierra." Such overt displays of accommodation may have concealed a larger Ndé policy goal. Several days later Governor Vargas found a group of Plains Apaches guarding the entrance to a funnel canyon where an at-large Taos Pueblo ranchería had camped, which suggests that the principal objective of this Ndé leader and his people was to protect their Pueblo allies from Spanish attack. Finally, the following May, an ancestral Lipan group known as Chilpaines, whose summer camp was probably on the Canadian River, traded at Picuris Pueblo and solidified an alliance there with Spaniards in October.[49]

To the southwest, however, things still proved more volatile. Despite the creation of a Spanish and O'odham-manned flying column headed by General Domingo Jirónza in March 1693 (or perhaps precisely because of it), Apaches, Jocomes, Janos, Sumas, and "barbarous" apostates continued to raid for Spanish livestock, kill Spaniards, and, most recently, helped paralyze "the transportation of ore from the mines." In late September, a Spanish official in Parral described three well-traveled raiding routes taken by Apaches and their allies into resource-depleted Sonora through the Caaguiona, Bavispe, and Teuricache Valleys. The Indians' "constant raids" through these points of entry caused the Real de Nacozari mining camp to be "nearly depopulated."[50]

Once in the province, Apaches and their allies tried to minimize their losses by not simply waging an all-out war. Depending on the circumstance, they alternated between resource raids and revenge raids, which the most astute Spanish observers recognized more than two centuries earlier than American anthropologists would. When the Indians sought horses, mules, and cattle, they employed stealth, traveling in small groups of three to four men, and watching "the ranches and pastures, and upon the slightest carelessness, they drive off all the animals." By the time Spaniards could mobilize a response, the Indians typically had a twenty- to thirty-league head start, and sought refuge "in the roughest parts of the mountains," where it was impossible for cavalry to reach them. If they did happen to be overtaken, which was most likely to happen if they were driving off slow-moving cattle, they would typically kill some of the animals with arrows "in order afterwards to come and eat them." In their more violent attacks, Apaches and their allies most commonly targeted Spanish wagon trains along the Camino Real. Employing the same kinds of guerrilla tactics as in their resource raids to minimize their losses, they would fall on the most weakly guarded pack trains "in the narrowest and mountainous passes," where Spanish horses could not travel quickly. After first "striking down the horses" with arrows, the Indians then proceeded to capture or kill the defenseless escorts, depending on their level of advantage.[51]

Frustrated Janos acting commander Juan Fernández de la Fuente, who knew these raiding Indians very well, lamented another rebel Indian raiding strategy, which Apaches would rely on for centuries. The officer noted that Apaches had united and "always travel together" with "Janos, Jocomes, Mansos, Sumas, and Chinarras" through the undefended and impenetrable mountainous extension of their homeland along the territorial border between Nueva Vizcaya and Sonora "where they always have their habitations."⁵² This represented significant southward territorial expansion for Apaches in this time period.

In June 1695 Spanish officers tried to negotiate peace terms with many of the rebel Indians. On the afternoon of June 17, Generals Domingo Terán de los Rios and Juan Fernández de la Fuente left Janos presidio in command of a mixed force of Spanish troops and Yaqui, Seri, Tepoca, Ópata, and O'odham allies. After a brief skirmish on a Sonoran hilltop near the confluence of the Cajón Bonito and San Bernadino Rivers with a group of Indians that included Suma, Chinarra, and Jano families carrying only food, they trailed the group to their camp in the Chiricahua Mountains, where several captives and an emissary led them to believe they would find all of the Indians – Janos, Jocomes, Sumas, Chinarras, Mansos, Apaches, and their Ópata captives. By the time General Fernández and a seriously ill General Terán reached that sierra on June 29 and met with Jocome leader El Tabobo ("Great Chief"), however, they learned that only two Apache rancherías remained among them. Fernández initially found the interethnic force of Janos, Jocomes, Mansos, Sumas, and Chinarras to be well armed with muskets, swords, and lances and some to be "mounted on Spanish saddles." After visiting the Indians' freshly swept camp, which they had arranged to look like a church, Spanish soldiers reported seeing "a high cross and three very small ones," which El Tabobo explained symbolized "their desire for peace." From the Spaniards' camp along Turkey Creek near modern Paradise, AZ, General Fernández then regaled Suma, Janos, and other native male and female emissaries with rations of meat, pinole, tobacco, and flour through three rounds of peace talks. Ultimately, however, the two sides failed to reach an agreement because of mutual mistrust and the fact that the neighboring O'odham had launched their own rebellion to the west several months earlier.⁵³

Sonoran troops and Jesuit priests had helped to precipitate this latest round of indigenous violence through their own aggressive and coercive practices. In 1694 Lieutenant Antonio Solis from the recently founded Fronteras presidio unethically murdered three Piman-speaking men near San Xavier del Bac who he thought were eating stolen horse flesh, but were actually only consuming venison, and then treacherously massacred fifty unarmed Christian O'odham Indians from mission San Pedro de Tubutama in the Altar River Valley after promising to grant peace to them. Although the Indians at Tubutama had revolted prior to this and killed three Christian Ópatas, their actions were in direct response to Spanish coercion perpetrated by Jesuit priests, who employed heavy-handed

Christian Ópatas as O'odham overseers at the mission. These abusive and excessively violent practices led to an escalation and expansion of O'odham violence, as O'odham from Oquitoa and surrounding villages joined those from Tubutama, destroying Altar and murdering the Sicilian-born Jesuit father Francisco Xavier Saeta at Caborca on Holy Thursday. Not to be outdone, former New Mexico Governor and General Domingo Jironza's Sonoran flying company and some Seri allies launched a punitive campaign into the Pimería, killing innocent women and children and destroying their crops at Caborca, which led to a full-fledged O'odham rebellion. But this was not all. Recognizing that they had failed to kill those responsible for killing Father Saeta, Father Kino and the Spanish military worked together to punish them in the middle of peace proceedings by beheading one and killing nearly fifty others, who included several innocent O'odham leaders, most notably the peaceful headman of mission El Tupo. Now a full-scale O'odham-Spanish war broke out until August 1695, which, given the similarity of causes, seems like an extension of the Pueblo Revolt.[54]

At the same time that Fernández and his men rushed westward to help Sonoran troops quell the O'odham uprising, a group of "fourteen young men" from an intermarried Jocome and Apache ranchería captured horses from the Ópata pueblos of Bacanuchi and Teuricachi. What El Tabobo considered to be young men hunting livestock to feed their hungry people, General Fernández regarded as acts of "war" that violated their "truce" and justified Spaniards waging war "with fire and blood." The truth of the matter, however, is that the two sides never reached an agreement, and Apache leaders whom Fernández considered to be "in a state of rebellion" by not attending the peace talks were actually following a policy of neutrality, which should not have resulted in Spanish aggression.[55] If this hunting or raiding party was guilty of anything, it was violating Spanish law, and a reasonable Spanish response would have been to reacquire the stolen animals, return them to their rightful owners, and have El Tabobo punish the men involved on their own terms. But in the midst of a widening interethnic Native rebellion, which Jocomes and Apaches had indeed participated in, Spanish officers viewed even the smallest indigenous transgressions as acts of war, which perpetuated a cycle of reciprocal violence and ensured an ongoing state of war.

In September 1695 Spaniards confirmed through their own observations that several Apache families had been living in the Chiricahua Mountains with equestrian Sumas, Janos, and Jocomes. As they walked through the Indians' hastily abandoned camp, Spanish soldiers and their

Native allies learned that these Indians had acquired branded "horses, mares, and a burro" from the Ópata mission of Cuquiarachi, which was located thirty miles south of modern Agua Prieta on a tributary of the Fronteras River. The Indians were mounted, eating the horses for food, and the women had been tanning hides, which likely came from these same animals. From native informants General Fernández learned that the perpetrators of this raid were from the Apache leader El Salinero's ranchería, which Jocomes had joined, and were camped "on the west side of the Santa Rosa Mountains" (today's Pinaleño Mountains). Another Ndé ranchería was camped in the woods along the Gila River near modern Safford, AZ, with Mansos, Sumas, Janos, and Chinarras. As one female Indian captive clearly stated, "the Apaches had been friends with the Janos, Jocomes, Sumas, and Mansos for a long time and always traveled together."[56]

On September 16, 1695, the Jocomes at last agreed to make peace with General Fernández under the same terms discussed two months previously at Turkey Creek. Both sides were war weary and suffering from illness. The Jocome governor and two emissaries were too ill to participate in the negotiations and Generals Fernández, Terán, and Jironza were all too sick to ride a horse. The symptoms, which an untold number of rebel Indians, Spanish soldiers, and Indian allies were also suffering from, included fever, chills, and convulsions. By late September, approximately 170 Piman-speaking O'odham and Ópata allies, constituting 85 percent of a mixed force of O'odham, Ópata, and Concho auxiliaries, deserted the Spaniards, while others, including General Terán, became so sick that they died. According to one Spanish officer, they contracted the illness from drinking stagnant water "poisoned by enemy Indians," but the more likely source was a virus from the contaminated water itself. After decades of fighting rebellious mission Indians and their allies, Spanish troops and two hundred Indian allies had made one of their deepest penetrations into the Apachería. Camped near modern Apache Pass, they stood a mere thirty leagues from their adversaries along the Gila River. But in a most profound irony, both sides were bedridden with the same deadly illness and compelled to make peace with one another. After collecting as much information as he could from his compliant captives, who consisted of three male Jocomes and two female Indians, and having them baptized, General Fernández promptly ordered them shot and hanged in front of his entire disease-ridden camp, in an attempt to foster honesty and loyalty via fear.[57]

Meanwhile, as Governor Vargas's reconquering force reentered New Mexico from El Paso, recently pacified Pueblo leaders kept them off balance by spreading rumors of impending pan-Indian attacks. In the spring of 1696, for example, Governor Bartolomé de Ojeda of the Keres pueblo of Santa Ana stated that a group of "Chilmo and Faraón Apaches, Tanos, and Mansos" were gathered at Acoma Pueblo and were waiting for the Zunis and Hopis (Moquis) to join them so that they could collectively "destroy this kingdom." Although this was an exaggeration, it contained elements of truth. El Chilmo's Chihenes, Mansos, and the Keres Pueblos of Acoma were allies, and Pueblos knew that preying on Spanish fears of Apaches by playing up Apache violence was an effective way to divert Spanish attention. The fact that some pacified Pueblo groups did revolt again in July and made their way to well-watered and game-plentiful Navajo territory to the northwest and El Cuartelejo to the northeast also demonstrates that at the very least the rumor of forthcoming indigenous coalescence, if not actual violence, bore truth. Further evidence of the ongoing harmonious relations between Pueblos and Apaches east and west of the Rio Grande in 1696 is that Governor Vargas sought to break up an alliance between Acoma Pueblo and "Faraón and Salinero Apaches, the rancherías of the sierra of Gila, and the Chilmo Apaches, who command all the Apaches of this sierra."[58]

In spite of the strong trend of indigenous alliance-building, Spaniards managed to regain a foothold in New Mexico over the next two years and subsequently rebuild alliances with Apache groups east and west of the Rio Grande. Governor Diego de Vargas and the Spaniards had reasserted control of Santa Fe by January 1694, and his successor, Governor Pedro Rodríguez Cubero successfully quelled a second Pueblo revolt launched in June 1696, and pacified the Pueblos of the upper Rio Grande Valley in December 1698. By April 1702, eastern Ndé groups and El Chilmo's Chihenes were all at peace with Spaniards in New Mexico.[59]

From an Ndé perspective, making peace with the Governor of New Mexico had no bearing on their relations with Spaniards in Nueva Vizcaya and Sonora. Confederated Apaches, Jocomes, Janos, Sumas, and Mansos targeted the corn and livestock-rich villages of the Spanish-allied Sobaipuri and Akimel O'odham in seasonal acts of war in early 1698. After sacking and burning Cocóspera pueblo and wounding Father Ruiz de Contreras in late February, they then destroyed the Sobaipuri ranchería of Santa Cruz de Gaybanipitea at dawn on Easter Sunday in late March 1698, which prompted the usual retaliatory expeditions by Spaniards and their Piman-speaking O'odham allies. This time, however, the O'odham were unusually successful. El Coro, the principal Sobaipuri leader from neighboring Quiburí, had just returned from San Xavier del

Bac, and engaged the Apaches and their allies at Santa Cruz with five hundred O'odham armed with poisoned arrows, killing between 168 and 300 Indians, who were predominately Janos and Jocomes. Despite the fact that El Coro's Sobaipuris immediately relocated farther westward out of fear of Apache- and Jocome-led retaliation after this victory, they had inflicted enough casualties on this confederation that several of these war-weary groups sought peace at Janos and El Paso.[60]

NEGOTIATING PEACE

By the spring of 1698, then, Spanish, Ópata, and especially O'odham offensives had taken their toll and the pan-Indian Great Southwestern Revolt was losing steam. In October a Jocome emissary initiated peace proceedings with General Juan Fernández at Janos presidio on behalf of a portion of independent Ndé and Janos, Jocomes, Sumas, and Mansos. As a symbol of their collective good faith, the Jocome leader gave General Fernández an intricately painted tanned deerskin, just as Chihene leader Sanaba had done for Friar Alonso Benavides more than sixty years earlier. The deerskin depicted a sun surrounded by twelve stripes, which symbolized the number of days that they had been in favor of making peace, and perhaps also was supposed to correspond with the number of Jesus's disciples. Six large circles near the sun delineated six Ndé tents who "come to give obedience to His Majesty" on behalf "of their nation." An additional "one hundred and twenty marks ... painted as jacals ... in four divisions" represented the General and "three principal chiefs" of the "four rancherías of Jano, Jocome, Manso, and Suma Indians with their families" who negotiated "the said peace." As a reciprocal sign of Spanish good faith, General Fernández had given gifts to these leaders, which were also depicted on the deerskin, and "two short stripes" symbolized that the treaty would commence within "the time of two moons." The deerskin also contained an image of Janos presidio and five drops of ink signifying the short five-day journey that the Indians had taken to reach it. If these symbols were all that the deerskin contained, they would seem representative of a potential enduring peace between the former adversaries. But the Jocome emissary explained that two stripes on a different part of the deerskin "are a sign that one who flees, once settled in peace" will be punished by "hanging." Taken at face value, these marks represented the Indians' desire to comply with Spanish law. The emissary's reference to "hanging," however, almost certainly referred to General Fernández's callous killing and hanging of innocent Jocome male and female informants in the fall of 1695. When viewed in conjunction with the events that followed, this likely indicated the confederacy's lack of trust in the capacity of this officer and the Spanish military to ensure a just peace.[61]

Following these talks, the Janos settled at Janos presidio, the Sumas (and probably the Mansos) at El Paso del Norte and Socorro, the Chihenes, and, most importantly, the Jocomes, remained independent. The Janos and Sumas agreed to serve as Spanish allies against any "hostile" O'odham. Although Chihenes remained in their homeland of Chi'laa, in early August 1699, Indians whom Father Kino called "Apaches nearest the Rio Colorado," who were either Western Apaches or Yuman-speaking Yavapais on the Verde River, followed the lead of the Janos, Jocomes, and Sumas to some extent by negotiating peace indirectly with him at the head mission of Nuestra Señora de los Dolores (Our Lady of Sorrows) at Cosari in the Pimería Alta. Kino himself had initiated the accord from San Andrés in March by sending a "cross, letter, gifts, and messages" to these "Apaches" via the Hopis, and the Indians responded by making peace with the Yuman-speaking Opas and Cocomaricopas and the O'odham, and sending emissaries from these three groups to present Father Kino with "four buckskins," on behalf of all four pacified groups, in the tradition of Sanaba and the recent Jocome leader at Janos.[62]

In late August Father Kino's superior, Father Antonio Leal optimistically believed "that the Apaches were going to be reduced and embrace our holy faith" as part of a "choice Christendom," and, for a while, Chihene actions seemed to bear this out. Regardless of what language Kino's Verde River-dwelling "Apaches" spoke, the key point is that they were successful in negotiating peace with the Chihenes, and a Chihene delegation traveled to Dolores with the Sobaípuris to meet with Kino in October 1699. Nine years later in 1708 Kino himself still believed that the O'odham conversions would lead to "the reduction and conversion of the neighboring Apachería" and expanded northeastern trade networks with Hopis, Zunis, and New Mexico. In 1716 Kino's successor, Father Luis Velarde, similarly believed that Apaches and all surrounding Indians could be converted if only "there were enough priests." But there is no record of any more Ndé visits to the Jesuits after October 1699. Jesuit priests enjoyed far more success in pacifying and converting the O'odham than the Apaches.[63]

Although Apaches and Jocomes did not enter Spanish missions or camp near Spanish presidios, their leaders apparently still did their best to honor their peace agreements with Spaniards by remaining independent, reducing their raiding and warfare, and adopting a policy of neutrality toward them. This is a significant change, especially in combination with missionized Janos and Sumas also remaining at peace. According to Jesuit Father Luis Velarde in 1716, ever since the Sobaipuri defeat of the confederated Apaches, Jocomes, Janos, and Sumas at Santa Cruz de Gaybanipitea in late March 1698, "there have been no enemies disturbing" any Sonoran town, which suggests peace had endured in that province for at least eighteen years.[64]

Yet, not all first-hand observers agreed with Father Velarde. In 1703, Velarde's predecessor, Father Eusebio Kino, noted that Apaches, Jocomes, Janos, and Sumas continued pushing deeper southward into Sonora and farther westward into the Pimería every year, as they had been doing since at least the Janos uprising of 1696, and, more accurately, since the Suma uprising of 1684. This trend of seasonal southward and westward raiding would continue, with periodic cycles of peace and more intensified revenge raids, for most of the eighteenth century. In February 1701, more than two hundred Apaches, Jocomes, Janos, and Sumas renewed their assault on the semisedentary Ópatas, attacking the exposed rancho of Saracachi on the San Miguel River, which lay fifty miles south of Cocóspera, killing six, wounding seven, sacking all but two homes, and carrying off horses, mares, and "all the sheep and goats."[65]

Most Spaniards, however, believed they had reached a turning point in pacifying surrounding Native peoples as of 1698. Regardless of the fact that Apaches and the remaining confederated and affiliated former mission Indians remained independent and outside of Spanish control, the seemingly endless series of revolts by missionized Indians across northern New Spain – the Great Southwestern Revolt – had ceased. Spanish officials in Sonora viewed the 1720s and 1730s as decades of relative peace. Missionized Indians would not rebel against Spaniards again until the Yaqui and Mayo uprising of 1740, and Apache raids would not reach the same level of intensity as the 1690s until the 1750s in conjunction with the O'odham rebellion of 1751.[66] In the meantime, enough O'odham, Ópata, Tarahumara, and Pueblo men were serving Spanish interests as Indian allies to reassert control of New Mexico's Rio Grande Valley and of northern Nueva Vizcaya and Sonora and to prevent Apaches from completely overrunning the region.

From an Ndé standpoint, a less clear-cut turning point had been reached.[67] Their most significant postcontact cultural transformations had occurred after 1670, when Ndé men became equestrians and expanded their territory southward, eastward, and westward in conjunction with the creation of new Ndé subgroups. This transpired most rapidly and enduringly west of the Rio Grande, as Chihenes expanded their territory southwestward into western Nueva Vizcaya and Sonora in conjunction with Chokonen and Western Apache ethnogenesis. At the same time, bison-hunting eastern Ndé groups expanded southeastward, pressuring Jumanos, Coahuiltecans, and Caddos to seek protection in Spanish missions in South and East Texas in the early 1680s. By 1686 ancestral Jicarillas, Mescaleros, and Lipans of the central and southern plains, whom Spaniards called Palomas, Cuartelejos, Carlanas, Jicarillas, Faraones, Natagés, and Ypandes, were the "owner[s] and possessor[s] of all of the plains" of "*Cíbola*." The majority of these groups maintained peaceful commercial relations with Spaniards and Pueblo groups in New Mexico, while defending their central position in the regional political economy against surrounding Jumanos, Caddos, Wichitas, and Pawnees and encroaching Utes and Comanches between the 1680s and 1720s. This escalating war over control of the regional buffalo, horse, and slave trade would prove much more transformative and disruptive than any peace agreements or military engagements with Spaniards in New Mexico, Texas, Nueva Vizcaya, or Sonora prior to 1750.[68]

Out of these intertribal wars, the Jicarilla, Lipan, and Mescalero groups would emerge. In the first half of the eighteenth century Ndé groups would continue to target Spanish livestock at missions, presidios, and ranches in seasonal raids, while doing their utmost to protect their women, children, and elderly and retain control of their territory. As long as Spanish troops and their growing number of Indian allies continued to campaign against Ndé families, and Spanish missionaries and presidial officers failed to offer Ndé families the same gifts, livestock, housing, and protection they offered their other Native allies, the Ndé believed they were completely justified in reciprocally taking these resources for themselves and offsetting their own captured, killed, and enslaved kinsmen by capturing Spanish and Indian women and children. Attempting to resolve this contradiction, some Spanish priests and military officers negotiated mutually beneficial agreements with Apache leaders after 1700, much like Friar Alonso de Benavides and Sanaba had once done in 1628. The next chapter explores the origins of this understudied pattern and the development of Spanish-run reservations for Apaches by the 1780s.

Notes

1 Alonso de Benavides, *Benavides' Memorial of 1630*, ed. Cyprian J. Lynch, trans. Peter P. Forrestal (Washington, DC: Academy of Franciscan History, 1954), 41–42; Alonso de Benavides, *The Memorial of Fray Alonso de Benavides, 1630*, ed. Frederick Webb Hodge and Charles Fletcher Lummis, trans. Mrs. Edward E. Ayer, (Albuquerque, NM: Horan and Wallace, 1965), 130–131. For other treatments of Sanaba, see Forbes, *Apache, Navaho, and Spaniard*, 117; Elizabeth A. H. John, *Storms Brewed in Other Men's Worlds: The Confrontation of Indians, Spanish, and French in the Southwest, 1540–1795* (College Station: Texas A&M University Press, 1975), 75; Blyth, *Chiricahua and Janos*, 33.
2 Benavides, *Benavides' Memorial*, 43–44; Benavides, *Memorial*, 264, 133–136. Chihene Nde Nation of New Mexico Chairman Manuel P. Sanchez believes that Sanaba's pueblo lay near Monticello Box Canyon along Cañada Alamosa Creek (personal communication). Offering no citation, Frederick W. Hodge believed Sanaba's "pueblo of Xila" lay "probably about the head of Corduroy canyon in Socorro County." See Benavides, *Memorial*, 42. Hodge's statement dates back to the first published version of Benavides' Memorial of 1630. See Mrs. Edward A. Ayer, trans., Frederick W. Hodge, ann., and Charles F. Lummis, ed., "Early Western History: Benavides's Memorial of 1630," *The Land of Sunshine* 13 (December 1900): 439. As Sanchez has correctly determined, however, Corduroy Canyon is much farther west than the fourteen-league (approximately forty-two-mile) distance from mission San Antonio de Senecú that Friar Benavides gave for the location of Sanaba's pueblo (personal communication). The Athapaskan word "Chi'laa" and definition are from Lorraine Garcia (personal communication). For Gila Apache territory encompassing "southwestern New Mexico," see Schroeder, *Apache Indians IV*, 235.
3 Benavides, Alonso de, *Fray Alonso de Benavides' Revised Memorial of 1634*, ed. and trans. Frederick W. Hodge, George P. Hammond, and Agapito Rey (Albuquerque: University of New Mexico Press, 1945), 83; Forbes, *Apache, Navaho, and Spaniard*, 117. On celestial bodies as sources of spiritual power, see Opler, *An Apache Life-Way*, 194.
4 Benavides, *Fray Alonso de Benavides' Revised Memorial*, 84–85, 307. Quotation is on p. 85.
5 Benavides, *Benavides' Memorial*, 52, 55–56; Benavides, *Memorial*, 151, 154–156; Forbes, *Apache, Navaho, and Spaniard*, 120.
6 Benavides, *Fray Alonso de Benavides' Revised Memorial*, 92; Forbes, *Apache, Navaho, and Spaniard*, 121; Forbes, *Apache, Navaho, and Spaniard*, 121. For a contrary view of Apache relations with Spaniards and Pueblos in this period, see Blyth, *Chiricahua and Janos*, 33.
7 Morris Edward Opler, *Myths and Tales of the Chiricahua Apache Indians* (1942; reprint, Lincoln: University of Nebraska Press, 1994), 1–2; Ball, *In the Days of Victorio*, 68; Thomas E. Mails, *Secret Native American Pathways: A Guide to Inner Peace* (1988; reprint, Tulsa, OK: Council Oak Books, 2003), 127–128; David La Vere, *The Texas Indians* (College Station: Texas A&M Press, 2004), 45. I thank Michael Paul Hill for his assistance with this story.

On the Christian influence on Southern Apache creation stories, see Opler, *An Apache Life-Way*, 194–199. For other versions of Ndé creation stories, see, for example, S. M. Barrett, *Geronimo, His Own Story: The Autobiography of a Great Patriot Warrior*, new edition (1906; reprint, New York: Penguin, 1996), 50–53; Ball, *In the Days of Victorio*, 68–70; Harry Hoijer, *Chiricahua and Mescalero Apache Texts* (Chicago, IL: University of Chicago Press, 1942), 14–15; Opler, *Myths and Tales of the Chiricahua*, 3-21; James L. Haley, *Apaches: A History and Culture Portrait* (Garden City, NY: Doubleday, 1981), 14–15.

8 William B. Carter, *Indian Alliances and the Spanish in the Southwest, 750–1750* (Norman: University of Oklahoma Press, 2009), 21–23, 29–32; B. Sunday Eiselt, *Becoming White Clay: A History and Archaeology of Jicarilla Apache Enclavement* (Salt Lake City: University of Utah Press, 2012), 39, 42, 48, 69; Britten, *Lipan Apaches*, 34, 41; Robinson, *I Fought a Good Fight*, 14–15; Opler, "Apachean Culture Pattern," 371, 381–384; Haley, *Apaches*, 10.

9 Michael Paul Hill and Lorraine Garcia (personal communication); Opler, "Apachean Culture Pattern," 369–370; Grenville Goodwin, "The Southern Athapascans," *The Kiva* 4 (1938): 8; La Vere, *Texas Indians*, 86–87; Keith H. Basso, *Wisdom Sits in Places: Landscape and Language among the Western Apache* (Albuquerque: University of New Mexico Press, 1996), xv–vi, 115, 153, 157.

10 Carter, *Indian Alliances*, 22; La Vere, *Texas Indians*, 35–36; Barrett, *Geronimo*, 67; Goodwin, "The Southern Athapascans," 6; Edward F. Castetter and Morris E. Opler, *The Ethnobiology of the Chiricahua and Mescalero Apache*, University of New Mexico Bulletin, Biological Series (Albuquerque: University of New Mexico Press, 1936), 25–26. For brush blinds, see "[Vicente de Zaldívar Mendoza's] Account of the Discovery of the Buffalo, 1599," in Herbert Eugene Bolton, ed., *Spanish Exploration in the Southwest, 1542–1706*, Original Narratives of Early American History Series, (New York: Charles Scribner's Sons, 1916), 230.

11 Goodwin, *Western Apache Raiding and Warfare*, 52, 227–239; Opler, *An Apache Life-Way*, 340–341; Andrée F. Sjoberg, "Lipan Apache Culture in Historical Perspective," *Southwestern Journal of Anthropology* 9 no. 1 (Spring 1953): 88–90; Britten, *Lipan Apaches*, 38–40; Haley, *Apaches*, 109–114. For bone-tipped arrows, see Maestas, "Culture and History of Native American Peoples of South Texas," 55. For Turkish-style bows, see "[Vicente de Zaldívar Mendoza's] Account of the Discovery of the Buffalo, 1599" in Bolton, *Spanish Exploration*, 230; Alonso de Posada, *Alonso de Posada Report, 1686: A Description of the Area of the Present Southern United States in the Seventeenth Century*, ed. and trans. Alfred B. Thomas, Spanish Borderlands Series (Pensacola: Perdido Bay Press, 1982), para. 37, 41.

12 Castetter and Opler, *Ethnobiology*, 34–52; Wendy C. Hodgson, *Food Plants of the Sonoran Desert* (Tucson: University of Arizona Press, 2001), 17–18, 33, 40; Goodwin, "The Southern Athapascans," 6; La Vere, *Texas Indians*, 33–35. According to Castetter, sotol and soapweed or palmilla were prepared

and utilized in virtually the same manner as mescal. On the importance of agaves to indigenous cultures of the Chihuahuan and Sonoran deserts, see Cynthia Radding, "Agaves, Human Cultures, and Desert Landscapes in Northern Mexico," *Environmental History* 17 (January 2012): 84–115.

13 Benavides, *Memorial*, 267n45; Frank D. Reeve, "Early Navaho Geography," *New Mexico Historical Review* 31 (October 1956): 299–300; William E. Doolittle, *Cultivated Landscapes of Native North America* (New York: Oxford University Press, 2000), 38, 111, 160, 368; Keith H. Basso, "Western Apache," in *Handbook of North American Indians: Southwest*, Vol. 10, ed. Alfonso Ortiz (Washington, DC: Smithsonian Institution, 1983), 465; Winfred Buskirk, *The Western Apache: Living with the Land Before 1950* (Norman: University of Oklahoma Press, 1986), 79; Opler, "Cause and Effect," 1135–1136; Ann L. W. Stodder and Debra L. Martin, "Health and Disease in the Southwest before and after Spanish Contact," in *Disease and Demography in the Americas*, ed. John W. Verano and Douglas H. Ubelaker (Washington: Smithsonian Institution Press, 1992), 56. For arguments for and against Apaches being agriculturalists prior to arriving in the Southwest, see Opler, "Apachean Culture Pattern," 370; Buskirk, *The Western Apache*, 60; Harry T. Getty, "Changes in Land Use among the Western Apaches," in *Indian and Spanish American Adjustments to Arid and Semiarid Environments*, ed. Clark S. Knowlton (Lubbock: Texas Technological College, 1964), 27–28. For Western Apache subgroups, O'odham, and Akimel O'odham naming and territory, see Jacoby, *Shadows at Dawn*, 12–13, 285–286, 289.

14 On early Ndé material culture, see Francisco Vázquez de Coronado to the King, Province of Tiguex, October 20, 1541, and "The Relación del Suceso (Anonymous Narrative), 1540s," in *Documents of the Coronado Expedition, 1539–1542*, eds. Richard Flint and Shirley Cushing Flint (Dallas: Southern Methodist University Press, 2005), 319, 501; Flint and Flint, eds., *Documents*, 596; Goodwin, "The Southern Athapascans," 7. On Ndé exchange networks, see Carter, *Indian Alliances*, 32, 38, 67–68; Opler, "Apachean Culture Pattern," 380; Forbes, *Apache, Navaho, and Spaniard*, 25; Robinson, *I Fought a Good Fight*, 15.

15 Carter, *Indian Alliances*, 46–47, 64–67, 77.

16 On the frequency and intensity of warfare in precontact Native North America, see Keeley, *War Before Civilization*, 17–20, 157, 174. On the potential Ndé role in the destruction of Casa Grande and the frequency and intensity of their precontact raiding and warfare, see Juan Mateo Manje, *Unknown Arizona and Sonora, 1693–1721: From the Francisco Fernández del Castillo version of Luz de Tierra Incógnita*, ed. Harry J. Karns (Tucson: Arizona Silhouettes, 1954), 86, 287–288; Forbes, *Apache, Navaho, and Spaniard*, 27; Donald E. Worcester, "The Beginnings of the Apache Menace of the Southwest," *New Mexico Historical Review* 41 (January 1941): 1–3; Albert H. Schroeder, "Documentary Evidence Pertaining to the Early Historic Period of Southern Arizona," *New Mexico Historical Review* 27 (April 1952): 139; Dolores A. Gunnerson, *The Jicarilla Apaches: A Study in Survival* (DeKalb: Northern Illinois University Press, 1974), 6–8; Nancy P. Hickerson, "The War for the South Plains, 1500–1700," in *The Coronado Expedition: From the*

Distance of 460 Years, ed. Richard Flint and Shirley Cushing Flint (Albuquerque: University of New Mexico Press, 2003), 188; Blyth, *Chiricahua and Janos*, 16.

17 For peaceful Ndé-Spanish encounters prior to 1667 with the exception of the Diné (Navajos), see Forbes, *Apache, Navaho, and Spaniard*, 7–9, 25, 160–161; Stan Hoig, *Came Men on Horses: The Conquistador Expeditions of Francisco Vásquez de Coronado and Don Juan de Oñate* (Boulder: University Press of Colorado, 2013), 95–96, 181, 231. For the first two quotations, see "The Relación de la Jornada de Cíbola, Pedro de Castañeda de Nájera's Narrative, 1560s (copy, 1596)," part 2, chapter 7 in Flint and Flint, *Documents*, 423. For the third quotation, see "Hearing of December 11, 1665," in Charles Wilson Hackett, ed., *Historical Documents Relating to New Mexico, Nueva Vizcaya, and Approaches Thereto, to 1773*, vol. III (Washington, DC: Carnegie Institution of Washington, 1937), 266.

18 On the Ndé acquisition of horses, see Albert H. Schroeder, "Shifting for Survival in the Spanish Southwest," *New Mexico Historical Review* 43 (October 1968): 297. For the mistaken claim that "the earliest record of the Spaniards bartering horses to the Plains Indians" was when Plains Apaches acquired them at Pecos in the 1650s, see Kenner, 16, citing Tyler and Taylor, ed. and trans., "The Report of Fray Alonso de Posada" *NMHR* 33 (October 1958): 301–303. For the Taos Pueblo role in El Cuartelejo, see Carter, *Indian Alliances*, 173–174; Charles L. Kenner, *A History of New Mexican-Plains Indian Relations* (Norman: University of Oklahoma Press, 1969), 15; Forbes, *Apache, Navaho, and Spaniard*, 137. For "The Far Quarter," see Phil Carlson, *Across the Northern Frontier: Spanish Explorations in Colorado* (Boulder, CO: Johnson Books, 1998), 33, 203. For an alternative translation of "fortified buildings," see James F. Brooks, *Captives and Cousins: Slavery, Kinship, and Community in the Southwest Borderlands* (Chapel Hill: University of North Carolina Press, 2002), 57.

19 For the Santa Clara and Picuris Pueblo contribution to El Cuartelejo, see Fray Silvestre Velez de Escalante to Fray Juan Agustín Morfi, Santa Fe, April 2, 1778, translated in Ralph Emerson Twitchell, *The Spanish Archives of New Mexico*, vol. Two (Cedar Rapids, IA: Torch Press, 1914), para. 12, 279–280; Alfred Barnaby Thomas, ed. and trans., *After Coronado: Spanish Exploration Northeast of New Mexico, 1696–1727* (Norman: University of Oklahoma Press, 1935), 15–16; Forbes, *Apache, Navaho, and Spaniard*, 271; Brooks, *Captives and Cousins*, 57–59. For a parallel example of Pecos Pueblos joining "Faraon" Apaches on the plains and constructing wood and adobe houses, see "Testimony of Don Lorenzo," Santa Fe, July 22, 1715, in Thomas, *After Coronado*, 82.

20 Declaration of Diego López Sambrano, Hacienda of Luis Carbajal, December 22, 1681, in *Revolt of the Pueblo Indians of New Mexico and Otermín's Attempted Reconquest, 1680–1682*, ed. Charles Wilson Hackett and trans. Charmion Clair Shelby, Coronado Historical Series, vol. 2 (Albuquerque: University of New Mexico Press, 1942), 299; Forbes, *Apache, Navaho, and Spaniard*, 166; Kenner, *A History*, 16.

21 On the limits of Ndé violence in New Mexico prior to 1667, see Carter, *Indian Alliances*, 138–139; Forbes, *Apache, Navaho, and Spaniard*, 160–161;

Gunnerson, *Jicarilla Apaches*, 6. For contrary arguments, see Worcester, "Beginnings of the Apache Menace," 1–14; Worcester, *The Apaches*, 10–11; France V. Scholes, *Church and State in New Mexico, 1610–1650*, New Mexico Historical Society Publications in History (Albuquerque: University of New Mexico Press, 1937), 20–21, 69–70, 142. On eastern Ndé commerce and conflict, see Carter, *Indian Alliances*, 49; Hickerson, "War for the South Plains," 187–188; Nancy Parrott Hickerson, *The Jumanos: Hunters and Traders of the South Plains* (Austin: University of Texas Press, 1994), 117–118; Brooks, *Captives and Cousins*; Carroll L. Riley, *The Kachina and the Cross: Indians and Spaniards in the Early Southwest* (Salt Lake City: University of Utah Press, 1999), 196; Anderson, *The Indian Southwest*, 26–27; James H. Gunnerson and Dolores A. Gunnerson, "Apachean Culture: A Study in Unity and Diversity," in *Apachean Culture History and Ethnology*, ed. Keith H. Basso and Morris E. Opler, Anthropological Papers of the University of Arizona (Tucson: University of Arizona Press, 1971), 9. Quotation is from Worcester, "Beginnings of the Apache Menace," 13.

22 For the Ndé attacks on the Piro pueblos, see Forbes, *Apache, Navaho, and Spaniard*, 162–163,166; Schroeder, *Apache Indians IV*, 21–23. According to Schroeder, El Chilmo's Gilas were probably ancestors of Warm Springs Apaches. The Ndé belief that Pueblos intruded on their territory comes from Lorraine Garcia (personal communication). For the Ndé attacks on the Tompiro pueblos and their abandonment, see, "Petition [of Father Fray Francisco de Ayeta, Mexico, May 10, 1679," translated in Hackett, *Historical Documents*, vol. III, 298; Escalante to Morfi, Santa Fe, April 2, 1778, translated in Twitchell, *Spanish Archives*, para. 2, 269; Schroeder, "Shifting for Survival," 297; Bancroft, *History of Arizona and New Mexico*, 170.

23 For an excellent synthesis of the positive and negative effects of horses on indigenous cultures of the Great Plains, see Pekka Hämäläinen, "The Rise and Fall of Plains Indian Horse Cultures," *Journal of American History* 90 (2003): 833–862. For the merits of dogs versus horses and their persistence among Plains Apaches in 1626 and from 1687 to 1719, see Alan J. Osborn, "Ecological Aspects of Equestrian Adaptations in Aboriginal North America," *American Anthropologist* 85 no. 3 (September 1983): 565; Benavides, *Benavides' Memorial*, 54; Forbes, *Apache, Navaho, and Spaniard*, 119–120, 191; Francis Haines, "Where did the Plains Indians Get Their Horses?," *American Anthropologist* 40 no. 1 (January–March 1938): 116; Francis Haines, "The Northward Spread of Horses among the Plains Indians," *American Anthropologist* 40 no. 3 (March–April 1938): 432; Fray Agustín de Vetancurt, *Teatro Mexicano: descripción breve de los sucesos exemplares de la Nueva-España en el Nuevo Mundo Occidental de las Indias*, vol. III (First edition, Mexico, 1698 [1697]; Madrid: José Porrua Turanzas, 1961), 278, para. 56; Manje, *Unknown Arizona and Sonora*, 295; "Diary of the Campaign of Governor Antonio de Valverde against the Ute and Comanche Indians, 1719," in Thomas, *After Coronado*, 131.

24 Jack S. Williams and Robert L. Hoover, *Arms of the Apachería: A Comparison of Apachean and Spanish Fighting Techniques in the Later Eighteenth Century* (Greeley, CO: Museum of Anthropology, University of

Northern Colorado, 1983), 48–52; Goodwin, *Western Apache Raiding and Warfare*, 259.

25 D. E. Worcester, "The Weapons of American Indians," *New Mexico Historical Review* 20 no. 3 (July 1945): 227, 232–233; Thomas Frank Schilz and Donald E. Worcester, "The Spread of Firearms among the Indian Tribes on the Northern Frontier of New Spain," *American Indian Quarterly* 11 (Winter 1987): 1–2; Bolton, *Athanase de Méziéres*, vol. 2, 153; Thomas, *After Coronado*, 73.

26 D. E. Worcester, "The Use of Saddles by American Indians," *New Mexico Historical Review* 20 (April 1945): 139, 143; William E. Dunn, "Apache Relations in Texas, 1718–1750," *Southwestern Historical Quarterly* 14 (January 1911): 222; Frank Raymond Secoy, *Changing Military Patterns on the Great Plains (17th Century through Early 19th Century)*, Monographs of the American Ethnological Society (Locust Valley, NY: J.J. Augustin, 1953), 13, 17, 19.

27 For the quotation, see Blyth, *Chiricahua and Janos*, 34. For contrary perspectives, supporting a more active Ndé role in these conflicts, see Eiselt, *Becoming White Clay*, 78; Forbes, *Apache, Navaho, and Spaniard*, 163, 178–182, 190–193.

28 "March of the army from El Paso to La Isleta," November 5–December 8, 1681, in Hackett and Shelby, *Revolt of the Pueblo Indians*, 208.

29 "Opinion of Fray Francisco de Ayeta, Hacienda of Luis de Carbajal, December 23, 1681," in Hackett and Shelby, *Revolt of the Pueblo Indians*, 307.

30 "[Declaration] of Diego López [Sambrano, Hacienda of Luis Carbajal, December 22, 1681]," in Hackett and Shelby, *Revolt of the Pueblo Indians*, 293.

31 "Auto of Antonio de Otermín, Hacienda of Luis Carbajal, December 24, 1681," in Hackett and Shelby, *Revolt of the Pueblo Indians*, 337–339; Forbes, *Apache, Navaho, and Spaniard*, 188–189.

32 Forbes, *Apache, Navaho, and Spaniard*, 190–191, 196. For quotations, see "Letter of Antonio de Otermín," March 29, 1682, AGI, México, 53, translated in Forbes, *Apache, Navaho, and Spaniard*, 191. For "Sierra de Gila" as Pinos Altos and Mogollon Mountains, see Schroeder, *Apache Indians IV*, 27–28. Seminomadic Sumas lived in northern Nueva Vizcaya and southwest Texas and are of unknown linguistic affiliation. See William B. Griffen, "Southern Periphery: East," in *Handbook of North American Indians: Southwest*, Vol. 10, ed. Alfonso Ortiz (Washington, DC: Smithsonian Institution, 1983), 330; Frederick Webb Hodge, ed., *Handbook of American Indians North of Mexico*, Smithsonian Institution, Bureau of American Ethnology, Bulletin 30 (Washington, DC: Government Printing Office: 1907), II, 649.

33 Frank Secoy, for example, without citing any specific examples of Apache raiding, argues that Apache eastward expansion began in conjunction with Spanish enslavement of Apaches in Parral in 1659. See Secoy, *Changing Military Partterns*, 22–23.

34 "Opinions given in the junta de guerra, Hacienda de Luis Carbajal, December 23, 1681," in Hackett and Shelby, *Revolt of the Pueblo Indians*, 324.

35 "Reply of the Fiscal, Don Martín de Solís Miranda, Mexico, June 25, 1682," in Hackett and Shelby, *Revolt of the Pueblo Indians*, 377.
36 Forbes, *Apache, Navaho, and Spaniard*, 193. For quotation, see "Extract of a paper which Don Lope de Sierra wrote in regard to matters touching upon the kingdom of Nueva Vizcaya [undated; subsequent to the year 1683]," in Charles Wilson Hackett, ed., *Historical Documents Relating to New Mexico, Nueva Vizcaya, and Approaches Thereto, to 1773*, vol. II (Washington, DC: Carnegie Institution of Washington, 1926), 219.
37 On seventeenth-century Apache enslavement at Parral, see Rick Hendricks and Gerald Mandell, "The Apache Slave Trade in Parral, 1637–1679," *Journal of Big Bend Studies* 16 (2004): 59–81; Paul Conrad, "Captive Fates: Displaced American Indians in the Southwest Borderlands, Mexico, and Cuba, 1500–1800" (Ph.D. diss., University of Texas at Austin, 2011), 44–54; Chantal Cramaussel, *Poblar la frontera: la provincia de Santa Bárbara en Nueva Vizcaya durante los siglos XVI y XVII* (Zamora: El Colegio de Michoacán, 2006). Mansos were a semisedentary people of unknown linguistic affiliation possessing many Pueblo cultural traits, who resided in the lower Rio Grande Valley north of El Paso in the late seventeenth century; see Hodge, *Handbook of American Indians*, I, 801; Griffen, "Southern Periphery: East," 330. According to Lorraine Garcia, modern Manso descendants claim a Pueblo heritage despite the fact their ancestors resided on lands that overlapped with Chihene territory (personal communication).
38 Forbes, *Apache, Navaho, and Spaniard*, 200–202; Thomas H. Naylor and Charles W. Polzer, eds., *The Presidio and Militia on the Northern Frontier of New Spain, 1570–1700* (Tucson: University of Arizona Press, 1986), 485, 528n4; Captain Francisco Ramírez de Salazar to the viceroy the Marqués de la Luna, Casas Grandes Valley, April 14, 1685, in Naylor and Polzer, eds., Presidio and Militia: Vol 1, 528–529; Hendricks and Mandell, "Apache Slave Trade," 72. Nomadic Janos are of unknown linguistic affiliation and lived in territory west of the Mansos and north of the Sumas corresponding with today's northwestern Chihuahua, northeastern Sonora, southwestern New Mexico, and southeastern Arizona, which would become part of the Apachería, although Franciscans identified them distinctly from Apaches as late as the 1750s in the Janos mission records. See Griffen, "Southern Periphery: East," 330–331.
39 Captain Francisco Ramírez de Salazar to the viceroy the Marqués de la Luna, Casas Grandes Valley, April 14, 1685, in Naylor and Polzer, *Presidio and Militia*, vol. 1, 530.
40 For the quotation and the Ndé attacks on Bácerac, see Salazar to Luna, Casas Grandes Valley, April 14, 1685, in Naylor and Polzer, *Presidio and Militia*, vol. 1, 532, 532n17. For the fates of the sacked missions in Nueva Vizcaya and the mistaken argument that indigenous expansion into Sonora did not begin until 1686, see Forbes, *Apache, Navaho, and Spaniard*, 205, 207. For the 1685 raids, see "Declaration of the sergeant, captain, and head of the presidio," Roque de Madrid, El Paso del Norte, April 13, 1685 in Naylor and Polzer, *Presidio and Militia*, vol. 1, 541.
41 Forbes, *Apache, Navaho, and Spaniard*, 206–227; Susan M. Deeds, *Defiance and Deference in Mexico's Colonial North: Indians under Spanish Rule in*

Nueva Vizcaya (Austin: University of Texas Press, 2003), 90–91, 93. For the quotations, see "Testimony of Francisco," San Antonio de Casas Grandes, March 20, 1690, AGI, Patronato, 236, quoted in Deeds, *Defiance and Deference*, 91. Nomadic Jocomes spoke the same unknown language as Janos and lived with them in territory west of the Mansos corresponding with today's northwestern Chihuahua, northeastern Sonora, southwestern New Mexico, and southeastern Arizona. See Griffen, "Southern Periphery: East," 330–331; Hodge, *Handbook of American Indians*, 632.

42 For the quotation and the attacks on Santa Rosa pueblo, see Juan Nentvig, S. J., *Rudo Ensayo: tentativa de una prevencional descripción geográphica de la provincia de Sonora, sus terminos, y confines* (St. Augustine: [Albany, Munsell, printer], 1863), 189. For an English translation, see Juan Nentvig, S.J., *Rudo Ensayo: Arizona and Sonora in 1763* (1894; reprint, Tucson: Arizona Silhouttes, 1951), 139. See also Schroeder, *Apache Indians IV*, 20. This passage is omitted from the 1764 version of the document. For the multitribal confederation, see Forbes, *Apache, Navaho, and Spaniard*, 226–229; "Diego de Vargas to the Conde de Galve, El Paso, 14 August 1691, LS," in Diego de Vargas, *By Force of Arms: The Journals of Don Diego de Vargas, New Mexico, 1691–93*, ed. John L. Kessell and Rick Hendricks (Albuquerque: University of New Mexico Press, 1992), 77, 116n53. For Sonoran expansion, see José Manuel Espinosa, "The Legend of Sierra Azul," *New Mexico Historical Review* 9 no. 2 (April 1934): 129; Schroeder, *Apache Indians IV*, 27. Sobas were part of the Piman-speaking Tohono O'odham (Papago) who lived around Caborca in northwest Sonora. See Hodge, *Handbook of American Indians*, 608.

43 Forbes, *Apache, Navaho, and Spaniard*, 230–231. For the first quotation, see Letter of Juan Fernández de la Fuente, December 12, 1691, AGI, Guadalajara, 139, and for the remaining ones, see Report of Juan Fernández de la Fuente, April 29, 1692, AGI, Guadalajara, 139, both translated in Forbes, *Apache, Navaho, and Spaniard*, 230–231.

44 Forbes, *Apache, Navaho, and Spaniard*, 231–232.

45 For Gila Apaches and their home territory in the late seventeenth century, see Schroeder, "Documentary Evidence," 144–145; Espinosa, "Legend of Sierra," 129–130; "Diego de Vargas to the Conde de Galve, El Paso, 14 August 1691, LS," and "Declaration of Captain Antonio Jorge," El Paso, August 12, 1691, in Vargas, *By Force of Arms*, 76–77, 147. For allied Gilas, Janos, and Jocomes as ancestral Chiricahuas by 1700, see Schroeder, "Shifting for Survival," 300–301. For an intriguing but unproven argument that "Jocome" is a Spanish derivation of "Chokonen," and that Jocomes and the Athapaskan-speaking Chokonen or Chiricahua were the same people and occupied the same territory from the Chiricahua Mountains westward to the San Pedro River, see Jack Douglas Forbes, "The Janos, Jocomes, Mansos and Sumas Indians," *New Mexico Historical Review* 32 (October 1957): 322–324. For a fallacious counterargument "that the Jocomes, Sumas, and Janos were *in no way* related to the Apaches," see Schroeder, *Apache Indians IV*, 42 (italics are my own). Schroeder contends that Jocomes exhibited Yuman cultural characteristics and did not appear in northern Sonora until 1684. See Schroeder,

Apache Indians IV, 47, 53. Lorraine Garcia, while not going as far as Schroeder, still cautions about deeming the Janos and Jocomes to be Chihene or Chiricahua ancestors, when Mexican and Texas history place them in their place specific areas separate from *traditional* Apache areas (personal communication).

46 Forbes, *Apache, Navaho, and Spaniard*, 244–245; Rufus Kay Wyllys, ed. and trans., "Padre Luís Velarde's Relación of Pimería Alta, 1716," *New Mexico Historical Review* 6 no. 2 (April 1931): 238; Father Luis de Velarde, "description of the site, longitude and latitude of the nations of the Pimería and its northern adjoining nations, the land of California," May 30, 1716, in Manje, *Unknown Arizona and Sonora*, 247. For the meaning of Chiricagui, see Nentvig, *Rudo Ensayo*, 21n3; Schroeder, *Apache Indians IV*, 117.

47 Father Eusebio Francisco Kino, *Kino's Historical Memoir of Pimeria Alta: A Contemporary Account of the Beginnings of California, Sonora, and Arizona, 1683–1711*, ed. and trans. Herbert Eugene Bolton (1919; reprint, Berkeley: University of California Press, 1948), vol. I, 29, 162n170, 162; Herbert Eugene Bolton, *Rim of Christendom: A Biography of Eusebio Francisco Kino, Pacific Coast Pioneer* (New York: MacMillan, 1936), 27; Manje, *Unknown Arizona and Sonora*, 285–286, 122; Schroeder, *Apache Indians IV*, 346; Hubert Howe Bancroft, *History of the North Mexican States and Texas*, vol. 1 (San Francisco, CA: The History Company, 1884), 273.

48 Diego de Vargas to the Conde de Galve, El Paso, 30 March 1692, LS," and "Diego de Vargas, Campaign journal, 16 October–27 December 1692, DS," in Vargas, *By Force of Arms*, 173–174, 580–581, 585; Forbes, *Apache, Navaho, and Spaniard*, 232, 242–243; La Vere, *Texas Indians*, 93. The quotations are from 585. For the Sierra Peña Larga's location, see E. Richard Hart, ed., *Zuni and the Courts: A Struggle for Sovereign Land Rights* (Lawrence: University Press of Kansas, 1995), 257.

49 On the Spanish reoccupation of Santa Fe and subsequent alliances with eastern Apaches, see J. Manuel Espinosa, "The Recapture of Santa Fé, New Mexico, by the Spaniards, December 29–30, 1693," *Hispanic American Historical Review* 19 (1939): 443–463; Forbes, *Apache, Navaho, and Spaniard*, 250–257, 262. For the quotations, see Diego de Vargas, "Campaign journal[s]," "28 January–30 March 1694, DS," "30 April–7 May 1694, DS," and "28 June–16 July 1694, DS," "Diego de Vargas to the Conde de Galve, Letter of transmittal, Santa Fe, 1 September 1694, C," and "Vargas to the Conde de Galve, Santa Fe, 9 May 1695, C," in Diego de Vargas, *Blood on the Boulders: The Journals of Don Diego de Vargas, New Mexico, 1694–97*, ed. John L. Kessell, Rick Hendricks, and Meredith D. Dodge (Albuquerque: University of New Mexico Press, 1998), 177, 219, 292, 359, 628. The first two quotations are from 177, the third is from 219, and the remaining two are from 292. Historian Alfred B. Thomas mistakenly thought that this was the first use of the term "Faraon"; however, Spaniards had employed that word to describe Apaches living east of the Rio Grande from Pecos to El Paso since at least January 1675 because the Indians allegedly did not know or respect God. See Thomas, *After Coronado*, 23–24; Forbes, *Apache, Navaho, and Spaniard*, 171; Willem J. de Reuse, "Synonymy" in Opler, "Apachean Culture Pattern," 390. For Chilpaines as

ancestral Lipans, see Albert H. Schroeder, *A Study of the Apache Indians: Parts I, II, and III*, American Indian Ethnohistory: Indians of the Southwest Series, vol. I (New York: Garland, 1974), 343–344; Robinson, *I Fought a Good Fight*, 32.

50 For the respective quotations, see Manje, *Unknown Arizona and Sonora*, 5–6; The *maestre de campo* Don Joseph Marín to his Excellency the Count of Galve, Parral, September 30, 1693 in Hackett, *Historical Documents*, vol. II, 399.

51 For the classic articulation of mid-nineteenth-century Apache raiding and warfare tactics, see Goodwin, *Western Apache Raiding and Warfare*, 16–18. For the quotations, see the maestre de campo Don Joseph Marín to the Conde de Galve, Parral, September 30, 1693, in Hackett, *Historical Documents*, vol. II, 397. For Indian raids on Sonora's Camino Real, see Diego García de Valdés to the maestre de campo Don Joseph Francisco Marín, Parral, September 26, 1693, in Hackett, *Historical Documents*, vol. II, 379.

52 Captain Juan Fernández de la Fuente to Gen. and Gov. Gabriel del Castillo, Janos, October 6, 1695, in Naylor and Polzer, *Presidio and Militia*, vol. 1, 585–586. Chinarras lived in settlements that were desert-dwelling extensions of the river-dwelling Conchos in modern north-central Chihuahua. See Griffen, "Southern Periphery: East," 331.

53 Captain Juan Fernández de la Fuente to Gen. and Gov. Gabriel del Castillo, Janos, October 6, 1695, in Naylor and Polzer, *Presidio and Militia*, vol. 1, 587–596, 594n26, 648, 651. For quotations, see 594–595 and for "Great Chief," see 648.

54 Spicer, *Cycles of Conquest*, 124–125; Forbes, *Apache, Navaho, and Spaniard*, 147; Naylor and Polzer, *Presidio and Militia*, vol. 1, 486; Wyllys, "Velarde's Relación," 144; Jacobo Sedelmayr, *Sedelmayr's Relacion of 1746*, ed. and trans. Ronald L. Ives, Bureau of American Ethnology, Bulletin 23 (Washington, DC: Smithsonian Institution, 1939), 102; Jacoby, *Shadows at Dawn*, 25–26. The cycle of indigenous violence spread to missionized Ópatas in 1696, who rebelled against Spanish appropriation of Ópata land, forced labor practices, and the enslavement of Ópata children in private homes, and to the Rarámuri (Tarahumaras) as well. See Spicer, *Cycles of Conquest*, 34–35; Forbes, *Apache, Navaho, and Spaniard*, 261–262.

55 Captain Juan Fernández de la Fuente to Gen. and Gov. Gabriel del Castillo, Janos, October 6, 1695, in Naylor and Polzer, *Presidio and Militia*, vol. 1, 641–651. For the quotations, see 643, 651.

56 Captain Juan Fernández de la Fuente to Gen. and Gov. Gabriel del Castillo, Janos, October 6, 1695, in Naylor and Polzer, *Presidio and Militia*, vol. 1, 640–641, 641n82, 643, 648. For quotations, see 640, 644. On Apache women's hide tanning, see Nicolás de Lafora, *The Frontiers of New Spain: Nicolás de Lafora's Description, 1766–68*, ed. George P. Hammond, Quivira Society Publications (Berkeley, CA: Quivira Society, 1958), 80; Laverne Herrell Clark, "Early Horse Trappings of the Navajo and Apache Indians," *Arizona and the West* 5 (Autumn 1963): 246.

57 Captain Juan Fernández de la Fuente to Gen. and Gov. Gabriel del Castillo, Janos, October 6, 1695, in Naylor and Polzer, *Presidio and Militia*, vol. 1,

642–646, 643n84, 648, 653. For the quotation, see 643. On Ópatas, as Piman-speaking, see Hodge, *Handbook of American Indians*, 138.

58 For the first two quotations, see "Diego de Vargas to fray Francisco de Vargas, Reply to petition, Santa Fe, 8 March 1696, DS," in Vargas, *Blood on the Boulders*, 679. For the July 1696 uprising, see "Diego de Vargas to Juan de Ortega Montañés, Santa Fe, 30 July 1696, C," in Vargas, *Blood on the Boulders*, 861. For the last quotation, see "Diego de Vargas to the Conde de Moctezuma, Letter of transmittal, 24 November 1696, Santa Fe, DS," in Vargas, *Blood on the Boulders*, 1065.

59 Matthew Liebmann, *Revolt: An Archaeological History of Pueblo Resistance and Revitalization in 17th Century New Mexico*, The Archaeology of Colonialism in Native North America (Tucson: University of Arizona Press, 2012), 190, 217; Andrew L. Knaut, *The Pueblo Revolt of 1680: Conquest and Resistance in Seventeenth-Century New Mexico* (1995), 182–183; John, *Storms Brewed*, 132, 142; Espinosa, "Recapture of Santa Fé," 463. On the reassertion of Spanish control of the upper Rio Grande valley, see Forbes, *Apache, Navaho, and Spaniard*, 274; John, *Storms Brewed*, 146. On the 1702 peaceful relations, see Schroeder, *Apache Indians IV*, 22.

60 Kino, *Kino's Historical Memoir*, vol. I, 176, 176n211, 233; Eusebio Francisco Kino, "The Remarkable Victory which the Pimas-Sobaípuris Have Won Against the Enemies of the Province of Sonora," Nuestra Señora de Dolores, May 3, 1698, in Fay Jackson Smith, John L. Kessell, and Francis J. Fox, S. J., *Father Kino in Arizona* (Phoenix: Arizona Historical Foundation, 1966), 48–49; Bolton, *Rim of Christendom*, 380–382, 385–386; Manje, *Unknown Arizona and Sonora*, 96–98. 247; Forbes, *Apache, Navaho, and Spaniard*, 274; Bancroft, *History of the North Mexican States and Texas*, 274; Spicer, *Cycles of Conquest*, 127, 235–236; Schroeder, *Apache Indians IV*, 40, 49; Deni J. Seymour, *A Fateful Day in 1698: The Remarkable Sobaipuri-O'odham Victory over the Apaches and Their Allies* (Salt Lake City: University of Utah Press, 2014), 39.

61 For the quotations, see "Juan Fernández de la Fuente's Letter, September 12, 1698," [Janos], Parral Archives, translated and transcribed in Seymour, *A Fateful Day in 1698*, 24–25, 250–251. See also Carl Sauer, *The Distribution of Aboriginal Tribes and Languages in Northwestern Mexico* (Berkeley: University of California Press, 1934), 75–76; Forbes, *Apache, Navaho, and Spaniard*, 278; Manje, *Unknown Arizona and Sonora*, 98, 175; Kino, "The Remarkable Victory," Nuestra Señora de Dolores, May 3, 1698, in Smith et al., *Father Kino*, 50; Blyth, *Chiricahua and Janos*, 46.

62 Kino, *Kino's Historical Memoir*, 181, 202; Wyllys, "Velarde's Relación," 138; Velarde, "description," May 30, 1716, in Manje, *Unknown Arizona and Sonora*, 122, 248; Schroeder, *Apache Indians IV*, 40. The quotation is from 202. For a contrary argument that Jocomes made peace at Janos, see Manje, *Unknown Arizona and Sonora*, 175. Historian Jack D. Forbes omits the fate of the Mansos and Father Kino's 1699 peace agreements with Native peoples in the Pimería Alta and Apachería from his study. See Forbes, *Apache, Navaho, and Spaniard*, 250–280. O'odham guides told Manje in 1699 that the headwaters of the Verde River was within Apache territory; however,

Bolton contends that these Indians were Yavapais, who were inaccurately called Mohave Apaches. See Bolton, *Rim of Christendom*, 424.
63 For Leal's quotation, see Father Antonio Leal to Father Eusebio Kino, August 29, 1699, quoted in Kino, *Kino's Historical Memoir*, 202. For Gila Apaches traveling to Dolores, see Bolton, *Rim of Christendom*, 424. For Kino's 1708 quotation and thoughts on trade, see Kino, *Kino's Historical Memoir*, vol. II, 256–257; Bolton, *Rim of Christendom*, 576, 574. For Velarde's quotation, see Velarde, "description," 30 May 1716 in Manje, *Unknown Arizona and Sonora*, 264.
64 Wyllys, "Velarde's Relación," 138.
65 Kino, *Kino's Historical Memoir*, vol. I, 166, 175–179, 233, and vol. II, 25–26; Schroeder, "Shifting for Survival," 300–301; Spicer, *Cycles of Conquest*, 233–239. For one of the earliest examples of Apache-Spanish peace in Sonora in 1716, see Velarde, "description," May 30, 1716, in Manje, *Unknown Arizona and Sonora*, 248. For the quotation, see Father Melchor Bartytomo to Father Eusebio Kino, Cucurpe, February 1, 1701, translated in Kino, *Kino's Historical Memoir*, vol. I, 267.
66 José Refugio de la Torre Curiel, *Twilight of the Mission Frontier: Shifting Interethnic Alliances and Social Organization in Sonora, 1768–1855* (Stanford and Berkeley, CA: Stanford University Press and Academy of American Franciscan History, 2012), 17; Spicer, *Cycles of Conquest*, 51–52, 129–130; Nentvig, *Rudo Ensayo*, 120–128. As of 1700, the Ndé-led confederation of groups west of the Rio Grande fits James C. Scott's conception of hill peoples purposefully adapting to imperial states "while remaining outside of their firm grasp." See Scott, *Art of Not Being Governed*, 337.
67 For examples of scholars who have regarded 1700–1706 as the beginning of a new phase of Ndé history, see Herbert Eugene Bolton, ed. and trans., *Athanase de Mézières and the Louisiana-Texas Frontier, 1768–1780*, vol. I (Cleveland, OH: Arthur H. Clark, 1914), 24; Alfred Barnaby Thomas, ed. and trans., *Forgotten Frontiers: A Study of the Spanish Indian Policy of Don Juan Bautista de Anza, Governor of New Mexico, 1777–1787* (Norman: University of Oklahoma Press, 1932), 58; Forbes, *Apache, Navaho, and Spaniard*, 280; Schroeder, "Shifting for Survival," 301–302; Haley, *Apaches*, 30. For a notable exception by a scholar examining Ndé groups west of the Rio Grande, see Spicer, *Cycles of Conquest*, 236.
68 For the quotation, see Posada, *Alonso de Posada Report, 1686*, para. 37, 41. On eastern Ndé territorial expansion from 1686–1715, see also Juan Antonio de Trasviña Retis, *The Founding of Missions at La Junta de los Rios*, ed. Reginald C. Reindorp, Supplementary Studies of the Texas Catholic Historical Society (Austin: Texas Catholic Historical Society, 1938), 18–19; Jack D. Forbes, "The Appearance of the Mounted Indian in Northern Mexico and the Southwest, to 1680," *Southwestern Journal of Anthropology* 15 no. 2 (Summer 1959): 205; Forbes, *Apache, Navaho, and Spaniard*, 196; Anderson, *The Indian Southwest*, 95–97, 110–111; La Vere, *Texas Indians*, 98–102; Maestas, "Culture and History of Native American Peoples of South Texas," 149; Robinson, *I Fought a Good Fight*, 28. For Comanche and Ute intrusions, see Hämäläinen, *Comanche Empire*, 28.

2

Precedents

In July 1779, a delegation of Mescalero allies met with Commander-in-Chief of the Interior Provinces of New Spain, Teodoro de Croix, in Chihuahua. Seeking protection from their Lipan and Comanche enemies and from Coahuila Governor Juan de Ugalde's warring troops, these Indians petitioned Croix to establish "pueblos formales," or formal towns, for their people at the former mission site of La Junta de los Rios, at the confluence of the Conchos and Rio Grande, near Presidio del Norte in northern Nueva Vizcaya (modern Ojinaga, across the river from Presidio, Texas). Farther north, other Apache groups joined the Mescaleros near presidios along the Rio Grande Valley. The headman Bigotes' Mescalero band from the Pecos River, whom Spaniards called Salineros, solicited peace in July and settled at San Elizario and Nantan Chafalote's Chihene band, whom Spaniards called Chafalotes, settled at El Paso.[1]

The Spanish military, under Croix's leadership, had just succeeded in establishing the first system of garrisoned agricultural communities for Apaches that did not involve missionaries. Croix clearly recognized the birth of a new system, for beginning in May 1780 he delineated an important new subheading within his monthly reports on Indian activities: "Recent news occurred with the *Mescaleros de paz* ['peaceful Mescaleros'], and state of the new *establecimientos* ['establishments' or 'settlements'] in Nueva Vizcaya." Croix's pueblos are significant because they served as the most immediate precedent for the Spanish military's larger system of garrisoned Apache reservations and ungarrisoned Comanche and Navajo pueblos in the late 1780s.[2]

This chapter explores the local, regional, and global factors that influenced the creation of Apache reservations by viewing Spanish efforts to incorporate Apaches through Teodoro de Croix's eyes and using the most enduring of his establecimientos – the Mescalero pueblos at La Junta – as a case study. A French native and career Spanish officer, Croix had risen from ensign to captain during a twenty-year European tour in Italy and Flanders. After accompanying his uncle, the Marqués de Croix, to New Spain in 1766, Croix served an additional five years at the rank of brigadier, during his uncle's tenure as viceroy. Croix was a close student of Spanish–Indian relations on the northern frontier. After assuming office as commander-in-chief of the interior provinces in January 1777, he spent four months, from March 31 until his departure for Arizpe in August, studying documents in the archives in Mexico City, which dated back to at least 1740.[3]

If Croix also examined earlier documents treating Spanish–Indian relations, he would have found numerous precedents for establishing reservations for equestrian native groups across the Spanish empire, from the Chichimecas in New Spain to the Berbers in North Africa. On the heels of a grueling, highly expensive forty-year war, Spanish officers took on new roles as Indian agents after 1590 by negotiating and maintaining peace with nomadic and seminomadic Pames, Guamares, Zacatecos, and Guachichiles who inhabited a vast region known as the Gran Chichimeca, which stretched from the eastern to the western Sierra Madre ranges southward of a line from Saltillo to Durango.[4]

These so-called Chichimecas settled in reservation-like *poblaciones* (settlements) near the presidios, which functioned as Indian agencies for the distribution of rations and gifts to them. The Indian settlements received maize from incorporated Indian towns and beef from haciendas in the region. The Indians also acquired a wide range of "peace goods" from Mexico City, including clothing, household utensils, blankets, agricultural tools, games, reading primers, and even musical instruments. Finally, veteran presidial soldiers served as *labradores* (husbandmen) and instructed the Chichimecas in farming. Through these efforts, Spanish officers hoped to transform equestrian *indios bárbaros* (wild, or unpacified, Indians) into agrarian *gente del rey* (subjects of the king).[5]

The *moros de paz* (peaceful Moors) at the Spanish-controlled port of Oran on the North African coast were another possible precedent for Apache reservations. These tribes of Berbers had sought Spanish protection from hostile Berbers and Bedouins, whom Spaniards called *moros de guerra*, and from the Turks since the Spanish conquest of Oran began in the early sixteenth century. Before the first Spanish evacuation of Oran in 1708, moros de paz had settled on Spanish-run reservations that extended for twenty leagues around the walls of the presidio. Many of the male moros de paz served as scouts and auxiliaries and guided Spanish campaigns into the Berbería (Berber Country), much like Apaches de paz would later do in the Apachería.[6]

The success Spaniards had in converting seminomadic Berbers into semisedentary agriculturalists at Oran might have influenced Croix to try the same in New Spain, especially given the fact that he commanded numerous Spanish officers who had served previously in that region. Colonel Diego Ortiz Parrilla, for example, who commanded San Sabá presidio in 1758, served as a presidial soldier for four years in Oran and Ceuta before coming to New Spain and noted that horse-mounted Comanches and Apaches "bear some resemblance to the Moors, in their way ... of fighting and making war." More broadly, this comparison is emblematic of the similarities Spanish officers drew between the perceived nomadic lifestyles of bison-hunting Apaches and Arabs that dates back to first contact during the Coronado expedition.[7]

The North African system continued to function through the early nineteenth century concurrently with the Apaches de paz program in New Spain. When Spanish King Carlos IV negotiated a peace treaty with the Dey de Argel and surrendered Oran and Masalquivir in 1791, the moros de paz moved to Ceuta, where they continued to serve Spanish interests for over twenty-five years, even though Spanish officers reduced their rations. The Spanish military dissolved the company for good in 1817, although ten former moros de paz remained at Ceuta as interpreters.[8] Croix's successors, then, also might have known of the moros de paz.

BUENA ESPERANZA: THE PRELUDE

With no apparent hesitation, Croix agreed to the Mescaleros' request for villages at La Junta, provided that they continue to serve as faithful auxiliaries, and he worked out a preliminary agreement with them in Chihuahua. Croix named the headman Dajunné ("consoled man"), whom Spaniards called Alonso, *gobernadorcillo* ("petty governor") of a town to be established at the abandoned mission site of San Francisco and Domingo Alegre *capitán de guerra* ("war chief") of another new village to be established nearby. After bestowing the same title on two other Mescalero leaders, Patule and Juan Tuerto, Croix granted them permission to bring their bands to settle with Alonso at San Francisco. The three headmen requested that Croix send "their relatives," Suma and Julimeño mission Indians from El Paso and Peyotes pueblo in Coahuila, to help them construct their homes and raise their crops, which indicates that Mescaleros, like Chihenes and Chokonens, maintained kinship ties with missionized tribes. The three leaders also asked for rations for a year, for military protection from their enemies, and that Lieutenant Colonel Manuel Muñoz be named "the chief to command them." Croix agreed to all of these requests and even offered to provide the Apaches with interpreters to serve as their liaisons with the Spaniards. In exchange, the Mescaleros promised to continue obeying Croix's orders, to serve as faithful vassals of the king, and to campaign as auxiliaries against any hostile Apache group, including those within their own tribe. As a sign of his commitment to the agreement, Croix then provided the Mescalero leaders with European clothing and trade goods and ordered Muñoz to make a formal treaty with them at El Norte presidio. Croix called this initial agreement a "capitulación," which in this context suggests a surrender, but Muñoz would call the final one a "tratado de paz" or peace treaty.[9]

During negotiations for the final treaty in late October 1779 at El Norte presidio, Gobernadorcillo Alonso and his delegation of five Mescalero headmen succeeded in extracting further concessions from Colonel Muñoz. After deciding on the precise locations of the new Apache towns, Muñoz had hoped to hold the Mescaleros to the same terms they had negotiated with Croix in Chihuahua. Instead, in response to their requests for meat and for protection from the Comanches, Muñoz agreed to provide them food, cigars, knives, and a ten-man military escort to hunt buffalo on the Texas plains. Prior to their departure, Alonso tested Muñoz again. Although Spaniards had already begun constructing a pueblo and planting wheat for his people at the abandoned mission of San Francisco, he preferred to choose his own place to settle. Alonso soon located a suitable half-acre site on a hill northeast of the presidio, which Muñoz named "El Pueblo de la Buena Esperanza" or the town of Good Hope. After returning from the plains in January, several other Mescalero leaders asked to join Alonso's forty-five-member band in the same town, and the commander increased the area to forty-one acres.[10]

When Buena Esperanza was finally completed in late November 1779, the site consisted of 113 adobe houses protected by two bastions. Although a smallpox outbreak and limited rations kept many Mescaleros away during the first winter, Alonso and his people remained at peace, alternating between living in the pueblo and inside El Norte presidio. By spring at least three other bands under the leadership of Domingo Alegre,

Patule el Grande, and Volante joined Alonso's group at Buena Esperanza, which Croix now called an "establecimiento." In March Croix reported that three of the four Mescalero rancherías at Buena Esperanza were "living happily in their houses," and by May Spanish troops and mission Indians had planted crops for them. Yet Croix remained pessimistic about the long-term prospects for peace with the Mescaleros as a whole, fearing that they would form an alliance with the Lipans and together demonstrate "infidelity to their peace."[11]

APACHE MISSIONS

Had Croix been able to put aside his preconceptions about Apache behavior, he might have had more reason for optimism. Although mutual violence and hostility had dominated Spanish–Apache relations for most of the eighteenth century, Croix and other Spanish officers could learn valuable lessons from the efforts of Franciscan priests in Texas and New Mexico to use missions to pacify Apaches beginning in the 1710s. From a Spanish perspective, this experiment was somewhat surprising. In nearly every province of northern New Spain except California, Spanish attempts to convert Indians had caused widespread Native uprisings. These began with the Tepehuan Revolt of 1616 in Nueva Vizcaya, peaked during the tumultuous Pueblo and Great Southwestern Revolts of 1680–98, and resurged with the Tarahumara and Pima Rebellions of 1748 and 1751 in Nueva Vizcaya and Sonora.[12]

The long-term prospects for the success of any mission, then, were dubious at best, and the possibility of missionizing Apaches and other mobile equestrian groups seemed even more remote. In apparent ignorance of the early missionizing success Alonso de Benavides enjoyed with Apaches in the 1620s, Fray Damián Massanet lamented in 1691, Apaches "have always had wars with the Spaniards of New Mexico, for although truces have been made, they have endured little."[13] Indeed, fear of Apache raids was one of the biggest reasons that other Indians decided to seek shelter in Spanish missions in the first place. However, the alliances and kinship ties eastern Apaches forged with many of those same missionized tribes, as well as Apaches' own material and spiritual needs, gave Franciscans new opportunities to Catholicize them.

As we have seen, since becoming equestrians in the late seventeenth century, Ndé groups expanded their territory and raiding and trading networks southward. By 1715, an ancestral Mescalero ranchería of sixty families lived above and below the missionized pueblos of La Junta.

Ancestral Lipans reached Spanish Texas by 1720 and Coahuila by 1735, and subsequent groups of ancestral Mescaleros reached Nueva Vizcaya by 1741 and Coahuila by 1746 (see Map 2.1).[14]

Like their kinsmen to the west, eastern Ndé groups sought horses and mules for commercial exchange and their own transportation and subsistence. The major difference, however, is that during the early eighteenth century surrounding French-armed Caddos, Wichitas, Pawnees, Utes, and Comanches collectively posed a much more serious threat to the territorial, economic, and subsistence base of eastern Apache groups than neighboring Navajos, Tohono and Akimel O'odham, Ópatas, Hopis, and Pueblos did for Apaches west of the Rio Grande, even when supplied with Spanish arms and ammunition. Eastern Ndé groups used a combination of creative adaptive survival strategies to hold their ground for close to seventy years, which included settling near Spanish missions in order to obtain provisions, protection, and spiritual and healing power.[15]

In response to Ndé requests, Franciscans in Texas and New Mexico together converted more Apaches between 1715 and 1771 than they ever had previously. The first Ndé Catholic convert within the region encompassing modern Texas was baptized by Fray Andrés Ramírez prior to June 1715 at the La Junta missions at the confluence of the Rio Grande and Conchos Rivers. Although his motives are unclear, this ancestral Mescalero (probably Faraon) leader converted on good terms as a close friend of the missionized Opoxmes (Oposmes) at San Francisco pueblo. He promised to have the rest of his people catechized and baptized as soon as teaching missionaries arrived; however, members of his ranchería contracted smallpox soon after this, and apparently stayed away.[16]

More than five hundred miles to the north, in 1733 Franciscan Fray José Ortiz de Velasco founded a mission at Taos Pueblo for a friendly Ndé group whom Spaniards called "Apaches de la Xicarilla" or Jicarillas. Named in 1700 for a hill in their territory northeast of Taos (probably Mt. Capulín) that was shaped like a little chocolate cup (*jícara*), they were closely related to eastern Ndé groups Spaniards previously called Achos, Colorados, Conejeros, Sierra Blancas, and Carlanas, as well as Navajos, Quinias, and Manases west of the Rio Grande. Seeking Spanish protection and military assistance in their ongoing wars against Comanches and Utes, Jicarillas had made repeated requests to receive baptism and for the establishment of missionized pueblos in their homeland in the Valley of La Jicarilla from 1719 to 1727. Some Jicarillas were baptized at mission San Gerónimo de los Taos in 1719 and 1722, and in 1727 Jicarillas, along with some of their Carlana, Cuartelejo, and Paloma kinsmen, began

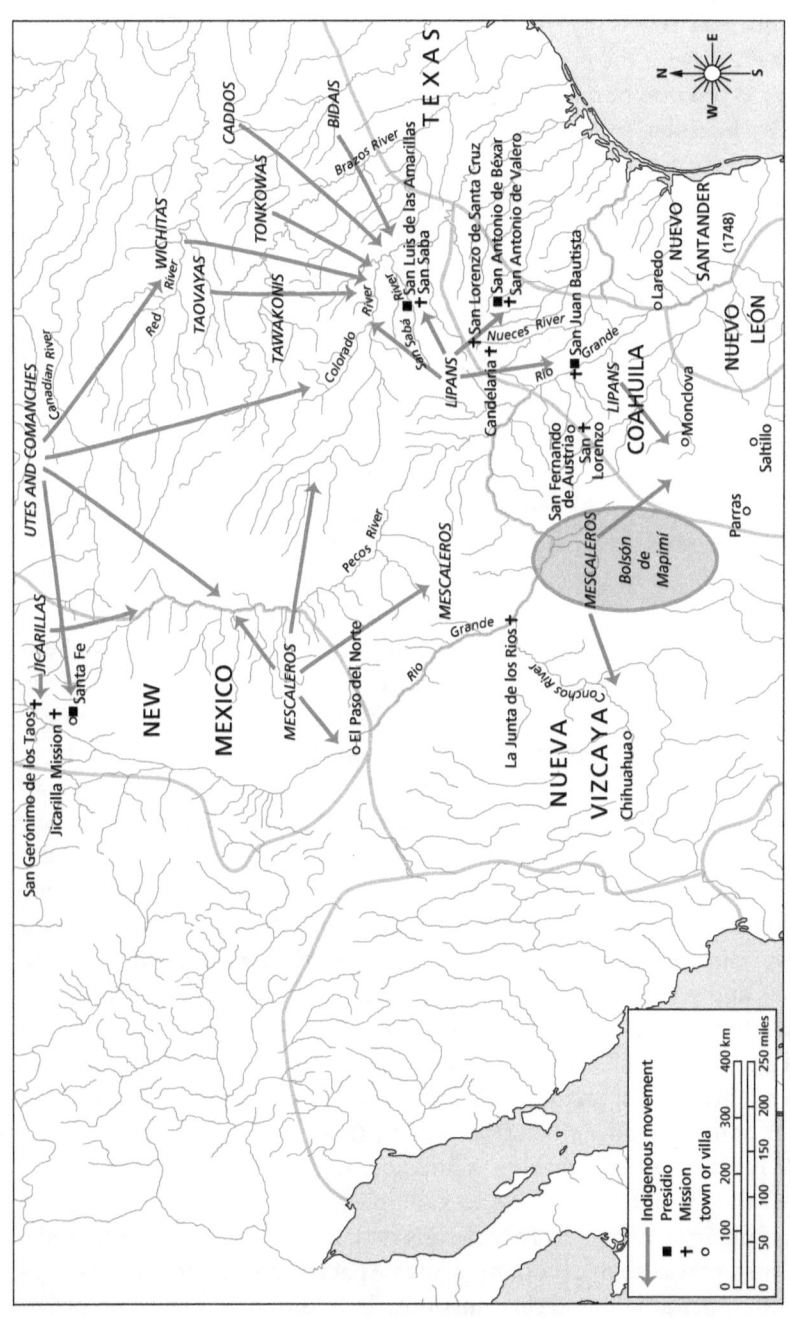

MAP 2.1 Eastern Apache movements and resettlement in missions, 1715–1766.

Source: Adapted from Stanley A. Arbingast, et al., *Atlas of Texas*, 5th edition (1976), 45, available online at www.lib.utexas.edu/maps/atlas_texas/texas_spanish_missions.jpg; Gerhard, *North Frontier of New Spain*, 196, 326; Moorhead, *Presidio*, 7.

settling along the Río de las Trampas (modern Rio Grande de Ranchos) and requested that Fray Juan José Pérez de Mirabal visit them at La Jicarilla. Although the precise location of the Jicarilla mission established by 1733 is unknown, it likely stood at or near modern Ranchos de Taos, with 130 Jicarillas still residing there in 1734. Ironically, New Mexico's own Governor Gervasio Cruzat y Góngora unwittingly killed the project by imposing harsh restrictions on the Indian hide trade. Although the governor intended the measure to restrict the Jicarillas' Ute and Comanche enemies, it deeply affected missionized Jicarillas as well, causing them to return to their territory.[17]

In addition to these localized and short-lived attempts, Franciscan priests in Spanish Texas also made more sustained efforts at Apache conversion and resettlement between 1723 and 1771. These began with attempts to convert ancestral Lipans, whom Spaniards called Ypandes, at mission San Antonio de Valero. In 1723 and 1724, Fray Joseph González tried to make peace with them at San Antonio. In 1725 Fray Francisco Hidalgo requested permission to travel northwest of San Antonio to work with the Ypandes in their own territory. In 1733, perhaps based on the establishment of the Jicarilla mission at Taos, Fray Gabriel de Vergara advocated that separate missions be established for Apaches in southern Texas, and a decade later Fray Benito Fernández de Santa Ana asked the viceroy to permit missions to be established within the Apachería.[18] Despite taking these positive steps to encourage Ypandes to settle in missions, Franciscan missionaries and Spanish military officers at San Antonio ultimately did more to undermine Apache–Hispanic relations during the 1720s than help them.

Franciscan priests cited several reasons for establishing missions for ancestral Lipans. These included curtailing their livestock raids around San Antonio, protecting the growth of its settlement and surrounding missions and settlement, and using the Apaches as a buffer against potential invasion by the French or British. Fray Vergara also believed that it would be more beneficial for Spaniards to try to convert Apache captives whom soldiers seized on their military campaigns rather than imprisoning them at San Antonio de Béxar or selling them to residents as domestic slaves. Finally, by establishing a mission in the Apachería, Spaniards believed they would gain access to valuable gold and silver deposits.[19]

The primary reason that Franciscans remained so vigilant and optimistic, however, was their recognition that Apaches had their own motives for making peace and entering missions. In addition to obtaining provisions, spiritual and healing power, and Spanish protection and military assistance against their enemies, at times Apaches promised to enter missions during peace negotiations in order to recover their captured kinsmen whom Spaniards held as captives and slaves. Following long-established practices in New Mexico, Nueva Vizcaya, and Sonora, Spanish officers in Coahuila and Texas authorized and led military offensives into the Apachería. Although these expeditions were usually in response to Ndé aggression against Spaniards, this was not always the case. During the early 1690s, for example, the French and the Spanish conducted joint campaigns with the Hasinai Caddos (Tejas) against eastern Apaches on the southern plains. Although eastern Apache groups and Caddos were embroiled in their own war over access to bison and horses at this point, there is no evidence that these Ndé groups committed any prior aggression toward Spaniards or Frenchmen in Texas. Thus, twenty-five years before the founding of San Antonio in 1718, ancestral Lipans and Mescaleros already had a perfectly legitimate reason to be hostile toward Europeans entering their territory.[20]

During the early 1720s allied Ypandes and ancestral Mescaleros (Natagés) who lived along the headwaters of the Red, Brazos, and Colorado Rivers of the Llanos de los Apaches (Apache Plains and today's central and southern plains) and in the bordering Lomería de los Apaches (Apache Hill Country and today's Texas Hill Country) began targeting San Antonio's recently established missions for livestock and for captives and sporadically attacking Spanish mule trains traveling along the Camino Real de los Tejas between presidios San Antonio de Béxar and San Juan Bautista in northern Coahuila. According to a forty-year-old female Apache captive in 1723, her people attacked Spaniards and stole their horses not based on revenge or an innate hatred for Spaniards but for commercial reasons, selling captive Spaniards and Spanish horses to "other Spaniards" far to the north, who were most likely French traders.[21] Regardless of the precise reasons for these raids, Spaniards believed they now had legitimate cause to launch a retaliatory offensive campaign against Apaches.

Opportunistic Franciscan priests in San Antonio frequently supported and sometimes participated in such expeditions in order to acquire potential Apache converts. Toward this end, in August 1723 San Antonio de Valero missionary Fray Joseph González supplied Captain Nicolás Flores and his force of thirty soldiers with thirty mission Indians for their two-month, two-hundred-mile punitive campaign into the Apachería. Although Flores and his men were responding to an Apache raid on the Béxar presidio horse herd, they simply targeted the first Apache group they came upon in late September, which happened to be a ranchería of 200 that included ancestral Lipans camped north of the San Sabá River (near modern Brownwood, TX). After killing thirty-four Indians, including a headman, taking twenty captive women and children, and seizing 120 horses and mules and an untold number of allegedly stolen saddles, bridles, and weapons, Flores's force returned with far more Apache people and resources than the eighty horses the Ndé raiding party initially took. Fray González himself was Flores' harshest critic, accusing him of attacking, capturing, and killing innocent Apaches who were trying to escape, which four soldiers confirmed. As Flores' behavior was deplorable, he was eventually punished for it, and the viceroy's royal regulations of 1729 "forbade any attack on Indians, whether friendly, hostile, or neutral," until Spanish officers had exhausted "every possible means to persuade them to peace."[22] The more surprising precedent is Fray González's decision to use military force, including his own mission Indians, to obtain potential Apache Catholic converts. This questionable decision, despite the regulations' ban on the separation of indigenous families captured in war, would be repeated by Fray González's successors, who also participated in several coordinated military campaigns into the Apachería between 1732 and 1745.

In spite of the inauspicious and violent beginning to Spanish–Apache relations in San Antonio, Ypandes still came to that community repeatedly during the 1740s to request that Franciscans build a mission for them. Most likely, this was because of their need to protect their elderly, women, and children during ongoing wars with Comanches and Caddoans. In response to a 1746 Comanche alliance with the Caddoan-speaking Taovaya Wichitas, in August 1749, Apaches forged an alliance with their former enemies, the Kadohadachos, in order to acquire French arms and ammunition. In the same month, following a less violent Spanish-led punitive expedition into the Apachería in which Béxar presidial commander Toribio de Urrutia took care to capture but not kill Apaches, ancestral Lipans negotiated terms for peace at San Antonio with Captain Urrutia and the Franciscans. After persuading Captain Urrutia to return all of his Apache prisoners to the Ypandes, Fray Santa Ana helped broker a lasting peace treaty ratified on November 29 that Lipans would faithfully honor for nearly twenty years from 1749 to 1767. Following the pact, Fray Santa Ana made two simple and powerful observations. What the Ypandes "value most," he wrote, "is the liberty of the prisoners from their nation," and "bloody campaigns would only make their conversion more difficult."[23]

Over the next several years small groups of Apaches, primarily women and children, braved the risks posed by smallpox and resident mission Indians and began staying at the San Antonio missions. These included the niece of Ypande nantan Boca Comida and nine other Apache women who intermarried with mission Indian men at San Antonio de Valero between 1749 and 1753 and a total of 129 baptized Apaches from 1721 through the 1780s.[24] Soldiers and settlers quickly recognized that the cost of maintaining peace was extremely high. Between 1749 and 1756, missionaries at San Antonio issued Apaches more than 2,670 bushels of maize, 133 steers, 76 horses, 60 bushels of beans, 91 strings of pepper, and large quantities of salt, sugar, and tobacco. They received 4,555 yards of cloth, 239 hats, 642 blankets, 458 knives, 196 bridles, 17 kettles and boilers, and 132 pesos' worth of ribbons, beads, and other gifts.[25] Pleased that Apaches finally decided to enter the missions, Franciscans believed they were on the verge of success.

Their further efforts at courting eastern Apaches, however, produced more meager results. In 1750, at Nantan Pastallenao's request, Fray Alonzo Giraldo de Terreros founded the first Ypande mission at San Juan Bautista on the Coahuilan shore of the Rio Grande, but they deserted it on the first night after their arrival. Four years later, in response to another direct request from Ndé, leaders of groups that Spaniards called Natagés, Cíbolas, and Tucubantes, Terreros established mission San Lorenzo near the Coahuilan town of San Fernando de Austria (see Map 2.1). By the end of March 1755, after three months of operation, eighty-three Apaches, including Nantans El Gordo, El de Godo, and Bigotes had settled at San Lorenzo, and Terreros employed an Ypande interpreter named Francisco del Norte to ease communication. On October 4, 1755, however, the Apache residents revolted by burning all the buildings and deserting permanently.[26] Frontier soldiers and settlers saw these revolts as clear signs of the natural fickle and inconstant nature of the Apaches, and Teodoro de Croix, who undoubtedly knew about this incident, would have concurred. Franciscans, however, believed that the sole problem was that the missions were situated too far south. If they established a mission farther north and closer to Apache hunting grounds, they believed the semisedentary Ypandes would remain at the mission more consistently throughout the year, as it would serve as a centrally located base for their seasonal hunting and wild plant gathering.

By January 1757, the prospects for building a more northerly mission in the Apachería itself appeared quite good. That year Fray Alonso Giraldo de Terreros' wealthy cousin Don Pedro agreed to finance personally all expenses for an Apache mission on the San Sabá River for three years, and the crown agreed to fund a presidio to protect it. Terreros encouraged the Apaches to speak Spanish and employed nine Tlascalan Indian families from Saltillo to stimulate their farming. Demonstrating initial receptiveness to the plan, two Ypande bands met with Colonel Diego Ortiz Parrilla at mission San Antonio de Valero and assured him that they wanted to enter the mission and become Spanish subjects. Parrilla then presented their two headmen with canes to symbolize their status as *alcaldes* (mayors) under Spanish law, and Terreros and Dolores offered them presents. After remaining at San Antonio for three days, the two Ypande leaders promised to assemble at San Sabá as soon as Spaniards finished constructing the mission buildings.[27]

In the spring of 1757, Franciscans constructed Santa Cruz de San Sabá on the southern bank of the San Sabá River (near present-day Menard) and soldiers began building a wooden stockade, San Luis de las Amarillas, along the north bank of the river. Although Spanish officials had envisioned San Sabá as an innovative mission–presidio complex reflecting the latest developments in European enlightened thinking, the reality was starkly different. Fearful that soldiers might corrupt their Apache converts, Franciscans insisted that the presidio be located across the river and three miles from the mission.[28]

By mid-June, 3,000 Ypandes gathered near the San Sabá mission. Terreros thought the dream of an Apache mission had finally been realized, but only El Chico and a few other leaders remained willing to remain there. Most ancestral Lipans had a very different purpose for seeking Spanish allegiance. The nantan Casablanca explained to Terreros that in May his Ypandes had been defeated by Hasinais along the Colorado River, and they sought Spanish protection for their annual summer buffalo hunt and campaign against Comanches, Hasinais, and other Caddoan-speaking groups whom Spaniards collectively deemed Norteños, or "Nations of the North." If the Spaniards agreed to escort them, then afterward, Casablanca claimed, he and his people would settle at San Sabá and accept the Catholic faith.[29]

Throughout the summer and fall small bands of Apaches stopped by San Sabá for a few days to replenish their supplies, but they refused to remain permanently for several reasons. First, they were at war with Comanches and their Norteño allies. Furthermore, the Ypandes had heard rumors that these same Indians planned to attack the mission – rumors that turned out to be true. Many Apache bands, then, preferred to remain south of the Rio Grande for safety, leading three of Father

Terreros' associates to lose hope in Ypande sincerity and to ask permission to leave the mission. According to these priests, the Apaches wanted a "workless" mission that functioned as a trading post. "Having fully learned the wishes of the Indians," fathers Joachín de Baños and Diego Ximénez complained, "we find no other motive (for friendship) than the hope of receiving gifts." These statements failed to take into account not only the military pressure the Lipans faced, but also the debilitating epidemic that ravaged their camps from October to December of 1757.[30]

On March 16 at dawn two thousand Hasinai, Taovaya, Wichita, Comanche, Bidai, and Tonkawa warriors carried out their previous threats and attacked the mission. Dressed in full war regalia, the Caddoan-led war party circled the stockade and fired French muskets in the air. After the *padres* inexplicably opened the front gate for this angry throng, the intruders killed Terreros, his assistant Fray José de Santiesteban, at least two other priests, and six Spanish soldiers. The few remaining missionaries and two Ypande Indians remained holed up in the mission church, and Parrilla's small presidial garrison failed to come to their aid.[31] Possessing superior numbers and facing little opposition, the attackers sacked the mission and burned it to the ground. The Comanches and Norteños claimed to be seeking revenge against the Apaches for killing some of their people near the Rio Concho; however, Fray Miguel de Molina believed their true purpose was to punish the Spaniards for befriending their enemies.[32]

In the wake of this attack, Father Molina believed that the Comanche and Norteño threat made it impossible to reduce and settle Apache Indians along the San Sabá. Molina understood that, unknowingly, Spaniards had established the San Sabá mission in the Comanchería rather than the Apachería and that the Lipan homeland lay farther south "closer to our settlements along the rivers." As a result, it would be "an inhuman action to try to reduce them in this region" and the Ypandes "are certain to try to escape" the danger from "their more numerous and warlike barbarian enemies."[33]

Taking heed of Molina's advice, in the winter of 1762 the Franciscans made two final efforts to convert Ypandes, whom Spaniards now called Lipans, farther south along the Nueces River. On January 23, the missionaries founded mission San Lorenzo de la Santa Cruz for the Lipan leader Cabezón's band on an upper branch of the Nueces at El Cañon (modern Camp Wood, TX). In February they founded a second mission, Nuestra Señora de la Candelaria, five leagues downstream for Nantan

Turnio's band. Although these missions survived for seven and four years, respectively, they were never officially approved by Spanish officials, offered insufficient rations and protection, and failed to convert a single Apache.[34]

In light of these events, by the late 1760s, many Bourbon policy makers had given up on converting Apaches to Catholicism in missions. In the summer of 1769 Franciscans working on the Apache frontier reported the poor results of their efforts to Visitor-General José de Gálvez. "Not one real conversion has been confirmed," Gálvez wrote. In his view, Apaches remained a "total impediment to the progress of the extension of the faith, and without removing the barrier they constitute, it will be very difficult for the missions to move forward, nor will these dominions of the King be freed from the continuous scourge of the Apaches." Although missions continued to function in Texas until 1794 and in the Californias until 1833, most Bourbon officials, whether enlightened or not, realized that pacifying Apaches required a different strategy.[35]

Three Spanish policy decisions – the expulsion of the Jesuits in 1767, the Marqués de Rubí's inspection of the presidial line from 1766 to 1768, and King Carlos III's regulations of 1772 – together demonstrated the military's expanded role in controlling Apaches and other equestrian Native peoples who lived along New Spain's northern frontier. Most infamously, Rubí advocated that Spaniards, Comanches, and Caddoan Norteños work to achieve "the total extermination" of Lipan Apaches "or at least their complete reduction," through the extradition of those who "seek asylum in our missions and presidios" to interior Mexico (see Figure 2.1). Although the Spanish military never achieved either goal, several officers, including Inspector-in-Chief Hugo O'Conor, Commander-in-Chief Teodoro de Croix, and Coahuila Governor Juan de Ugalde sometimes tried to accomplish those goals in practice.[36]

Yet Spanish Indian policy was multidimensional and predicated on peace as well as violence. The repeated stated objective of waging offensive war against Indians in Spanish policies during the 1770s was to achieve peace. By the time Teodoro de Croix took office in 1777, even Franciscans conceded that the Spanish military should assume responsibility for the pacification of these groups. In contrast to missionaries, who believed that conversion should be the critical first step toward "civilization," enlightened Bourbon reformers preferred to turn pacified Indians into productive members of society *before* Christianizing them. As Croix noted in 1778 independent Apaches visited "the missions of Texas and

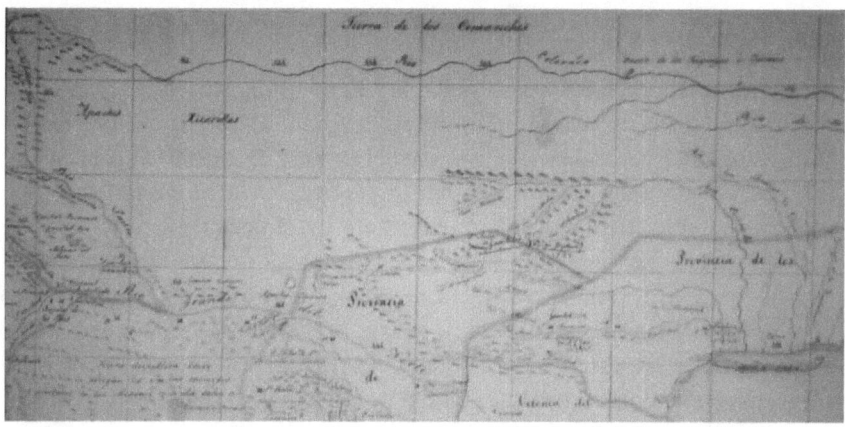

FIGURE 2.1 Detail of Nicolas de Lafora's 1771 Map depicting the outcome of the Marqués de Rubí's 1768 policy recommendations, with eastern Apache groups confined to the margins of the southern plains and Comanches north of the Red River.
Source: Mapa de la frontera del virreynato de Nueva España nuevamente construido por el ingeniero ordinario Don Nicolas de Lafora ... en esta capital el dia 27 de Julio de 1771, Huntington Manuscript 2047. Courtesy of the Huntington Library, San Marino, CA.

Coahuila" frequently to trade for seeds and livestock, but they had little incentive to reside in them permanently. "They enter in the huts of the neophytes," he continued, "see their misery, and their lack of rations, and that only the Padres make the exchanges: they compare their labor with their own troubles, their poverty with their abundance, and conclude with evidence, that it is the greatest misfortune to be reduced."[37]

APACHE PEACE PACTS AT PRESIDIOS

Officially, Spanish military policy discouraged all peace-seeking Indians from permanently settling at presidios prior to 1779. The royal regulations of 1729 and 1772 permitted presidial commanders to use their posts only as temporary internment camps for peaceful Indians caught stealing livestock or for enemy Indians captured in battle before extraditing and imprisoning them indefinitely in Mexico City.[38] In practice, however, some post commanders sometimes departed from policy and tried to congregate Apaches permanently near presidios prior to 1779. From a Spanish perspective, the practice of settling Apaches in pueblos and on reservations may have emerged as a logical solution for relocating Apache groups who voluntarily surrendered in war.

In the midst of the Pueblo Revolt in the fall of 1693 Maestre de Campo Joseph Marín offered a little-known early revision to Spanish Indian policy in northern New Spain that may have influenced late eighteenth-century Spanish Apache policy. Rather than allowing peace-seeking Native peoples to choose to live in their own "locations and sites" as the Spanish military had been doing previously, Marín advised Spanish officers to exercise more control over them by requiring them to settle in poblaciones or settlements "in sight of the presidios." With the aim of transforming the Indians from alleged mountain-dwelling nomads into riverside sedentary agriculturalists, Marín proposed that Spanish soldiers encourage the relocated Indians "to build their houses correctly, to raise chickens, and to plant their cornfields" so that they developed "an attachment" to their new Spanish-style communities. An additional benefit, in Marín's fanciful view, is that these poblaciones would serve as buffers to prevent Indian raids across the Spanish frontier and promote "complete tranquility and peace."[39] Given the high level of interethnic indigenous violence in northern New Spain, it is doubtful that Spanish officials had the opportunity to act on Marín's suggestions. Nevertheless, his thinking is remarkably similar to the Apache policies implemented by Teodoro de Croix and other Spanish military officials in the late eighteenth century.

Ndé groups residing west of the Rio Grande conducted widespread raids across Nueva Vizcaya and Sonora in the early eighteenth century. "The Apaches have stolen and slaughtered great numbers of cattle and horses," Fronteras Captain Juan Bautista de Anza (the Elder) lamented in August 1735. In addition to conducting resource raids, Anza claimed Apaches "murdered Spaniards and friendly Indians, and have besieged villages" since at least 1715. As a result, settlers abandoned several cattle and horse ranches, whose ruins, Anza noted, "are still visible." Anza neglected to mention why Apache groups committed these acts and whether any Spanish activities prompted them. As a general rule, Ndé men did not intentionally kill their enemies unless they lost kinsmen of their own, and that was the scenario in this instance. Anza boasted that he had "punished our enemies in various ways" for their murders "in order to curb their attacks."[40]

One might think that Anza's efforts would have backfired and simply encouraged Apache groups to raid more intensely; however, instead they caused some of them to seek peace. In 1732, for example, Apaches requested peace from Captain Don Antonio Becerra at Janos presidio because of Anza's campaigns and Becerra's own offerings of food rations and other gifts in an effort "to attract them to a more civilized life."

Seeking to recover their women and children, whom Anza had captured in a prior attack, another Ndé band offered to make peace with Captain Anza at Fronteras in October 1733. Two days after the commander returned them, the Apaches sent a delegation to the presidio. Anza offered them "horses, loads of food, coarse cloth, blankets, and knives." His troops also planted a field of corn for the Apaches near the presidio. The result was that as many as eighty Apache men and women "camped within four gunshots" of Fronteras with other families nearby.[41] Apache men at Janos and Fronteras, for their part, appreciated the handouts but preferred to use them for sustenance on their equestrian raids for livestock, rather than as a means of becoming more like Spaniards (see Map 2.2).

At the same time he courted Apaches at the presidio, Captain Anza continued to launch offensive campaigns into their camps in the Sierra de las Espuelas twenty leagues northeast of Fronteras along the Continental Divide. He "punished" those men who refused to surrender, presumably by seizing them and taking them as captives. But he noted that his successes were sporadic because the Apaches were so adept at concealing themselves in rugged, impenetrable mountains.[42]

Exaggerating their depredations, Anza wrote that Apaches "offered peace in order to massacre its inhabitants." Yet he acknowledged that in all of their recent raids, they had only killed one person – an Indian from Cumpas pueblo in Sonora. He was a bit more accurate when he wrote, "peace was just a ploy for them to rob at liberty, as they had been doing." Unprovoked Ndé groups did not seek to kill Spaniards, and, although they took livestock, they did not view such routine acts as robbing or stealing, but as appropriating resources that they regarded as rightfully their own. Obviously, frontier Spaniards, such as Anza, thought otherwise and likely reacted so strongly out of a combination of anger and fear. Despite his complaints, Anza recognized the difference between Apache raiding and warfare. "When they come to plunder," he explained, "it is in small groups" and "they spy out horses, mules, and cattle." But on other occasions, "they gather in large numbers to mount a major attack against travelers, soldiers, or settlements," often in multiple bands.[43]

Interestingly, even though Becerra's and Anza's efforts to permanently congregate Apaches near presidios appeared to go against the royal regulations of 1729, they claimed to be abiding by royal policy. Anza maintained that he and Becerra followed "the repeated mandates" issued by King Felipe V, "the instructions of Viceroy Marqués de Casafuerte, and the requirements of Christian charity."[44] It is unclear how this could be the case. Perhaps the truces they offered the Apaches were only

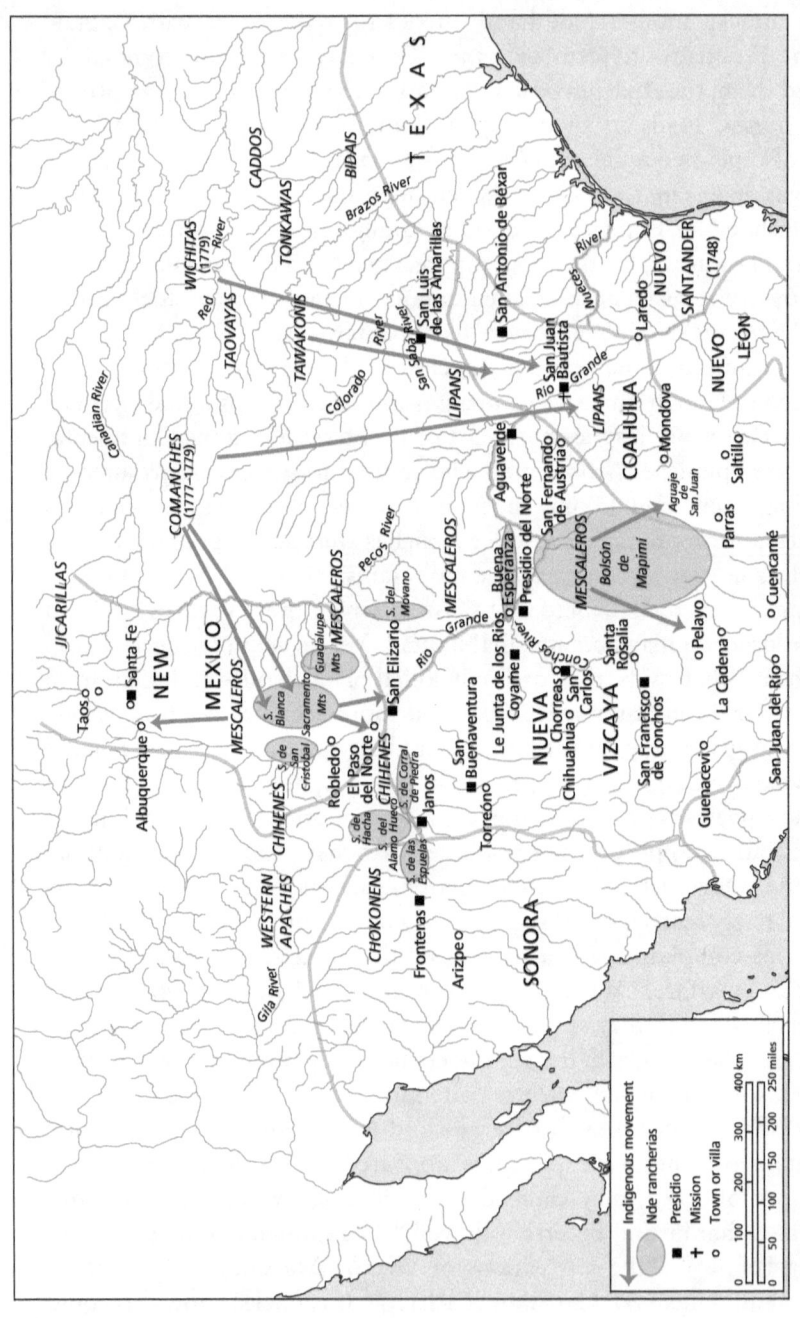

MAP 2.2. Ndé movements, peace pacts, and resettlement near Presidios, 1732–1783.
Source: Adapted from Moorhead, Apache Frontier, 171, 201; Presidio, 7; Jack D. Forbes, Apache, Navaho, and Spaniard, 77; William B. Griffen, Apaches at War and Peace: The Janos Presidio, 1750–1858 (1988; reprint, Norman: University of Oklahoma Press, 1998); Gerhard, North Frontier of New Spain, 192, 196, 280, 315, 326.

temporary or maybe the viceroy's policy was different from the king's. In any event, Anza denied instituting a new policy at the local level.

Much like Becerra and Anza, in 1741 Captain José de Berroterán negotiated peace with ancestral Mescaleros north of Parral at San Francisco de Conchos presidio in Nueva Vizcaya. After initially reporting that "four hundred Apaches had overrun the area" between 1730 and 1741, Berroterán later clarified that the Indians had "not begun to rob and murder yet, due to the peace their chief, Pascual, has made with me." In contrast to Becerra and Anza, Berroterán specifically noted that his actions were in accordance with Article 193 from the royal regulations, which stated that any hostile Indian who sought peace at a presidio should be granted it. Pascual's people were living "in the pocket of land that is free of hostile Indians," and had entered into a "friendly relationship" with the presidial captain, trading deerskins and serving as auxiliary troops in exchange for Spanish horses, goods, clothing, and provisions.[45]

Prior to Nueva Vizcaya's declaration of war against Apaches in 1748, Pascual's Apaches and another undesignated Ndé band under El Ligero ("the swift one") helped Berroterán's garrison recapture runaway mission Indians seeking refuge in and around the arid Bolsón de Mapimí (see Map 2.2). These apostate Indians were likely joining the dwindling number of war and disease-ravaged allied groups fighting for their survival against Spanish colonialism, who included the Concho-speaking Chisos subgroup of Sisimbles, Toboso-speaking Cocoyomes, and Coahuileños. Pascual and El Ligero's troops, then, represent the first groups of Apache auxiliaries to serve Spanish interests at presidios, which would eventually become one of the most important obligations for Apache men in the system of Spanish reservations.[46]

As of 1748 Pascual and El Ligero's people were among three Ndé groups, probably all ancestral Mescaleros, at peace with the mission Indians of La Junta. The third group Spaniards called Natagés, which they probably derived from the Lipan word *nátahé* for "mescal people" or Mescaleros. Although Captain Berroterán had set an important precedent in utilizing Apache men as auxiliary troops, it would be temporarily forgotten as the officer unfairly blamed Pascual, El Ligero, and the four hundred Ndé living between Coahuila and Nueva Vizcaya for all of the violence in the region. In 1749, in the same year that Ypandes had negotiated an enduring peace treaty with Captain Toribio Urrutia in San Antonio, Berroterán initiated the first military campaign against Pascual and El Ligero's people on Governor Puerta y Barrera's orders. Perhaps this is not so surprising, given that Pascual and El Ligero were in close contact with Natagés, who had opted not to make peace with Spaniards at San Antonio and had little desire to settle in missions.[47]

By the early 1770s, Apache groups residing south and west of the Rio Grande voluntarily surrendered in war and agreed to settle in towns. In November 1772, for example, a Mescalero (Natagé) Apache nantan and two companions sought peace with Inspector-in-Chief Hugo O'Conor in Chihuahua on behalf of their bands and those of nine other Mescalero leaders residing in the Bolsón de Mapimí. In exchange for returning all of the captive Spaniards they had taken during the last fifteen years by the end of January, and all horses and mules taken in the last six years, "they would be settled in towns along the shores of the Rio Grande." In spite of the harsh conditions, the Mescaleros agreed to the terms and O'Conor rewarded each headman with "a scarlet-colored suit with silver trim, a matching hat, shirt, stockings, shoes, and other articles of clothing."[48] It is unclear precisely where these towns were to be located, whether Spaniards ever constructed them, and whether the Mescaleros entered them.

Two years later, in the fall and winter of 1774–75, O'Conor led a series of offensives into the sierras of Alamo Hueco, El Hacha, and Corral de Piedra north of Janos and negotiated a similar agreement with some Chihene Apaches. They sought peace at El Paso on January 19, 1775, and agreed to live in a settlement under Spanish protection. Although O'Conor was skeptical of their promises, he went to El Paso personally to negotiate with them. The initial talks went well, but problems arose once the Chihene leaders returned to the Apachería to review the terms with their people. El Paso's presidial commander reported that a raiding party of these same Indians took thirty cattle and thirty mules from the jurisdiction and escaped into the Organ Mountains to the northeast. As a result, O'Conor and Viceroy Bucareli decided to abandon negotiations with the Chihenes and to reduce them by military force.[49] Although O'Conor's efforts to settle Apaches in pueblos failed, they set a precedent that Croix seems to have followed.

CROIX'S WAR COUNCILS AND THE DECISION TO SETTLE APACHES IN PUEBLOS

From the winter of 1777 through the summer 1778 Teodoro de Croix convened three successive war councils of leading frontier administrators and military officers. Held at Monclova in December, San Antonio in January, and Chihuahua in June and July, these meetings addressed

Indian policy in Coahuila, Texas, and Nueva Vizcaya, respectively. From them Croix devised a strategy to pacify the eastern Apaches by bolstering Spanish military forces, forging alliances with Comanches and their Caddoan allies, and attacking Mescaleros, Plains Apaches, and Lipans in their own camps. These aggressive measures were necessary, the Monclova council unanimously agreed, because administrative reforms and changes in presidio locations had not quelled Apache attacks, which were more frequent and intense than ever before. The council also unanimously agreed that, rather than extermination, the goal of this policy was for Apaches to "surrender to the mercy of our Catholic arms" and "seek asylum and safety" at the edge of Spanish territory along the presidial line. Presidial captains promised to protect those Apaches who voluntarily surrendered and to treat them "with all the mildness recommended by the king," while continuing to punish those who refused. Caught "between two fires" – the Comanches and Caddoan Norteños on one side and Spanish forces on the other – Spaniards hoped that these Apaches, too, would eventually surrender. In short, this council recognized that, in the near future, "even though the total subjection of the Apaches should not be effected," they still might "be reduced to a small number, conquerable with fewer troops and less anguish" than at present.[50]

In the wake of the Monclova and San Antonio councils, Croix made an important change in policy: truces would no longer be granted to Apaches. Because of Apaches' tendency to raid after making peace, post commanders should only grant them peace if they agree to settle permanently in formal pueblos assigned by Croix. This policy went into effect on February 12, 1778, and stemmed from Croix's frustration with the truce Janos presidial commander Narciso de Tapia had granted Chihene leaders. According to Croix, all Apache groups were "unsubduable" because "every Indian is an independent republic." "Accustomed to living wildly," he went on, they "never stopped robbing," "were unable to keep the good faith," and were incapable of "settling down to a rational and Christian life." Given his ethnocentric view of Apache culture, it should not be surprising that Croix's preference, as the previous war councils had advised, was to attack and defeat Apaches by force. Because of the lack of Spanish troops, however, Croix still granted peace to Apaches who promptly agreed "to be reduced voluntarily to live in formal populations."[51]

Croix put his policy change into effect immediately because numerous Apache groups were seeking peace across the northern frontier. Three days earlier El Paso Lieutenant Governor José Antonio de Arrieta requested that his successor Narciso Muñiz permit the Mescalero nantan Josef's band to settle in peace and "to form a pueblo" for them at San Elizario. On the same day he issued his order, Croix instructed Inspector-in-Chief José Rubio to follow the new terms with Nantan Chafalote's son Natanijú and two other Chihene headmen, Pachatijú and El Zurdo, who had been seeking peace at Janos and San Buenaventura presidios intermittently since the previous August, and with Mescalero Apaches from the Sierra Blanca at Albuquerque. After months of negotiations hampered by sporadic raiding and disagreements over prisoner exchange, in April 1778 these same Chihene leaders finally agreed to settle their bands in a pueblo at Janos and to raise their own crops, provided that Spaniards supplied them with rations for the first year.[52]

Early in the same month Commander-in-Chief Croix reported to Minister of the Indies José de Gálvez the strict conditions under which all Apaches, including the Chihenes at Janos, would now be admitted to peace. First, they had to surrender all Spanish captives, although they could keep their stolen horses. Then, Apache families were to settle in well-organized pueblos and help build homes subject to the orders of a Spanish official, who in most cases was a presidial captain. Although they could select one of their own leaders as their governor, they could not leave the pueblo without Spanish permission. Each family would receive necessary farming tools, horses for work and transportation, and weekly rations for one year. Apparently unaware of the division of labor in Apache culture, the Spaniards chose to give the residential and farming plots to each male family head and expected all Apaches, including men and children, to help farm. This was a serious change from customary Apache gender roles. Generally, neither Apache men nor children were expected to farm on a daily basis, although the men did help the women with the heaviest labor in the spring and fall. Finally, in a departure from previous mission policy, only Apache children were required to become Catholic. Adult Apaches were free to make up their own minds, most likely because Spaniards had experienced such difficulty attempting to Christianize them in the past.[53]

Perhaps as a way of showing their displeasure, the Chihenes refused to abide by Croix's demands and stepped up their raiding. Still, these negotiations were significant because they reveal that Spanish officers had finally developed a uniform peace policy and were committed to following it. At the same time, however, Spanish forces continued to punish Apaches west of the Rio Grande in their own territory with coordinated expeditions from presidios in Nueva Vizcaya and Sonora from the south and from Santa Fe and Zuni from the north.[54]

At Teodoro de Croix's third and final war council held at his home in Chihuahua in June and July 1778, frontier officials made several revisions to the Monclova council's findings. Although they concurred with Croix that progress could be made against Apaches with the 2,000 additional troops he requested, the members of the council determined that they needed 4,000 troops to actually defeat them. Part of the reason so many more troops were needed was because the Monclova council's estimate of 5,000 Apache warriors was too low. According to New Mexico governors Pedro Fermín de Mendinueta and Juan Bautista de Anza (the younger), when Apaches waged war, "an equal number of women ... form regularly a reserve corps" and "round up the horses while the men attack our troops." These officials also noted that, aside from this practical purpose, Apaches used women to bolster their numbers and give them a psychological edge against their enemies. Mendinueta and Anza explained, "by increasing the number of individuals" in a war party, Apaches succeeded "in creating the well-founded idea that they are more formidable."[55]

Aside from these two revisions, however, the Chihuahua council essentially upheld the strategies of the Monclova council. Most notably, they agreed peace should not be extended to the Apaches in any of the provinces "because their friendship will always produce very funereal effects. Experience confirms this every time it is done." According to the council members, the Chihenes had recently demonstrated that they could not be trusted. After seeking peace at Janos and San Elizario presidios and the towns of El Paso and Albuquerque, the council's secretary Antonio de Bonilla explained, they had "treacherously" caused "serious injuries" to frontier Spaniards "in the very spots where they sought peace."[56] In short, the council believed that granting peace to Apaches, especially the Chihenes, or so-called Gileños, was a complete waste of royal funds.

Frontier realities, however, dictated a slightly different course of action toward eastern Apaches. The council recommended that while Croix waited for additional royal troops to carry out his military offensives, he make peace with Mescaleros in Nueva Vizcaya in order to entice them to attack the Lipans. At the same time, the council advised making peace with Lipans in Coahuila and having them attack the Mescaleros.[57]

Meanwhile, as frontier officials reacted to alleged Chihene "duplicity" by authorizing offensive war, José de Gálvez approved the terms Croix had drawn up in April for settling Apaches in pueblos in a royal order of July 18, 1778. As Croix later explained to Gálvez, the minister of the Indies' response arrived too late.[58] Croix had already tried to offer peace to the Chihenes, and they had dishonored the agreement by raiding. So he was proceeding with the council's murderous recommendation of inciting Mescaleros and Lipans to kill one another.

INDIGENOUS AND SPANISH MILITARY PRESSURE

Rather than responding to any centralized Spanish policy, Teodoro de Croix offered to settle Apaches in pueblos primarily because Apaches themselves sought peace. Indeed, Croix and other Spaniards understood that eastern Apaches did so because of military pressure from Caddoans and Comanches. In practice, Croix was unable to forge the Comanche alliance his war councils had advised because of Indian agent Athanase de Mézières' death in November 1779 and a lack of royal funds for gifts.[59] In spite of these setbacks, however, confederated Caddoan Norteños and Comanches attacked Lipans and Mescaleros independently of Spaniards. At the same time, as Croix's councils had advised, Spanish troops from Coahuila and Nueva Vizcaya launched a series of punitive expeditions with Apache auxiliaries against independent Lipans and Mescaleros. Without this combined military pressure, which came largely from Indians, Croix could not have established his establecimiento for the Mescaleros at El Norte (see Map 2.2).

As we have seen, Caddoans and Comanches had already pushed Lipans and the Spanish mission frontier south of San Antonio by the 1760s. They continued to pressure Lipans and Mescaleros in the 1770s in an effort to control access to the southern plains buffalo herd, which served as a vital resource for food, shelter, and trade. Prior to November 1776, Comanches attacked three hundred Apaches fleeing from Spanish troops and, according to Spanish reports, only one Apache and one Spanish captive escaped. Since this battle took place on the edge of Mescalero territory, east of the Guadalupe Mountains and the Sierra Blancas along the Rio Colorado in Texas, these Apaches were probably Mescaleros. The fact that Spaniards also found buffalo meat at the scene suggests the Indians may have been encroaching on Comanche hunting grounds. Although it is going too far to say that this single battle broke Apache power in Texas, it must have reduced *eastern* Apache authority on the southern plains and helped to reinforce Comanche dominance in the region (see Map 2.2).[60]

By December 1777, at the same time Spanish officers were meeting at Monclova, the Comanches had moved southwestward into the Sierra Blanca and were driving the Mescaleros from their own territory. According to one Spanish sergeant, Apaches all along the Rio Grande between El Paso and Robledo feared the Comanches. El Paso Lieutenant Governor José Antonio de Arrieta reported that Mescaleros from the Sierra Blanca came to settle at San Elizario pueblo in early February 1778 because Comanches had attacked them while they were hunting on the plains. Fearful of returning to their former hunting grounds, these Mescaleros were suffering from "much hunger and tiredness," Arrieta revealed. As further proof of their desperation, Arrieta reported that the Mescalero women have loaded many horses with wood "to sell to the *vecinos* [townsfolk] for corn and other seeds." Finally, he explained that he was unable to help them "at the present" because "I find myself still without the necessary sustenance for my own family."[61]

This last statement suggests that regional drought in combination with Comanche military pressure influenced these Mescaleros to seek peace. Although Teodoro de Croix failed to acknowledge that drought was a factor, he at least recognized that part of Apache motivations for negotiating stemmed from "the repeated assaults that the Comanches gave them." By the end of February the Mescaleros, who asked for peace at El Paso pueblo and San Elizario presidio, had abandoned the Sacramento Mountains and moved onto the empty hill ten leagues from El Paso.[62]

In January 1779 the Comanches and their allies struck again, killing or capturing 300 Lipans. As a result of this attack, Teodoro de Croix wrote, "they were defeated (as never before) in Coahuila and Texas, and that in spite of their fundamental suspicions of our friendship, they lent their support" against the Mescaleros. Clearly, without this sustained military pressure from Apaches' Comanche and Caddoan enemies, Croix would have been in no position to coax the Mescaleros and Lipans into attacking each other. Croix hoped that by pitting Mescalero allies in Nueva Vizcaya against independent Lipan bands in Coahuila and Lipan allies against independent Mescaleros, he could weaken both groups to the point that they would no longer pose a significant military threat. Then, Croix believed, these eastern Apaches would finally agree to settle in pueblos and make a "less deceitful peace." Furthermore, Croix hoped that by maintaining peace with the "Nations of the North," the Lipans, and the Mescaleros, he could attract Apaches west of the Rio Grande to also make peace. Then, with their major enemy pacified, Croix's presidial troops, who numbered less than 1,500 men in all of Nueva Vizcaya and Coahuila, could confine their activities to "purely defensive operations."[63]

Commander-in-Chief Croix had first tested out this policy in 1778, when the Lipans offered to deliver two Mescalero rancherías to Aguaverde presidial captain Francisco Martínez. But when the Lipans joined the campaign, they went back on their promise and warned the Mescaleros ahead of time, most likely because of the kinship ties the two groups shared. Croix thought this was "traitorous," and it may explain why he turned to making peace with the Mescaleros instead.[64]

Spaniards had better luck in 1779. In late spring Coahuila Governor Juan de Ugalde began carrying out Croix's shrewd but diabolical policy. Forming an alliance with the Mescaleros, he led a combined force of Spaniards and Mescaleros against the Lipans, resulting in heavy Apache losses on both sides and the destruction of 600 horses. On July 8, Presidio del Norte commander Manuel Muñoz and the Mescaleros, including Patule, attacked a small Lipan ranchería, killing five warriors and taking five captives. After learning the location of several more Lipan bands from one of their captives, Muñoz's force attacked them in a large forest at dawn. The Lipans, who numbered 500, were ready for them, however, and the battle lasted all morning. Although the Lipans killed one Spaniard and one Mescalero, Muñoz and the Mescaleros had compelled them to retreat north of the Rio Grande and took eight captives, sixty loads of meat, and 640 animals. Thus, the campaign was successful, and it was after these two operations that the Mescaleros presented themselves to Commander-in-Chief Croix in Chihuahua, in the apparent belief that they now enjoyed a strong negotiating position.[65]

THE ROYAL ORDER OF 1779 AND THE AMERICAN REVOLUTION

The few scholars who have offered an explanation for Croix's first Apache settlement at Presidio del Norte suggest that it simply resulted from José de Gálvez's royal order of February 20, 1779.[66] Yet, as we have seen, Hugo O'Conor had already begun this practice in the early 1770s, and this monocausal explanation ignores the impact of Croix's three war councils on Spanish Indian policy, Croix's personal responses to Apache requests for peace during this period, and military pressure from Comanches and Norteño allies. Most significantly, this interpretation misconstrues the provisions of the royal order of 1779 itself.

Rather than embracing pueblos as a means of pacifying Apaches, José de Gálvez's order specifically forbade Croix from settling Apaches and other peace-seeking nomadic Indians in pueblos. It is "appropriate and of strict justice," Gálvez wrote, "to leave them in their complete liberty." Much as his nephew Bernardo would argue in 1786, José de Gálvez believed that over time Indians would simply start coveting Spanish goods and homes and would see the advantages of their "rational life." Unable to live without these goods, they would "reduce their rancherías to a type of villages" independently first, and only as a subsequent step would they then join Spanish populations. In this pacified state they would not only adopt clothing and begin farming, they would also begin to use Spanish arms for hunting and even for defending themselves against their enemies. As a result, José de Gálvez argued, they would forget how to use the bow and arrow, and the Indians would become dependent "vassals of the king."[67]

As previous scholars have shown, when the royal order of 1779 finally arrived in Croix's hands in July, it did prevent him from carrying out his planned military offensives into the eastern Apachería. Without the 2,000 additional troops Croix asked for, he was unable to place enough sustained pressure on the Apaches to attract them to pueblos in significant numbers. Yet Croix still wanted those 2,000 troops for defensive purposes as he moved forward with his preconceived plan of Apache resettlement. It was not until September 30 – long after the Mescaleros had solicited peace in Chihuahua and agreed to settle at Buena Esperanza – that Croix learned from Gálvez that Spain had declared war on England on June 21 and entered the American Revolution as an ally of Bourbon France. From this he concluded that getting those additional troops was impossible. Still Croix went on with his plan to settle the Mescaleros in pueblos. He believed, in the best scenario, his peace with the eastern Apaches could open the door to a general peace with all Apaches, including those who lived west of the Rio Grande, or it could be the key to waging a decisive war against the Apaches.[68]

BUENA ESPERANZA: THE DENOUEMENT

By June 1780 one hundred Mescalero families had joined Gobernadorcillo Alonso and *Capitanes* (chiefs) Alegre, Volante, and Patule at Buena Esperanza. Cornfields now surrounded their settlement. Although the Mescalero leader Barbitas had left after a disagreement with Domingo Alegre, he and his people remained at peace in the Sierra del Movano (possibly the Delaware Mountains), where they harvested mescal and hunted deer.[69]

Then disaster struck. In July the Conchos River flooded and destroyed the majority of their crops, leaving the remaining Mescaleros just a few squash and some corn to harvest. Then a smallpox epidemic broke out in mid-August and ravaged them through the fall. This was apparently a strain of the deadly North American smallpox epidemic of 1775–82, which had spread north from Mexico City and reached Chihuahua by July 1780. By October, Spanish officials lamented that the Mescaleros de paz had completely abandoned the pueblo, and only Alonso and his family remained inside Presidio del Norte.[70]

El Norte commander Manuel Muñoz came away from this experience with a profound distrust in Apaches. By the end of 1780, he had spent more than 1,000 pesos on the construction of the town and maintenance of the fields and more than 4,000 pesos on food and other supplies. Puzzled by Apache cultural practices, Muñoz complained to Croix that the remaining Mescalero leaders were only content if they were receiving gifts and lacked the authority to retain their families at Buena Esperanza. The only thing he was sure of was that they tended to say one thing and do another. This was especially true when it came to farming. Apache headmen, such as Domingo Alegre, routinely made promises to become sedentary farmers and failed to carry them out. Muñoz called this leader and his "brother" Volante "sons of liberty, vice, and plunder."[71]

In spite of his skepticism of Apache sincerity and ignorance of their gendered division of labor, Muñoz could also point to several benefits that the Presidio del Norte experiment provided Spaniards. On October 12, on the heels of the smallpox epidemic, thirty-two Mescalero auxiliaries, including Alonso, Domingo Alegre, Patule, and Volante, helped Muñoz's forces ambush a Chihene ranchería near San Elizario. Although the Mescaleros only captured one Chihene warrior, a musket, and thirty horses, Muñoz was impressed with the intensity of their fighting, and as late as November 19, he reported that he had no reason to question their faithfulness. In contrast to the others, Bigotes and Patule's bands had found little sustenance around El Norte, Muñoz observed, but he did not accuse them of raiding, for, if they had, he wrote, then he would know about it.[72]

Even those Mescaleros de paz who refused to settle down and farm at Buena Esperanza, he recognized, only raided sporadically. Although the province of Nueva Vizcaya suffered a considerable loss of livestock from Mescalero raids, Muñoz wisely recognized that these losses were "fewer than those it would suffer by declaring them enemies all at once." Muñoz also noted that the Spaniards took forty-two prisoners from the peace and baptized six of them. Thirty-two remained at peace and served as auxiliaries, but Muñoz was not sure if they would attack other Mescaleros. Another benefit from the Spanish perspective is that Muñoz persuaded Mescalero auxiliaries to kill some of their own people. For example, in

June of 1781 Mescaleros de paz killed the disloyal headman Juan Tuerto, who failed to comply with Spanish peace terms and had launched a series of raids in Nueva Vizcaya and Coahuila.[73]

Muñoz also offered an insight into Apache behavior and their resistance to sedentary life. "The lack of a meat supply is what these Apaches feel the most," Muñoz explained, "and not being able to live without it they desire the freedom to supply themselves on their hunts."[74] Here, then, Muñoz revealed that there was a lot more to Apache raiding than simple duplicity and insincerity. Spaniards did not always provide them with sufficient rations; Apaches needed to hunt.

Like Muñoz, Croix was not willing to give up on the Mescaleros yet. "It is more convenient to keep peace than to declare war," Croix wrote. Demonstrating a sincere effort to help Mescaleros meet their subsistence needs, Croix indicated in late July that some Sumas from El Paso and Julimeños from Peyotes mission had joined the Mescaleros in their two towns to teach them how to cultivate the land. His goal was simply to attract those Mescaleros who wanted to make peace voluntarily initially and then attract the rest gradually "with gifts, with proper flattery, and by overlooking their slight faults."[75]

In an effort to cut the costs of rations and provisions, Croix issued new regulations for Muñoz to follow with the Mescaleros in late July. In early September, Muñoz, San Elizario commander Diego Borica, and San Carlos commander Juan Gutiérrez de la Cueva reviewed the guidelines with Gobernadorcillo Alonso and Capitanes Domingo Alegre and Patule. Five of Croix's "nuevas capitulaciones de paz" focused on distributing rations in a more cost-efficient and systematic way to all Mescalero groups at peace in Nueva Vizcaya. In addition to those who lived in the town of Buena Esperanza, Croix identified three other Mescalero pueblos at Coyame, Chorreas, and San Elizario. Regarding all four as part of the same system, Croix made three fundamental distinctions in ration distribution based on Apaches' degree of acculturation and loyalty. In his view, the only Apaches who should receive weekly rations were those who settled in these four pueblos and then only during the first year. Town-dwelling Apaches who also served faithfully as auxiliaries would be paid a salary of three *reales* a day or the equivalent in food, horses, and supplies for military service. As an added incentive to serve Spanish military interests, Croix also exempted town-dwelling auxiliaries from all farm labor. Apaches who refused to live as Spaniards but still served faithfully as auxiliaries against all Spanish enemies, including the Chihenes, would only receive rations and gifts on a provisional basis as a reward for good service. Finally, those Apaches who remained independent and refused to become sedentary or serve Spanish interests Croix deemed "hostiles" who should receive no aid whatsoever.[76]

In the remaining two articles, Croix addressed Mescalero subsistence in the towns. Although he would permit Apache men to hunt for limited periods with the permission of the Spanish commander, he required the majority of each family to provide for themselves within municipal boundaries. To assist in this effort, during the first year of settlement, Spanish soldiers would help Mescalero families, "particularly the children," tend to their crops.[77] Clearly, then, Croix did not focus exclusively on turning Apache adults into Spaniards. Instead, he targeted the next generation.

Although Teodoro de Croix intended these terms to be absolute, Mescalero headmen Alonso, Domingo Alegre, and Patule, not surprisingly, extracted several concessions from the Spaniards during and after final negotiations at El Norte in September 1781. First, the Spaniards agreed to pay a double salary or six reales a day in currency or provisions to any Apache chieftain who served as an auxiliary with ten of his men. Second, Alonso, Domingo Alegre, and Patule once again left on a prolonged twenty-day mission "to convene their people, and to find out if they had embraced peace." According to one skeptical officer, Patule asked for so much time because he needed that long simply to find Bigotes and his people in the Bolsón de Mapimí, which both leaders used as a base for hunting and raiding. This meant the Mescaleros de paz had kinsmen to the south as well as to the north of Presidio del Norte and that Spaniards had not effectively "subdued" the Mescaleros. After returning in mid-September, the more trusted Alonso and Domingo Alegre continued to remain at peace, but not exactly as the Spanish had envisioned. Only Alonso settled in the town of Buena Esperanza with very few followers. Instead of settling in San Francisco pueblo as he initially promised, Domingo Alegre moved his ranchería across the river, farther away from the watchful eyes of the Spaniards, to live with more freedom.[78]

Spanish officers issued weekly rations of corn, beans, and *cigarros* (cigars) to the women of each Apache family residing in pueblos. *Capitancillos* (chieftains) received four reales worth of cigars and, once a month, twenty reales worth of meat. They also were to receive articles of Spanish clothing "to attract them more" and "to distinguish them from the men." Interestingly, Muñoz also issued clothing to some Mescalero leaders who were faithful allies and did not live in towns, which went against Croix's orders.[79] Although frontier officials tried to implement a uniform policy toward Apaches across the northern frontier, ultimate authority continued to rest with the Apache leaders and officers with whom they negotiated on the local level.

According to several well-informed Spanish officers, seasonal flooding, rather than Apache or Spanish treachery, was the biggest threat to any long-term peace. As Captain Gutiérrez de la Cueva revealed, "in most years, the river carries away the cornfields." Thus, Spaniards would either have to continue to issue rations to the Mescaleros de paz or the Indians would resort to hunting and raiding for their subsistence. These same officers also believed that the agreement was an overall success, however, because "we have experienced fewer" and less intensive Apache attacks since its inception. Although the Mescaleros de paz continued to conduct small-scale raids, the majority of Apaches who still raided in Nueva Vizcaya were Chihenes.[80]

Indeed, several Mescalero bands continued to demonstrate their good faith in the fall of 1781. Domingo Alegre, Volante, and Manuel Cabeza returned to Buena Esperanza with their people and remained loyal into early November. In October Domingo Alegre and twelve Mescalero auxiliaries accompanied Colonel Muñoz and 109 Spanish troops on an expedition against independent Mescaleros in the Guadalupe Mountains and took forty-nine prisoners in three engagements.

After their return, however, on November 10, Domingo Alegre and Volante's rancherías fled the settlement with nineteen of the prisoners. A Spanish detachment under Lieutenant Juan Antonio de Arce followed them, and after Domingo Alegre refused to surrender, Arce's forces killed the Mescalero's brother-in-law, who was a Lipan, and took eleven captives and ninety animals. Amazingly, however, Manuel Cabeza and "some of his relatives" still remained at Presidio del Norte, where they would continue to be esteemed for "their faithful conduct" through March of 1783.[81]

While Alegre, Volante, and Manuel Cabeza remained at peace, the rest of the Mescaleros, including many former Mescaleros de paz, stepped up their raiding throughout interior Nueva Vizcaya in October, hitting Torreón, Guanaceví, Santa Rosalía, San Juan del Río, and Dolores. By November the remaining Mescaleros abandoned the pueblo of Buena Esperanza and joined the Mescalero warfare. Peace had clearly broken down as Mescaleros intercepted the weekly mail to Durango, and in groups of more than two hundred took thousands of horses, mules, and sheep from haciendas across Nueva Vizcaya and Coahuila.[82]

Because of these raids, Spaniards in Coahuila treated Mescaleros de paz in Nueva Vizcaya as hostiles. Colonel Juan de Ugalde, the governor of

Coahuila, launched a series of campaigns against the Mescaleros from late November 1781 through 1783. After a less than spectacular winter campaign in the arid Bolsón de Mapimí, between March and May 1782 his forces encountered numerous formerly peaceful Mescaleros in the field, including Patule and Buena Esperanza gobernadorcillo Alonso, whom they wounded at the Aguaje de San Juan. Ugalde also identified several other Mescalero headmen during his expedition, including Dajate, Tagadachilé, Quiéfiéquijá, and Pechollé.[83] To the Ndé, it would appear that Ugalde was simply a rogue war leader, whom they had no reason to treat well because he had not offered them gifts or peace terms.

In April 1782 a Mescalero nantan who had been leading raids in the desolate Bolsón de Mapimí along the Coahuilan eastern border requested peace in El Paso, he said, because of Ugalde's attacks. Croix agreed, provided that he and other Mescaleros ceased their raiding at Mapimí and Cuencamé and surrendered. Three headmen and 134 other Apaches complied; however, Croix deceived them by ordering them to be extradited and imprisoned in interior New Spain.[84]

A June 27 royal order merely confirmed the current frontier reality that Spaniards would abandon defensive war and resume offensive war as a strategy. As recently as August 14, Croix had given permission for the capitancillo Manuel Cabeza to be admitted to peace at El Norte. Instead, acting pragmatically, they sought temporary refuge from repeated attacks on their camps from Spanish officers. Following Ugalde's lead, in September Muñoz and his forces attacked Bigotes' ranchería in the Sierra de San Cristóbal and killed three Apaches, captured another, and recovered six horses. In October, they returned again, killing Bigotes and nearly destroying the entire camp. It now seemed clear to Croix that the Mescaleros did not really want to make peace, as he angrily wrote that Alegre's and Volantes' bands had joined other Mescalero Apaches in "cruelly attack[ing]" Nueva Vizcaya and Coahuila.[85] Given the Spanish military's increased aggression and recent unwillingness to distinguish between peaceful, neutral, and bellicose Apache bands, however, it is hard to blame Apaches for their behavior.

Seeking to avoid Ugalde in the Bolsón de Mapimí, Patule, his brother, and another Mescalero sought peace at San Carlos presidio that fall. Recognizing Patule's role in Apache hostilities, however, the San Carlos commander promptly placed him in the stocks. He then took these formerly peaceful Apaches, along with fifty-five other Mescalero men, women, and children who surrendered in the Sierra de los Murcielagos, including Capitancillo Alonso and a new leader named Zapato Tuerto, to

Presidio del Norte. At Presidio del Norte, thirty-five more Mescaleros asked for peace, but Croix ordered them held as prisoners instead.[86]

Having lost all faith in the Mescaleros, Croix had all ninety-five Mescalero prisoners at Presidio del Norte, including Alonso and Patule, transported to Mexico City via Chihuahua. Although forty-seven Mescaleros successfully escaped the *collera* (chain gang) south of Chihuahua in late January 1783 and presumably returned to the Apachería, Spanish troops killed nine, including Patule. Only one Mescalero leader, Manuel Cabeza, remained at peace and if he violated any of Croix's treaty terms or tried to return to his people, he would suffer the same fate.[87]

Croix tried to justify his harsh actions by stating that the Mescaleros he apprehended were responsible for the killings and robberies in the districts of Saltillo and Parras and, thus, were guilty of making peace in bad faith. Although Patule and some Mescalero men had indeed raided and killed in those areas, it is doubtful whether the more than thirty-five women and children whom Croix deported had participated. In addition, as Croix himself noted, the Mescalero men who allegedly committed the raids in Coahuila did so "after the rupture of the peace agreements" in Nueva Vizcaya. Thus, they violated neither Apache nor Spanish customs by attacking Spanish settlements in a period of war. Croix was on more solid ground, however, in accusing Patule of making peace at San Carlos under false pretensions. Clearly, even on Ndé terms, the Mescalero nantan had no legitimate reason for seeking peace at that presidio when he was raiding in the very same area. But those Mescaleros who continued to seek peace in Nueva Vizcaya likely saw no conflict in raiding in Coahuila while "leaving their families secured at Presidio del Norte."[88]

Croix understood that this was their strategy, but in contrast to Bernardo de Gálvez in 1786, Croix refused to accept localized peace. "These Indians presented themselves in peace," he wrote, "but with their hands stained with the blood of their Christian victims that have been sacrificed to their fury."[89] Croix had not completely replaced the carrot with the stick, however. He still granted Manuel Muñoz the authority to accept or refuse peace offers from other Apache groups. Thus, considerable power still rested at the local level.

THE COSTS OF PEACE AND WAR

At first glance, from an economic standpoint, it hardly seemed worthwhile for Spaniards to make peace with Apaches. In three years of peace with the Mescaleros, from 1779 to 1782, Croix spent more than 7,000 pesos on gifts, rations, and houses. But the total value of Spanish losses from Mescalero raids from Saltillo to Durango stood at more than three times that amount. Punitive expeditions were not cost-effective either. In almost six months of campaigning from September 1782 to March 1783, Juan de Ugalde killed six Apaches, took twelve prisoners, recovered one Spanish captive, and redeemed 144 horses. Although he lost only one man, as a result of the harsh climate and terrain, his troops' horses were so worn out that they were unusable. Even more telling, while he was busy searching for Apaches in their camps, war parties of eighty to ninety men made off with six hundred horses of their own from Pelayo, Cadena, Cuencamé, and San Juan del Río and killed forty-five Spaniards and took several captives. Exasperated with the high costs of Ugalde's negligent, unauthorized campaigning, in the spring of 1783 Croix dismissed the governor from office.[90]

It is not hard to understand Croix's decision. Attacking the highly mobile Apaches in their own territory, while leaving the frontier undefended, made no sense. Thus, as other historians have intimated, a "peace by purchase" strategy, or a bad peace, was preferable to an all-out war. Viceroy Bernardo de Gálvez would make this critical insight the cornerstone of his frontier Indian policy in 1786.[91]

As we have seen, Croix turned to military-run establecimientos for Apaches because of lack of military manpower and because missionaries had proven unreliable. Croix's solution was a practical experiment that had at least two potential precedents on other frontiers: military-run settlements for Chichimecas and moros de paz. He also likely drew on previous local practices, especially the pueblos that O'Conor had planned to settle eastern Apaches in previously. Spaniards, however, did not solely determine when and where these reservation-like communities would be established and how they would function. To get a more complete picture of why they came about, it is also necessary to examine Ndé motives for settling on them.

Notes

1 For the quotation, see Croix to Minister of the Indies José de Gálvez, Informe General, July 29, 1781, AGI, Guadalajara, 279, para. 205; Croix to Gálvez, General Report, Arizpe, October 30, 1781, AGI, Guadalajara, 278, Alfred Barnaby Thomas, ed. and trans., *Teodoro de Croix and the Northern Frontier of New Spain, 1776–1783: From the Original Document in the Archives of the Indies, Seville* (Norman: University of Oklahoma Press, 1941), 125, para. 201; Moorhead, *Presidio*, 245–246; Moorhead, *Apache Frontier*, 202, 204. For the location of "Ojinaga," see Jefferson Morgenthaler, *La Junta de*

Los Rios: The Life, Death and Resurrection of an Ancient Desert Community in the Big Bend Region of Texas (Boerne, TX: Mockingbird Books, 2007), 49. For "other Apache groups," see Croix to Gálvez, Informe General, Arizpe, January 23, 1780, AGI, Guadalajara, 278, MLMC, para. 109. For Chafalotes as Chihenes ("Gileños"), see Thomas, *Forgotten Frontiers*, 156; Griffen, *Apaches at War and Peace*, 29. For Salineros as a Mescalero group living on the Rio Salado (Pecos River) in 1745, see Willem J. de Reuse's synonymy in Opler, "Apachean Culture Pattern," 389. For Mescaleros, Salineros, and Natagés as "one in the same Indians," see Dunn, "Apache Relations in Texas," 266. For Salineros and Mescaleros at Presidio del Norte as distinct Apache groups, see Luis Navarro García, *Don José de Gálvez y la Comandancia General de las Provincias Internas del norte de Nueva España* (Seville: Escuela de Estudios Hispano-Americanos, 1964), 372.

2 For quotation, see Croix, "Extracto de novedades ocurridas en las provincias internas de Nueva España en los meses de abril y mayo," Arizpe, May 23, 1780, AGI, Guadalajara, 271, Seville. For Croix's La Junta establecimiento as a reservation, see Moorhead, *Presidio*, 243–248; Morgenthaler, *La Junta*, 132; Mark Santiago, *The Jar of Severed Hands: Spanish Deportation of Apache Prisoners of War, 1770–1810* (Norman: University of Oklahoma Press, 2011), 52. As with Croix's Apache pueblos, Spanish officers used "pueblos formales," "poblaciones formales," and "establecimientos" to describe Navajo and Jupe Comanche pueblos, but these were self-sustaining agricultural communities rather than reservations because they lacked presidios to serve as Indian agencies. See, for example, Commander-in-Chief Jacobo Ugarte to Gov. Juan Bautista de Anza, Chihuahua, October 5, 1786; Ugarte to Gov. Fernando de la Concha, Chihuahua, July 22, 1788; Concha to Ugarte, Santa Fe, November 12, 1788; and Ugarte to Concha, Valle de San Bartolomé, January 28, 1789, SANM-HL, roll 11, fr. 1043–1057, and roll 12, fr. 84–86, 106–107, 138–139. On Comanche and Navajo pueblos, see Alfred B. Thomas, "San Carlos: A Comanche Pueblo on the Arkansas River, 1787," *Colorado Magazine* 6 (May 1929): 79–91; Weber, *Bárbaros*, 194–195; Joaquín Rivaya-Martínez, "San Carlos de los Jupes: Une tentative avortée de sédentarisation des bárbaros dans les territoires frontaliers du nord de la Nouvelle-Espagne en 1787–1788," *Recherches amérindiennes au québec* 41 no. 2-3 (2011): 29–59.

3 Thomas, *Teodoro de Croix*, 17–18, 20, 27, 21; Croix to Gálvez, General Report, Arizpe, October 30, 1781, AGI, Guadalajara, 278, in Thomas, *Teodoro de Croix*, 202–203, paras. 472–473.

4 Powell, *Soldiers, Indians, and Silver*, 33. For "Chichimeca" word origins and its inaccurate extension to sedentary tribes, see Charlotte M. Gradie, "Discovering the Chichimecas," *The Americas* 51 (July 1994): 67–88, esp. 68–69, 76–79. For further detail on the Spanish use of the term, see Philip Wayne Powell, "The Chichimecas: Scourge of the Silver Frontier in Sixteenth-Century Mexico," *Hispanic American Historical Review* 25 (August 1945): 318–320. For "Gran Chichimeca," see Powell, *Soldiers, Indians, and Silver*, 234–235.

5 Philip Wayne Powell, "Genesis of the Frontier Presidio in North America," *Western Historical Quarterly* 13 (April 1982): 135, 137; Powell, *Soldiers, Indians, and Silver*, 218–221; Philip Wayne Powell, "Peacemaking on North America's First Frontier," *Americas* 16 (January 1960): 242–243.

6 Henri-Léon Fey, *Historia de Orán. Antes, durante y después de la dominación española* (Málaga: Editorial Agazara, 1999), 183–184; Arques and Gibert, *Los mogataces*, 8, 12–14, 45; Cortés, *Views from the Apache Frontier*, 7, 126. On the long history of Spanish use of "moros de paz" from at least the 1240s, see Brian Catlos, *Muslims of Medieval Latin Christendom, c. 1050–1614* (New York: Cambridge University Press, 2014), 79, 538; Henk Driessen, "The Politics of Religion on the Hispano-African Frontier: An Historical-Anthropological View," in *Religious Regimes and State Formation: Perspectives from European Ethnology*, ed. Eric R. Wolf (Albany: State University of New York Press, 1991), 254; Fernand Braudel, *The Mediterranean and the Mediterranean World in the Age of Philip II*, Vol. II (New York: Harper & Row, 1973), 819.

7 Col. Parrilla to the Marqués de las Amarillas, San Luis de las Amarillas, April 8, 1758, in Lesley B. Simpson, ed. and Paul D. Nathan, trans., *The San Sabá Papers: A Documentary Account of the Founding and Destruction of San Sabá Mission* (San Francisco, CA: John Howell Books, 1959; reprint, Dallas, TX: Southern Methodist University Press, 2000), 137–138. For early Apache (Querecho)–Arab comparisons, see "The Relación de la Jornada de Cibola, Pedro de Castañeda de Nájera's Narrative [of the Coronado Expedition], 1560s (copy, 1596)," in Flint and Flint, *Documents*, 408, 423, 679n302, 381; Worcester, "Beginnings of the Apache Menace," 2.

8 Arques and Gibert, *Los mogataces*, 72, 79, 82, 85.

9 For "Dajunné" as "hombre consolado," see Commander-in-Chief Teodoro de Croix to Minister of the Indies José de Gálvez, Arizpe, October 7, 1782, AGI, Guadalajara, 282, quoted in Navarro García, *Don José de Gálvez*, 377, paras. 147–152. For Croix's agreement, see Croix to Gálvez, Informe General, July 29, 1781, AGI, Guadalajara, 279, Seville, paras. 205–208; Croix to Gálvez, General Report, Arizpe, October 30, 1781, AGI, Guadalajara, 278, in Thomas, *Teodoro de Croix*, 125–126, paras. 201–204; Moorhead, *Presidio*, 246. For Muñoz's treaty, see Lt. Col. Manuel Muñoz to Croix, Cuartel de Dolores, June 16, 1781, AGI, Guadalajara, 282, MLMC. On the subtleties in Spanish pacts with Indians, see Weber, *Bárbaros*, 208.

10 Muñoz to Croix, Cuartel de Dolores, June 16, 1781, AGI, Guadalajara, 282, MLMC; Moorhead, *Presidio*, 246–247.

11 For "establecimiento," see Croix, "Extracto de novedades ocurridas en provincias internas de Nueva España en enero y febrero," Arizpe, March 26, 1780, AGI, Guadalajara, 271, Seville. For the Apache bands, see Moorhead, *Presidio*, 247. For first quotation, see Croix, "Resumen de las muertes y robos que han ocurrido en las provincias internas de Nueva España desde marzo hasta el día de la fecha," Arizpe, May 23, 1780, AGI, Guadalajara, 271, Seville. For crop planting, see Croix, "Extracto de novedades ocurridas en las provincias internas de Nueva España en los tiempos que se expresan," June 23, 1780, AGI, Guadalajara, 271, Seville. For Mescalero fighting strength and the Lipan alliance, including the final quotation, see Croix to Gálvez, General Report, Arizpe, October 23, 1781, AGI, Guadalajara, 278, in Thomas, *Teodoro de Croix*, 129, para. 212.

12 Charlotte M. Gradie, *The Tepehuan Revolt of 1616: Militarism, Evangelism, and Colonialism in Seventeenth-Century Nueva Vizcaya* (Salt Lake City:

University of Utah Press, 2000), 1–4, 153–172; Forbes, *Apache, Navaho, and Spaniard*, 177–280; Weber, *Spanish Frontier*, 133–141, 199; Spicer, *Cycles of Conquest*; Cynthia Radding, *Wandering Peoples: Colonialism, Ethnic Spaces, and Ecological Frontiers in Northwestern Mexico, 1700–1850* (Durham, NC: Duke University Press, 1997), 283–286, 299; Deeds, *Defiance and Deference*, 97, 69–70, 86–99, 119–120, 169.

13 Fray Damián Massanet, "Diario de los Padres Misioneros," 1691, in *Memorias de Nueva España*, Vol. 27, f. 100, quoted in Dunn, "Apache Relations in Texas," 203.

14 For ancestral Mescaleros near La Junta, see Trasviña Retis, *Founding of Missions*, 19. For evidence of ancestral Lipan presence in Texas by 1720 and Coahuila in 1735, see Dunn, "Apache Relations in Texas," 205, 241n4. For evidence of ancestral Mescalero presence in Nueva Vizcaya in 1741 and Coahuila by 1746, see Capt. Joseph de Berroterán to Viceroy Juan Francisco de Guemes y Horcasitas, Marqués de Casafuerte, Mexico, April 17, 1748, translated in Diana Hadley, Thomas H. Naylor, and Mardith Schuetz-Miller, eds., *The Presidio and Militia on the Northern Frontier of New Spain, Vol. 2, Part 2: The Central Corridor and the Texas Corridor* (Tucson: University of Arizona Press, 1997), 193–194, 200.

15 On the military threat to eastern Apaches posed by their French-armed neighbors from 1719 to 1766, see Herbert Eugene Bolton, *Texas in the Middle Eighteenth Century* (Berkeley: University of California Press, 1915), 34–36, 68–69, 79; Schroeder, "Shifting for Survival," 301–302; John, *Storms Brewed*, 255, 265–266, 312, 317–318, 338–341, 362–363, 381; Anderson, *The Indian Southwest*, 123–126; Hämäläinen, *Comanche Empire*, 24–37, 39–40, 48, 57–67. On the dominance of Apache groups west of the Rio Grande over their surrounding indigenous neighbors from the 1670s to 1786, see Spicer, *Cycles of Conquest*, 233–239; Schroeder, "Documentary Evidence," 141–145, 151–152; Schroeder, "Shifting for Survival," 300–301; John, *Storms Brewed*, 272–273, 297–298. On eastern Apache resilience against their French-armed northern and eastern indigenous neighbors and dominance over their southern ones, see Robinson, *I Fought a Good Fight*, 66–67; Dunn, "Apache Relations in Texas," 222–223; William C. Foster, *Spanish Expeditions into Texas, 1689–1768* (Austin: University of Texas Press, 1995), 267; John, *Storms Brewed*, 261, 271–273. For an excellent summary of Indians' multiple motives for entering missions, see Deeds, *Defiance and Deference*, 197–199. For a discussion of Lipans and other Indians of the southern plains using missions as a place of refuge for ethnogenesis, see Anderson, *The Indian Southwest*, 91–92.

16 Trasviña Retis, *Founding of Missions*, 18–19, 26. Oposmes were part of the Concho confederation of 1645. See William B. Griffen, *Indian Assimilation in the Franciscan Area of Nueva Vizcaya* (Tucson: University of Arizona Press, 1979), 34. For Faraons as equivalent to Athapaskan Sejines [Sejen-ne], as well as Chipaynes [Chilpaines] and Limitas [Lemitas], see "Testimony of Don Gerónimo," Santa Fé, July 20, 1715, and Thomas, "Historical Introduction," in Thomas, *After Coronado*, 80, 24. On Sejen-ne as Faraon, see Matson and Schroeder, "Cordero's Description," 336. For Faraons and Natagés as

ancestral Mescaleros, see Opler, "Apachean Culture Pattern," 390; Schroeder, *Apache Indians I*, 525. On Faraon territory extending from near Santa Fe southward to the jurisdictions of El Paso and La Junta as of 1720, see Antonio de Valverde Cosio to the Marquis de Valero, Santa Fé, October 8, 1720, in José Antonio de Pichardo, *Pichardo's Treatise on the Limits of Louisiana and Texas*, ed. Charles Wilson Hackett, Vol. I (Austin: University of Texas Press, 1931), 198, para. 278.

17 Fray Juan de la Cruz to Viceroy Marqués de Valero, [Taos, 1719]; Gov. Juan Domingo Bustamente to Viceroy Marqués de Casa Fuerte, Santa Fe, January 10, 1724; Brigadier Pedro de Rivera to Viceroy Marqués de Casa Fuerte, Presidio del Paso del Río del Norte, September 16, 1727 in Thomas, *After Coronado*, 137–138, 201, 211–212;"Declaration of Fray Miguel de Menchero," Santa Bárbara, May 10, 1744 in Hackett, *Historical Documents*, Vol. III, 403; José Antonio de Pichardo, *Pichardo's Treatise on the Limits of Louisiana and Texas*, ed. Charles Wilson Hackett, ed., and trans., Vol. II (Austin: University of Texas Press, 1934), 521, para. 1506; Bancroft, *History of Arizona and New Mexico*, 242; Gunnerson, *Jicarilla Apaches*, 154, 157–158, 167, 183–184, 199–200, 203–204, 215–222, 252–253; Eiselt, *Becoming White Clay*, 73–75, 120–121; Veronica E. Tiller, "Jicarilla Apache," in *Handbook of North American Indians: Southwest*, Vol. 10, ed. Alfonso Ortiz (Washington, DC: Smithsonian Institution, 1983), 447, 459–460; Morris E. Opler, "A Summary of Jicarilla Apache Culture," *American Anthropologist* 38 (April–June 1936): 202–205; Opler, "Apachean Culture Pattern," 387–392; John, *Storms Brewed*, 256.

18 Dunn, "Apache Relations in Texas," 255–256; William E. Dunn, "Missionary Activities among the Eastern Apaches Previous to the Founding of the San Sabá Mission," *Southwestern Historical Quarterly* 15 (January 1912): 188.

19 Dunn, "Apache Relations in Texas," 235, 259; William E. Dunn, "The Apache Mission on the San Sabá River: Its Founding and Failure," *Southwestern Historical Quarterly* 17 (April 1914): 382–383.

20 Dunn, "Apache Relations in Texas," 203–204, 239.

21 Notes of Fray Jesús María Casañas, 1691, in Pichardo, *Pichardo's Treatise*, Vol. II, 175, para. 803; Dunn, "Apache Relations in Texas," 202. For ancestral Lipans at San Antonio in 1720 and raids south of it in 1721, see Dunn, "Apache Relations in Texas," 205. For a first-hand account of an Ndé raid on San Antonio de Béxar in August 1723, see the Parecer de Juan de Olivar de Rebolledo, México, January 27, 1724, Biblioteca Nacional de México, Fondo Reservado, Colección Archivo Franciscano, available from http://lyncis.dgsca .unam.mx/franciscanos/busquedaDocumento.html, accessed August 19, 2006. For the captive's testimony and quotation, see Carlos E. Castañeda, *Our Catholic Heritage in Texas, 1519–1936*, The Chicano Heritage Series (1936; reprint, New York: Arno Press, 1976), 191.

22 Dunn, "Apache Relations in Texas," 207–208.

23 Fray Benito Fernández de Santa Ana to Fray Guardian Alonso Giraldo de Terreros, Mission Concepción de Acuña, December 4, 1745; Fray Benito Fernández de Santa Ana to the Lord Captain, Mission Concepción de Acuña, February 1, 1746; and Fray Benito Fernández de Santa Ana to Viceroy Conde

de Revillagigedo, Mexico, February 23, 1750, in Benito Fernández de Santa Ana, *Letters and Memorials of the Father Presidente Fray Benito Fernández de Santa Ana, 1736–1754: Documents on the Missions of Texas from the Archives of the College of Querétaro*, ed. and trans. Fr. Benedict Leutenegger O.F.M. (San Antonio, TX: Our Lady of the Lake University, 1981), 55, 57, 163–165; Dunn, "Apache Relations in Texas," 259, 261–262; Curtis D. Tunnell and W. W. Newcomb, Jr., *A Lipan Apache Mission: San Lorenzo de la Santa Cruz, 1762–1771*, Bulletin of the Texas Memorial Museum, vol. 14 (Austin: Texas Memorial Museum, July 1969), 157–158; Hämäläinen, *Comanche Empire*, 43; Fray Benito Fernández de Santa Ana to Auditor of War Juan Rodríguez de Albuerne, Marqués de Altamira, Mexico City, February 23, 1750, in Hadley et al., *Presidio and Militia*, Vol. 2, Part 2, 479. The quotations are from Fray Benito Fernández de Santa Ana to Viceroy Conde de Revillagigedo, Mexico, February 23, 1750. The first is taken from Hadley et al., *Presidio and Militia*, Vol. 2, Part 2, 484, and the second from Fernández de Santa Ana, *Letters and Memorials*, 64–65. On this agreement being a "tratado de paz," rather than a truce, see Auto de Toribio de Urrutia [to the Conde de Revilla Gigedo], San Antonio de Béxar, November 28, 1749, Biblioteca Nacional de México, Fondo Reservado, Colección Archivo Franciscano, available from http://lyncis.dgsca.unam.mx/franciscanos/busquedaDocumento.html, accessed August 19, 2006.
24 Fray Benito Fernández de Santa Ana to Auditor of War Juan Rodríguez de Albuerne, Marqués de Altamira, Mexico City, February 23, 1750, in Hadley et al., *Presidio and Militia*, Vol. 2, Part 2, 483, 485.
25 Dunn, "Apache Mission," 381.
26 Dunn, "Missionary Activities," 196–200; John, *Storms Brewed*, 294–295.
27 Dunn, "Apache Mission," 390–392.
28 Weber, *Spanish Frontier*, 188–89.
29 Dunn, "Apache Mission," 399.
30 Dunn, "Apache Mission," 401–402; John, *Storms Brewed*, 297. Quotation is from Fray Joaquín de Baños and Fray Diego Jiménez to the Guardian of the College of Querétero, July 5, 1757, quoted in Dunn, "Apache Mission," 401.
31 Depositions of Sgt. Joseph Antonio Flores and Fray Miguel de Molina, San Luis de las Amarillas, March 22, 1758 in Simpson and Nathan, *The San Sabá Papers*, 46–60, 84–92; Juliana Barr, *Peace Came in the Form of a Woman: Indians and Spaniards in the Texas Borderlands* (Chapel Hill: University of North Carolina Press, 2007), 180–181; John, *Storms Brewed*, 298–299; Robert S. Weddle, *The San Sabá Mission: Spanish Pivot in Texas* (Austin: University of Texas Press, 1964), 73, 102. Borderlands scholars have devoted considerable attention to the founding and destruction of the San Sabá Mission. For the most comprehensive monograph, see Weddle, *The San Sabá Mission*. For primary documents in English, see Simpson and Nathan, *The San Sabá Papers*. Pekka Hämäläinen omits the Wichitas proper and Bidais from the attack and does not mention that it was Caddoan-led. See Hämäläinen, *Comanche Empire*, 59.
32 Deposition of Fray Miguel de Molina, March 22, 1758, in Simpson and Nathan, *The San Sabá Papers*, 88.

33 Simpson and Nathan, *The San Sabá Papers*, 91.
34 For the first Spanish use of the term "Lipans" by Capt. Felipe de Rábago y Terán in July 1761, see Maestas, "Culture and History of Native American Peoples of South Texas," 249; Robinson, *I Fought a Good Fight*, 93; Bolton, *Texas in the Middle Eighteenth Century*, 94; Lafora, *Frontiers of New Spain*, 12; Tunnell and Newcomb, *A Lipan Apache Mission*, 3, 141, 184; Weber, *Spanish Frontier*, 191. For a detailed secondary account of these two missions, see Weddle, *The San Sabá Mission*, 156–166. For further information on the shortcomings of these missions, see Fray Diego Jimenez to the Comisario General, Fray Manuel de Nájera, Presidio de San Sabá, November 4, 1761; Capt. Felipe de Rábago y Terán to the Marqués de Cruillas, San Sabá, October 15, 1762; Jiménez to Rábago y Terán, Misión de la Santa Cruz, October 8, 1762; and Jímenez and Fray Martín de Cuevas to [the virrey?], Misión de Santa Cruz, January 24, 1763, Biblioteca Nacional de México, Fondo Reservado, Colección Archivo Franciscano, all available from http://lyncis.dgsca.unam.mx/franciscanos/busquedaDocumento.html, accessed August 19, 2006.
35 Quotations are from Gálvez to Capt. Lope de Cuellar, Alamos, July 4, 1769, AGI, Guadalajara, 416, Seville. On Bourbon efforts to reduce the role of missions, see Weber, *Bárbaros*, 102–109. For the end of missions in Texas, see Weddle, *The San Sabá Mission*, 190–191. For the California missions, see Francis F. Guest, "Mission Colonization and Political Control in Spanish California," *Journal of San Diego History* 24 (Winter 1978).
36 Brinckerhoff and Faulk, *Lancers for the King*, 7; Moorhead, *Apache Frontier*, 116–117; Marqués de Rubí, *Dictamen*, Tacubaya, April 10, 1768, translated in Jack Jackson and William C. Foster, eds., *Imaginary Kingdom: Texas as Seen by the Rivera and Rubí Military Expeditions, 1727–1767* (Austin: Texas State Historical Association, 1995), Aricle 16, 181–182. For a published Spanish version of Rubí's *Dictamen*, see María del Carmen Velásquez, ed., *La frontera norte y la experiencia colonial* (Mexico: Secretaría de Relaciones Exteriores, 1982), 29–84. Rubí advocated the extermination of Lipans specifically, not all Apaches, as a majority of Borderlands specialists have mistakenly suggested. See Weber, *Spanish Frontier*, 220; John, *Storms Brewed*, 440; Moorhead, *Presidio*, 60–61; Moorhead, *Apache Frontier*, 16–17; Park, "Spanish Indian Policy," 330; Bolton, *Texas in the Middle Eighteenth Century*, 381–382. For a notable exception, which is still not evident in the actual text, see Weber, *Bárbaros*, 325n64.
37 Park, "Spanish Indian Policy," 338; Weber, *Bárbaros*, 104. For peace as the goal of offensive war, see King Carlos III, "The Royal Regulations of 1772," translated in Brinckerhoff and Faulk, *Lancers for the King*, title 10, article 1, 31; Hugo O'Conor, *The Defenses of Northern New Spain: Hugo O'Conor's Report to Teodoro de Croix, July 22, 1777*, ed. and trans. Donald C. Cutter (Dallas, TX: Southern Methodist University Press/DeGolyer Library, 1994), para. 188, 81. For quotations, see Croix to Gálvez, Chihuahua, September 23, 1778, AGI, Guadalajara, 270, Seville.
38 Navarro García, *Don José de Gálvez*, 372; Moorhead, *Presidio*, 244–245.
39 Maestre de Campo Don Joseph Marín to His Excellency the Count of Galve, Parral, September 30, 1693, in Hackett, *Historical Documents*, Vol. II,

400–401, 405. The last quotation is from p. 405 and all others are from p. 401. This edition contains English and Spanish versions of the document.

40 For quotations, see "Juan Bautista de Anza (the Elder) to Manuel Bernal de Huidobro, Ures, August 13, 1735," in *The Presidio and Militia on the Northern Frontier of New Spain: A Documentary History: Volume 2, Part I: The Californias and Sinaloa-Sonora, 1700–1765*, ed. Charles W. Polzer and Thomas E. Sheridan (Tucson: University of Arizona Press, 1997), 305, para. 2. For a transcription of the original Spanish document, see ibid., 309–312. On various translations of this document and the life of Juan Bautista de Anza (the Elder), see Donald T. Garate, *Juan Bautista de Anza: Basque Explorer in the New World* (Reno: University of Nevada Press, 2003), 262. On Apache war parties killing to avenge the death of slain kinsmen, see Opler, *An Apache Life-Way*, 336; Goodwin, *Western Apache Raiding and Warfare*, 16, 18.

41 "Anza to Huidobro, Ures, August 13, 1735," 305, paras. 3–4.

42 "Anza to Huidobro, Ures, August 13, 1735," 306, 309, paras. 5, 13.

43 "Anza to Huidobro, Ures, August 13, 1735," 305, 307, paras. 4–5, 8–9; Griffen, *Utmost Good Faith*, 182; Griffen, *Apaches at War and Peace*, 11; Opler, *An Apache Life-Way*, 334; Ball, *In the Days of Victorio*, 12; Goodwin, *Western Apache Raiding and Warfare*, 17.

44 "Anza to Huidobro, Ures, August 13, 1735," 305, para. 4.

45 Capt. Joseph de Berroterán to Viceroy Juan Francisco de Guemes y Horcasitas, Marqués de Casafuerte, Mexico, April 17, 1748 in Hadley et al., *Presidio and Militia*, Vol. 2, Part 2, 191, 193–194. Quotations are from 191, 193. For English and Spanish versions of Article 193 of the royal regulations of 1729, see Viceroy Marqués de Casafuerte, The *Reglamento de 1729*, México, April 20, 1729 in Thomas H. Naylor and Charles W. Polzer, S. J., eds., *Pedro de Rivera and the Military Regulations for Northern New Spain, 1724–1729: A Documentary History of His Frontier Inspection and the Reglamento de 1729* (Tucson: University of Arizona Press, 1988), 279, 330.

46 Sara Ortelli, *Trama de una guerra conveniente: Nueva Vizcaya y la sombra de los apaches (1748–1790)* (Mexico City: El Colegio de México, 2007), 16–17, 25–26, 50–51. For the languages of the Sisimbles and Cocoyomes, see William B. Griffen, *Culture Change and Shifting Populations in Central Northern Mexico*, Anthropological Papers of the University of Arizona (Tucson: University of Arizona Press, 1969), 134–135.

47 Ortelli, *Trama de una guerra conveniente*, 40n80; Navarro García, *Don José de Gálvez*, 78. For the three Apache groups at peace with La Juntans in 1748, see Griffen, *Indian Assimilation*, 17–18. On the meaning of Natagés, see Willem J. de Reuse's and Ives Goddard's respective synonymies in Opler, "Apachean Culture Pattern," 392; Opler, "Mescalero Apache," 438. On Natagés opting out of peace at San Antonio prior to 1749, see Fray Benito Fernández de Santa Ana to Viceroy Conde de Revillagigedo [no location], November 11, 1749, in Fernández de Santa Ana, *Letters and Memorials*, 156, para. 55; Dunn, "Apache Relations in Texas," 259; Hadley et al., *Presidio and Militia*, Vol. 2, Part 2, 483n4.

48 [Viceroy Antonio Bucareli y Ursua], "Extracto de las noticias que se han recibido de las Provincias internas hasta el dia de la fecha," Mexico, December 27, 1772, AGI, Guadalajara, 416, Seville.

49 Thomas, *Forgotten Frontiers*, 8.
50 Manuel Merino, "Report of the Council at Monclova," December 11, 1777, in Bolton, *Athanase de Méziéres*, Vol. 2, 150, 156, 158–159; Moorhead, *Apache Frontier*, 46. Quotations are from 156, 158, and the last three 159.
51 For the policy change, see Thomas, *Forgotten Frontiers*, 16. For the quotations, see Croix to Inspector-in-Chief Joseph Rubio, Valle de Santa Rosa, February 12, 1778, AGI, Guadalajara, 276, Seville.
52 For the quotation, see Lt. Gov. José Antonio de Arrieta to Lt. Gov. Narciso Muñiz, Carrizal, February 9, 1778, AGI, Guadalajara, 276, Seville. On the Chihene (Gila) peace at Janos, see Croix to Gálvez, Valle de Santa Rosa, February 15, 1778, AGI, Guadalajara, 276, Seville; Thomas, *Forgotten Frontiers*, 14–18; Griffen, *Apaches at War and Peace*, 38–39, 42.
53 Croix to Gálvez, Chihuahua, April 3, 1778, AGI, Guadalajara, 276, Seville; Thomas, *Forgotten Frontiers*, 17–18. On gender roles in Western Apache farming, see Buskirk, *The Western Apache*, 50–51.
54 Thomas, *Forgotten Frontiers*, 18–19.
55 Croix et al., "Council of War," Chihuahua, June 9-15, 1778 in Alfred Barnaby Thomas, ed. and trans., *The Plains Indians and New Mexico, 1751–1778: A Collection of Documents Illustrative of the History of the Eastern Frontier of New Mexico* (Albuquerque: University of New Mexico Press, 1940), 194, 206, 199. All quotations are from 199. Two distinguished borderlands scholars have mistakenly written that this council met in 1779. See Thomas, *Teodoro de Croix*, 47; Moorhead, *Presidio*, 83–84.
56 Both quotations are from Croix et al., "Council of War," Chihuahua, June 9-15, 1778, in Thomas, *Plains Indians*, 199.
57 Croix et al., "Council of War," Chihuahua, June 9-15, 1778, in Thomas, *Plains Indians*, 200. See also Thomas, *Teodoro de Croix*, 37–38; Moorhead, *Apache Frontier*, 47–48, 120.
58 Croix to Gálvez, Informe General, Arizpe, July 29, 1781, AGI, Guadalajara, 279, Seville, para. 204; Croix to Gálvez, General Report, Arizpe, October 30, 1781, in Thomas, *Teodoro de Croix*, 124–125, para. 200.
59 Thomas, *Teodoro de Croix*, 45; John, *Storms Brewed*, 554.
60 Historian Alfred Barnaby Thomas claims from this single battle, "Undoubtedly thus was broken Apache power in Texas." See Thomas, *Forgotten Frontiers*, 13, 64. The analysis is my own.
61 Arrieta to Muñiz, Paso del Rio del Norte, February 8, 1778, AGI, Guadalajara, 276, Seville.
62 Croix to Gálvez, Valle de Santa Rosa, February 15, 1778, and Rubio to Croix, Chihuahua, February 27, 1778, AGI, Guadalajara, 276, Seville. The quotation comes from the first document.
63 Croix to Gálvez, General Report, Arizpe, October 30, 1781, in Thomas, *Teodoro de Croix*, 92–93, 91, paras. 74, 68; Croix to Gálvez, Informe General, Arizpe, January 23, 1780, AGI, Guadalajara, 278, MLMC, paras. 28, 96, 103, 149. Quotations are from para. 68 of the first document and paras. 96 and 103 of the second.
64 Croix to Gálvez, General Report, Arizpe, October 30, 1781, in Thomas, *Teodoro de Croix*, 89–90, paras. 60–61. Quotation is from para. 61. For

evidence of kinship ties between Mescaleros and Lipans, see Moorhead, *Apache Frontier*, 233, 252–253.
65 Croix to Gálvez, General Report, Arizpe, October 30, 1781, in Thomas, *Teodoro de Croix*, 125, para. 200; John, *Storms Brewed*, 535; Croix to Gálvez, Arizpe, May 23, 1780, AGI, Guadalajara, 278, Seville.
66 Navarro García, *Don José de Gálvez*, 372; Moorhead, *Presidio*, 244–245.
67 All quotations are from Gálvez to Croix, El Pardo, February 20, 1779, Biblioteca Nacional de México, Fondo Reservado, Colección Archivo Franciscano, available from http://lyncis.dgsca.unam.mx/franciscanos/busquedaDocumento.html, accessed August 19, 2006. Interestingly, Moorhead had gotten this right in a previous study, when he wrote, "Croix was not to force them to settle in the Spanish towns or even to form permanent villages of their own, but was to leave them in their just and natural liberty." See Moorhead, *Apache Frontier*, 122. He offered no explanation in this work, however, for the development of a system of Apache resettlements in Croix's time.
68 For a concise summary of Croix's overall Apache policy, see Weber, *Bárbaros*, 156–159. For detailed summaries of the royal order itself, see Moorhead, *Apache Frontier*, 120–123; Thomas, *Teodoro de Croix*, 43–45. For Spain's role in the American Revolution, see Weber, *Spanish Frontier*, 265–270. For Croix's thoughts on the Mescalero peace, see Croix to Gálvez, Informe General, Arizpe, January 23, 1780, AGI, Guadalajara, 278, MLMC, para. 110.
69 Croix, "Extracto de novedades ocurridas en las provincias internas de Nueva España en los tiempos que se expresan," Arizpe, July 23, 1780, AGI, Guadalajara, 271, Seville; O'Conor, *Defenses of Northern New Spain*, xix.
70 For the North American smallpox epidemic of 1775–82, see Elizabeth A. Fenn, *Pox Americana: The Great Smallpox Epidemic of 1775–82* (New York: Hill and Wang, 2001), 148–150. For the effects of this epidemic on New Mexico, see Marc Simmons, "New Mexico's Smallpox Epidemic of 1780–1781," *New Mexico Historical Review* 41 (October 1966): 319–326. On the Mescalero response, see Croix, "Resumen de las muertes y robos que han executado los indios enemigos en las provincias internas de Nueva España," Arizpe, September 23, 1780, AGI, Guadalajara, 271, Seville; Muñoz to Croix, Cuartel de Dolores, June 16, 1781, AGI, Guadalajara, 282, MLMC; Navarro García, *Don José de Gálvez*, 373–374.
71 Muñoz to Croix, Cuartel de Dolores, June 16, 1781, AGI, Guadalajara, 282, MLMC.
72 Muñoz to Croix, Cuartel de Dolores, June 16, 1781, AGI, Guadalajara, 282, MLMC; Croix, "Extracto de novedades ocurridas en las provincias internas de Nueva España en los tiempos que se expresan," Arizpe, December 23, 1780, Seville.
73 For Mescalero raiding and the quotation, see Muñoz to Croix, Cuartel de Dolores, June 16, 1781. On the killing of Juan Tuerto, see Croix to Gálvez, General Report, Arizpe, October 30, 1781, in Thomas, *Teodoro de Croix*, 129, para. 213. See also Navarro García, *Don José de Gálvez*, 375.
74 Muñoz to Croix, Cuartel de Dolores, June 16, 1781, AGI, Guadalajara, 282, MLMC.

75 All quotations are from Croix to Muñoz, Arizpe, July 26, 1781, AGI, Guadalajara, 282, MLMC.
76 Croix to Muñoz, Arizpe, July 26, 1781, AGI, Guadalajara, 282, MLMC; Muñoz, Capt. Diego de Borica, Capt. Juan Gutiérrez de la Cueva, and Capt. Francisco Xavier de Uranga, "Articles of peace read to the Mescaleros," Presidio del Norte, September 5, 1781, AGI, Guadalajara, 282, MLMC.
77 Muñoz et al., "Articles of peace read to the Mescaleros," Presidio del Norte, September 5, 1781, AGI, Guadalajara, 282, MLMC.
78 For the "double salary," see Muñoz et al., "Articles of peace read to the Mescaleros," Presidio del Norte, September 5, 1781, AGI, Guadalajara, 282, MLMC. For the quotation, see Muñoz to Croix, Presidio del Norte, September 12, 1781, AGI, Guadalajara, 282, MLMC. For the "skeptical officer" and Mescalero activities after their return, see Gutiérrez de la Cueva to Croix, Chihuahua, September 15, 1781, AGI, Guadalajara, 282, MLMC.
79 Muñoz, Borica, and Cueva, "Statement of presents to be distributed to the Mescaleros," Presidio del Norte, September 6, 1781, AGI, Guadalajara, 282, MLMC.
80 Borica to Croix, Chihuahua, September 14, 1781, AGI, Guadalajara, 282, MLMC; Gutiérrez de la Cueva to Croix, Chihuahua, September 15, 1781, AGI, Guadalajara, 282, MLMC. Quotations are from second document.
81 Croix to Gálvez, Arizpe, October 7, 1782, AGI, Guadalajara, 282, MLMC; Croix, "Extracto de novedades de enemigos ocurridas en las provincias internas de Nueva España," Arizpe, January 26, 1782, AGI, Guadalajara, 268, Seville. See also Moorhead, *Presidio*, 250.
82 Navarro García, *Don José de Gálvez*, 375–376.
83 Navarro García, *Don José de Gálvez*, 377.
84 Thomas, *Teodoro de Croix*, 62.
85 For the June 27 royal order and Muñoz's fall attacks, see Navarro García, *Don José de Gálvez*, 359, 378. For Croix's thoughts and actions and the quotation, see Croix to Muñoz, September 12, 1782, AGI, Guadalajara, 282, MLMC.
86 Croix to Gálvez, Arizpe, October 7, 1782, AGI, Guadalajara, 282, MLMC.
87 Croix to Gálvez, Arizpe, October 7, 1782, AGI, Guadalajara, 282, MLMC; Thomas, *Teodoro de Croix*, 62; Max L. Moorhead, "Spanish Deportation of Hostile Apaches: The Policy and the Practice," *Arizona and the West* 17 (Autumn 1975): 211–212; Santiago, *Jar of Severed Hands*, xi, 51–52.
88 Croix to Gálvez, Arizpe, October 7, 1782, AGI, Guadalajara, 282, MLMC.
89 Croix to Gálvez, Arizpe, October 7, 1782, AGI, Guadalajara, 282, MLMC.
90 Croix to Gálvez, Arizpe, October 7, 1782, AGI, Guadalajara, 282, MLMC, para. 104; Navarro García, *Don José de Gálvez*, 377–378; John, *Storms Brewed*, 633; Thomas, *Teodoro de Croix*, 61–62.
91 For a lucid and comprehensive comparison of these policy options, see Weber, *Bárbaros*, 156–159. See also Moorhead, *Apache Frontier*, 125, 229; Bernardo de Gálvez, *Instructions for Governing the Interior Provinces of New Spain, 1786*, ed. and trans. Donald E. Worcester (Berkeley, CA: Quivira Society, 1951), para. 20, 29.

3

Ambivalent Compromise

Within the first seven months after Viceroy Bernardo de Gálvez issued his well-known "Instructions for Governing the Interior Provinces of New Spain" in late August 1786, three Ndé groups sought peace at Spanish presidios in Sonora and Nueva Vizcaya. The Chokonens acted first. On September 10, 1786, several of these bands requested peace with Ensign Domingo de Vergara in their Chiricahua mountain homeland north of the presidial line in Sonora. Vergara, a native of Eibar in the Basque Country of Spain, was an effective and well-respected field officer and diplomat in the Ópata garrison at Bacoachi pueblo. After more than three weeks of talks in the Apachería, Nantan Isosé and twenty-three Chokonen emissaries, including some captive Spaniards who had married into the tribe, accompanied Vergara to Fronteras presidio, where they discussed the prospects of settling near Bacoachi. In December twenty Chokonen families camped near the garrisoned town, and by mid-March 1787, more than a hundred families had moved into the district, constituting well over four hundred people.[1]

Simultaneously, three hundred miles to the east, eight Mescalero headmen, whose bands numbered more than two hundred families, made peace with Captain Domingo Díaz at Presidio del Norte in northeastern Nueva Vizcaya, requesting to live at La Junta once again. Last, as the snow began to melt off the highest peaks of the western Sierra Madre, the Chihene Mimbres, whom Spaniards called Mimbreños, sought peace in northwestern Nueva Vizcaya. Two Mimbres headmen, Chafalote's son Natanijú and Inclán (known as El Zurdo or "the left-handed one" to the Spaniards), presented themselves to Lieutenant Colonel Antonio Cordero at Janos presidio that same March, stating that they wished to settle at

El Paso del Norte and in the San Buenaventura Valley. By early April two Mimbres camps stood within half a league of San Buenaventura presidio, and a month later Cordero estimated that five hundred peaceful Mimbreños had moved into the surrounding valley.[2]

Although scholars have produced several case studies of individual Apache establecimientos, they have not adequately addressed the reasons why so many Ndé groups from the Rio Pecos to the Rio Gila simultaneously decided to give up their independence and frequent livestock raids on Spanish settlements, which they had enjoyed for more than a century, to settle on reservations.[3] I argue that Apaches settled in these fixed locations for three main reasons: protection from Spanish soldiers and Indian enemies, material benefits gained within the system, and to manipulate the system to work in their favor. In other words, Apaches settled on reservations for many of the same reasons that Indian groups across Spanish America entered Catholic missions. That soldiers tried to make Indians materially dependent rather than convert them to Catholicism as the first step in the acculturation process serves as the principal difference between Spanish reservations and missions. Spanish officers ordered post chaplains "not to interfere in the governing of the Apache Indians" until "they are more civilized."[4]

Just as in 1779, those Ndé groups who opted to settle near Spanish presidios did so in part because of the policy change authorizing Spanish officers to make that offer. Yet Bernardo de Gálvez's "Instructions" of 1786 were more derivative, vague, and unevenly enforced than some historians have recognized. Although José and Bernardo de Gálvez's policies each marked a return to a combined strategy of peace and war to pacify the Indians, more hawkish viceroys temporarily undermined these advances by advocating policies of all-out war on Apaches from 1782 to 1785 and 1787 to 1789. An important similarity in the two policies was that in each "capitulation" or peace agreement Spanish officers hoped to satisfy Apaches' desire for material goods by issuing them items needed for food, hunting, and war to "attract them" and eventually "put them under our dependency." A critical difference in Gálvez's "Instructions," however, was that Spanish troops would engage in ceaseless offensive rather than defensive war "against the Apaches who have declared it." The viceroy hoped that such "incessant campaigns" into the Apachería would cause "one or more" Apache groups to become intimidated and disheartened enough to "sue for peace" under standardized Spanish terms.[5] As we have seen, however, Ndé leaders and frontier commanders routinely shaped those conditions in practice.

As Apaches gradually became dependent on Spanish aid, Gálvez believed there were two possible outcomes. First, as a result of their alleged "warlike inclinations" and some Spanish encouragement, Apaches could use Spanish arms to fight each other to the point of "their mutual destruction." Here Gálvez borrowed directly from Hernán Cortés's tried-and-true method of using the Tlascalans to conquer the Mexicas, which Spanish officers had recently used to turn the Mescaleros and Lipans against each other. Gálvez hoped to extend the policy by encouraging "anger" between these two groups "and other bands of Apaches" so that the tribe would "weaken itself" and would be that much easier for Spaniards to conquer. Gálvez knew that Spanish efforts alone would not achieve this end and that the help of Comanches, their Caddoan allies, and other indigenous groups was needed to achieve "the extermination of the Apaches." The second possibility, Gálvez wrote, was that Apaches might "improve their customs" by following our example" and "*voluntarily* embracing our religion and vassalage."[6]

Gálvez's "Instructions" offered few specifics for Spanish officers on the administration and resettlement of Apache groups near presidios. Although seasoned presidial officers could draw on the Regulations of 1779 and Teodoro de Croix's Apache pueblos as potential blueprints, they were unable to prevent Apaches from coming and going from the presidios in the early years. Spanish officials continued to implement policy too late. It would take another five years before Commander-in-Chief of the Interior Provinces Pedro de Nava finally refined the policy of the deceased viceroy. In the interim, both groups would continue to shape the emerging system.

PROTECTION

Portions of all Ndé groups sought protection from the intensified offensives of Spanish soldiers and their growing number of Indian allies between 1786 and 1793. The Mescaleros made peace at Presidio del Norte in 1787 partly because it offered refuge from the military operations of Spanish troops and their Indian allies, including the Comanches and Jicarillas. The situation west of the Rio Grande was more complex. Spaniards intended to squeeze the Chokonens and Chihene Mimbres between three pincers: Spanish, O'odham (Pima), and Ópata garrisons from the south; Spanish troops, Pueblo auxiliaries, Navajos, and Utes from the north; and Comanches from the east.[7] Not all, however, went as planned. Spaniards and Indians succeeded in pushing many bands southward. Apaches could still find food in the pine–oak forests of the western Sierra Madre and free-range cattle herds of exposed Spanish ranches, and very few of those groups living west of the Rio Grande requested peace because of military pressure alone (see Map 3.1).

After nearly a century of prolonged warfare between Spaniards and Apaches in northern New Spain, the accommodation they reached in the late 1780s represented a profound military change, which borderlands scholars have generally attributed to Spanish military pressure. "Probably the greatest military advantage which the Spaniards enjoyed over the Indians," Donald Worcester argued, "was their organization and discipline. Even the most warlike tribes rarely could resist a well-concerted charge." Worcester's statement ignores the Spanish military's limited success in making well-concerted charges on Apaches for most of the eighteenth century because of the tribe's high degree of organization in their raiding and warfare. Apaches outnumbered Spanish troops and were difficult to engage directly. After striking quickly at night, Ndé warriors retreated to remote and rugged regions of the sierras, where the Spanish could not easily surprise them, horses traveled with difficulty, and water sources were hard to find. As a result, Spanish *presidiales* (presidio troops) frequently returned from campaigns with their horses and provisions completely exhausted, waiting several months to be resupplied.[8]

By the 1780s, however, Spaniards had abandoned the "well-concerted charge." Rather than relying on European tactics to defeat Apache men in open battle, frontier officers began reforming their approach to warfare by employing guerrilla or Indian-style tactics. Although Bourbon bureaucrats in Madrid and Mexico City encouraged the heightened militarization of New Spain's northern frontier in the late eighteenth century, the impetus for many of the reforms stemmed from the periphery rather than the core. Commander-in-Chief Teodoro de Croix, for example, responded to the poor state of the region's defenses by increasing northern New Spain's troops by 932 men between 1776 and 1783. A large percentage of the addition consisted of companies of *tropa ligera*, or light troops, who wore lighter armor and carried fewer weapons and horses and more mules than typical presidial soldiers. These troops could move more quickly than ordinary cavalry whether on horseback in flat terrain or on foot in rugged terrain. Field officers continued to standardize guerrilla tactics under the leadership of Commanders-in-Chief Felipe de Neve and Jacobo Ugarte in the 1780s. Tucson Captain Pedro de Allande, for example, wrote that he and his men often spent "the cold nights

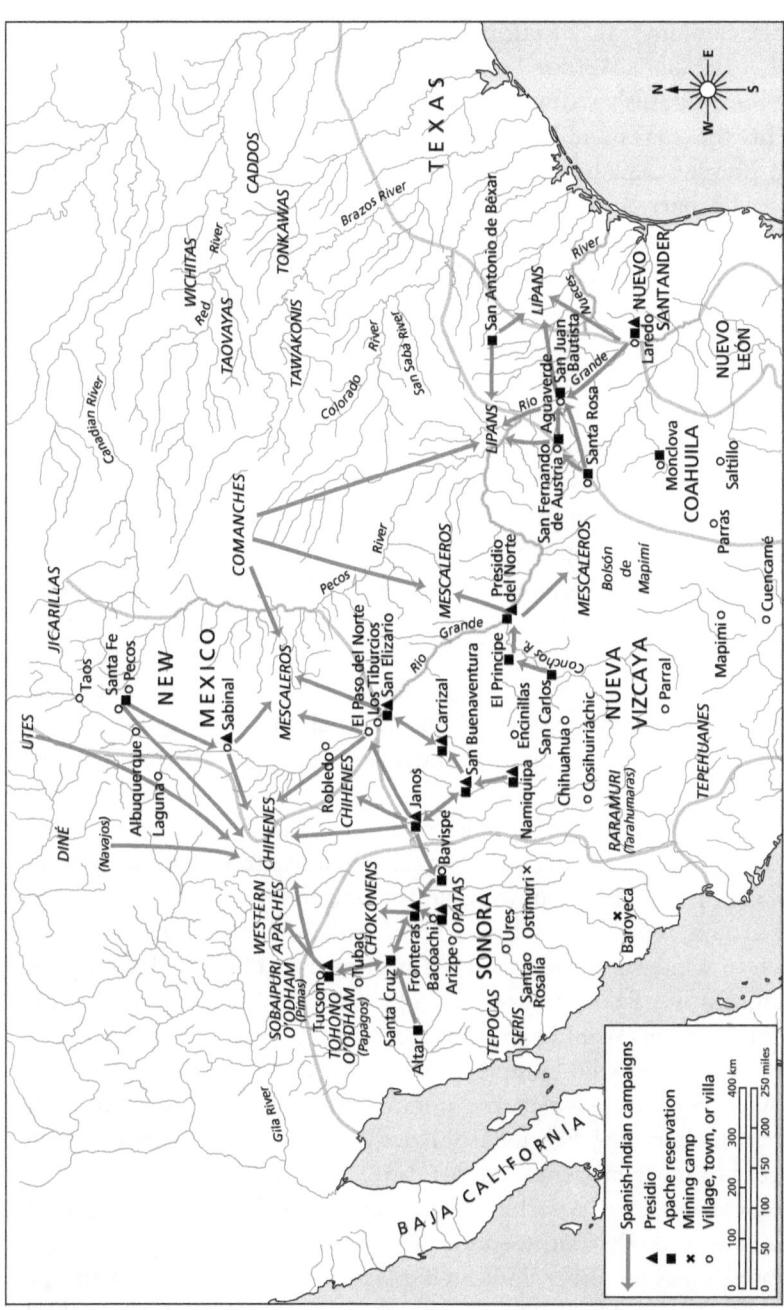

MAP 3.1 Spanish–Indian military campaigns into the Apachería, 1786–1798.
Source: Adapted from the same sources as Map 2.1; Matthew Babcock, "Turning Apaches into Spaniards: North America's Forgotten Indian Reservations," Ph.D. diss., Southern Methodist University, 2008), 106; Sidney R. Brinckerhoff and Odie B. Faulk, "The Last Years of Arizona, 1786–1821," *Arizona and the West* 9 (Spring 1967): 10–11; and Spanish military reports.

without a campfire" in an effort to "more surely surprise and punish" Apaches. Coahuila governor Juan de Ugalde took even further steps. His frontier-born Spanish scouts wore buckskin breeches and jackets and carried brown cloaks and blankets, which Ugalde believed was "the best color to prevent their being seen from afar." Similarly, his men carried muskets with barrels of blued steel to prevent their flashing in the sunlight. When attacking the Mescaleros, his scouts even wore Mescalero moccasins so that their tracks would not alert the enemy of their presence. Ugalde also employed other Indian tactics, such as advancing only at night when his troops were close to Apache rancherías, attacking at dawn, and dividing into separate squads of fourteen men each to maximize surprise and avoid detection.[9]

Like these other frontier officers, Viceroy Gálvez, who had personally fought Apaches before assuming office in Mexico City in 1785, believed that attacking Apaches in their own camps was the only effective way of punishing them and bringing peace to the frontier. To increase the effectiveness of these operations, Gálvez advocated additional tactical changes. First, he wanted small parties of regular troops commanded by seasoned frontier officers to do the fighting. By keeping the detachments between 150 to 200 men and further dividing them upon attack, he hoped that he could retain an element of surprise. He also believed that regular troops were better at finding pasture and water and staying quiet than frontier militia.[10]

Along with stealth, timed offensives and increased coordination were two of the key tactical changes that enabled Spanish troops to reach more Apache families in their camps. Spanish officers were well aware that Apache groups typically traveled southward to lower elevations at the approach of winter and then returned northward to higher elevations in the spring. On July 22, 1777, Irish-born Inspector-in-Chief Hugo O'Conor reported that troops would carry out special punitive campaigns "against the western Apaches who inhabit the sierras of Chiricagui, Gila, and that of the Mimbres, from which the immoderate colds of the months of December, January and February oblige them therefore to seek refuge in other areas of more moderate temperature." O'Conor wanted three divisions to converge on Apaches in the Sierra del Hacha (the Hatchet Mountains in today's southwestern New Mexico) from different directions, "where, as in other indicated places, they will surely find the enemies occupied making mescal, which forms a great part of their subsistence." O'Conor also aimed to capitalize on the next Apache migratory shift. He understood that in mid-April these same Indians returned northward with their mescal crop to the Sierra de las Mimbres (today's Black Range) "to plant their corn, beans, and squash in the canyons of that same sierra." Here, O'Conor thought, was a second chance to ambush the Apaches: when they were sedentary and most vulnerable. O'Conor believed 250 men commanded by an officer who knew their territory would be sufficient to accomplish the task.[11]

When New Mexico governor Fernando de la Concha lengthened the duration of these expeditions into the Apachería in 1788, they became even more effective. In 1784 Concha's predecessor, Juan Bautista de Anza, had initiated a system of monthly campaigns, departing between July 15 and early November, into the Gila and Mimbres mountains. Concha, however, quickly recognized the futility of the policy. Given that the ranges lay more than one hundred leagues from Santa Fe and took two weeks to reach on a one-month campaign, troops only fought for two days. Instead, in the summer of 1788, Concha implemented a new tactical plan: departing in late August, two columns converged on the same mountain ranges and operated for sixty to seventy days.[12]

In general troops from Nueva Vizcaya, Sonora, and New Mexico effectively organized their offensives to maximize military pressure on the Apaches. Forces in Coahuila and Texas, because of policy differences toward the Apaches, worked together much less efficiently. Finally, the least successful coordination was demonstrated in defensive operations in all of these provinces. The increased level of offensive cooperation in the late colonial period stands in marked contrast to the highly localized offensive and defensive Indian campaigns that presidiales waged previously and to which northern Mexican militias would revert between 1821 and 1846.[13]

In addition to tactical changes, Spanish officials made important personnel changes in their military offensives in the 1770s and 1780s. Their primary goal focused on the use of peaceful Indians, including Apaches de paz, as auxiliaries to intimidate and dishearten independent Apaches "to such a degree that one or more of the Apache groups sue for peace." Between 1777 and 1784, Croix and Neve pragmatically increased the overall fighting strength of northern New Spain's chronically undermanned presidial troops by employing Ópata and O'odham mission Indians as soldiers in their own separate fighting units, rather than as auxiliaries alongside Spanish troops. Commanded in the field by their own elected officers, these Native-manned flying companies proved especially effective in combatting Apache groups west of the Rio Grande in the 1780s from posts at Bavispe, Bacoachi, and Tubac in Sonora.[14]

Although Croix primarily utilized these troops to defend their settlements from Apache attacks, the succeeding commanders-in-chief, beginning with Neve, employed them offensively in the Apachería. In contrast to Spanish presidiales, Neve wrote in 1783, "Indian companies ... have the known advantage of not casting shadows, making noise, or making a cloud of dust; they conceal themselves with ease, even in flat terrain, and they discover the enemy and are able to surprise them with more frequency and certainty." As infantry, these Indians were especially valuable in operations against Native camps hidden in the Apachería's remote and broken terrain, where Spanish cavalry could not penetrate. Thus, Ópata and O'odham mission Indians, who were motivated to fight for the Spaniards because they, too, suffered grievously from Apache raids, made significant headway against Apache groups west of the Rio Grande and helped influence some bands to make peace.[15]

In the late 1780s, when the majority of Apaches first entered the establecimientos, these mixed ethnic forces from Sonora and Nueva Vizcaya worked in tandem with Pueblo auxiliaries and Spanish troops who operated from New Mexico and drove Chihene groups southward. Much like the O'odham and Ópatas in Sonora, Pueblos had loyally served Spanish interests for most of the eighteenth century, beginning with their first unified campaign against an ancestral Mescalero subgroup that Spaniards called Faraons in the Sandia Mountains in the spring of 1704. By the mid-eighteenth century, Spaniards had organized them into separate infantry units with the same command structure later employed by Croix and increasingly used them in offensive military campaigns. Although Pueblo auxiliaries did not utilize firearms or horses to any significant degree until after 1800, Spanish officials praised their agility, physical stamina, and knowledge of Apache territory and fighting tactics. They provided the backbone of Native assistance to New Mexicans in their Chihene campaigns from 1786 to 1788 and clearly influenced some Apaches to seek peace.[16]

In addition to employing mission Indians, as part of Ugarte's so-called grand strategy for bringing the Apaches to peace, Spanish officers formed military alliances with different Native groups. Texas governor Domingo Cabello signed a peace treaty with eastern Comanches in San Antonio in October 1785, and New Mexico governor Anza reached a similar agreement with western Comanche divisions in Santa Fe in February 1786. Helping Spaniards fight Apaches was in no way a concession on the Comanches' part. They had been waging war on Apaches since their arrival on the southern plains from the Great Basin in the early eighteenth century. In the fall of 1776, Comanches dealt a significant blow to eastern Apaches when they slaughtered three hundred families who were butchering buffalo along the Rio Colorado in Texas. Indeed, responding to confederated Comanche and Caddoan, rather than Spanish territorial expansion, the Jicarillas, Lipans, and Mescaleros eventually chose to move to the southern and western peripheries of the buffalo plains.[17]

Jicarilla Apaches and Utes, who had guided and fought alongside Anza's New Mexican forces against the Comanches in 1779, also agreed to join Spanish military campaigns against the Apaches in New Mexico. The Jicarillas strengthened their alliance in New Mexico by campaigning with Santa Fe presidial soldiers against Mescalero Apaches in the Sierra Blanca in October 1787 in exchange for Spanish military protection on their fall buffalo hunt into the Comanchería. The Utes had been loyal Spanish allies in New Mexico since at least 1735 and had served as auxiliaries against Comanches since at least the 1760s. Perhaps because the smallpox epidemic of 1781 nearly exterminated them, the Utes agreed to an alliance with the Comanches in 1786. Now with the Comanches at peace, Governor Anza urged the Utes to redirect their campaigns to southwest of Santa Fe against the Chihenes.[18]

Finally, on the western front, Governor Anza succeeded in weakening the nine-year Chihene Gila–Diné (Navajo) alliance, which Spaniards had been trying to break up since 1783. Combining the threat of Comanche attacks with a trade ban, Anza pressured a faction of the Athapaskan-speaking Navajo into severing their alliance with the Chihenes in March 1786 and waging war on them instead. The Navajo leaders Carlos and Antonio Pinto told Anza that their people had suffered from famine as a result of the ban, indicating that the reestablishment of trade with Pueblos and Spaniards appears to have been a strong motivation for making peace.[19] Comanche and Navajo armed men eventually launched a series of attacks on eastern and western Apache rancherías both with Spanish forces and independently between the summer of 1786 and the summer of 1790.

In practice, however, no matter how impressive these alliances appeared on paper, Comanche, Navajo, and Ute manpower contributed little to Spanish campaigns against Chihenes and Chokonens. In four joint campaigns from New Mexico in 1786 and 1787, Comanche, Spanish, Pueblo, and Navajo armed men killed or captured only twenty-five Apaches living west of the Rio Grande, while Comanches alone suffered thirteen casualties. Comanches might have been more excited about fighting alongside Spaniards had they received the quantity of weapons and supplies promised them in the 1786 treaty. Instead, because of budget limitations, Commander-in-Chief Jacobo Ugarte could only afford to furnish the most well-known chiefs with muskets, and he ordered presidial captains to supply Comanche allies with cigarros sugar, and the bare minimum of food to sustain them on their campaigns. Comanches also lost faith in the dependability of Spanish troops when Ensign Salvador Rivera's men retreated during the heat of battle in September 1787, leaving only Comanches to fight the Chihenes. Finally, no evidence indicates that Utes served on any expeditions against the Apaches. Instead Utes and Comanches continued to attack each other after 1786, and eventually broke their unstable alliance in early 1792.[20]

Just as they did prior to 1786, Comanches achieved the best results against eastern Apaches when fighting them independently from the Spaniards. In late April 1787, after Lieutenant Colonel Juan de Ugalde had spent months tracking eastern Apache bands unsuccessfully, Comanches wiped out a large Mescalero band at a waterhole where tobacco grew, near El Paso del Norte. At the end of July 1787 ninety-five Comanche allies under Chief Ysampampi led a successful campaign against the Mescalero (Faraon) Apaches at the southern end of the Sierra Blanca range. The Comanches killed five Mescaleros, took thirty-five captives, and captured sixteen horses, while suffering only five casualties of their own. By mid-January 1788, Ugarte believed that the Comanches had successfully driven the Apaches out of the Sierra Blanca and noted that they also pursued them in the Rio Grande Valley.[21]

The extent of the Spanish-Navajo alliance in the west should also not be exaggerated. In June 1785, prior to the negotiation of an alliance by New Mexico governor Anza, Navajo men participated in their most successful punitive expedition, during which five headmen led 150 Navajo and 94 Pueblo auxiliaries from Laguna Pueblo to Chihene camps in the Datil Mountains, west of Socorro. The expedition killed more than forty Chihenes with only two Navajo casualties. The high number of Chihene casualties probably resulted from the Navajos divulging the hidden locations of the Apaches. At this time, Navajos had a strong incentive to comply with Spanish interests: they wanted Anza to resanction Spanish trade in New Mexico. The majority of the Diné, including their principal diplomat Antonio El Pinto, however, continued to honor their raiding and trading alliances with Apache groups west of the Rio Grande.[22] To that end, Navajos may have used Spanish horses, muskets, and ammunition for their own purposes either in raids against Spaniards or in exchanges with Apaches.

"Suffering no doubt from the invasions of their mountain strongholds by Anza's New Mexican forces and new Navaho allies," the Chihene Mimbres, according to one scholar, requested peace at Janos in May 1787. Yet no hard evidence supports this statement. As we have seen, Navajos launched only one significant attack on western Apache camps in 1785. Furthermore, the Diné had close kinship and political ties to multiple Ndé groups, including the ones that made peace. The Diné headman Kasgoslan, for example, was the brother of the prominent "peaceful" Chokonen nantan El Compá, who settled first at Bacoachi and later at Janos. At the Chihene headman El Zurdo's request, Kasgoslan and several other Diné leaders even took part in the peace proceedings with the Chihene Mimbres at Janos in the spring of 1787.[23] Thus, the Diné could exert geopolitical influence in a variety of ways beyond the bounds of Spanish control.

More important was that although each Indian alliance had its own limitations, they worked well enough together, combined with the Comanches' efforts east of the Rio Grande, to influence most Mescaleros and some Southern and Western Apache bands to move southward. By employing Hugo O'Conor's and Fernando de la Concha's tactical changes and relying on the scouting skills of Indian allies, these coordinated multiethnic expeditions succeeded in reaching Apache camps more frequently in the 1780s than ever before – sometimes with devastating effect. On May 24, 1786, for example, after spotting Apache fires in the Florida Mountains, Spanish and Ópata troops attacked the camp, killing five Indians and "burn[ing] down the ranchería with an incredible amount of pillage without even leaving the poles of the huts." When troops failed to kill or capture Apaches or destroy their homes, they targeted their crops. In September 1788, Antonio el Pinto guided Concha to a "half matured" Chihene cornfield near the Mimbres Mountains. Although the Apaches remained beyond his troops' grasp, Concha "had the ears pulled off the stalks and trampled by the horses before the eyes of three Apaches" who stood on a nearby mountaintop. Five days later, when Concha's scouts looked for Apache tracks, they "found and destroyed a cornfield in the direction of the Tecolote [probably the Cuchillo Negro Mountains]." As Concha undoubtedly knew, corn began to ripen in late September, and Apaches harvested it in October.[24] Clearly, then, as Spaniards intensified their offensives on Chihene camps just before harvest time, they disrupted their food supply. Targeting Apache crops, however, unwittingly encouraged many Ndé men to resort to raiding for subsistence at the same time that other Spanish officials were asking presidiales to "teach" settled Apaches how to farm outside the presidios. The Ndé, then, still had options besides making peace with Spaniards.

Some Spanish officials, such as Commanders-in-Chief Croix and Neve, also hoped to deprive Apaches of their staple mescal plant. In 1780, after researching the plant as carefully as a twenty-first-century botanist, however, Croix's legal advisor Pedro Galindo Navarro determined in 1780 that mescal was far too abundant to wipe out. The plant "naturally increased without cultivation, nor any care in almost all of the lands of these provinces," Galindo Navarro wrote, and "it is so prevalent that the Apaches subsist on it during the seasons." Coordinated Spanish campaigns threatened their safety, especially in their low-elevation winter camps, but Mescalero and Southern Apaches continued to eat mescal during this period. As Galindo Navarro observed, some Apache groups made "their annual harvest (which they call *mescalear*) in the Paraje de la Boca and other harvests not far from Janos presidio, where the plants reproduce with the most abundance." Safely accessing seasonal harvest locales within their homeland, then, represented another reason some Ndé groups likely sought peace. Women and children, who were especially vulnerable to capture when they gathered mescal along southward-facing arroyos and mountain slopes from November to May, could clearly benefit from Spanish protection. Apache women also needed a reliable water source to process mescal hearts, and presidios were generally situated along river valleys.[25]

Once Apaches de paz began joining Spanish offensives in the late 1780s, independent Apaches' need for protection grew stronger. During the winter of 1788 Chokonens at peace at Bacoachi began guiding Spaniards northward to Chihene Mimbres camps. The captive Spaniard José Gonzales commanded the Apache auxiliaries on the expedition and personally killed or captured ten Apaches. Ugarte promoted Gonzales to ensign and noted that the Chokonens' intimate knowledge of the Apachería enabled Spaniards to locate numerous hidden Apache camps for the first time. *Chokonens de paz* also demonstrated their effectiveness south of the presidio line in Nueva Vizcaya, where their efforts in the western Sierra Madre directly influenced the Chihene Mimbres leader Yagonglí, or Ojos Colorados ("Red Eyes"), as the Spaniards called him, to seek peace at Janos in March 1790. Finally, after settling at Tucson in January 1793, Nantan Nautilnilce's Tsézbiné ("Black Rocks People") auxiliaries, whom Spaniards called Aravaipas, killed seven "rebellious" Western Apaches in April "whose heads he presented to the commander." This attack, along with repeated Tsézbiné offensives made in conjunction with Spanish troops, persuaded Nantans Quitolá and Quinanzos and sixty-nine Western Apaches confronted along the San Carlos River to make peace at Tucson in spring 1793.[26] Although mission and independent Indians initially operated together to elevate the success of Spanish campaigns in the West, the addition of Apaches de paz clearly finished the process.

The scenario east of the Rio Grande was different in one major respect: the most intense military pressure came from the north rather than from the south. Based on their own testimony to Spanish officials, the overriding reason that Mescalero Apaches sought peace with Spaniards at posts in Nueva Vizcaya was because they wanted protection from Comanche aggression. Two high-ranking Spanish officers explained that no single Spanish or Comanche attack prompted the Mescaleros to request peace initially from Ensign Juan Francisco Granados in February 1787. Instead, the Indians realized that they were trapped between these two superior military forces, the Comanches posing a greater threat than the Spaniards. Like numerous other eastern Apache groups since the mid-eighteenth century, the Mescaleros specifically told Captain Domingo Díaz that they sought relief from Comanche attacks and asked that Spanish troops escort them for their annual fall buffalo hunt northward into the Comanchería. Inspector-in-Chief José Antonio Rengel further validated the Mescaleros' claim when he offered two of their headmen, Patule el Grande and El Quemado, the option of settling in the abandoned agricultural community of Los Tiburcios near El Paso in present-day Chihuahua. In large part, Rengel presented this opportunity to the Apache leaders, so they would be farther away from the Comanches' rapid southward expansion. Finally, in December 1787, after the Mescaleros had been residing at Presidio del Norte for nine months, Ugarte reported, "The Mescaleros did not dare to retreat to the North out of fear of meeting Comanche groups that cross in pursuit of them and the Gileños [Chihenes]."[27]

Other Mescalero bands sought peace at El Paso for the same reasons. On May 22, 1787, an Ndé nantan camped north of the Rio Grande in the Sacramento or Organ Mountains asked Rengel to settle at El Paso. The headman told Rengel he feared the Comanches, who had just wiped out a large Mescalero band in late April, and promised to return in three days with his people.[28] This story, then, shows a clear correlation between a Comanche attack and Apaches seeking peace for protection.

Spanish military pressure was also a factor in the Mescalero decision to make peace at Presidio del Norte in 1787, but it came from the south, rather than the north. According to Nantan Quijiequsyá (Zapato Tuerto or "Twisted Shoe"), as soon as they learned that Coahuila Governor Juan de Ugalde was returning to the frontier in February to attack them, they started negotiating. In fact, the "skittishness" the Mescaleros displayed in their initial encounter with Ensign Juan Francisco Granados' men near San Carlos presidio by abandoning ten horses and six loads of buffalo hides and antelope skins and racing across Las Varas mesa may have been a consequence of their mistaking him for Ugalde. Even after Granados dispelled this initial concern, however, the Mescaleros still had good reason to be suspicious. Less than five years earlier, in April 1782, a Mescalero headman who had been leading raids in the rugged and desolate Bolsón de Mapimí that stretched across Coahuila, Nueva Vizcaya, and Durango claimed that he had requested peace in El Paso because of Ugalde's attacks. Commander-in-Chief Croix agreed to discuss peace with him, provided that the Mescaleros cease their raiding at Mapimí and Cuencamé and surrendered. Three headmen and 137 Apaches surrendered; however, Croix deceived them and deported them to the interior as prisoners. This brutal prior experience and others like it among Chokonens and Chihenes are vital to understanding why peace-seeking Ndé people were initially so distrustful of Spanish troops despite promises of humane treatment.[29]

The need for Spanish military protection alone was enough for some Ndé headmen to sit down at the bargaining table, but they only agreed to settle on reservations with a lot of reassurance and many diplomatic concessions from Spaniards. Although the Mescaleros had previously settled at Presidio del Norte in 1779, two months of preliminary negotiations passed before Spaniards convinced them to return there. Even then, the Mescaleros carried a copy of the 1779 agreement with them for leverage in the proceedings. Only after significantly modifying the initial terms of the treaty to suit their needs did the Mescaleros agree to come to Presidio del Norte again.[30]

Similarly, Chokonens and Chihene Mimbres drove hard bargains with Ensign Vergara before portions of those groups agreed to settle at Bacoachi and Janos respectively. In March 1787, at Janos, for example, Ugarte sent Vergara three Apaches de paz and two Spanish soldiers to assure the Chihene Mimbres residing in the Sierra de la Boca that Spaniards would not kill or imprison their emissaries again. Four days later, Vergara, accompanied by the leader El Zurdo, four young men, and four women, returned from the Mimbres camps. "The famous chief Natanijú," who had solicited peace at Janos with El Zurdo in 1778, promised to come down soon and settle in the San Buenaventura Valley. Shocked at the Apaches' compliance, Ugarte told José de Gálvez, "I confess to your Excellency that I am amazed ... by the wonderful judgments of God." Ugarte thought the Apaches west of the Rio Grande had "the best intentions of settling in formal towns, ceasing their hostilities all at once on our side and theirs." In Ugarte's view, Vergara deserved most of the credit. During his "repeated departures" to their camps, Vergara had "courted them with what he had been able to attract them with" and had won "their confidence and affection." Ugarte rewarded Vergara for his efforts with a promotion to first lieutenant and even recommended him for captain. Ugarte also recommended that the king bestow special recognition on Vergara for "his zeal, aptitude for war, generosity with which he has spent as much as he had until he persisted, [and] thought and confidence that he warrants from the Apaches, having been the principal instrument that God has chosen to put them in the good state that they are in."[31]

THE FRUITS OF PEACE

After more than a century of violent conflict and treacherous acts on both sides, faithful diplomacy was essential to building trust between Apaches and Spaniards. In addition to seeking Spanish military protection, Apaches also wanted as many material benefits within the establecimientos as Spaniards were willing to offer them. These consisted of food rations, gifts, spoils from battle, trading privileges in neighboring pueblos, and, most importantly from an Ndé perspective, the recovery of captured kinsmen. In exchange Apaches agreed to return their captive Spaniards and unbranded livestock, stop their raids into Spanish territory, and help Spaniards defeat other independent Ndé groups.

Apaches east and west of the Rio Grande requested food rations when their provisions were low as a result of environmental stress or from the strains of war. As a condition for making peace at Presidio del Norte in spring 1787, the Mescaleros persuaded Captain Domingo Díaz to issue the bands rations although Ugarte's initial terms forbade this. Chokonens and Chihene Mimbres also asked for rations at Bacoachi in the fall of 1786 and at Janos in the spring of 1787.[32]

Apaches likely sought these provisions for three reasons. First, they wanted to avoid the risk of ambush by their enemies, particularly the Comanches, while hunting, gathering, or farming in their own territory. Second, a prolonged regional drought may have diminished their food supply. The Mescalero "Nation," Captain Domingo Díaz explained, exists "in total poverty as much from the small number of horses they have, as from the scarcity of rains of these past years, [for] the harvest has not supplied them with their fruits, with which they sustain themselves for part of the year." Spanish troops also suffered from this drought. Owing to "the scarcity of corn and other provisions" at Presidio del Norte, for example, Díaz ordered three hundred *fanegas* (a measure that is approximately 1.5 bushels) of seeds from El Paso to supply the Mescaleros de paz for the rest of April and May.[33] Finally, early frosts wiped out Spanish crops and probably ravaged Ndé plantings as well. The most devastating frost struck Nueva Vizcaya on August 27, 1786, completely destroying the fall harvest. That same year, Gálvez wrote that Nueva Vizcaya was "a province notably afflicted with the rigors of war and with illness and the scarcity of food." These losses created a food shortage, prices skyrocketed, and famine and disease spread across the region. According to Bishop Esteban Lorenzo de Tristán, half of Nueva Vizcaya's population died. Gálvez, in fact, died of a fever from this same epidemic in 1786.[34]

The trend of drought, disease, and early frost continued in 1788 and lasted until 1789. Scholars have argued that Indian raiding increased because of these environmental pressures.[35] Yet, the large number of Ndé people requesting rations at the establecimientos suggests that some Indians responded to these same environmental stresses by making peace.

Like other Native peoples of the Southwest, peace-seeking Ndé bands also routinely sought gifts from Spanish officials as a sign of their friendship. During the fall of 1786, small groups of Chokonens filed into Fronteras, Sonora, to verify their people's resettlement at Bacoachi and to test Spaniards' willingness to help them. Several Chokonen men, for example, requested and received Spanish horses to transport their families to Bacoachi. The Mescaleros seemed even more adept than the Chokonens at extracting Spanish concessions. When Rengel met with Mescalero nantans El Quemado and Patule in El Paso the following spring, he issued horses to both men, a Spanish suit to El Quemado (Patule had received one already), and hats or shirts to each of the six young men accompanying the headmen. Likewise, instead of giving gifts to a single principal chief as Ugarte had intended, Díaz bestowed gifts on all eight Mescalero band leaders at El Norte and their kinsmen in June. These Spanish overtures held symbolic importance for Ndé people. Whenever someone gave a gift outright without requesting one in return, the Ndé recipient held the gift-giver in high esteem for his or her generosity and wealth.[36]

By serving as scouts and auxiliaries in Spanish military campaigns, Apache men could also acquire unbranded horses and other spoils from battle. Although they usually attacked rival Ndé groups in addition to their own kinsmen, peaceful Apache scouts and auxiliaries could still enhance their prestige by redistributing these items as status goods among their people. These material benefits translated into social and political power; peaceful Apache leaders and young men of rising status agreed to perform this service both in the treaty proceedings and in practice. They also had valuable resources at their disposal to exchange as commodities with Spaniards and Native allies, including the Rarámuri (Tarahumaras) and Diné.[37]

Finally, Spanish officials granted Apache men and women passports that enabled them to trade their animal skins, mescal, and other products with vecinos in neighboring communities. In the treaty terms at Bacoachi in 1786, Chokonens had secured an important concession: "to exchange and sell their goods" in all Spanish towns without injury. Spanish officials had typically tried to restrict all trade with Apaches because of the ongoing war against them and their incorrect notion that Apaches were incapable of producing any trade goods other than stolen livestock, the Indians' main exchange commodity when under siege from all sides. Under normal circumstances, however, Southern Apaches manufactured a variety of trade products, including deer and antelope skins, mescal, coiled basketry, and pottery. From an Ndé perspective, gift exchange served as an important activity for leaders seeking to enhance their political and social prestige and for the establishment of fictive kinship ties with Spaniards. Western Apaches called the custom *tedó'dí* ("to exchange gifts"), and it could be done at any time between members of the same sex. Its key component was usually reciprocity: when an Apache man or woman gave a gift, such as a horse, knife, or dress, they typically expected the other person to give something in return. The parties involved did not need to exchange the same type of item or even one of equal value. In fact, part of the fun was trying to obtain the best bargain.[38]

Perhaps recovering their kinsmen, captured by Spanish soldiers and their Indian allies on military campaigns, represented the most important reason for Ndé groups to make peace. In response to Mescalero demands at Presidio del Norte, Ugarte ordered that all Mescalero men, women, and children imprisoned in Chihuahua and Santa Rosa and employed against their will in the workhouses of Encinillas, Mexico, be returned to their people in April 1787. During the fall of 1788, in another extraordinary case, Chokonen nantan El Compá, named principal chief of the peaceful Apaches at Janos by Commander-in-Chief Nava three years later, surrendered to Santa Cruz Captain Manuel de Echeagaray near the Gila River. El Compá and his children wanted to be reunited with their wife and mother, whom Echeagaray held captive. Similarly, during negotiations with Lieutenant Colonel Antonio Cordero in Chihuahua in April 1791, Chihene Mimbres headmen demanded that Cordero return eleven prisoners, mostly women and children, before their bands would agree to settle at establecimientos near Carrizal and Namiquipa.[39]

Unfortunately, owing to chronic supply problems, Spanish presidial commanders frequently failed to meet adequately the subsistence and commercial needs of peaceful Apaches. Although seriously flawed, the establecimiento system still offered Ndé men the opportunity to hunt game and Ndé women the opportunity to harvest mescal without fear of military attack.[40]

OTHER MOTIVES

Prior to settling on reservations, Apaches already recognized that they could manipulate the system to suit their own needs. They could draw on over a century's worth of Spanish contact experiences that included converting to Catholicism and settling near missions and in pueblos, negotiating short-term peace agreements at presidios, and, of course, raiding for livestock and captives around these same locations. By making peace with Spaniards, Ndé men and women knew that they could gain advance knowledge of Spanish troop movements to help protect those bands who remained independent. In addition, Ndé men understood that they could use the establecimientos as bases for small-scale livestock raids in Spanish territory.

During the late eighteenth century, numerous Spanish officials accused Apaches of using peace as a pretext for obtaining information. When an emissary appeared before the Governor of El Paso to ask for peace on behalf of the Chihene nantan Chafalote in December 1778, Croix later concluded that "these pretensions had no other purpose, than of making, as long as they lasted, their exchanges and acquiring information about our ideas." Similarly, in November 1786, two Lipan leaders and six families tried to reinitiate trade with Pecos, New Mexico, which they had not had for more than thirty-five years. Commander-in-Chief Jacobo Ugarte suspected, based on past history in Coahuila, that "the commercial interests that they claimed were not their true motive." Noting the

Lipans are "the most refined and astute heathen Indians that we know," he believed they were intent on "finding out with this motive, the state of our friendship and alliance with the Comanches."[41] Although recovering captives and obtaining trade goods and information were viable motives for short-term peace agreements, these reasons alone were insufficient cause for Apaches to remain at the presidios. Similarly, both Apaches and Spaniards learned useful information about the other's plans, movements, and resources from restored captives.

Finally, many Apaches continued to raid Spanish settlements even after seeking peace. Spaniards had purposely positioned the majority of the presidios along Apache raiding routes (see Map 3.2). Opportunistic Ndé men saw the establecimientos as a convenient way to keep their women and children safe, while they raided for livestock and captives in other provinces. In the past, the vast majority of Spanish officials, such as Janos lieutenant Narciso de Tapia in 1778, had viewed truces with Athapaskans as "feigned and deceitful peaces" and commonly regarded Apache allies as "fake friends." In his "Instructions" of 1786, Viceroy Bernardo de Gálvez correctly noted that the "inconveniences" of making peace with seminomadic Apaches including the warriors "leav[ing] their families in safety" in order to carry out their raids "with greater peace of mind" and "greater confidence, because they are better informed concerning our ideas, customs, and movements." Gálvez, however, urged presidial commanders to tolerate such raids. As Apaches themselves had maintained many times, "they do not offend their friends by the harm which they impute to other subjects of the king who live in territories where actually no peace has been made." In short, Gálvez believed, "the deceitful peace pacts of the Indians produce better results than open war."[42] Thus, his policy of "peace by deceit," which embraced peace at the local, rather than the provincial or state, level, constituted peace on Native terms.

In general, Spaniards tended to exaggerate the extent of Apache raiding in northern New Spain and used Apaches as scapegoats for raiding groups that comprised multiple indigenous groups and even Spaniards themselves. Raiding and rustling were especially heavy in periods of drought-induced famine and epidemic disease, such as in Sonora in the summer of 1781. In the first six months of that year, unidentified "Indians" killed sixty-eight Spaniards and captured forty-seven. When Spaniards redeemed eleven of these captives, the captives reported, "most of the aggressors were captives, O'odham, Ópatas, Yaquis, gente de razón, a few Seris, and very few Apaches."[43]

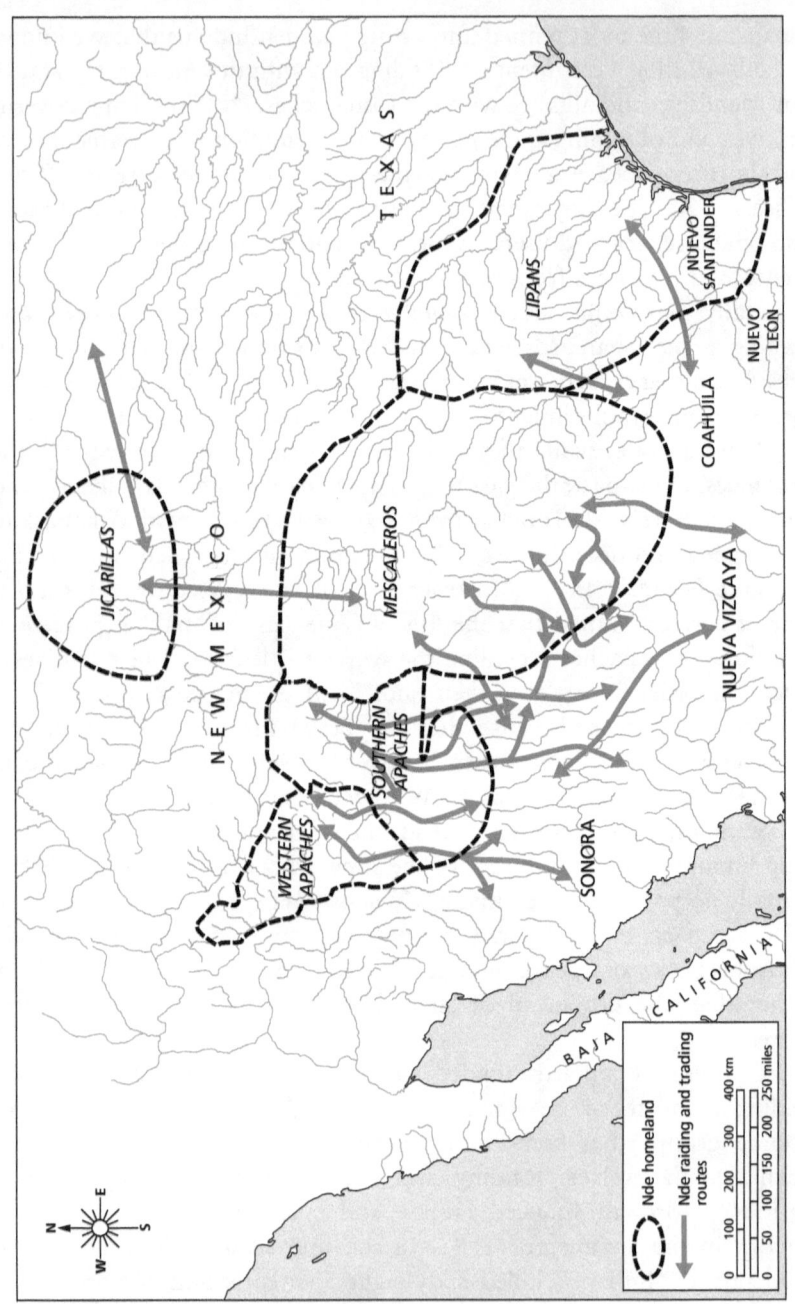

MAP 3.2 Ndé homeland and raiding and trading routes, 1766–1846.
Sources: Nicolás de Lafora, *The Frontiers of New Spain, Nicolás de Lafora's Description, 1766–68*, ed. and trans. by Lawrence Kinnaird (Berkeley, CA: Quivira Society, 1958), 76–78, 156; Ralph A. Smith, "Indians in American-Mexican Relations before the War of 1846," *Hispanic American Historical Review* 43 (February 1963): 36; Ralph A. Smith, "Apache 'Ranching' Below the Gila, 1841–1845" *Arizoniana* 3 (Winter 1962): 1–17; Sidney B. Brinckerhoff and Odie B. Faulk, ed. and trans., *Lancers for the King: A Study of the Frontier Military System of Northern New Spain, with a Translation of the Royal Regulations of 1772* (Phoenix: Arizona Historical Foundation, 1962): 68; *Apache Indians IV: A Study of the Apache Indians, Parts IV and V*, ed. David Agee Horr (New York: Garland, 1974), 130; Morris E. Opler, "Lipan Apache" in *Handbook of North American Indians: Plains*, Vol. 13, Pt. 2, ed. Raymond J. DeMallie (Washington, DC: Smithsonian Institution, 2001), 942; Opler, "Mescalero Apache" and "Chiricahua Apache" in *Handbook of North American Indians: Southwest*, Vol. 10, ed. Alfonso Ortiz (Washington, DC: Smithsonian Institution, 1983), 402, 419; Grenville Goodwin, *The Social Organization of the Western Apache* (Chicago, IL: University of Chicago Press, 1942), 4.

Throughout the 1780s Spanish criminals, escaped convicts, delinquents, and "other classes of lost and vagabond people" joined forces with independent Rarámuri (Tarahumaras), Topios, and Tepehuanes from the Sierra Madre, and fugitive Indians from the missions and pueblos to raid and kill across Nueva Vizcaya and Sonora. While some Apache men also joined these interethnic bands prior to 1786, which Spaniards called *quadrillas*, or "gangs" of "enemigos domestics," most of the time, Commander-in-Chief Felipe de Neve revealed, they falsely blamed their "insults, thefts, and killings" on "the enemy tribes, who have not committed them, nor even taken notice of them." Ironically, these men conducted many of their illicit activities at the same time they were supposed to be serving Spanish interests in search parties to recover stolen livestock from Apaches. Apparently, instead of tracking down the Apaches, they found it much easier to raid for branded free-range livestock themselves and say that they recovered it from Apaches. The gangs also killed a lot of Spaniards. After being captured, Nueva Vizcayan gang leader Joseph Armenta bragged that his *banditos* had killed 197 people, and he had personally killed seventeen. Thus, Neve concluded that the Apaches "cannot be the perpetrators of all the hostilities" in Nueva Vizcaya and Sonora. Instead, he said Armenta's gang and at least two others had been doing most of the killing and livestock stealing for the last ten to twelve years in Nueva Vizcaya and rebel bands of Seris and Tepocas committed similar raids in Sonora.[44]

As Spanish and Comanche military pressure increased on Ndé groups in the late 1780s, many more of them moved south, including disgruntled

Apaches de paz, and forged alliances with this cultural mosaic of Nueva Vizcayans. Jacobo Ugarte reported that throughout the spring and summer of 1787 small and large raiding parties of Rarámuri and other "Indians in revolt" hid out in the Sierra Madre and converged on the mining camps and settlements around Chihuahua, Parral, and in the Ostimuri district bordering the Sierra Tarahumara to conduct livestock raids. Given that they killed only five Spaniards from mid-April to July 20, it appears that resources were their principal aim. According to Ugarte, the renegade Nueva Vizcayans served Apache interests as guides and auxiliaries, and the Ndé headman Queyeyá and his ranchería, who were admitted to peace at Bavispe, had moved south through the western Sierra Madre and joined these raiders.[45]

A critical bond between Apaches and these interior groups appears to be the Chihene Gila–Rarámuri alliance, which had endured for roughly fifty years. In the 1730s Chihenes forged an alliance with the Rarámuri and embarked on joint raids in northern Nueva Vizcaya. Apaches always needed horses and mules, and the Rarámuri could either exchange them or serve Chihene interests as guides and auxiliaries and raid with them. In addition, both groups shared common grievances toward Spaniards. Spaniards appropriated their lands for grazing, established mines in their territory, and raided their rancherías for laborers and servants.[46]

As of the spring of 1773, the Chihenes had an alliance with 1,700 supposedly pacified Rarámuri people living in thirty-five towns near Chihuahua. The Rarámuri stole horses and mules from Chihuahua presidio and traded them to the Chihenes. The exchanges took place in the Sierra de Rosario, where the Rarámuri pastured their stolen livestock, and received chamois and arrows from the Chihenes. In late November 1778, Croix noted that the Rarámuri committed hostilities in alliance with Apaches and independently. Bernardo de Gálvez later evaluated this alliance and suspected that not all Rarámuri allied with the Apaches, but he suspected some "fugitive Tarahumaras [Rarámuri]" united with them.[47]

Apaches at war and peace appear to have coordinated policy of strategic raiding. The Ndé and Rarámuri "gangs" escalated their raiding before and after the Chihene Mimbres peace talks with Antonio Cordero in the San Buenaventura Valley in 1787. In April, prior to seeking peace, confederated Ndé and Rarámuri destroyed more than 500 head of livestock in Nueva Vizcaya. Then in May, as Mimbres–Spanish negotiations began in earnest, they captured only sixty-one and killed none. Once peace broke down in June, they killed 240 more animals. According to one Spanish officer, these mixed Athapaskan-led bands preferred to raid rather than make peace because they feared Spanish troops would intern them as prisoners.[48] Although scholars have correctly noted the multi-ethnic makeup of these bands, it seems clear that their members were culturally indigenous. The poorly understood Nednhi Apache band of the western Sierra Madre may have also developed from these groups and Apaches de paz.[49]

Mescaleros and Chihenes vociferously voiced their displeasure with Spaniards' aggressive offensives into the Apachería during the summer and fall of 1788 by intensifying their raids south of the presidial line from Coahuila to Sonora, launching their heaviest assaults in Nueva Vizcaya. As one anthropologist has aptly noted, "the presidio line was a sieve through which the Apaches penetrated at will," and this was especially true when they were responding to enemy assaults on their families. In late June 1788 Viceroy Manuel Flores reported that rebel Mescaleros attacked Coahuila and that all Apache groups attacked Nueva Vizcaya, including allied Rarámuri, Tepehuanes, and renegade *mestizos*. According to testimony from Spanish troops and officials at Parras and Saltillo, Chihene and renegade Rarámuri armed men – not former Mescaleros de paz – carried out these raids in eastern Nueva Vizcaya. Meanwhile, Mescaleros and Lipans continued to carry out livestock raids in Coahuila on a much smaller scale.[50]

Although Apaches clearly targeted Spanish livestock, one should not assume that Spaniards owned every horse, mule, and cow Apaches captured. At the height of Spanish–Apache hostilities in the late 1760s, Apaches had destroyed so many Spanish ranches and towns and stampeded such a large number of horses and cattle that wild herds quickly formed across vacant hills and plains. As Nicolás de Lafora traveled through Sonora in the spring of 1767, he noted "an infinite number of stray and wild cattle" grazed on the Cerro de Quisuani around Santa Rosalía and other abandoned pueblos near Las Ures mission. In the wake of abandoned mining settlements, wild horse herds could also quickly form. Lafora observed that near the mining town of Baroyeca, "There are still droves of mares, notwithstanding that the enemies have driven off a great many." The line between wild and domesticated horses and cattle, then, could often be very thin. In general, wild herds sought out good water sources, which made them easy targets for Apaches, who knew where to find them.[51]

Ndé groups also had a variety of other motives for moving south of the presidio line besides raiding for Spanish livestock and captives. For decades Mescaleros and Lipans had used Nueva Vizcaya, Nuevo León, Nuevo Santander, and Texas "as a refuge and asylum" from the attacks of Comanches and Caddoans. In 1789 or 1790 an unidentified Spanish official, most likely Antonio Cordero, noted that numerous Chihene Mimbres bands had moved southward into the uneven terrain from the presidial line to the districts of Cosihuiriáchic and Chihuahua. They came here, he explained, to avoid military pressure from Spanish patrols, "to live more comfortably than in their country because of the multitude of mescal that abounds in the mountains," and to raid for the livestock in the well-supplied haciendas in the region.[52]

When Ndé war parties launched their most damaging attacks on Spaniards they had specific reasons for doing so. As Spanish detachments from Janos and San Buenaventura approached Namiquipa in February 1789, unidentified Apaches ambushed them from a rocky hill. Assaulting the troops with a shower of arrows, they killed one soldier, wounded four, and wounded two horses. Spanish troops managed to kill two Apaches and wound several others. After returning at 8 P.M. that night with more men on horseback, Apaches killed another soldier, wounded seven, and killed six horses. In the two attacks, the Apaches killed two soldiers and a vecino; wounded fifteen soldiers and eight vecinos; and captured, wounded, or killed twenty-six Spanish horses. The Spaniards killed only two Apaches. Although Spanish troops failed to recognize any familiar faces, they suspected these Apaches were "Mimbreños," including those from El Chiquito, Quesicha, and Vívora's bands, who were avenging a prior attack on their people near the plains of Babícora led by Captain Manuel de Casanova.[53]

NDÉ MOTIVES FOR PEACE: BEYOND NUMBERS

Those Mescalero, Southern, and Western Apache groups that decided to make peace and submit to Spanish authority from 1786 to 1793 sought to protect their people from Spaniards and other Indians, recover relatives, and reap the material benefits of the establecimientos. Finding ways to make the system work in their favor undoubtedly facilitated that major step. Some borderlands scholars have focused too exclusively on Spanish soldiers in the field, but the coordinated military pressure from Spaniards, Comanches, Navajos, and Indian flying companies after 1786 clearly placed extreme pressure on Apaches east and west of the Rio Grande. Although the voices of Ndé groups west of the Rio Grande are mostly silent, the Mescaleros acknowledged that Comanche attacks were their primary motive for seeking peace. According to Commander-in-Chief Jacobo Ugarte, a combination of diplomacy and war brought about the peace with the Chokonens, Chihene Mimbres, and Mescaleros. He also maintained that Apaches had reduced their raiding because of the repeated Spanish-led punitive expeditions that had transpired on a monthly basis year-round.[54]

Gathering a large quantity of Apache captives and prisoners of war constituted the principal military profit Spaniards and their Indian allies achieved in the wars against Apaches after 1786. From April 19, 1786, to December 31, 1787, in all five Interior Provinces, Spaniards took 365 Apache prisoners, while Apaches and their allies took only 30 Spaniards (see Table 3.1). By June 12, 1789, Spanish forces in Nueva Vizcaya, Sonora, and New Mexico had captured 665 Apaches, over 90 percent of whom were women and children.[55] The disparity grew even wider once the reservation system solidified. From 1792 to 1795, independent Apaches reported only eight Spanish captives, while Spaniards, with plenty of help from Apaches de paz, took 674 Apache prisoners (see Table 3.1).

This Spanish military victory was hardly absolute. The killing on both sides was nearly even. Between 1786 and 1787, Spaniards killed 328 Indians, while Apaches and their allies killed 310 Spaniards, more than 75 percent of whom were in Nueva Vizcaya. Most important, independent Apaches and their allies maintained a corresponding advantage in stolen livestock. Apaches and their allies captured 5,306 Spanish horses, mules, and cattle and Spaniards recovered less than half (see Table 3.1). With such a large surplus, Ndé headmen had a means of bargaining with Spanish officers to recover their captives. Those Apache families who retrieved their relatives often chose to make peace, while those who did not either remained neutral or made war. Just as Spaniards combined diplomacy and war, so did Apaches.

Cold winter temperatures and spring and fall frosts affected all peoples of the Southwest during the tumultuous 1780s and prompted Ndé groups to come to the presidios to harvest mescal. Drought possibly helped influence the Mescaleros to make peace at Presidio del Norte in 1787, but Spanish military protection, the Indians' principal need, enabled their collection of food, even in dry periods. Spaniards, however, could not guarantee the Apaches' protection, especially if the Indians' camps were dispersed in surrounding mountains, where they were vulnerable to attack from other Spaniards, Comanches, or independent Apaches. Apaches de paz were also distressed by Spanish Indian policy. The Chihene Mimbres nantan Ojos Colorados resented the Spaniards' supposedly

TABLE 3.1 *Summary of Apache and Spanish Hostilities in the Interior Provinces of New Spain, 1778–95 (Selected Years)*

Dates	Spaniards killed by Apaches	Spaniards captured by Apaches	Animals captured by Apaches	Apaches killed by Spaniards	Apaches captured by Spaniards	Captive Spaniards recovered	Animals captured by Spaniards
1778	85	28	1721	22	18	12	1047
1779	90	14	5052	19	0	1	100
1780	112	17	3700	77	87	2	1131
1781	194	78	2343	23	68	22	958
1782	10	1	337	1	8	0	0
1783	82	2	1383	48	40	8	1256
1786	159	13	3273	157	68	14	1569
1787	151	17	2033	171	291	11	739
1792	35	0	511	60	57	4	641
1793	36	3	484	67	240	1	449
1794	66	5	1767	131	291	3	492
1795	69	0	672	153	86	0	581
TOTAL	1089	178	23276	929	1254	78	8963

*Texas, Coahuila, New Mexico, Nueva Vizcaya, Sonora

Sources: Data come from summary military reports from the Commander-in-Chiefs of the Interior Provinces of New Spain of deaths, killings, and thefts in the Interior Provinces for the years indicated from Legajos 267, 268, 270, 271, 276, 282, 284, 289, and 290 of Audiencia de Guadalajara, Archivo General de Indias, Seville, Spain, and Legajos 7022–7025, 7031, 7042 of Guerra Moderna, Archivo General de Simancas, Simancas, Spain. See Matthew Babcock, "Rethinking the Establecimientos: Why Apaches Settled on Spanish-Run Reservations" *New Mexico Historical Review* (Summer 2009): 383–387 for the individual document citations.

"just policy" of combining peaceful diplomacy with unrelenting warfare because it meant that they made war on his people at the very same time that they asked for the Indians' loyalty and friendship.[56]

Finally, Apaches found a variety of ways to gain advantages both during and after the peace process. They extracted material advantages through trade and gifts. By retaining at least a semisedentary mode of living and refusing to become sedentary agriculturalists, Apaches maintained more cultural independence than Spaniards initially intended. Some Apaches de paz continued to raid for livestock south of the presidial line in conjunction with confederated Ndé and Rarámuri bands, just as they had in the past. Once the establecimiento system solidified in the 1790s, these transgressions occurred less frequently and intensely across the northern frontier of New Spain, much like Gálvez had hoped.

Even though Apaches had clear motivations for settling on Spanish-run reservations, they never did so with the intention of becoming sedentary agriculturalists as the Spanish had envisioned. By continuing to gather wild plants, hunt game, and conduct livestock raids on a small scale, these peaceful Apaches met their subsistence needs when rations fell short and ensured their cultural independence for more than forty years. At the same time, Spaniards benefited from avoiding the expense of a full-blown Apache war and from an overall reduction in the frequency and intensity of Apache raids throughout the northern frontier of New Spain, allowing their population and economy to grow and prosper.

More than a half century before the U.S. Army established their first Indian reservations at military posts in the American West, Spanish officers had implemented the earliest and most extensive system of military-run reservations in the Americas.[57] By 1793 approximately two thousand Ndé people, from a variety of groups that Spaniards called Mescaleros, Faraones, Mimbreños, Gileños, Chiricaguis, and Aravaipas, had settled in eight establecimientos situated near seven presidios in Nueva Vizcaya and Sonora, and in the sparsely inhabited agricultural community of Sabinal in New Mexico, south of Belen, on the Rio Grande in New Mexico. Lastly, from 1793 to 1799 Lipans remained at peace in Texas, Coahuila, Nuevo León, and Nuevo Santander, and in the fall of 1798 three Lipan rancherías under Nantans Conoso, Moreno, and Chiquito settled in a ninth establecimiento along the banks of the Salado River in Coahuila near Laredo presidio, and their people resettled there the following spring. Some of these bands would remain at peace well into the Mexican national period until presidial troops stopped issuing rations to them in 1832.[58] The next chapter examines how this system functioned in practice.

Notes

1 For Gálvez's policy, see Gálvez, *Instructions*, which contains a transcription of the original Spanish document. On the Chokonen peace at Bacoachi, see Commander-in-Chief Jacobo Ugarte to Capt. Juan Perú, October 9, 1786, Chihuahua, roll 9, microfilm, Janos Historical Archives, Special Collections, University Library, University of Texas at El Paso Library (hereafter JHA-UTEP); Gov. Pedro Corbalán and Lt. Col. Roque de Medina to Ugarte, "Extracto deducido de los partes que ... solicitaron los Apaches del poniente bajo el nombre de Gileños," Chihuahua, February 1, 1787, Audiencia de Guadalajara, Legajo 286, Archivo General de Indias, Seville, Spain, Max Leon Moorhead Collection, Western History Collections, University of Oklahoma, Norman (hereafter AGI, Guadalajara, Legajo number, MLMC); Ugarte to the Marqués de Sonora [Minister of the Indies José de Gálvez], no. 59, Chihuahua, February 1, 1787, AGI, Guadalajara, 286, MLMC; Navarro García, *Don José de Gálvez*, 438, 458; José Luis Mirafuentes Galván, "Los dos mundos de José Reyes Pozo y el alzamiento de los apaches chiricahuis (Bacoachi, Sonora, 1790)," *Estudios de Historia Novohispana* 21 (2000): 104.

2 Capt. Domingo Díaz to Ugarte, Presidio del Norte, March 29, 1787; Ugarte to the Marqués de Sonora, no. 77, Arizpe, April 16, 1787; Ugarte to the Marqués de Sonora, no. 88, Arizpe, May 14, 1787; Lt. Col. Antonio Cordero to Ugarte, San Buenaventura, May 1, 1787; and Cordero, "Diario de ocurrencias, May 1–21," May 22, 1787, San Buenaventura, AGI, Guadalajara, 287, MLMC.

3 Case studies of individual establecimientos include Dobyns, *Spanish Colonial Tucson*, 92–112; "The Sabinal Apaches" in Simmons, *Coronado's Land*, 56–60; Hendricks and Timmons, *San Elizario*; Griffen, *Apaches at War and Peace*; Blyth, *Chiricahua and Janos*. Well-respected regional studies that also omit this question include Brooks, *Captives and Cousins*; John, *Storms Brewed*; Oakah L. Jones, Jr., *Pueblo Warriors and Spanish Conquest* (Norman: University of Oklahoma Press, 1966). For exceptions, see Moorhead, *Apache Frontier*, 170–290; Moorhead, *Presidio*, 232–234; Griffen, "Apache Indians," 183–195; Weber, *Bárbaros*, 193–194; Matthew Babcock, "Turning Apaches into Spaniards: North America's Forgotten Indian Reservations" (Ph.D. diss., Southern Methodist University, 2008); Jacoby, *Shadows at Dawn*, 157; Matthew Babcock, "Rethinking the Establecimientos: Why Apaches Settled on Spanish-Run Reservations, 1786–1793," *New Mexico Historical Review* 84 (Summer 2009): 363–397. Much of this chapter derives from the last cited article.

4 For Indians' selective use of Spanish missions and their adaptations to them, see Deeds, *Defiance and Deference*, 197–198; Weber, *Spanish Frontier*, 115–117. For the quotation, see Commander-in-Chief Pedro de Nava, "Instructions for Dealing with the Apaches at Peace in Nueva Vizcaya, Chihuahua, October 14, 1791," in Hendricks and Timmons, *San Elizario*, 109, para. 35. For the original document, see ff. 363–77, microfilm, Archivo General de la Nación, Provincias Internas, legajo 66, Bancroft Library, University of California, Berkeley (hereafter AGN, PI, legajo number, BL-microfilm). Additional copies are in AGI Guadalajara 289 and the Ciudad Juárez Municipal Archives II, r. 133, 1788, bk. 1, ff. 325–349, available on microfilm at UTEP.

5 Gálvez, *Instructions*, 34, 36, 40–41, paras. 20, 24–25, 39–42. The fourth quotation is from 34, para. 20. All others are from 36, para. 24. The majority of scholars have argued that Gálvez's policy represented a clear synthesis of Spanish Indian policies since 1768 that also contained some innovations. See Weber, *Bárbaros*, 183–184; Weber, *Spanish Frontier*, 229; Moorhead, *Apache Frontier*, 123; Park, "Spanish Indian Policy," 340–341. Others have emphasized the newness of this policy without, as David J. Weber has pointed out, adequately explaining what was truly new about it. See Bancroft, *History of the North Mexican States and Texas*, 648–649; Faulk, "The Presidio: Fortress or Farce?," 27; Moorhead, *Presidio*, 100–101; Weber, *Spanish Frontier*, 444n116. For the hard line advocated by Spanish viceroys, see Moorhead, *Presidio*, 92–98, 108–109. Most U.S. military officers also viewed force as the only way to subdue and begin to acculturate Indians. See Sherry L. Smith, *The View from Officers' Row: Army Perceptions of Western Indians* (Tucson: University of Arizona Press, 1990), 92, 106.

6 Gálvez, *Instructions*, 37–39, 41, 44, paras. 29–30, 34, 42, 53–54. The first and last two quotations are from para. 42, the second is from para. 34, the next three are from para. 53, and the sixth is from para. 54. The italics are my own. For Nava's policy, see Pedro de Nava, "Instructions for Dealing with Apaches at Peace in Nueva Vizcaya, Chihuahua, October 14, 1791," in *San Elizario: Spanish Presidio to Texas County Seat*, ed. Rick Hendricks and W. H. Timmons (El Paso: Texas Western Press, 1998), 102–109.

7 For O'odham, see Jacoby, *Shadows at Dawn*, 13, 289.

8 For quotation, see Donald E. Worcester, introduction to Gálvez, *Instructions*, 1. On the proficiency of Apaches at raiding and warfare and the ineffectiveness of Spanish fighting techniques against them, see Gálvez, *Instructions*, 81–83, paras. 203–205, 208, 210; Matson and Schroeder, "Cordero's Description," 345–348; Williams and Hoover, *Arms of the Apachería*, 22–23. Scholars arguing that Apaches sought peace exclusively because of military pressure from Spaniards and their Indian allies include Alfred Barnaby Thomas, "Historical Background" in Thomas, *Forgotten Frontiers*, 54, 72; Brinckerhoff, "Last Years of Spanish Arizona," 8–9; Park, "Spanish Indian Policy," 341–342. Moorhead adds that some "Apache warriors surrendered voluntarily ... to become reunited with their captured families." Moorhead, *Apache Frontier*, 274. Anthropologist William B. Griffen suggests that drought may have been a possible cause. See Griffen, *Apaches at War and Peace*, 63.

9 For the influence of independent Indians and frontier Spanish officials on Spanish Indian policy in these years, see David J. Weber, "Bourbons and Bárbaros: Center and Periphery in the Reshaping of Spanish Indian Policy," in *Negotiated Empires: Centers and Peripheries in the Americas, 1500–1820*, ed. Christine Daniels and Michael V. Kennedy (New York: Routledge, 2002), 79–103; Wayne E. Lee, "Projecting Power in the Early Modern World: The Spanish Model?," in *Empires and Indigenes: Intercultural Alliance, Imperial Expansion, and Warfare in the Early Modern World*, ed. Wayne E. Lee, Warfare and Culture Series (New York: New York University Press, 2011), 7. For the effectiveness of Croix's reforms, see Moorhead, *Presidio*, 82–83, 92;

Weber, *Spanish Frontier*, 226. For a contrary argument, see Sidney B. Brinckerhoff and Odie B. Faulk, "The Spanish Military System in the Interior Provinces: *An Appraisal*," in Brinckerhoff and Faulk, *Lancers for the King*, 91. For the possible influence of European light cavalry on Croix's tropa ligera, see Geoffrey Parker, *The Military Revolution: Military Innovation and the Rise of the West, 1500–1800*, 2nd ed. (New York: Cambridge University Press, 1996), 149; Luis Alberto García, *Guerra y frontera: el ejército del norte entre 1855 y 1858* (Monterrey, Mexico: Fondo Editorial de Nuevo León, 2007), 21–22. For quotations, see Capt. Pedro de Allande to the King of Spain [Carlos III], Tucson, n.d. [ca. 1786] in McCarty, *Desert Documentary*, 46; Juan de Ugalde, "Diary [of first campaign]," March 24, 1787, quoted in Al B. Nelson, "Campaigning in the Big Bend of the Río Grande in 1787," *Southwestern Historical Quarterly* 39 (January 1936): 207.

10 Gálvez, *Instructions*, 34, 82–83, paras. 20, 206–207; Kieran McCarty, "Bernardo de Gálvez on the Apache Frontier: The Education of a Future Viceroy," *Journal of the Southwest* 36 (Summer 1994): 103–130.

11 For Ndé seasonal movements, see Harry W. Basehart, "Mescalero Apache Band Organization and Leadership," in *Apachean Culture History and Ethnology*, ed. Keith H. Basso and Morris E. Opler (Tucson: University of Arizona Press, 1971), 39; Grenville Goodwin, *The Social Organization of the Western Apache* (Chicago, IL: University of Chicago Press, 1942), 158; Robert N. Bellah, *Apache Kinship Systems* (Cambridge, MA: Harvard University Press, 1952), 85. For quotations, see O'Conor, *Defenses of Northern New Spain*, 87–88, paras. 215, 220.

12 Ugarte to Viceroy Manuel Antonio Flores, Chihuahua, July 31, 1788, Archivo General de la Nación, Provincias Internas, Legajo 65, Center for Southwest Research, Zimmerman Library, University of New Mexico (hereafter, AGN, PI, 65, CSWR-UNM); Ugarte to Gov. Fernando de la Concha, Chihuahua, July 22, 1788, AGN, PI, 65, CSWR-UNM; and Concha to Ugarte, no. 34, Santa Fe, June 24, 1788, AGN, PI, 65, CSWR-UNM.

13 Moorhead, *Apache Frontier*, 74–78; Cuauhtémoc Velasco Ávila, "Negociaciones con los lipanes a fines del siglo XVIII: avances y retrocesos," in *52nd Congreso de las Americanistas* (Universidad de Sevilla, Spain: July 17–21, 2006); Gálvez, *Instructions*, 60, paras. 120–121; DeLay, *War of a Thousand Deserts*, 145–148.

14 For the quotation, see Gálvez, *Instructions*, 39, para. 34; Croix, "General Report of 1781," Arizpe, April 23, 1781, in Thomas, *Teodoro de Croix*, 156–157, 159–160, paras. 330, 340, 344, 346; Commander-in-Chief Felipe de Neve to J. de Gálvez, Arizpe, December 1, 1783, paras. 42–43, AGI, Guadalajara, 520, MLMC.

15 For the quotation, see Neve to J. de Gálvez, Arizpe, December 1, 1783, paras. 41–42, AGI, Guadalajara, 520, MLMC; Navarro García, *Don José de Gálvez*, 440; Mirafuentes Galván, "Los dos mundos de José Reyes Pozo," 79; Croix, "General Report of 1781," in Thomas, *Teodoro de Croix*, 199, para. 461; Radding, *Wandering Peoples*, 256–263; Spicer, *Cycles of Conquest*, 101–102, 133.

16 Oakah L. Jones, Jr., "Pueblo Indian Auxiliaries and the Reconquest of New Mexico, 1692–1704," *Journal of the West* 2 (July 1963): 275; Oakah L. Jones, Jr., "Pueblo Indian Auxiliaries in New Mexico, 1763–1821," *New Mexico Historical Review* 80 (April 1962): 96–97, 102, 106.

17 Moorhead, *Apache Frontier*, 140; Nava "Treaty with the Eastern Comanches, October 1785," Chihuahua, July 23, 1799, in *Border Comanches: Seven Spanish Colonial Documents, 1785–1819*, ed. and trans. Marc Simmons (Santa Fe, NM: Stagecoach Press, 1967), 21–22; Gov. Juan Bautista de Anza, "The Spanish-Comanche Peace Treaty of 1786," Santa Fe, July 14, 1786, in Thomas, *Forgotten Frontiers*, 329–332; Hämäläinen, *Comanche Empire*, 107–24; Thomas, "Historical Background," in Thomas, *Forgotten Frontiers*, 15, 64.

18 Ronald Benes, "Anza and Concha in New Mexico, 1787–1793: A Study in New Colonial Techniques," *Journal of the West* 4 (January 1965): 68; John, *Storms Brewed*, 313, 330, 467; Navarro García, *Don José de Gálvez*, 386. For the Ute–Comanche alliance and the Ute role in the Comanche peace proceedings, see Pedro Garrido y Durán, "An Account of the Events Concerning the Comanche Peace, 1785–1786," Chihuahua, December 21, 1786, in Thomas, *Forgotten Frontiers*, 294–321; Brooks, *Captives and Cousins*, 158–159; Blackhawk, *Violence over the Land*, 103–105.

19 Interim Commander-in-Chief José Antonio Rengel to Anza, Chihuahua, August 27, 1785; Ugarte to the Marqués de Sonora [J. de Gálvez], Chihuahua, December 21, 1786; and Garrido y Durán, "An Account of the Events Concerning the Dissolution of the Gila–Navajo Alliance, 1785–1786," Chihuahua, December 21, 1786, in Thomas, *Forgotten Frontiers*, 266, 343, 345–351; Donald E. Worcester, "The Navajo during the Spanish Regime in New Mexico," *New Mexico Historical Review* 26 (April 1951): 113; Moorhead, *Apache Frontier*, 174–178.

20 Inspector-in-Chief Rengel, "Diary," El Paso, December 4, 1787, AGN, PI, 65, CSWR-UNM; "Tally Sheet: Record of a Comanche Apache Battle 1786," in Thomas, *Forgotten Frontiers*, 324–325; Moorhead, *Apache Frontier*, 156–160, 164–166, 189–190; John, *Storms Brewed*, 687, 737, 754. For Diné, see David M. Brugge, Ives Goddard, and Willem J. de Reuse, "Synonymy," in David M. Brugge, "Navajo Prehistory and History to 1850," in *Handbook of North American Indians: Southwest*, Vol. 10, ed. Alfonso Ortiz (Washington, DC: Smithsonian Institution, 1983), 496.

21 Nelson, "Campaigning in the Big Bend," 225; Ugarte to Concha, Arizpe, January 23, 1788, and Anza to Ugarte, Santa Fe, October 20, 1787, AGN, PI, 65, CSWR-UNM.

22 Rengel to Minister of the Indies [J. de Gálvez], Chihuahua, August 27, 1785, in Thomas, *Forgotten Frontiers*, 257; Moorhead, *Apache Frontier*, 176.

23 For the quotation, see Moorhead, *Apache Frontier*, 186; Cordero, "Diario de ocurrencias y novedades [2–15 April]," San Buenaventura, April 16, 1787, AGI, Guadalajara, 287, MLMC.

24 For the first quotation, see Rengel to Ugarte, "Diario de las operaciones," Janos, May 29, 1786, roll 9, JHA-UTEP. For the remaining quotations, see

Adlai Feather, ed., "Colonel Don Fernando de la Concha Diary, 1788," *New Mexico Historical Review* 34 (October 1959): 297, 300. For corn ripening and harvesting, see Basso, "Western Apache," 469.

25 For quotations, see Assessor Pedro Galindo Navarro to Croix, Arizpe, February 23, 1780, Audiencia de Guadalajara, Legajo 276, Archivo General de Indias, Seville, Spain (hereafter, AGI Guadalajara, Legajo number, Seville). For Felipe de Neve's similar intentions, see Neve to J. de Gálvez, Arizpe, December 1, 1783, AGI Guadalajara 520, MLMC. For a description of a successful attack on Apache winter camps during the spring of 1785, see Navarro García, *Don José de Gálvez*, 448. On mescal processing, see Hodgson, *Food Plants*, 17–18, 33, 40.

26 Ugarte to Flores, Valle de San Bartolomé, no. 417, January 5, 1789, ff. 389–89v, AGN, PI, 76, BL-microfilm; Lt. Col. Diego de Borica to Capt. Ramón Marrujo, Chihuahua, March 28, 1790, F6A, S1, JPR-UTA; Lt. Col. Manuel de Echeagaray to Nava, Arizpe, January 21, 1793, in Dobyns, *Spanish Colonial Tucson*, 98–99; Moorhead, *Apache Frontier*, 198–199. For the quotations, see Nava, "Extracto y resumen de hostilidades," Chihuahua, May 30, 1793, AGS, GM, 7022, Exp. 2, Simancas.

27 Moorhead, *Apache Frontier*, 166, 207, 218, 220, 238; Hendricks and Timmons, *San Elizario*, 23. Comanches had compelled Apaches to make peace with the Spaniards before. See Dunn, "Missionary Activities," 188; Croix, "General Report of 1781," in Thomas, *Teodoro de Croix*, 73, para. 3; Gov. Tomás Vélez Cachupín to the Conde de Revillagigedo [Viceroy Francisco de Güemes y Horcasitas], Santa Fe, September 29, 1752, and Gov. Pedro Fermín de Mendinuetta to the Marqués de Croix [Carlos Francisco de Croix], Santa Fe, June 18, 1768, in Thomas, *Plains Indians*, 124, 111–112. For quotation, see Ugarte to Flores, "Informe General," Arizpe, December 10, 1787, para. 32, AGN PI 76, BL-microfilm.

28 Ugarte to Flores, "Informe General," Arizpe, December 10, 1787, para. 32, AGN, PI, 76, BL-microfilm; Ugarte, "Extracto de las novedades ocurridas en la paz con los Apaches," Arizpe, July 15, 1787, AGI, Guadalajara, 287, MLMC.

29 Nelson, "Campaigning in the Big Bend," 212; Thomas, *Teodoro de Croix*, 62; Moorhead, *Apache Frontier*, 207–208; Gov. Pedro Corbalán and Lt. Col. Roque de Medina to Ugarte, "Extracto deducido de los partes," Chihuahua, February 1, 1787, AGI, Guadalajara, 286, MLMC; and Ugarte to the Marqués de Sonora [J. de Gálvez], no. 75, Janos, March 20, 1787, AGS, GM, 7031, Exp. 9, Simancas.

30 Díaz to Ugarte, Presidio del Norte, March 29, 1787, AGI, Guadalajara, 287, MLMC; Moorhead, *Apache Frontier*, 212–213, 220; Nelson, "Campaigning in the Big Bend," 212.

31 For the first four quotations, see Ugarte to the Marqués de Sonora [J. de Gálvez], no, 75, Janos, March 20, 1787, AGS, GM, 7031, Exp. 9, Simancas. For the final quotation, see Ugarte to the Marqués de Sonora [J. de Gálvez], no. 59, Chihuahua, February 1, 1787, AGI, Guadalajara, 286, MLMC.

32 Moorhead, *Apache Frontier*, 212, 213, 220; Corbalán and Medina to Ugarte, "Extracto deducido de los Partes," Chihuahua, February 1, 1787, AGI,

Guadalajara, 286, MLMC; Cordero to Ugarte, San Buenaventura, May 1, 1787, F3, S1, JPR-UTA.

33 For the first quotation, see Díaz to Ugarte, no. 77, Presidio del Norte, March 29, 1787, AGI Guadalajara, 287, MLMC; Lt. Gov. José Antonio de Arrieta to Capt. Narciso Muñiz, El Paso, February 8, 1778, El Paso, F3, S1, JPR-UTA. For the second quotation, see Díaz to Ugarte, Guajoquilla, April 13, 1787, AGI, Guadalajara, 287, MLMC; Rengel to Díaz, El Paso, April 27, 1787, AGI Guadalajara 287, MLMC.

34 Gálvez, *Instructions*, 65, 72, 35, paras. 141, 65, 21–22. Quotation is from 65, para. 141; Ross Frank, *From Settler to Citizen: New Mexican Economic Development and the Creation of Vecino Society, 1750–1820* (Berkeley: University of California Press, 2000), 119–120, 288; Ortelli, *Trama de una guerra conveniente*, 193.

35 For scholars who argue that Indian raiding increased because of environmental concerns, see Spicer, *Cycles of Conquest*, 166; Ortelli, *Trama de una guerra conveniente*, 193–194.

36 Gov. Pedro Corbalán and Medina to Ugarte, "Extracto deducido de los partes," Chihuahua, February 1, 1787, AGI, Guadalajara, 286, MLMC; Moorhead, *Apache Frontier*, 218, 220; Goodwin, *Social Organization*, 549; Weber, *Bárbaros*, 192.

37 Griffen, *Apaches at War and Peace*, 104. For a discussion of the difference between status and consumer goods among Apaches, see Anderson, *The Indian Southwest*, 106–107. For Rarámuri, see Spicer, *Cycles of Conquest*, 23.

38 For quotation, see Gov. Pedro Corbalán and Lt. Col. Roque de Medina to Ugarte, "Extracto deducido de los partes," Chihuahua, February 1, 1787, AGI, Guadalajara, 286, MLMC; Moorhead, *Apache Frontier*, 209; Opler, "Chiricahua Apache," 412–413; Basso, "Western Apache," 468–469; Goodwin, *Social Organization*, 549; Opler, *An Apache Life-Way*, 33, 439–440.

39 Moorhead, *Apache Frontier*, 274–275, 219, 194; Griffen, *Apaches at War and Peace*, 60, 62; Dobyns, *Spanish Colonial Tucson*, 94; Cordero to the Janos commander, El Paso, August 12, 1791; [Cordero], "Noticia de los prisioneros solicitados por los capitancillos Mimbreños," Chihuahua, April 18, 171; Cordero to Capt. Manuel de Casanova, Chihuahua, January 17, 1791; and Nava to Casanova, Chihuahua, July 7, 1791, all in F7, S1, JPR-UT Austin.

40 Griffen, *Apaches at War and Peace*, 27.

41 For the first quotation, see Croix, "Resumen de las muertes y robos executadas por los enemigos en las provincias internas de Nueva España," Chihuahua, January 23, 1779, AGI, Guadalajara, 270, Seville; Anza to Ugarte, no. 507, Santa Fe, November 18, 1786, AGN, PI, 65, CSWR-UNM; and for the last two quotations, see Ugarte to Anza, Chihuahua, January 26, 1787, AGN, PI, 65, CSWR-UNM.

42 For the first two quotations, see Tapia to Capt. Narciso Muñiz, Janos, February 11, 1778 and Tapia to Muñiz, Janos, February 28, 1778, F3, S1, JPR-UTA. For the remaining quotations, see Gálvez, *Instructions*, 42, 41, paras. 46, 45, 43.

43 Croix, "Resumen de las muertes y robos" and "Extracto de novedades ocurridas con los indios enemigos en las provincias internas de Nueva España, desde el mes de enero último hasta el de la fecha," Arizpe, June 30, 1781, AGI, Guadalajara, 267, Seville. The quotation is from the second document.

44 For the first quotation, see Ugarte to Díaz, Chihuahua, January 4, 1787, AGI, Guadalajara, 287, MLMC; Neve to Gálvez, Arizpe, December 1, 1783, paras. 14, 6, 51, 9, AGI, Guadalajara 520, MLMC. The remaining quotations are from paras. 14 and 51. For a more comprehensive look at the Ndé role within interethnic bands in Nueva Vizcaya and Sonora, see William L. Merrill, "Cultural Creativity and Raiding Bands in Eighteenth-Century Northern New Spain," in *Violence, Resistance, and Survival in the Americas: Native Americans and the Legacy of Conquest*, ed. William B. Taylor and Franklin Pease (Washington, DC: Smithsonian Institution Press, 1994), 124–152; William L. Merrill, "La economía política de las correrías: Nueva Vizcaya al final de la época colonial," in *Nómadas y sedentarios en el norte de México: homenaje a Beatriz Braniff*, ed. Marie-Areti Hers et. al. (Mexico: UNAM, 2000), 623–668; Deeds, *Defiance and Deference*, 97, 119–120, 185–195; Ortelli, *Trama de una guerra conveniente*, 112–115, 125; Sara Ortelli, "Enemigos internos y súbditos desleales: La infidencia en Nueva Vizcaya en tiempos de los Borbones," *Anuario de Estudios Americanos* 61 (2004): 467–489; Sara Ortelli, "Crisis de subsistencia y robo de ganado en el septentrión novohispano: San José de Parral (1770–1790)," *Relaciones 121* 31 (2004): 24–25; Torre Curiel, *Twilight of the Mission Frontier*, 123–139; José Refugio de la Torre Curiel, "'Enemigos encubiertos': bandas pluriétnicas y estado de alerta en la frontera sonorense a finales del siglo XVIII," *Takwá* 14 (October 2008): 11–31.

45 For the quotation, see Ugarte to the Marqués de Sonora [J. de Gálvez], no. 129, Arizpe, August 14, 1787, AGS, GM, 7031, Exp. 9, Simancas; Ugarte to Flores, no. 175, Chihuahua, May 15, 1788, AGN, PI, 76, BL-microfilm. For a similar argument that the primary objective of these bands was to acquire animals for subsistence and trade in Nueva Vizcaya and Sonora, see Torre Curiel, *Twilight of the Mission Frontier*, 132; Ortelli, *Trama de una guerra conveniente*, 98.

46 Spicer, *Cycles of Conquest*, 36; Deeds, *Defiance and Deference*, 119–120.

47 For the quotation, see Gálvez, *Instructions*, 62, para. 128; Thomas, *Forgotten Frontiers*, 6; Croix, "General Report of 1781," Arizpe, October 30, 1781 in Thomas, *Teodoro de Croix*, 122, para. 190.

48 [No signature] to Ugarte, no date [1790], roll 10, JHA-UTEP; Ugarte to Cordero, Arizpe, May 4, 1787, roll 9, JHA-UTEP.

49 Precisely when the Nednhi formed and who they were remains poorly understood. For speculation on Nednhi origins, see Edwin R. Sweeney, *Mangas Coloradas: Chief of the Chiricahua Apaches* (Norman: University of Oklahoma Press, 1998), 5, 14–16.

50 For the quotation, see Spicer, *Cycles of Conquest*, 238; Moorhead, *Apache Frontier*, 191, 243, 250–252; Griffen, *Apaches at War and Peace*, 62–63. For evidence of Chihene (Gileño and Mimbreño) raiding in Nueva Vizcaya from May through November 1788, see Jacobo Ugarte, "Extracto de hostilidades

ocurridas en las provincias internas del poniente de Nueva España," Chihuahua, July 3, 1788, AGS, GM, 7042, Exp. 1, Simancas; Cordero, "Diario de operaciones de guerra," Janos, June 14, 1788, F5, S2, JPR-UTA; Claudio Serna to [no recipient], San Buenaventura, July 29, 1788; [Cordero] to the Commander-in-Chief [Ugarte], Janos, September 16, 1788; Ugarte to Cordero, San Buenaventura, October 2, 1788, roll 9, JHA-UTEP; [Cordero] to Ugarte, Janos, November 17, 1788 and Ugarte to Cordero, Salvador de Orta, December 2, 1788, F5, S2, UTA. For evidence of Apache raiding in Sonora in August, see Lt. José Tato to the Janos commander, Bavispe, August 22, 1788, roll 9, JHA-UTEP.

51 Lafora, *Frontiers of New Spain*, 121.
52 For the first quotation, see Teodoro de Croix, "General Report of 1781," Arizpe, October 30, 1781, in Thomas, *Teodoro de Croix*, par. 57, 89. For the second quotation, see [no signature] to Ugarte, Janos, no date [1790], roll 10, JHA-UTEP. For the intriguing but unsupported claim that these raids were carried out by groups of Mescaleros de paz from Presidio del Norte, see Int.-Gov. Felipe Díaz de Ortega to Antonio Valdés y Baran, Durango, December 6, 1787, AGS, GM, 6952, Exp. 58, Simancas.
53 Ensign Antonio Torres to Cordero, Namiquipa, February 15, 1789; Phelipe Perú to Lt. José Manuel Carrasco, Namiquipa, February 15, 1789; Marrujo to Cordero, Namiquipa, February 15, 1789, all in JHA, roll 9, JHA-UTEP. For the identification of these Apaches as Chihenes (Mimbreños), see Marrujo to Cordero, Namiquipa, February 15, 1789, and [no signature: Cordero?] to Ugarte, Janos, February 19, 1789, roll 9, JHA-UTEP.
54 Ugarte to Flores, "Informe General," Arizpe, December 10, 1787, paras. 38–39, AGN, PI, 76, BL-microfilm.
55 Ugarte, "Noticia de los enemigos muertos y apresados por las armas del Rey," Chihuahua, May 29, 1789, f. 165, AGN, PI, 193, microfilm, Mexico City, courtesy of Brian DeLay (hereafter, Mexico microfilm).
56 Cordero to Lt. Antonio Muñoz, April 25, 1790, San Buenaventura, F6A, S1, JPR-UTA. On cold and drought in the 1780s, see Georgina H. Endfield, *Climate and Society in Colonial Mexico: A Study in Vulnerability* (Malden, MA: Blackwell, 2008), 179–180.
57 For the connection between Spanish and U.S. military-run reservations, see Perry, *Apache Reservation*, 4; Hurt, *Indian Frontier*, 49–51, 247.
58 Nava, "Estado que manifiesta el número de rancherías Apaches existentes de paz en varios parajes de las provincias de Sonora, Nueva Vizcaya, y Nuevo Mexico," Chihuahua, May 2, 1793, Audiencia de Guadalajara, Legajo 289, Archivo General de Indias, Seville, Spain (hereafter, AGI, Legajo number, Seville); Navarro García, *Don José de Gálvez*, 491; Moorhead, *Presidio*, 260–261; Griffen, *Apaches at War and Peace*, 267–268; Dobyns, *Spanish Colonial Tucson*, 98. For Lipans, see Nava, "Extracto y resumen de hostilidades ocurridas en las Provincias Internas," May 30, 1793–December 4, 1796; Nava to Minister of War Juan Manuel Alvarez, Chihuahua, June 6, 1797–September 10, 1799; Viceroy Miguel Joseph de Azanza to Alvarez, Mexico, April 6–December 23, 1799, AGS, GM, 7022–7029, Simancas; Nava, "Extracto y resumen de hostilidades ocurridas en las Provincias

Internas," September 5, 1793–December 4, 1794, AGI, Guadalajara, 289–290, Seville; Azanza to Alvarez, Mexico, August 27 and September 26, 1798; April 26 and June 26, 1799, AGS, GM, 7029, Simancas. For the cessation of rations in 1832, see Ensign Rafael Carbajal to Commander-in-Chief Ramón Zuñiga, Janos, January 22, 1832, roll 25, microfilm, Janos Archives, Main Library, University of Arizona (hereafter JA-UA); Griffen, *Utmost Good Faith*, 30.

4

Acculturation and Adaptation

On October 29, 1790, Lieutenant Ventura Montes's Spanish patrol escorted Nantan Volante's group of Mescaleros off their protected reservation at Presidio del Norte and onto the open and exposed southern plains to hunt buffalo. Volante knew this territory well because Mescaleros had once controlled it, and he hoped that Spanish troops might help them reclaim it from their Comanche archenemies. Upon making camp south of San Antonio along the Nueces River in late November, Volante and his people breathed a sigh of relief. Six Mescalero women, held captive in Coahuila and recently released by Commander-in-Chief of the Interior Provinces Jacobo Ugarte, had arrived to help prepare the hides and meat. But their reconciliation was short-lived. The women explained that "a party of Comanches" had killed their escort, the interpreter Francisco Pérez, in a driving "snow and hail storm." Incensed at this unprovoked violent act and unbeknownst to Lieutenant Montes and his troops, Volante and the Mescaleros ambushed a Comanche ranchería the following day, "which they attacked repeatedly, killing three and taking various captives of both sexes" before returning to their reservation.[1]

This chaotic series of events highlights the complicated nature of Indian relations on early North American frontiers, and reveals the blurred cultural and spatial borders between Apaches, Comanches, and Spaniards in the colonial Southwest. As a well-respected historian has argued, through the acquisition of new values, skills, sensibilities, and technologies, enlightened Bourbon officials and powerful independent Indians were relating to each other in new ways across the frontiers of the Americas in the late eighteenth century.[2] Yet what was transpiring between Spaniards, Apaches, and Comanches on the ground in the fall of 1790 was not what any of the parties, especially Bourbon policy makers, intended. Several key questions come to mind: How did the Spanish-run reservations that Mescaleros and other Ndé groups agreed to live on function in practice? Why were Spaniards, who had negotiated peace treaties with Comanches in Texas and New Mexico, escorting Mescaleros into the Comanchería to hunt buffalo? And what efforts, if any, would these groups make to reconcile relations?

Spanish officials had intended to pacify Apaches by offering them a clear-cut choice between peace and war. Carrying out the enlightened Indian policies of Viceroy Bernardo de Gálvez and Commander-in-Chief of the Interior Provinces Pedro de Nava, presidial commanders offered gifts, rations, protection, and plots of "fertile land" to those Apache bands who requested peace in the hope of curbing their livestock raids and turning them into productive sedentary farmers subject to the crown's authority. At the same time, however, Spanish troops and their Indian allies, including Apache auxiliaries, were to wage incessant offensive campaigns into the Apachería to compel the remaining independent Ndé bands to "sue for peace" under standardized Spanish terms. Finally, the most resistant Apaches who refused to submit were to be "removed from land where they can be dangerous" and supposedly transported "humanely and gently" southward to interior Mexico and Cuba as prisoners.[3] Regardless of Spanish rhetoric, this part of the policy was reminiscent of the British exiling of Wampanoag captives to the West Indies after King Philip's War, of the French shipping of Fox deportees to Martinique and Guadeloupe from 1660 to 1760, and of the American extraditing of Apache and other American Indian prisoners to Fort Marion and Alcatraz in the late nineteenth century.[4]

In reality, peace and war were inseparable. At the heart of this blending lay a contestation over the meaning of the establecimientos themselves. From a Spanish perspective they constituted a unified system of reservations built on established precedents on colonial frontiers in Europe, Africa, and North America. As we have seen, these included the Spanish military's efforts to resettle Chichimecas in "peace camps" in the 1580s, their seldom-recognized relocation program for moros de paz around presidios in North Africa from 1739 to 1803, and their numerous attempts to resettle Apaches in missions and pueblos in the eighteenth century. In 1791 Commander-in-Chief Nava explicitly ordered, "The territory that each [Apache] ranchería occupies should be specified, as well as the distance from the principal post." Each month Indian agents recorded the total numbers of Apaches in each band, noting marital status, gender, and age, and if Apaches left their specified boundaries for any reason, they had to obtain a written passport from the commander.[5]

From an Ndé standpoint, establecimientos constituted resource-rich zones of safety. Spanish presidios, like U.S. forts, provided reservation-dwelling Indians with a potentially abundant but chronically inconsistent supply of rations and gifts. Instead of remaining in fixed locations, Ndé families preferred to receive the free handouts Indian agents offered them and continue hunting, raiding, and gathering on a seasonal basis. For Mescalero men this included lobbying post commanders for Spanish escorts to hunt buffalo in the Comanchería and using the establecimientos as bases for small-scale livestock raids in Spanish territory, which were both clear-cut violations of imperial Bourbon policy. Never content to be exclusively farmers, Ndé women also sought to harvest mescal and raise their children without fear of military attack from Spaniards or Indian enemies.[6] Rather than a radical first step toward civilization, then, from an Ndé perspective, settlement on protected reserves represented an opportunity to fulfill temporary needs, rebuild their population, and circumvent the overambitious incorporation efforts of Spanish and Mexican officials.

Even though most Apaches de paz resisted Spanish efforts to become sedentary farmers, however, Spaniards and a core group of Apaches benefited from the reservation system by adapting its provisions to suit their own interests. Taking advantage of the reduction in Apache raiding, Spaniards Hispanicized a select group of Apaches by employing, baptizing, adopting, and educating them. At the same time, laborers and entrepreneurs from interior New Spain moved north to the frontier, fueling demographic and economic expansion across the region. Meanwhile, the vast majority of reservation-dwelling Apaches used Spanish protection, rations, and gifts to rebuild their war-ravaged culture and reassert their independence.

Chokonens who negotiated peace and personally chose to settle at the garrisoned Ópata pueblo of Bacoachi provide a good case in point. Although inadequate rations and attacks from independent kinsmen influenced some of the Indians to return to the Apachería prior to 1790, at least nineteen families remained there continuously from December 1786 onward, and an average of sixty families received weekly rations there through January 1790. Looking back on the Chokonen experience at Bacoachi from the fall of 1786 to the spring of 1789, Commander-in-Chief

Ugarte suggested that a small degree of Hispanicization had already occurred. At first the Apaches de paz camped a league outside of Bacoachi and entered it daily; then they settled on a mountaintop on the outskirts of the town; and, finally, they lived in houses inside the town. "Some families," Ugarte noted, "work hard at sowing small plots of land." Bacoachi, then, was the most immediate successful precedent for the developing larger system of reservations, a point several scholars have overlooked.[7]

HISPANIC BENEFITS

Even though most peaceful Apaches never farmed, hundreds of Apaches and redeemed captives of Christian parents served Spanish interests as scouts, interpreters, and auxiliaries, and a handful of these allies and an untold number of Apache children became productive laborers in Spanish society. Three beneficial results of the Apache peace from a Spanish perspective, then, were Hispanicization, demographic expansion, and economic growth.

Spanish documents reveal that at least some of the "Apache" men who agreed to serve as scouts, interpreters, and auxiliaries were former captive Spaniards who voluntarily surrendered to Spanish troops in the field in an effort to avoid being shipped southward to Mexico City or Havana as "hostiles." Aguaverde soldier Joaquín Gutiérrez, for instance, was captured by the Mescaleros in the Santa Rosa Valley when he was six or seven years old and spent roughly twelve years in captivity before escaping from them in 1779. He then agreed to employ his language skills and geographical knowledge as an interpreter and scout for Governor Juan de Ugalde in Coahuila and loyally served his interests for more than a decade. After Gutiérrez helped Ugalde treacherously ambush, kill, and imprison a delegation of peace-seeking Mescalero leaders and their families at Santa Rosa presidio in late March 1789, the governor recommended him for the rank of sergeant.[8]

Apache women also offered to serve as scouts for Spaniards and their Indian allies. In the spring of 1789, for example, Sergeant Josef Tato retained an Apache woman for this purpose with the Ópata garrison at Bavispe. Some of these women were daughters of prominent chiefs and others, like the men, were former captive Spaniards. Proving just as resourceful as their male counterparts, female scouts not only revealed the locations of enemy camps but also described the military strength of enemy rancherías to Spanish officers and informed them of Apache movements, thus directly influencing Spanish military strategy in the field.[9]

Spaniards rewarded those redeemed captive men who served most effectively as scouts and auxiliaries, such as the Sonoran-born ex-Apache captive José María González, by making them paid presidial soldiers. After González voluntarily surrendered to the Spaniards, Commander-in-Chief Jacobo Ugarte pardoned him. Ugarte then rewarded him for his "excellent courage" and compliance in killing several independent Ndé men in battle by making him a salaried soldier in the Bacoachi company of Ópatas and issuing him the standard four-peso daily salary. At the same time, the Chokonens continued to respect González because he understood them and knew their territory. Within a year, González had risen to the rank of ensign and had led a group of fifteen to twenty Chokonen scouts who punished independent Ndé bands with increasing efficiency.[10] Military service was one of the most valuable assets captive men offered Spaniards in the establecimiento system. At the same time captives themselves benefited from their rise in social status.

The most Hispanicized Apaches at peace were not all necessarily captives, however. The most favored Apaches, such as the Chokonen nantan El Compá, were not only excellent soldiers but also savvy politicians. Like many other Apache scouts, El Compá began serving Spanish interests after voluntarily surrendering to Spanish troops in 1788 so that he could be reunited with one of his wives and his children, whom Spaniards had captured and held as a bargaining chip. He and his family settled first at Bacoachi and then moved to Janos in 1790, where some of them would remain for more than thirty years. Prior to dying from natural causes at age 52 in July 1794, El Compá was the most loyal and trusted Apache scout, informant, and cultural broker on any reservation. He launched repeated military campaigns into the Apachería with Spanish troops and independently with Chokonen auxiliaries, and he used his diplomatic prowess in peace proceedings with independent Chokonen leaders to bolster the numbers of peaceful Apaches in Nueva Vizcaya and Sonora.[11]

For such efforts, Spaniards rewarded El Compá and several of the most loyal first-generation peaceful Apache headmen with adobe homes outside the presidio. In addition, in August 1791 Lieutenant Colonel Antonio Cordero increased El Compá's political authority by naming him "principal chief of the Apaches at Peace" at Janos and further distinguished him by calling him *El Capitán* Compá in contrast to other Apache headmen who were merely *capitancillos* (chieftains). In exchange for his continued loyal service, Spaniards offered him horses, clothing, playing cards, liquor, cows for stock raising, and additional daily rations of half a sheep for his three wives. Perhaps most significantly of all, by June 1793 El Compá's Chokonen band moved inside the walls of Janos presidio: this was the only Apache band known to have done so after 1786.[12]

El Compá's two sons Juan Diego (Nayulchi) and Juan José, who lived at Janos for decades, offer further evidence of Hispanicization and accommodation. Juan Diego, who was twenty-two years old and married when his father died in 1794, took over his father's band and continued to live inside the presidio. Meanwhile, in the same year El Compá's seven-year-old son Juan José began attending the presidio school for sons of Spanish soldiers, the only Apache known to have done so. By the early nineteenth century both Compá brothers were fluent in Spanish, and Juan José was also fully literate. In the summer of 1804 Commander-in-Chief Nemesio Salcedo even issued him a one-peso reward for having the best handwriting at the presidio school and expressed interest in having Juan José serve Spanish interests as a scribe. Because of their language skills and demonstrated loyalty, the Compá brothers, like their father, often served unofficially as interpreters, spies, and cultural brokers between Apaches and Spaniards, which further distinguished them from their kinsmen. As a result, some independent Apaches distrusted these peaceful Apaches and may have even questioned their Athapaskan identity. Nevertheless, Spaniards and Mexicans referred to the Compás as Apaches at the time, and in his twentieth-century interviews with Eve Ball, Nednhi Nantan Asa Daklugie did as well.[13]

If the Compás made the most documented progress in Spanish literacy, the Chihene headman Jasquenelté's people achieved one of the greatest successes in farming. After negotiating preliminary terms with Governor Fernando de la Concha in Santa Fe in late June 1789, the following July the four Chihene nantans Jasquenelté, Jansquiedetcho, Hansgesni, and Nasbachonil signed a peace treaty on behalf of mountain-dwelling Apaches residing in the Gila, San Mateo, Ladrones, Magdalena, Tecolote, Fray Cristobal, Caballo, Robledo, and Mimbres ranges, which stretched across most of today's southern New Mexico, from Zuni Pueblo in the northwest to El Paso in the southeast. In late May 1791, Jasquenelté, a resident of the San Mateo Mountains whom Concha named "General," had relocated "eighteen ranchos" of his people from the San Mateo, Gila, and Mimbres ranges to within half a league of Sabinal pueblo, a Rio Grande farming community located south of Belen.[14]

For four straight years these Chihenes, whom Spaniards called Gileños and Mimbreños, seasonally farmed near Sabinal during the growing season, using Spanish farming implements and the existing acequias for irrigation. After meeting with the Apaches at Sabinal in late April 1792, the governor reported that the two groups resided in separate settlements on either side of the Rio Grande and that vecinos from the Rio Abajo district were assisting the Chihenes in sowing three cornfields in an effort to ensure that the Indians complied with the treaty terms. By December Sabinal's close to "three hundred" Apache residents were receiving "a small weekly ration of maize and meat at the King's expense."[15] Despite Sabinal's brief existence as an Apache reservation, Governor Concha's successful farming experiment is noteworthy because it reflects the high level of accommodation that Apaches and Spaniards reached in this era, and Apaches could draw on their experience in their future dealings with Mexicans and Americans.

Apache baptisms, while infrequent, demonstrate that a small group of Apaches and frontier Spaniards adapted and reached an accommodation in the 1790s. In May 1792, Commander-in-Chief Nava ordered that Janos chaplain Francisco Atanasio Domínguez cease baptizing Apache children for the sole purpose of "pleasing their parents" because of the "risk of profaning the sacraments." The only exceptions were Apache children who voluntarily accepted Catholicism and whose parents permitted them to be "reared and educated" among the Spaniards. Domínguez, however, continued to defy the orders of his superior officers by complying with the requests of numerous favored Apache chiefs to baptize their *parbulos* or young children without Captain Manuel de Casanova's knowledge.[16]

In spite of the general policy discouraging baptism, then, post chaplains baptized the most favored Apache men on a discretionary basis and, most commonly, Apache children. One anthropologist has pointed out that the number of recorded Apache baptisms at Janos is so small that Apache Christianization can only be considered on an individual basis.[17] Even so, it still seems worth examining the motives behind the practice and pointing out that some Apaches did become Catholic, Spanish-speaking subjects of the crown after all.

A predominant trend, especially in the late 1780s, was that Apaches sought baptism when suffering from illness. A Franciscan friar, Antonio Rafael Benites, the *ministro doctrinero* at the mission of San Miguel de Bacoachi, baptized six Apaches who were "feeling ill" and "at risk" (three women, a young girl, and a young boy) from the fall of

1785 through the winter of 1787, and all of them died. What did Apaches have to gain from seeking baptism on the verge of death? It may have been an attempt to acquire supernatural healing power to fight off illness, which Apaches believed could be caused by witchcraft, an angry god, or an offended force of nature. In contrast to the Algonquian-speaking Montagnais, who perceived French Jesuit priests as shamans with the power to cure them, young Ndé warriors preferred to harness the power of God and the Christian saints themselves to enhance their spiritual and political prestige among their kinsmen.[18]

In addition to seeking baptism as a last resort, small numbers of Ndé parents asked for their healthy children to be baptized at the establecimientos, and some of them were incorporated into Spanish frontier society as mission Indians or as adopted children in Spanish households. At Janos eleven of the fifteen recorded Apaches baptized from 1799 to 1802 were babies and young children that reservation-dwelling Apache parents "voluntarily" sold to Spanish military and civilian families in exchange for a horse, a calf, a scarf and a blanket, or a small sum of four to ten pesos. The other four were young girls between the ages of four and seven whom Spaniards captured on military campaigns in the Apachería. In this situation, the Spanish post commander either adopted the orphaned girls himself or gifted or sold them to Spanish officers. After Domínguez baptized the children, he gave them Christian names, usually José and María, and he advised the godparents of their obligation to raise and educate their Apache children as Catholics. Not surprisingly, the majority of Spanish godfathers (ten of fifteen or two thirds) were enlisted and retired officers and soldiers. The remaining third consisted of Spanish settlers who were on good terms with the post commander.[19] The fate of these fifteen Apache adoptees is unknown. Presumably, if they did not die prematurely from disease, the boys became presidial soldiers and the girls became servants in their godparents' households.

Not all Apaches whom Spaniards attempted to incorporate into the workforce had the privilege of remaining on the frontier. In the 1790s Spanish soldiers routinely extradited the most bellicose and recalcitrant Apache male and female *prisioneros* (prisoners) southward to Mexico City and Cuba. In October 1789, the second Conde de Revillagigedo, who succeeded Manuel Antonio Flores as viceroy, ordered all prisoners, from Indians to vagabonds, including those already in Mexico City, to be sent to Veracruz and shipped to Havana for forced labor. Commander-in-Chief Nava's frontier Apache policy, however, only called for "childless adult women and the adult males" to be removed from the frontier because of their tendency "to flee," and evidence indicates that he did his best to follow this in practice. When an Apache *collera* (chain gang) of prisoners arrived in Chihuahua from San Elizario (along the Rio Grande south of El Paso) in August 1794, for example, Nava fulfilled Casanova's request that the Apache woman Can-slude and her three sons be separated and returned to Janos to be reunited with her sister María, the widow of deceased chief El Compá.[20]

A small number of exiled Apache women worked as laborers in Spanish households and businesses from Chihuahua to Mexico City and some of the men worked on fortifications in Havana, Cuba, alongside Spanish convicts. The vast majority of Apache prisoners, however, either escaped and fled back to the Apachería or died from malnutrition, fatigue, and disease, and thus remained unincorporated into Spanish society. Based on my own calculations, Spaniards exiled at least 979 Apache men, women, and children to interior Mexico and Havana from 1739 to 1805. After peaking at 300 in 1788, the number of Apache prisoners dropped to between 50 and 100 as the reservation system solidified in the 1790s. Of the 371 who are identifiable by age, more than 80 percent were adults. Of the 214 adults identifiable by gender, 67 percent were women. Of the 247 whose fate is identifiable, 59 percent escaped and returned to the Apachería, 23 percent remained in interior Mexico and Cuba, and 17 percent died either en route or soon after arrival. Of the 23 percent who remained in the interior, 81 percent worked in Mexico City or Havana and 19 percent were distributed in private homes north of Mexico City.[21]

Were any of these Apaches slaves? Although Spanish officers sometimes referred to captured Apaches as *piezas* (slaves), given their wide range of fates, they are better understood as war captives or prisoners until they actually began forced labor. Just like so-called *genízaros* in New Mexico, a minority of removed Apache women did work as slaves in Spanish households and businesses such as *obrajes* (textile workshops) from Chihuahua to Mexico City, and a minority of the men worked as criminalized slaves on fortifications in Havana, Cuba, alongside Spanish convicts.[22]

As a matter of policy, Spaniards tried to divorce the forced removal and enslavement of "hostile" Apaches from the admittance of "peaceful" Apaches at presidios. According to Colonel Cordero, the reservation system "does not aspire to the destruction or slavery" of the Apaches, but instead "it seeks their happiness by the most efficacious means." In practice, however, peaceful and exiled Apaches were members of the same Apache groups, rancherías, and families, and they shared common interests. One of the most important reasons that independent Apaches chose to resettle in establecimientos was to recover their kinsmen whom Spanish soldiers and their Indian allies had captured on military campaigns. At the same time, a "peaceful" Apache who committed a serious crime such as murder could find himself quickly extradited to Mexico City, as was the case when the Chokonen headman Tadiya (Estidaya), whom Spaniards knew as El Padre, turned himself in at Janos after killing a vecino in 1793. Yet he was lucky enough to return two years later.[23]

Despite the high number of Apache fatalities and escapes, Spaniards still garnered clear-cut benefits from the establecimiento system, although many were unintended. At its height in the early 1790s, approximately 2,000 Apaches resided on eight reservations across the frontiers of Nueva Vizcaya, New Mexico, and Sonora, with 782 Chihenes and Chokonens at Janos alone in 1795 (see Map I.1). Much of the system's demographic and territorial expansion in Nueva Vizcaya stemmed directly from the burgeoning Apache population at Janos. This makes sense, given that Janos was situated within Chihene territory and subgroups that Spaniards called Mimbreños and Gileños camped in the surrounding mountains each winter to harvest mescal and hunt game. Officers took the first Apache census in March 1792, which consisted of 325 persons in eleven rancherías. By December the numbers rose to 450. The numbers would have been even higher, but in the arid colonial Southwest presidios could only support a limited number of people. To prevent the land from exceeding its carrying capacity and to limit disagreements between certain Apache leaders, Captain Antonio Cordero began permitting some Apache groups at Janos to permanently settle at neighboring presidios in Nueva Vizcaya, including Carrizal, Namiquipa, and San Buenaventura. The establecimiento system not only expanded in Nueva Vizcaya during these years, but also in New Mexico and Sonora. Chihenes farmed at Sabinal from 1790 to 1794 and Tsézhinés (Aravaipas) settled at Tucson in 1793.[24]

As a result, the crown spent increasing amounts on rations and gifts in these years. Annual expenditures at Janos rose from 1,100 pesos between 1787 and 1790 to 13,011 pesos in 1796, which comprised about a quarter of the presidio's annual budget.[25] In spite of these high costs, the experiment clearly paid off for Spaniards economically. The system was still much cheaper than the combined cost of waging an all-out war and paying for lost resources from retaliatory raids.

Another way that the reservations benefited Spaniards is that they gave the most competent post commanders, whether Spanish- or American-born, the opportunity to showcase their administrative skills as higher officials. The Presidio del Norte commander Manuel Muñoz served as governor of Texas from 1790 to 1798 and the Fronteras commander Antonio Narbona, a native of Mobile in Spanish Louisiana (modern Alabama), was promoted to Commander of Arms of Sonora and then served as governor of New Mexico from 1825 to 1827. Most notable of all, Janos commander Antonio Cordero served as governor of Coahuila from 1797 to 1817, including a three-year term as acting governor of Coahuila y Texas from 1805 to 1808. Cordero was subsequently appointed Commander-in-Chief of the Western Interior Provinces in 1822 and was ultimately promoted to field marshal general, a position he held until his death in Durango, Mexico, in the spring of 1823.[26]

More importantly, as a result of the overall reduction in raiding and warfare, New Spain's northwestern frontier began to expand economically. Farming, mining, church building, and especially ranching all flourished in Sonora in the mid-1790s. The Franciscans, who criticized the army's reservation system because they thought they could do a better job themselves, benefited from the completion of beautiful missions at Tumacácori and San Xavier del Bac at Tucson, and Spanish-language oral tradition and a single Spanish document indicate that Apaches helped perform the work. Spanish and Mexican *rancheros* (ranchers) pushed into the San Pedro, Sonoita, and Santa Cruz Valleys into the 1820s, reoccupying many of the same sites where missionaries had previously established *visitas* (churches or settlements regularly visited by missionaries) and missions in the eighteenth century before surrendering them to the Apaches. This sustained growth demonstrates that Ndé raiding from Janos to Tucson did not pick up immediately with the onset of the Mexican War of Independence in the 1810s, as some scholars have mistakenly assumed. Rancheros would not have chosen to move their herds northward into Apache territory if they expected to be attacked by them (see Figure 4.1).[27]

As ranchers moved northward from Sonora, so did miners from Nueva Vizcaya. In 1803 and 1804 Spaniards founded the copper mining community of Santa Rita del Cobre (fifteen miles east of today's Silver City, New Mexico) and began extracting copper from the surrounding Sierra del Cobre, which lay just south of the Mogollon range in the Apachería. Operations lasted until 1838. Just as with the Chichimecas at Zacatecas two centuries earlier, folk history holds that Apaches discovered the deposits. Whatever the case, Spanish documents tell us that the highly

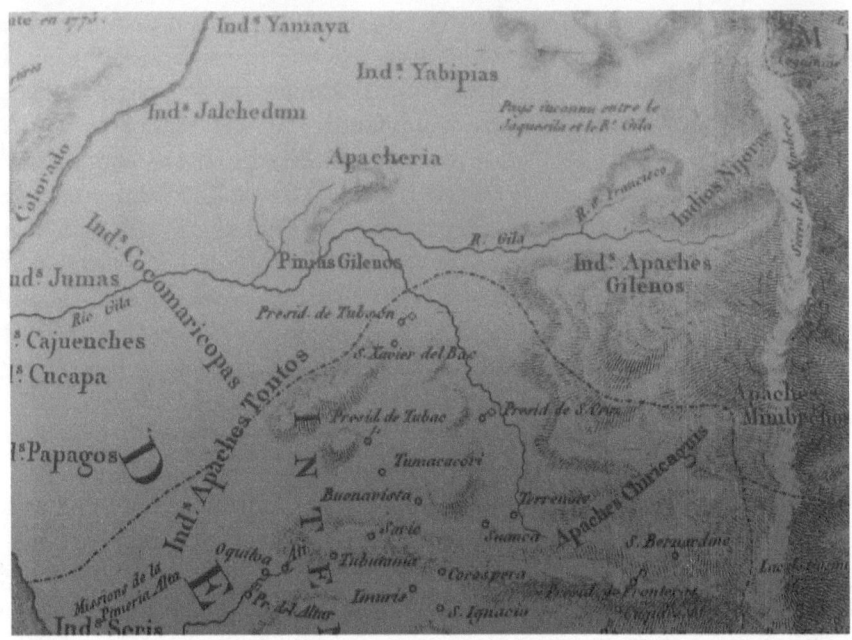

FIGURE 4.1 Detail of Alexander von Humboldt's 1804 Map of the Kingdom of New Spain, showing Apache groups west of the Rio Grande.
Source: Alexandre de Humboldt, "Carte Generale Du Royaume de la Nouvelle Espagne," in Alexander von Humboldt, Atlas géographique et physique du royaume de la Nouvelle Espagne (Paris, G. Dufour, 1812). Courtesy of the Huntington Library, San Marino, CA.

literate Chihene Mimbres leader Juan Diego Compá wrote a petition in Spanish asking permission to explore for gold and copper ore along the San Francisco River, which lay more than a hundred miles northwest of Santa Rita del Cobre in Chihene Mogollon territory. The Chihuahuan mining settlements of Corralitos and El Barranco followed during the 1830s, and Mexicans even began extracting salt from a mine in the Mogollon Mountains. While one might imagine that the Chihene Mogollons would have immediately responded to this encroachment with intensified raiding and warfare, instead they ratified a peace agreement with Spanish troops in 1816, and a portion of their tribe opted to receive weekly rations at Janos from 1818 until at least 1822.[28]

With the increased economic opportunity on a less violent frontier came demographic expansion. From 1800 to 1830 northern New Spain's population grew at three times the rate as the rest of New Spain. At Janos this same pattern of growth is evident from 1792 until at least 1822, when the Hispanic population more than tripled. Further evidence of stable relations between soldiers, settlers, and the Apaches at peace there is that census takers included the Apaches in the overall numbers in four consecutive censuses from 1812 to 1822. Janos residents also founded new communities, such as the neighboring settlement of Casas Grandes, near the ruins of the large pre-Columbian trade center of the same name that is today a World Heritage site. Casas Grandes helped supply the Janos presidio with corn and livestock. Although growth was much slower there, the population still rose from 110 people in 1795 to 167 people in 1812. Similarly, on the Sonoran frontier the populations of Tubac and Tucson grew and fueled demographic and territorial expansion northward into the Pimería Alta (today's southern Arizona).[29]

By adopting a wider geographical lens, we can connect the economic benefits of the Apache peace in Sonora and Nueva Vizcaya with that of the Comanche and Navajo alliance in New Mexico. One scholar has emphasized the importance of the Comanche alliance in fueling New Mexico's economic expansion. Although the Comanche peace did play a significant role, without securing simultaneous peace agreements with Navajos and Apaches, Athapaskan raiding parties would have continued to disrupt regional trade and little economic growth would have been possible. The Comanche peace enabled vecinos to apply for land grants and found new villages on the outskirts of Taos, Abiquíu, and the Mora Valley; however, the expansion south and west of Albuquerque, including Sabinal, stemmed directly from Apache peace accords.[30]

Finally, Tucson itself merits special attention because of its sustained growth during and after Mexican independence. Although most reservations either destabilized or continued to function at a low level of effectiveness during the transition from Spanish to Mexican rule, the Tucson reservation appeared to grow stronger. Peaceful Apaches there continued to serve royalist forces loyally during the Hidalgo revolt and helped ease the impact of troop depletion in Sonora. Moreover, in 1819 the program expanded when Nantan Chilitipagé and 236 Western Apaches from the T'iisibaan ("Cottonwood in Grey Wedge Shape People"), or Pinal band, settled at Tucson and apparently managed to coexist peaceably with the Tsézhinés already in residence. Although the reservation's numbers were reduced during a general Apache rebellion from 1832 to 1834, by 1835 the numbers had rebounded. Chief Antuna remained in residence with 488 Apache men, women, and children, all of whom received weekly rations of wheat. Apache bands continued to reside at Tucson and Tubac through the 1840s, despite increased raiding from independent Apaches. Some of those still at Tucson in the 1860s become scouts at Fort Goodwin where they intermarried with Dzilghą'é (White Mountain Apache) women on an American-run reservation.³¹

APACHE ADAPTATIONS

The trends of Hispanicization and Christianization described so far were pronounced only among a minority of Apaches during this time period. Although scholars in multiple disciplines have defined acculturation as a unidirectional linear process in which a colonized culture adopts the traits of the colonizer, it is in fact a dynamic reciprocal process. Apaches and Spaniards both adapted and modified their cultures as they came into contact with one another, demonstrating processes of mutual adaptation and acculturation, and the overall direction of culture change was never fixed. Most independent Apaches had only limited contact with Spaniards, and most Apaches de paz continued to subsist on their own procured fruits, nuts, and game, while receiving weekly rations of Spanish corn, meat, and tobacco simply as dietary supplements. In general, supposedly "peaceful" Apaches typically exhibited mixed loyalties, sometimes serving Spanish interests and other times subverting them.³²

Reservation-dwelling headmen and interpreters frequently started rumors. Sometimes they tried to incite their people to revolt by claiming that the Spaniards wanted to kill all of the Apaches. Most often, however, they reversed the tactic and warned of pending revolts or attacks from their kinsmen in order to strike fear in the hearts of Spanish troops and frontier settlers. Even Juan Diego Compá, despite living inside Janos presidio with his people, spread so many unsettling rumors at Janos that Commander-in-Chief Salcedo tried to move him permanently to another reservation in 1803.³³ Although his motives are unclear, he may have been voicing his displeasure at not being named principal chief like his father.

Operating out of their bases at establecimientos, the most influential peaceful Apache leaders served their people's interest by negotiating for the release of Apache war captives. Sometimes they even traveled to Spanish provincial capitals to meet with Spanish officials. In 1790 El Compá met with Commander-in-Chief Nava in Chihuahua and convinced him to keep several Apache relatives from being shipped to Mexico City. Two years later an unnamed Apache de paz traveled to Arizpe and brokered the release of a Christianized Apache girl from a Spanish family. Similarly, in 1819, after making peace at Tucson, the T'iisibaan headman

Chilitipagé traveled to Arizpe and successfully negotiated the release of an Apache woman and a boy imprisoned at Fronteras.³⁴

Spaniards did not return every prisoner the Apaches requested. When officers refused, peaceful Apache leaders used several methods to express their displeasure and convince Spaniards to change their minds, including refusing to serve as scouts or deserting their reservation. At the same time, reservation-dwelling Apaches were under no obligation to give up their most acculturated "Christian captives ... who were raised in their way and who remain with them as Apaches." By recovering their incarcerated relatives and retaining their most indoctrinated captives, Apaches reunited their families and began rebuilding their population at the establecimientos.³⁵

Demonstrating similar compassion for their closest kin, Apache scouts and auxiliaries did their best to spare the lives of the Ndé groups Spaniards asked them to attack. In February 1792, Commander-in-Chief Jacobo Ugarte tried to persuade the Chokonens at Bacoachi to fight the Chihenes to the northeast. But the auxiliaries were reluctant to do so because many of them and their wives had Chihene relatives. Although a group of the auxiliaries accompanied Spanish troops on an expedition, they purposely made noise to warn the Chihenes during the critical moment of their attack. It is misleading, then, to assume that scouts and auxiliaries always fought against their own people. In general, auxiliaries convinced members of their own bands to join them by peaceful means and preferred to attack Apaches outside their own band.³⁶

Apaches at peace also used Spanish rations and gifts for their own purposes. In the early 1790s Spanish officials gave Apaches livestock for breeding in an effort to reduce the costs of rations and promote self-sufficiency. But the Apaches simply consumed all of the animals. Year after year peaceful Apaches confounded Spanish officials by devouring their entire weekly food rations on the first day of issue, or selling, trading, or gambling their food rations and clothing away to Spanish settlers. Such allegedly gluttonous behavior prompted numerous Spanish priests and military officers to question whether they could ever transform equestrian Apaches into sedentary Spaniards.³⁷

Apaches, however, had good reasons for butchering and eating breeding animals quickly. Because of droughts, floods, and Indian raids, Spanish mule trains did not always arrive on schedule with adequate rations. Apache men attempted to compensate for the shortage and demonstrate their anger by eating whatever was available, whether breeding animals or in some cases even soldiers' own horses. Moreover, just as when hunting deer and buffalo in the Apachería, headmen sought to enhance their political status by slaughtering animals on the spot and redistributing meat among as many of their kinsmen as possible. When the often volatile Chihene Mimbres leader Ojos Colorados repeatedly complained that he was not receiving enough rations at Janos because Spanish officers were only issuing them to his immediate family members, he spoke the truth.[38]

In spite of some Apaches' legitimate need for more rations, their overall tendency to demand a wider range of rations and gifts than delineated in Spanish policy quickly drove up the costs of the system. At Janos in 1795 these not only included soldiers' abandoned mounts but also "deer hides, money, sheep, bull-hide shields, [and] corn cobs." Clearly, Spanish officials' fanciful hope that post commanders could economize by giving Apaches gifts "of little value" that were "highly esteemed" was not coming to fruition. Instead, Apaches were pressuring Spaniards into giving them items that they could actually use, while retaining their cultural identity. Apaches preferred horse meat to beef, and acquiring tanned deer hides saved them precious time and labor and eliminated the risk of off-reservation attacks from their enemies.[39]

Another way Apaches adapted to Spanish reservations was by allegedly adopting and building on the vices of frontier Spaniards and mission Indians. One of the best examples of this is gambling. Rather than becoming sedentary agriculturalists or pious Catholics, Chokonens at Bacoachi preferred to play cards with "Christians," which included both Spanish settlers and Ópata mission Indians. They made their own painted leather card decks and developed their own card games, which they incorporated into their already large repertoire of games of chance (see Figure 4.2). Another favorite Apache pastime was betting on foot racing. When the peaceful Apaches repeatedly outpaced Tucson settlers in an off-duty contest in 1825, Spanish residents complained that the Apaches had "fixed" the races and demanded the return of their bets. Other "Spanish" vices Apaches reportedly adopted included dancing, swearing, and concubinage. According to one Franciscan friar, Apaches exhibited all three of these evils at frequent fandangos in Bacoachi "in which a thousand improprieties are sung and the most evil movements are made." From a Franciscan perspective, then, Spanish subjects simply corrupted Apaches rather than helping them to Hispanicize in any morally acceptable way. But in reality this may have been a case of reciprocal acculturation – of Spaniards Apacheanizing (adopting Apache cultural traits). Gambling, especially horse racing, was a serious Apache enterprise, dancing held

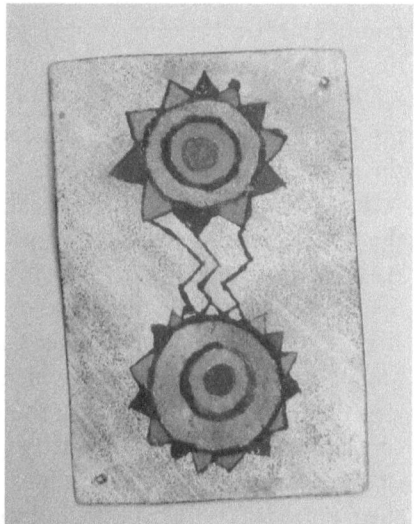

FIGURE 4.2 Ndé playing cards for the game Monte.
Source: Courtesy of the Southwest Museum of the American Indian Collection, Autry National Center, Los Angeles, CA.

spiritual significance, and acquiring more than one wife was a way for Apache men to raise their social rank.[40]

Not surprisingly, the most important way in which Apaches adapted to living at reservations was by moving off them. Like missions, close quarters on reservations fostered the transmission of infectious disease and, whenever an epidemic struck, Apaches tried to ensure their survival by moving to other reservations or back to the Apachería to avoid contracting it. In the spring of 1801, for example, Juan Diego and thirty-six kinsmen moved from Janos to Fronteras in Sonora because of a smallpox outbreak. Others went to Bavispe or returned to the Apachería. A subsequent smallpox outbreak in 1816 and a measles outbreak in 1826 caused further "restlessness" among Apaches.[41]

At other times peaceful Apaches returned to their homeland because of political instability. Sometimes they did this peaceably, such as in August 1794 at Janos. Within three weeks of El Compá's death, 40 percent of the nearly 500 peaceful Apaches left the presidio. Although one scholar has suggested the Apaches may have been following their custom of abandoning a camp after a kinsman's death, the fact that El Compá's entire family and band remained in residence inside the presidio points against that interpretation. What more likely happened, as one of El Compá's wives, María, personally attested, was that new Ndé leaders vying for influence tried to incite a general rebellion among the Apaches de paz in the midst of the power vacuum.[42]

In addition to internal political instability, peaceful Apaches also left the establecimientos because of political disagreements with independent Apache groups. Nantan Chiganstegé's independent Chokonens killed Spaniards' imposed Chief Isosé of the Chokonens de paz at Bacoachi in February 1788. Four years later Chihene Gila bands launched their own attack in the same month, which prompted nearly 90 percent of the 500 peaceful Apaches to leave the reservation. Although only a minority of Chokonen residents remained at Bacoachi after 1792, the vast majority of reservation-dwelling Tsézhinés and T'iisibaans at Tucson overcame their periodic conflicts with independent Western Apache groups prior to Mexican independence and continued to live near the presidio.[43]

Apaches sometimes deserted their reservations to seek revenge against Spanish troops for launching punitive expeditions into the Apachería. In March 1794, the Mescaleros left San Elizario after Spanish troops had launched several campaigns against independent Mescaleros. When a Spanish patrol tried to punish them for their insubordination, the once peaceful Mescaleros ambushed the Spaniards in the Organ Mountains, killing fourteen soldiers and settlers, including the post commander Manuel Vidal de Lorca. The following July, the Mescaleros at El Paso del Norte followed suit, killing fifty-seven Spanish soldiers and three officials in two days with only twenty-one losses of their own.[44]

In the wake of this Apache victory, Friar Diego Bringas reported, "there is no way to travel without being attacked." Like many critics of the establecimientos program, he believed that former Apaches at peace posed even more of a threat to frontier Spaniards than unpacified ones. Because they possessed "an intimate knowledge of all the provinces" and had learned how to use firearms, Bringas argued, they could "commit greater crimes" when "they return to the wilderness." In short, he considered the support of "those ignorant barbarians" to be a complete waste of royal funds.[45]

In the aftermath of this revolt, the former Mescaleros de paz reunited with their kinsmen and formed an alliance with independent Chihene bands. Such coordinated defense efforts reveal that distinct Apache groups were fully capable of working together and posed a significant obstacle to Spanish troops and their Indian allies, who continued to wage war against Mescaleros until at least 1799.[46] This prolonged conflict indicates that the Spanish–Mescalero peace was unstable long before Mexico's independence. The Mescaleros, it seems, were the first pacified Apache group to permanently abandon a reservation and reassert their cultural independence.

Most frequently, Apaches moved because of shortages of rations. From the reservation system's inception, Apaches had convinced Spanish officers to let them leave the presidios to hunt when rations were in short supply. As a means of distinguishing these Apaches on furlough from their independent kinsmen, post commanders issued Apaches passports to hunt for ten to twenty days in their own territory. As a Franciscan friar, Antonio Barbastro, reported in 1795, passports were "the main stumbling block" to a stable peace with the Apaches because they permitted supposedly loyal Apaches de paz "to roam about and steal under the pretext of going hunting." Thus, Mescaleros at peace in eastern Nueva Vizcaya often raided for horses in Coahuila and Chihenes at peace in western Nueva Vizcaya did the same in Sonora, often in conjunction with their relatives on other reservations or with independent kinsmen. If a Spanish or Mexican patrol confronted them, the Apaches simply showed the soldiers their passports, blamed the raids on independent Ndé groups, and gambled that they would be left alone. Once they had a sizeable number of Spanish horses, peaceful Apaches traded them either to independent Apaches or back to Spanish settlers near their reservation. Most frontier Spaniards were willing to tolerate such small-scale raids and illicit exchanges in the 1790s. The system began to rupture, however, in the 1810s as Spaniards diverted troops and money from the frontier during the Mexican War of Independence. It would deteriorate further when Mexican officials tried to cut costs by eliminating meat rations in 1822 and rations *in absentia* in 1824 and Apaches responded by raising the frequency and intensity of their raids.[47]

THE LEGACY OF PARTIAL PEACE

With all of the expansion and growth across northern Mexico in the late eighteenth and early nineteenth century, it is tempting to call this period the region's "Golden Age," as one borderlands historian has already concluded for Spanish Arizona. Franciscan friar Diego Bringas's optimistic statements confirm this assessment for Sonora. With the "ferocious nation" of Apaches now pacified, Bringas reasoned in the spring of 1796, some of Sonora's nine companies of troops "will be without work" and could be moved northward to the Gila River Valley. He further concluded, based on Sonora's "present happy state," that "no new expenses are necessary" and that "they never will be."[48] Although Commander-in-Chief Pedro de Nava failed to grant Bringas his request and continued to spend royal funds to maintain the Apache peace, the friar's observations remain instructive.

Spanish officers reporting from Nueva Vizcaya echoed Bringas's sentiments in the late 1790s. "At present the wise provisions of a just, active and pious government are bringing" the war with the Apaches "to a close," Lieutenant Colonel Antonio Cordero contended in 1796. Cordero believed Apaches de paz respected the justice of Spanish Apache policy, their power to enforce it, and even frontier Spaniards themselves. Three years later José Cortés, a member of an enlightened group of officials who thought Apaches were capable of becoming rational Spaniards, was even more optimistic. "It has been and continues to be our absurd and foolish belief," he argued, "that [Apaches] are impossible to force into peace and the customs of a rational life, but this is a most potent fallacy. They love peace and hate to lose it."[49]

If Bringas, Cordero, and Cortés had shifted their gaze farther east, however, they likely would have reached a different conclusion. Writing from Texas in 1804, Cadet Ramón de Murillo reported that across the two-hundred-league frontier of northern New Spain "exists the Frontier

Line of heathen Indians whom we have not yet been able to settle, and who wage such a destructive war against us that since the year 1770 there is a third less population than used to exist." He also maintained that troop performance had dropped. "Whereas in 1770 a detachment of 200 soldiers would attack and destroy an enemy force of 500 Indians," Murillo continued, "today the situation is just about the reverse."[50]

How do we reconcile such pessimistic statements with the glowing reports from Sonora and Nueva Vizcaya in these years? Murillo was apparently extending the lack of progress with the Mescaleros and Lipans in the eastern provinces to the whole frontier. As we will see, because of Comanche southward expansion and their ongoing wars with Mescaleros and Lipans, the peace on the southern plains periphery of eastern Nueva Vizcaya and Coahuila was less enduring, and the demographic and economic benefits were less pronounced. Still some expansion took place. In February 1801, for example, a group of Spanish vecinos and Tlaxcaltecans founded the *villa* (chartered municipality with a status ranking between a town and a city) of Nava near the presidio of San Juan Bautista de Rio Grande in Coahuila.[51]

Hispanic economic growth and demographic expansion in these years were real but uneven processes. In addition to taking into account Comanche southward expansion, they also need to be understood in the context of Spain's own monetary and supply problems, which produced some early cracks in the system. Spain's war with France from 1793 to 1795 meant that the Spanish crown diverted money and troops from the Apache frontier. As a result, Spanish officials were left in the unenviable position of reducing rations to peaceful Apaches and asking them to return to their homeland just as the program was stabilizing. Spanish officers and administrators hoped that Apaches would remain at peace, but had little to offer in exchange. Their enforcement of this abrupt policy change compelled the Chihenes to desert Sabinal after May 1795 and may have helped precipitate three Mescalero revolts at El Paso, San Elizario, and Presidio del Norte during 1794 and 1795. These same problems also likely prompted close to 70 percent of resident Chihenes and Chokonens to leave Janos in mid-1796. Although some of them came back, the numbers at Janos never again approached the more than 800 that lived near the presidio in 1795. Instead, Janos averaged around 234 individuals for the next three decades.[52]

Without question, in practice the Apaches de paz program turned out to be far more complicated and volatile than Spanish policy makers envisioned at the outset. These reservations had costs for both sides.

The heightened violence from independent Apaches and Spanish troops between 1786 and 1790 nearly prevented the system from being fully implemented. Even after its implementation, they were expensive to run, they were incubators for disease, and few Apaches ever farmed or even became sedentary Spaniards. From an Ndé perspective, as long as Spaniards failed to distinguish between neutral and hostile Apaches in the Apachería and continued to ship their men and women southward, this was not peace at all. Indeed, the vast majority of Apaches who settled at Spanish reservations did so only to fulfill temporary needs. Demonstrating minimal signs of Hispanicization, Christianization, and incorporation, they instead found ways to creatively adapt to maintain their cultural independence and retain dominion over the full extent of their territory.

This did not mean the system failed, however. After 1790 the number of extraditions declined, and by 1800 the military attacks became more localized and infrequent. This more controlled violence enabled a core group of Apaches and Hispanics, including Nantan Volante's Mescaleros and Spanish troops at Presidio del Norte, to work together to remake frontier colonial society in the southwest after 1790. When Volante's Mescaleros returned to Presidio del Norte with their Comanche captives, the post commander Domingo Diaz nearly destroyed their relationship by callously proposing to invite the Comanches to conduct a revenge raid on the Mescaleros de paz in order to maintain the Spanish–Comanche alliance. But cooler heads prevailed. Commander-in-Chief Nava vetoed Diaz's suggestion and restored twelve Spanish- and Mescalero-held Comanche captives, including Chief Ecueracapa's daughter, to the Comanches. At the same time the Mescaleros remained on their reservation, retaining a Comanche woman and several babies to raise as Apaches.[53] In the decades after the establecimiento system's collapse, a minority of Mexican and American politicians and military officers would continue to employ the diplomatic measures that were the hallmark of this era – including exchanging captives, issuing rations, and even reserving specific tracts of land – as a means of convincing war-weary Apache groups to make peace agreements at the local level.

Notes

1 Viceroy Conde de Revillagigedo to the Conde del Campo de Alange, Mexico, February 8, 1791, AGS, GM, 7020, Exp. 8, Simancas. For a brief summary in English, see Moorhead, *Apache Frontier*, 262–263.
2 Weber, "Bourbons and Bárbaros," 79.

3 For Gálvez's and Nava's enlightened Indian policies, see Moorhead, *Apache Frontier*, 97–99; Weber, *Spanish Frontier*, 228. Pedro de Nava, "Instrucción que han de observar los comandantes de los puestos encargados de tratar con los indios Apaches que actualmente se hallan de paz," Chihuahua, October 14, 1791, paras. 10, 16–18, 27, AGN, PI 66, BL-microfilm. The quotations are from paras. 27, 10, and 16. For an English translation, see Nava, "Instructions," 102–109. On Apache "deportation," see Santiago, *Jar of Severed Hands*; Conrad, "Captive Fates"; Weber, *Bárbaros*, 149–150; Christon I. Archer, "The Deportation of Barbarian Indians from the Internal Provinces of New Spain, 1789–1810," *The Americas* 29 (January 1973): 376–385; Moorhead, "Spanish Deportation of Hostile Apaches," 205–220.
4 Daniel R. Mandell, *King Philip's War: Colonial Expansion, Native Resistance, and the End of Indian Sovereignty* (Baltimore, MD: Johns Hopkins University Press, 2010), 118; Brett Rushforth, *Bonds of Alliance: Indigenous and Atlantic Slaveries in New France* (Chapel Hill: University of North Carolina Press, 2012), 10, 13; R. David Edmunds and Joseph F. Peyser, *The Fox Wars: The Mesquakie Challenge to New France* (Norman: University of Oklahoma Press, 1993), 80; Eve Ball, *Indeh: An Apache Odyssey* (1980; reprint, Norman: University of Oklahoma Press, 1988), 131–139; Troy R. Johnson, *The Occupation of Alcatraz Island: Indian Self-Determination and the Rise of Indian Activism* (Urbana: University of Illinois Press, 1996), 3.
5 Babcock, "Rethinking the Establecimientos," 366, 391–392; Weber, *Bárbaros*, 183, 193–195; Moorhead, *Presidio*, 243–266; Nava, "Instructions," 104–107, paras. 15, 23–24, 26. The quotation is from para. 26.
6 For "Spanish escorts to hunt buffalo" see, e.g., Lt. Col. Manuel Muñoz to Commander-in-Chief Teodoro de Croix, Cuartel de Dolores, June 16, 1781, AGI, Guadalajara, 282, MLMC; Moorhead, *Presidio*, 246–247; Moorhead, *Apache Frontier*, 212–213, 220. For a comparative Jicarilla case in New Mexico, see Benes, "Anza and Concha," 68. For raiding, see, e.g., Commander-in-Chief Jacobo Ugarte to the Marqués de Sonora, Arizpe, August 14, 1787, AGS, GM, 7031, Exp. 9, Simancas. For mescal harvesting, see Auditor of War Pedro Galindo Navarro to Croix, Arizpe, February 23 and April 23, 1780, AGI, Guadalajara, 276, Seville; and Griffen, *Apaches at War and Peace*, 27.
7 Mirafuentes Galván, "Los dos mundos de José Reyes Pozo," 104–105. For the quotation, see Ugarte to Flores, Chihuahua, March 21, 1789, folio 416, AGN, PI, 66, BL-microfilm. On Hispanicization, see William Roseberry, *Anthropologies and Histories: Essays in Culture, History, and Political Economy* (New Brunswick, NJ: Rutgers University Press, 1989), 87, 93–94; Spicer, *Cycles of Conquest*, 570. For examples of scholars overlooking Bacoachi as the first operating establecimiento in 1786, see John, *Storms Brewed*, 655–766; Griffen, "Apache Indians," 88; Cortés, *Views from the Apache Frontier*, 7.
8 Ugalde to Flores, Santa Rosa, April 1, 1789, AGN PI 159, ff. 237–261, Moorhead transcription, MLMC; Moorhead, *Apache Frontier*, 253; Moorhead, *Presidio*, 257–258.

9 Sgt. Josef Tato to Juan Caneva, Bavispe, April 24, 1789, roll 9, microfilm, JHA-UTEP; Cordero to Ugarte, San Diego, September 14, 1789, AGN, PI, 193, f. 251v; Lt. José Manuel Carrasco to Ugarte, Hacienda del Carmen, October 9, 1789, AGN, PI, 193, ff. 278–279, Mexico microfilm.
10 For Gonzalez, see Ugarte to Flores, March 13, 1788, AGN, PI, 128, ff. 363–366, summary and partial translation, MLMC; Ugarte to Flores, Chihuahua, February 28 and March 7, 1789, AGN, PI, 193, ff. 105–107, 162v, Mexico microfilm; Torre Curiel, *Twilight of the Mission Frontier*, 124. For the quotation, see Carrasco to Ugarte, San Buenaventura, May 25, 1789, AGN, PI, 193, f. 162, Mexico microfilm.
11 Ugarte to Gov. Juan Bautista de Anza, Hacienda de San Salvador de Orta, December 2, 1788, AGN, PI, 128, f. 522, Mexico microfilm; [Commissioner] Leonardo Escalante, "Padrón del número de Apaches bajos de paz," Bacoachi, December 1, 1788, AGN, PI, 193, ff. 4–4v, Mexico microfilm; Griffen, "Compás," 26, 30. For Mescalero service as military auxiliaries at Presidio del Norte from 1790–95, see Moorhead, *Presidio*, 259.
12 There is no evidence that any Apache leader who received a house at Janos ever occupied one. For rewards, see Griffen, *Apaches at War and Peace*, 105–106; Griffen, "Compás," 26–29. For comparative cases at Presidio del Norte in 1780, Bacoachi, and Sabinal respectively, see Moorhead, *Presidio*, 248; Moorhead, *Apache Frontier*, 185; Simmons, *Coronado's Land*, 58. For the quotation, see Cordero to Janos Commander, Pueblo del Paso, August 12, 1791, F7, S1, JPR-UTA. See also Nava, "Instructions," 103, para. 4. For similar privileging of T'iisibaan (Pinal) nantan Chilitipagé as "indio General" at Tucson, see Lt. Antonio Narbona to Commander-in-Chief Alejo García Conde, Arizpe, May 26, 1819, facsimile in Brinckerhoff and Faulk, *Lancers for the King*, 116.
13 Salcedo to the Janos commander, Chihuahua, July 21, 1804, F17, S2, JPR-UTA; William B. Griffen, "The Chiricahua Apache Population Resident at the Janos Presidio, 1792 to 1858," *Journal of the Southwest* 33 (Summer 1991): 153–154, 157; Griffen, "Compás," 33, 39; Richard J. Perry, *Western Apache Heritage: People of the Mountain Corridor* (Austin: University of Texas Press, 1991), 168; Ball, *Indeh*, 13n2, 22.
14 For the initial negotiations and treaty, respectively, see Gov. Fernando de la Concha to Flores, Santa Fe, July 6, 1789, fr. 94; Concha to Ugarte, no. 177, July 13, 1790, fr. 289–291, roll 12, microfilm, SANM-HL. For an English translation of the treaty, see Vine Deloria, Jr. and Raymond J. DeMallie, eds., *Documents of Indian Diplomacy: Treaties, Agreements, and Conventions, 1775–1979*, vol. 1 (Norman: University of Oklahoma Press, 1999), 136–137. As the historian David J. Weber has pointed out, these editors have reversed "sender and recipient." See Weber, *Bárbaros*, 342n112. For Jasquenelté's experience at Janos and his wide variety of name equivalents, which include Esquielnoctén and Squielnoctero at Janos and Arrieta and Hischa at El Paso, see Griffen, *Apaches at War and Peace*, 72, 74, 88–90, 105–106, 136n16; Willem J. de Reuse, "Apache Names in Spanish and Early Mexican Documents: What They Can Tell Us about the Early Contact Apache Dialect Situation," in *From the Land of Ever Winter to the American Southwest:*

Athapaskan Migrations, Mobility, and Ethnogenesis, ed. Deni J. Seymour (Salt Lake City: University of Utah Press, 2012), 166. For the quotations, see Concha, "Distribución de los caudales invertidos en la gratificación de las naciones aliados," Santa Fe, December 31, 1790; Concha to the Conde de Revillagigedo, Santa Fe, July 12, 1791, fr. 440–455, 560, roll 12, SANM-HL.

15 Concha, "Distribución de los caudales," Santa Fe, December 31, 1790; Interim Lt. Gov. Francisco Xavier Bernal to Concha, El Paso del Norte, May 30, 1791; Concha to the Conde de Revillagigedo, Santa Fe, July 1 and 12, 1791, fr. 440–455, 540–541, 549–550, 560, roll 12, SANM-HL; Concha to the Conde de Revillagigedo, Santa Fe, April 14 and July 22, 1792, fr. 54 and 114–115, roll 13, SANM-HL; Benes, "Anza and Concha," 72–73; Simmons, *Coronado's Land*, 58–60. For the contrast with officers in western Nueva Vizcaya, see Lt. Col. José María de Tovar to the Commander-in-Chief, no. 101 [copy], Janos, February 21, 1804, F17, S3, JPR-UTA. For the first two quotations, see Fernando de la Concha, "Advice on Governing New Mexico, 1794," *New Mexico Historical Review* 24 (July 1949): 240, para. 8. Worcester's translation, "*short* weekly ration" (my italics), is incorrect.

16 For the respective quotations, see Nava to Casanova, Chihuahua, June 8, 1792, F8, S1, JPR-UTA; Nava, "Instructions," 109, para. 35; Nava to Casanova, San Diego, May 14, 1792, roll 10, microfilm, JHA-UTEP. For a closer look at the long-standing debate over baptizing unacculturated Indians across Spanish America, see Weber, *Bárbaros*, 93, 103. For baptism of *parbulos*, see Domínguez to Nava, Janos, July 1, 1792, roll 10, JHA-UTEP. For the first identification of the trend of "peaceful" Apache headmen at Janos requesting baptism for their children in the 1790s, see Griffen, "Compás," 28.

17 For two Chokonen cases at Bacoachi, see Fray Pedro de Arriquibar to Fray Francisco Antonio Barbastro, Bacoachi, May 20, 1795, in Father Diego Bringas, *Friar Bringas Reports to the King: Methods and Indoctrination on the Frontier of New Spain 1796–97*, ed. Daniel S. and trans. Matson and Bernard L. Fontana (Tucson: University of Arizona Press, 1977), 121. Only 11 percent of the people (15 of 135) whom Janos chaplain Domínguez baptized between 1799 and 1802 were Apaches. See Domínguez, "Baptisms," Janos, April 30, 1799, to June 30, 1802, roll 14, JHA-UTEP. Of twenty-two baptisms performed by Mexican chaplains in the Janos district from 1833 to 1834, only one was an Apache. See Fray Rafael Echeverría and Fray Alejo Bermudes, Casas Grandes baptism book, F35, S3, JPR-UTA. For the anthropologist, see Griffen, *Apaches at War and Peace*, 110.

18 For the quotations, see Father Antonio Rafael Benites, Bacoachi, April 9, 1787, AGI, Guadalajara, 287, MLMC. In May 1785 an epidemic causing deaths from pleurisy or "inflammation of the lungs" struck New Mexico. See Stodder and Martin, "Health and Disease," 66. For "supernatural healing power," see Opler, "Apachean Culture Pattern," 373; Opler, *An Apache Life-Way*, 242–257. For the comparison with the Montagnais, see Kenneth W. Morrison, *The Solidarity of Kin: Ethnohistory, Religious Studies, and the Algonkian-French Religious Encounter* (Albany: State University of New York Press, 2002), 123–126, 143; H. Henrietta Stockel, *On the Bloody Road*

to Jesus: Christianity and the Chiricahua Apaches (Albuquerque: University of New Mexico Press, 2004), 85.
19 For baptism of Apache children," see Nava to Barbastro, Chihuahua, March 28, 1795; Barbastro to Nava, Aconchi, June 29, 1795, both in Bringas, *Friar Bringas Reports to the King*, 121, 128. For the quotation, see Domínguez, "Baptisms," Janos, April 30, 1799, to June 30, 1802, roll 14, JHA-UTEP.
20 For deportation, see Galindo Navarro to Nava, Chihuahua, December 9, 1796; Nava to Galindo Navarro, Chihuahua, December 20, 1796, both in Bringas, *Friar Bringas Reports to the King*, 74–75; Archer, "The Deportation of Barbarian Indians," 377. Quotations are from the second document in Bringas, 75. For an argument that the deportation policy began earlier in 1787, see Moorhead, "Spanish Deportation of Hostile Apaches," 208–209. For "collera" and the return of prisoners, see Barr, *Peace Came in the Form of a Woman*, 169; Nava to the Janos commander, Chihuahua, August 12, 1794, F10, S1, JPR-UTA.
21 The data are based on Spanish archival documents from JPR-UTA and JHA-UTEP; from AGN, PI, 76, BL-microfilm; from AGI, Guadalajara, 289, Seville, courtesy of David Weber; from the Archivo Parroquial de San Felipe El Real de Chihuahua, courtesy of Chantal Cramaussel; and from Moorhead, "Spanish Deportation of Hostile Apaches," 205–220. See also Mary Lu Moore and Delmar L. Beene, trans. and ed., "The Interior Provinces of New Spain: The Report of Hugo O'Conor, January 30, 1776," *Arizona and the West* 13 (Autumn 1971): 265–282; Dunn, "Apache Relations in Texas," 198–274. For similar percentages and a much higher estimate of 2,266 Apaches deported to Mexico City from 1773 to 1809 that omits the fates of captives extradited to Veracruz and Havana, see Santiago, *Jar of Severed Hands*, 201–203. For the finding that 70 percent of indigenous miners in Nueva Vizcaya in the 1680s, who included Apaches, were adult women, see Chantal Cramaussel, "The Forced Transfer of Indians in Nueva Vizcaya and Sinaloa: A Hispanic Method of Colonization," in *Contested Spaces of Early America*, ed. Juliana Barr and Edward Countryman (Philadelphia: University of Pennsylvania Press, 2014), 184–207.
22 For "pieza," see Brooks, *Captives and Cousins*, 374. Frontier Spaniards were likely borrowing from the term "pieza de india" for the perfectly healthy young adult male in the African slave trade. See Philip D. Curtin, *The Atlantic Slave Trade: A Census* (Madison: University of Wisconsin, 1969), 22. On captives' fates and the difference between war captives and slaves, see Catherine M. Cameron, "Introduction: Captives in Prehistory," in *Invisible Citizens: Captives and Their Consequences*, ed. Catherine M. Cameron (Salt Lake City: University of Utah Press, 2008), 2, 5, 20; Orlando Patterson, *Slavery and Social Death* (Cambridge, MA: Harvard University Press, 1982), 106–109; Daniel K. Richter, *The Ordeal of the Longhouse: The Peoples of the Iroquois League in the Era of European Colonization* (Chapel Hill: University of North Carolina Press, 1992), 69–70. On forced and salaried indigenous labor in Spanish America, see Weber, *Bárbaros*, 245–247. For a similar conclusion on Apache miners in late-seventeenth-century Nueva Vizcaya, see Cramaussel, "Forced Transfer," 184–207. For the comparative use of captive indigenous

labor in "obrajes" in New Mexico, see Ned Blackhawk, "Toward an Indigenous Art History of the West: The Segesser Hide Paintings," in *Contested Spaces of Early America*, ed. Juliana Barr and Edward Countryman (Philadelphia: University of Pennsylvania Press, 2014), 292, 294–295, 298; Blackhawk, *Violence over the Land*, 24.

23 For the quotations, see Cordero y Bustamante, "Noticias relativas a la nación apache," 379. For an English translation, see Matson and Schroeder, "Cordero's Description," 350. On "captured kinsmen," see Moorhead, *Apache Frontier*, 274–275. For Tidaya, see Nava, "Extracto y resumen de hostilidades," Chihuahua, April 24, 1793, AGI, Guadalajara, 289, Seville; Nava to Lt. Dionisio Valle, Valle de San Bartolomé, May 22, 1795, F11, S1, JPR-UTA.

24 Moorhead, *Presidio*, 260–261; Griffen, *Apaches at War and Peace*, 268–269, 72–73; Nava, "Estado que manifiesta el número de rancherías Apaches existentes de paz," Chihuahua, May 2, 1793, AGI, Guadalajara, 289, Seville; Dobyns, *Spanish Colonial Tucson*, 105; Benes, "Anza and Concha," 71–72. On Janos's location within Chihene territory and Chihene winter subsistence patterns, see Griffen, *Utmost Good Faith*, 14, 27; O'Conor, *Defenses of Northern New Spain*, 87–88, paras. 215, 220.

25 Asst. Inspector Diego de Borica to the Janos commander, Chihuahua, August 1, 1791, F7, S1, JPR-UTA; José Tapia, "Compañia de Janos: Distribución del primer medio … de tesoreria," Chihuahua, January 17, 1796, roll 10, JHA-UTEP; Capt. Joseph Manuel de Ochoa, "Cuenta seguida a los Apaches de paz," Janos, December 31, 1799, F15, S2, JPR-UTA.

26 Odie B. Faulk, *The Last Years of Spanish Texas, 1778–1821* (The Hague: Mouton, 1964), 29–31, 124; Donald E. Chipman, *Spanish Texas, 1519–1821* (Austin: University of Texas Press, 1992), 277; Navarro García, *Don José de Gálvez*, 513. For more on Antonio Narbona, including his role in an 1804 campaign against the Navajos, see Brian DeLay, "Blood Talk: Violence and Belonging in the Navajo-New Mexico Borderland," in *Contested Spaces of Early America*, ed. Juliana Barr and Edward Countryman (Philadelphia: University of Pennsylvania Press, 2014), 239–240, 247, 392n20; Dobyns, *Spanish Colonial Tucson*, 129.

27 For Tucson and its missions, see Dobyns, *Spanish Colonial Tucson*, 41–42, 105. For the Sonoran frontier, see James E. Officer, *Hispanic Arizona, 1530–1856* (Tucson: University of Arizona Press, 1987), 79–80. For the argument that Apache raiding increased in the 1810s, see Park, "Spanish Indian Policy," 343, and reprinted in Weber, *New Spain's Northern Frontier*, 231. Numerous borderlands scholars, drawing on Park, have inadvertently repeated this error. See, e.g., Brinckerhoff and Faulk, *Lancers for the King*, 92; Moorhead, *Apache Frontier*, 289; Moorhead, *Presidio*, 265. For exceptions, see Radding, *Landscapes of Power and Identity*, 288; Officer, *Hispanic Arizona*, 87, 108, 112; Ray H. Mattison, "Early Spanish and Mexican Settlements in Arizona," *New Mexico Historical Review* 21 (October 1946): 288.

28 Griffen, *Apaches at War and Peace*, 87, 120; Griffen, "Compás," 33. For the Chihene Mogollon peace and rations, see Capt. Laureano de Murga to Capt.

José Ignacio Ronquillo, Namiquipa, July 27, 1816, F22, S1; Capt. Miguel Ortiz to the Janos commander, Carrizal, August 27, 1816, F22, S1; Capt. Alberto Maynez to Bernardo Bonavia, Janos, October 3, 1816, F22, S1; Maynez to the Commander-in-Chief, Janos, October 9, 1816, F22, S1; Maynez, et al. "Ración," August 3, 1818, F23, S3; José Antonio Vizcarra, et al. "Ración," Janos, March 18, 1822, F25, S1; Ronquillo, "Hoja de Servicio," December 31, 1821, F24A, S2, JPR-UTA.

29 For northern New Spain, see Luis Aboites Aguilar, *Norte precario: poblamiento y colonización en México, 1760–1940* (Mexico: Colegio de México, Centro de Estudios Históricos: Centro de Investigaciones y Estudios Superiores en Antropología Social, 1995), 49. For Janos, see Janos censuses from January 1, 1793; December 31, 1799; December 31, 1800 (includes Casas Grandes); [no day, month] 1804; December 31, 1807; December 31, 1812; December 31, 1818; [no day, month], 1819; December 31, 1822, all in JPR-UTA; Janos censuses from December 31, 1798; Janos census from December 31, 1801 (includes Casas Grandes); all on roll 14, JHA-UTEP. For a closer look at the Pre-Columbian site of Casas Grandes (Paquimé), see Carter, *Indian Alliances*, 29, 46–49, 61; Curtis F. Schaafsma and Carroll R. Riley, "The Casas Grandes World: Analysis and Conclusion," in *The Casas Grandes World*, ed. Curtis F. Schaafsma and Carroll R. Riley (Salt Lake City: University of Utah Press, 1999), 246–48; Charles C. Di Peso, *Casas Grandes: A Fallen Trading Center of the Gran Chichimeca*, 3 vols. (Dragoon, AZ: Amerind Foundation, 1974). For Casas Grandes, see Griffen, *Apaches at War and Peace*, 120; Casas Grandes censuses from August 1, 1795; December 31, 1795; December 31, 1798; December 31, 1799; December 31, 1800; December 31, 1812, all in JPR-UTA; Census of Casas Grandes (including Janos presidio), December 31, 1801, roll 14, JHA-UTEP.

30 Frank, *From Settler to Citizen*, 119.

31 For Tucson's post-1810 growth, see McCarty, *Desert Documentary*, 134; Kieran McCarty, ed. and trans., *A Frontier Documentary: Sonora and Tucson, 1821–1848* (Tucson: University of Arizona Press, 1997), 51; Jacoby, *Shadows at Dawn*, 159, 289; Lt. José Romero to Narbona, Tucson, May 21, 1819, facsimile in Brinckerhoff and Faulk, *Lancers for the King*, 116. For the reconciliation with the Tsézhinés, see García Conde to the Count of Venadito, Durango, July 19, 1819, translated in Dobyns, *Spanish Colonial Tucson*, 104. For the 1840s, see Bancroft, *History of Arizona and New Mexico*, 402. For the 1860s, see David Longstreet's testimony in Goodwin, *Western Apache Raiding and Warfare*, 192. See also "Resumen breve y explicatoria de los pueblos del Partido de Arizpe," Boletín de la Sociedad de Geografía y Estadística (BSGE) (México), vol. II, 1861, reprinted in Escudero, *Noticias estadísticas*, 368.

32 On mutual acculturation or transculturation, see Ramón A. Gutiérrez and Elliott Young, "Transnationalizing Borderlands History," *Western Historical Quarterly* 41 (Spring 2010): 36; Lee, "Projecting Power," 7. For two examples among Southern Apaches, see Griffen, *Apaches at War and Peace*, 71.

33 For an example of the first rumor at Namiquipa, see Nava to the Conde de Revillagigedo, Chihuahua, July 29, 1791, f. 358, AGN, PI, 66, BL-microfilm.

For an example of reversing that tactic in 1793, see Rick Hendricks, "Massacre in the Organ Mountains: The Death of Manuel Vidal de Lorca," *Password* 39 (Winter 1994): 172; Hendricks and Timmons, *San Elizario*, 34, 37. For examples at Janos from Juan Diego and others from 1795 to 1817, see Griffen, *Apaches at War and Peace*, 80–81, 91–92; Griffen, "Compás," 32–33.

34 For Chihuahua, see Griffen, "Compás," 27. For Arizpe, see Fray Diego Bringas to the king, Apostolic College of Santa Cruz de Querétaro, 1796–97, translated in Bringas, *Friar Bringas Reports to the King*, paras. 95, 120. For Tucson, see Narbona to Gov. Cordero, Arizpe, March 8, 1819, translated in Dobyns, *Spanish Colonial Tucson*, 103.

35 Griffen, *Apaches at War and Peace*, 103. For the quotation, see Bringas to the king, in Bringas, *Friar Bringas Reports to the King*, 119, para. 92. For a similar discussion of Lipan Apaches and other southern plains Indians using missions as a place of refuge for ethnogenesis, see Anderson, *The Indian Southwest*, 91–92.

36 Garrido y Durán to the king, Madrid, February 8, 1792, AGI, Guadalajara, 390, Seville, para. 65. For further examples of Apache auxiliaries attacking groups outside of their own band, see Manuel de Echeagaray to Juan Bautista de Anza, camp of San Bernadino, November 9, 1788, AGN, PI, 128, MLMC, ff. 522–524; Griffen, *Apaches at War and Peace*, 103–104.

37 For Apache adaptive strategies, see Griffen, *Apaches at War and Peace*, 109; Arriquibar to Barbastro, Bacoachi, May 20, 1795, and Barbastro to Nava, in Bringas, *Friar Bringas Reports to the King*, 122, 126–127. For another translated excerpt of the Arriquibar document, see Dobyns, *Spanish Colonial Tucson*, 44–45. For "gluttonous behavior," see Bringas to the king, in Bringas, *Friar Bringas Reports to the King*, 119, para. 93.

38 For environmentally induced supply shortages, see Capt. Domingo Díaz to Ugarte, March 29, 1787, AGI, Guadalajara, 287, MLMC; Gálvez, *Instructions*, 165, para. 141; Ortelli, *Trama de una guerra conveniente*, 193; Moorhead, *Presidio*, 79, 212. For eating soldiers' horses, see Borica to the Janos commander, Chihuahua, July 23, 1792, F8, S1, JPR-UTA. For a parallel case of this among Apaches and Yavapais at San Carlos reservation in 1876, see Timothy Braatz, *Surviving Conquest: A History of the Yavapai Peoples* (Lincoln: University of Nebraska Press, 2003), 184. For enhancing political status, see Opler, *An Apache Life-Way*, 465. For Ojos Colorados, see Nava to the Janos commander, Chihuahua, November 10, 1796, roll 10, JHA-UTEP.

39 For the first quotation, see Lt. Col. Roque de Medina to the Janos commander, Chihuahua, January 17, 1795, F11, S2, JPR-UTA. For the remaining quotations, see Nava, "Instructions," 106, para. 22. On the Ndé preference for horse meat, see Paul Hagle, "Military Life on New Spain's Northern Frontier" (M.A. thesis, University of Texas at Austin, 1962), 33; Griffen, *Apaches at War and Peace*, 102.

40 Although Barbastro and Arriquibar use the term "Christians," Bringas states, "Apaches continue to suffer from the bad example of the other Indians." See Bringas to the king, in Bringas, *Friar Bringas Reports to the King*, 130, para. 99. For Ndé card decks and games, see Bringas, *Friar Bringas Reports*

to the King, 122. For "fixed," see Mayor José Leon, "The Republic of Tucson," February 1, 1825, in McCarty, *A Frontier Documentary*, 2. For the fandango quotation, see Arriquibar to Barbastro in Bringas, *Friar Bringas Reports to the King*, 122. For "Apacheanization," see Anderson, *The Indian Southwest*, 106. On the spiritual significance of Apache dancing, see Opler, *An Apache Life-Way*, 100–113. For an earlier Spanish take, see Cortés, *Views from the Apache Frontier*, 62–64. On gambling, see Virginia Wayland, Harold Wayland, and Alan Ferg, *Playing Cards of the Apaches: A Study in Cultural Adaptation* (Tucson, AZ: Screenfold Press, 2006), 53; Opler, *An Apache Life-Way*, 299. On polygyny, see Opler, *An Apache Life-Way*, 416–426; Goodwin, *Social Organization*, 352; Haley, *Apaches*, 145.

41 Griffen, "Compás," 32, 36; Griffen, *Utmost Good Faith*, 311; Griffen, *Apaches at War and Peace*, 81, 89.

42 Griffen, "Compás," 30. Although Griffen offers both interpretations, he fails to note the significance of El Compá's band's continued residence at Janos. See Griffen, *Apaches at War and Peace*, 78.

43 For Bacoachi, see Moorhead, *Apache Frontier*, 192–196; Sec. Pedro Garrido y Duran to the king, Madrid, February 8, 1792, AGI, Guadalajara, 390, Seville, Spain, para. 61, courtesy of David Weber. For Tucson, see Dobyns, *Spanish Colonial Tucson*, 45, 101–102; Jacoby, *Shadows at Dawn*, 158–160.

44 For the first Mescalero ambush, see Hendricks, "Massacre in the Organ Mountains," 174. For the second, see Bringas to the King, in Bringas, *Friar Bringas Reports to the King*, 120, para. 94; Navarro García, *Don José de Gálvez*, 493; Elizabeth A. H. John, ed., and John Wheat, trans., "Views from a Desk in Chihuahua: Manuel Merino's Report on Apaches and Neighboring Nations, ca. 1804," *Southwestern Historical Quarterly* 95 no. 2 (October 1991): 163.

45 All quotations are from Bringas to the king, in Bringas, *Friar Bringas Reports to the King*, 119–120, para. 94.

46 Navarro García, *Don José de Gálvez*, 493; Moorhead, *Presidio*, 259.

47 For evidence that inadequate rations were a significant factor in the initial Apache desertions at Bacoachi, see Int. Gov. Pedro Garrido y Duran to Escalante, February 8, 1788, AGN, PI, 234, translated in Dobyns, *Spanish Colonial Tucson*, 100. For the quotations, see Barbastro to Nava in Bringas, *Friar Bringas Reports to the King*, 127. For raiding and trading strategies, see Griffen, *Apaches at War and Peace*, 79; Lance R. Blyth, "The Presidio of Janos: Ethnicity, Society, Masculinity, and Ecology in Far Northern Mexico, 1685–1858" (Ph.D. diss., Northern Arizona University, 2005), 84. For the uneven breakdown of the system after 1810, see Weber, *Bárbaros*, 360n60; Zúñiga, *Rápida ojeada al estado de Sonora*, 22–26. For the ending of meat rations and the 1824 policy change, see Janos ration lists 1822–1827, JPR-UTA; Griffen, *Apaches at War and Peace*, 125, 131; Griffen, *Utmost Good Faith*, 21.

48 For the first quotation, see Brinckerhoff, "Last Years of Spanish Arizona," 14. For the remaining quotations, see Diego Bringas to Pedro de Nava, Chihuahua, March 13, 1796, in Bringas, *Friar Bringas Reports to the King*, 94.

49 Matson and Schroeder, "Cordero's Description," 350; Cortés, *Views from the Apache Frontier*, 66. See also Griffen, *Apaches at War and Peace*, 14; Weber, *Bárbaros*, 195.

50 Jesús F. de la Teja, ed. and John Wheat, trans., "Ramón de Murillo's Plan for the Reform of New Spain's Frontier Defenses," *Southwestern Historical Quarterly* 7 (April 2004): 511.
51 Navarro García, *Don José de Gálvez*, 513. On Comanche expansion and their Spanish-supported wars with eastern Apaches in these years, see Hämäläinen, *Comanche Empire*, 128–130. For "villa," see Kessell, *Spain in the Southwest*, 425.
52 For Sabinal, see Nava to the Governor of New Mexico [Fernando Chacón], Chihuahua, December 31, 1794, fr. 591–592; Nava to [Chacón], Chihuahua, June 26, 1795, fr. 708–71; [Chacón] to Nava, Santa Fe, July 15, 1795, fr. 735–736; Nava to [Chacón], Chihuahua, August 11, 1795, fr. 748–750, roll 13, SANM-BL; Griffen, *Apaches at War and Peace*, 81; Benes, "Anza and Concha," 73; Jack August, "Balance-of-Power Diplomacy in New Mexico: Governor Fernando de la Concha and the Indian Policy of Conciliation," *New Mexico Historical Review* 56 (April 1981): 156. For Janos, see Griffen, *Apaches at War and Peace*, 81–82.
53 Moorhead, *Apache Frontier*, 263.

5

Collapse and Independence

"The wives and families of the troops are in such nakedness that they can't leave their homes or go to mass," Janos commander Alberto Maynez lamented in late January 1818. The garrison had not received any clothing in twenty months. Although Lieutenant Colonel Maynez had managed to issue soldiers a single white shirt five months ago from locally purchased coarse cotton cloth, they were now completely used up and his troops "did not have shoes or hats." Apaches de paz were also affected by the supply problems. Suppliers from the Mexican interior had failed to send the cigars that roughly 400 Apaches and more than 130 soldiers were accustomed to receiving each week at the presidio. As Maynez explained, both groups were clamoring "because of the lack of assistance with the necessary ration, which they can't live without." Although the severity of the cigar shortage seems open to question, the accompanying depletion of ammunition must have posed a serious threat to the security of Apaches and Spaniards at the presidio. Maynez asked for three loads of lead for balls a year ago, and they still had not arrived.[1]

The fact that Janos and other presidios across Mexico's northern frontier were experiencing supply problems in 1818 was completely understandable considering the emerging nation was embroiled in its war for independence from Spain, and it suggests that the reservation system was in trouble during these years. Perhaps because of the resurgence of the presidial system under the Bourbons in the late eighteenth century, historians once assumed that presidios and the Apache reservations did not begin to break down until Mexican independence in 1821. Rather than a radical transformation after independence, Mexican officers' cries of receiving "nothing for seven months" and their garrisons being "reduced to the most deplorable state," which run rampant through documents in the 1820s, seem quite similar to conditions in the 1810s.[2]

I contend that the establecimientos began to decline much earlier than many scholars have asserted. Major transformations in the administration of Apaches transpired in the 1790s, at the precise moment when the Spanish military had achieved more control over Apaches than ever before and long before the Mexican War of Independence and the heightened political and economic instability in Mexico City in 1810. Spaniards, Mexicans, and Apaches all contributed to the breakdown. It began under Spanish rule in 1794 when Mescaleros at peace protested Spanish punitive expeditions against their independent kinsmen in the Apachería by deserting their reservations, reuniting with their people, and forming alliances with independent Ndé groups west of the Rio Grande. It continued in the 1810s, as Spaniards diverted troops and money from the frontier during the Mexican War of Independence and the Comanche alliance fell apart in Texas. Local environmental changes, such as drought and disease, also encouraged Apache desertion, which typically occurred in waves, rather than in a straightforward linear fashion. Mexican officials then made a declining situation worse, when they reduced meat rations in 1822 and eliminated rations *in absentia* in 1824 in an effort to cut costs. The system ultimately fell apart in 1832, rather than in 1831 as specialists previously argued, and, even then, the Mexican military continued to negotiate treaties at the state and local level with Apache groups through the 1840s.

EARLY SIGNS OF DECLINE

Decades before the supply shortages of the 1810s, in the midst of an unprecedented era of peace between Spaniards and Apaches in the 1790s, the reservation system was already beginning to crack. Even though the dominant trends in that decade were growth and expansion, as we have seen, Apaches still created many headaches for Spanish officers by adapting to the establecimientos in unexpected ways. Spaniards, their independent allies, and Apaches also faced a host of political and economic challenges in these years. All three groups experienced crises in leadership, which led to the temporary breakdown and permanent collapse of some reservations. At the same time, the commander-in-chief of the Western Interior Provinces, Pedro de Nava, faced increased pressure from the crown to cut costs. Consequently, he scaled back the reservations in the middle of the decade, which gave Apaches more freedom to move and undermined many of his own policy goals.

One of the earliest crises in leadership Spaniards faced was drunkenness, but not in the way most historians have argued. Although Bernardo de Gálvez advocated that Spanish officers bribe Apaches with liquor at the presidios in his 1786 policy, in reality Spanish officers rarely issued alcohol to Apaches de paz, and, when they did, it was to display affection toward favored chiefs rather than to corrupt them. The favored Chokonen nantan El Compá was the only Apache known to have received alcohol at any presidio and this was on a single occasion as a reward. The only known alcohol-related incident that transpired among peaceful Apaches prior to 1810 occurred at San Elizario in November 1807 when the inebriated Mescalero chief Dientón killed another Apache de paz.[3]

In the Bourbon era, drunkenness of Spanish officers was a more frequent and serious problem than that of Apaches. In November 1791 Nava forced Lieutenant Antonio Denojeant into early retirement as commander of the Ópata company at Bacoachi. From the time Nava first entered office in Chihuahua, he had been hearing rumors that Denojeant "was not fit to treat and manage" the Apaches de paz at that post, who "lived with too much freedom" because of the commander's "lack of resolve and integrity" and his propensity for excessive drinking. These were not mere fabrications. In June the resident Chokonens told Sonoran Governor Enrique de Grimarest that Denojeant's love for "strong drink" was affecting his ability to effectively manage them.[4]

In a subsequent trip to Bacoachi in October, Lieutenant Manuel de Echeagaray learned the Indians were upset that Denojeant did not punish or try to gain the respect of several Chokonens de paz who had allegedly conversed with independent Apaches prior to revolting on September 16. According to Echeagaray, in the four years that Denojeant had commanded the post, the Apaches "ha[d] lived with the same freedom that they would have without making peace," had failed to achieve "any advancement in civilization," and had scorned Spanish conventions and shown Denojeant a lack of respect.[5]

The situation at Bacoachi stood in marked contrast to the neighboring post of Fronteras, where the talented Captain Pedro de Mata Biñolas had managed Apaches so prudently that Spaniards were moving there without fear to search for mineral deposits in the surrounding mountains. As a result, Nava attempted to remove Denojeant to Altar and replace him with the more trustworthy and capable Biñolas, but, in an apparent effort to salvage his honor, Denojeant obtained the viceroy's permission to retire instead. Although Denojeant's abuse of alcohol and poor judgment had created temporary instability at Bacoachi, a competent officer happened to be available to replace him, and the reservation remained intact.[6]

A more serious crisis in leadership occurred when New Mexico Governor Fernando de la Concha retired because of deteriorating health and ceased administering the promising Apache reservation at Sabinal. Concha had already withstood one major political and diplomatic crisis to establish Sabinal in the first place. Both Comanche leaders and Commander-in-Chief Jacobo Ugarte voiced their displeasure with admitting Apaches to peace in New Mexico in 1788. Comanches complained that they would have no enemies to fight if Spaniards granted Apaches peace in the province. Ugarte, fearing the disruption of the Comanche alliance, on the one hand, and a lack of Apache compliance, on the other, forbade New Mexico's governors from making peace with any Apache group. Concha was still able to proceed with his Sabinal experiment, however, because Viceroy Manuel Antonio Flores and Ugarte's successor, Pedro de Nava, supported it.

The collapse of the Sabinal establecimiento is poorly understood. Comanches did not destroy the reservation, nor did it gradually wither away because Spaniards lost interest in fostering it.[7] For nearly a decade after the Spanish-influenced breakup of the Chihene Gila-Diné (Navajo) alliance in October 1786, Navajos, not Comanches, were the major indigenous threat to Chihenes. Navajos' repeated killing of Chihene adults and capturing of small children, including the treacherous assassination of Nantan Napachuli (also known as Tecolote or "Owl") and eight other Chihene men during peace negotiations in the Dinétah (Navajo homeland) in July 1791, did not ruin Sabinal either. Instead, the violence was likely a major reason that so many Chihene families relocated to the Rio Grande community under General Jasquenelté's leadership from 1790 to 1794 in the first place. In the fall of 1793 independent Chihenes successfully avenged Napachuli's assassination and subsequent Navajo attacks on their camps in the San Mateo Mountains by attacking them forty leagues from Laguna Pueblo in the Paraje de Guadalupe and killing General Antonio el Pinto.[8]

Concha's own deteriorating health and changes in Spanish policy, not Comanche- or Navajo-initiated violence, were the major factors precipitating Sabinal's collapse in late 1794. Suffering from a severe eye injury that had plagued him for at least three years and left him permanently disabled, the governor left office in the late fall of 1793 and rode south with the pack train to Chihuahua, where he became a patient at the army hospital. His successor, Fernando de Chacón, opposed Concha's efforts and offered no support to the Sabinal Apaches. Taking advantage of Concha's departure and his own late October policy change in Nueva Vizcaya, Commander-in-Chief Nava ordered Governor Chacón to have the Apaches at Sabinal and any other *indios de paz* in New Mexico settle thirty leagues from Spanish presidios and settlements or remain independent and be subject to Spanish attack.⁹

Political instability among Spanish Indian allies also posed a threat to the reservations. In the late summer or early fall of 1793 the prominent Kotsoteka Comanche chief Ecueracapa died from battle wounds inflicted by southward-pushing Pawnees, who threatened Comanche hegemony on the southern plains. When Chihene Apaches dealt the favored Navajo General Antonio el Pinto the same fate in November, Spanish officials had suddenly lost two of their most faithful Indian allies. Like Spaniards, Comanches and Navajos chose new leaders. But these chiefs, Encaguané and Baquienagage (José) respectively, were much younger and more unseasoned than their predecessors, who had played such key roles in solidifying peace accords with Spaniards in the 1780s. Of the two, the Comanche chief Encaguané was the stronger leader, and it was largely through his efforts that Pedro Vial was able to mediate an agreement between the Comanches and Pawnees in 1795. But the peace was short-lived and the chief did not remain in power long. The Comanches went through a flurry of leaders in these years with western divisions maintaining a more stable political organization than eastern ones.¹⁰

From an Ndé perspective, the Comanche and Navajo political instability must have been encouraging because it meant those groups would have more difficulty organizing offensive campaigns into the Apachería. For Spaniards, however, the breakdown in leadership was disconcerting. Protection from warring Comanches and Navajos was one of the main benefits Spaniards offered Apaches at the establecimientos. If either one of those groups severed their alliance with Spaniards, Apaches at peace would be more likely to return to their homeland. Comanches were the archenemies of Mescalero Apaches. As their past experiences had shown, the rugged sierras stretching from New Mexico to Coahuila offered them more protection against Comanche raids than they would have had remaining sedentary in easily accessible river valleys on the southern plains or near Spanish presidios at their periphery. Diné independence, on the other hand, offered Chihene Gilas an opportunity to reconcile their old alliance with their Athapaskan neighbors and tilt the balance of power back in their favor, which they did in April 1796.¹¹

Of course, consistent strong leadership was also a serious concern within the system of Apache reservations. Immediately following the deaths of Ecueracapa and Antonio, in July 1794, the influential Chokonen nantan El Compá died of natural causes at Janos. In contrast to the Comanche and Navajo cases, there is no evidence that any Ndé leader succeeded El Compá as principal chief at Janos. During their peace talks in Chihuahua in January 1791, Chihene Mimbres leaders from Janos specifically told Nueva Vizcaya's commander-in-chief, Antonio Cordero, that they did not like having a principal chief because they were used to having each leader live with his family and relatives. Janos commanders subsequently tried to confer the title of principal chief on the Chokonen El Guero in 1795 and the Chihene Mimbres Juan Diego Compá in 1803. The available evidence suggests that in each case the officer never followed through with his plan because he feared it would spark jealousy among the other headmen.[12] From an Ndé perspective, Spaniards' reluctance to appoint a principal chief was a sign of progress on their part and reflected a keener understanding of Apache culture. But in terms of following through with the primary goals of Spanish policy – fostering acculturation and maintaining control over Apaches de paz – it was a step backward. Rather than investing authority in a single leader, Spanish officers had to contend with the decentralized political structure of Apache bands.

The continued well-being of the reservation system not only depended on strong leadership from Spaniards, their Indian allies, and Apaches at peace; it also demanded adequate funds to deliver a consistent supply of rations and gifts, a willingness among Spanish officers to avoid dispensing them corruptly, and a willingness among Apaches to limit raids. In the 1790s, in response to budget restrictions and raids by Apaches de paz, Pedro de Nava implemented three major policy changes that damaged Spanish–Apache relations.

First, Nava attempted to ban Apache leaders from traveling to Chihuahua. In July 1791 Pedro de Nava issued a "confidential order" requesting that post commanders stop sending so many Apaches to Chihuahua because of the excessively high costs. In Nava's mind, the only Apaches who should be coming to see him were chiefs with specific complaints about how Spaniards were treating them and their people or to address a serious issue, and as few other Apaches as possible should accompany him. Although the cost cutting made sense from a Spanish administrative standpoint, Nava's behavior must have seemed off-putting to the Ndé, who understood their peace agreement with Spaniards to be built on a foundation of reciprocity. As anthropologist Marcel Mauss has argued in a classic essay, "To refuse to give, to fail to invite just as to refuse to accept, is tantamount to declaring war; it is to reject the bond of alliance and communality." In addition, Commander-in-Chief Nava was a less visible presence on the frontier than his predecessor, Jacobo Ugarte. With his headquarters in Chihuahua rather than Arizpe, he was more remote, and he paid far fewer visits to the presidios than Ugarte. On a rare visit to the frontier of Eastern Nueva Vizcaya in April 1795, Nava did not visit a single presidio harboring Apaches.[13]

The second and most significant change Nava made to the system of establecimientos in the 1790s was implementing a policy of removal. In December 1794 Nava revoked Article 18 of his 1791 Instructions, which required Apaches at peace to settle near the presidios on "assigned land," and instead required them to live thirty leagues from the presidios. Nava did this for two main reasons. First, he wanted to cut costs and lessen the pressure to admit so many Apaches to peace. Inflation was a major problem that affected presidio commanders across New Spain's northern frontier. In the fall of 1792, the price of sugar in northern New Spain quadrupled as a result of conditions in Europe. In addition, at the very same time that Spanish expenditures on Apaches peaked, the crown restricted Nava's Apache funds and reallocated them to help finance Spain's draining war with the French Republic from 1793 to 1795. In Nava's own words, the second and more significant reason for removing Apaches from the presidios was that Apaches "were not content" and "expressed disgust" in living peacefully and receiving Spanish support at the presidios. "Up until now," Nava wrote, "neither the young men nor their families are inclined to farm" nor to partake in any other productive industry.[14]

Three years after Nava issued his detailed regulations solidifying administrative policy within the program, some of the Apaches at peace at Fronteras and other posts were still leaving their camps to engage in clandestine raiding south of the presidio line. According to Nava, if Spanish officers discovered and punished them, it was impossible to manage the peace. By requiring Apaches to reside in their own barren lands thirty leagues away from the presidios and permitting them only to venture to the presidios once a week to receive rations, Nava reasoned, Apaches would be less tempted to raid because it would be easier for soldiers to detect their movements southward. In some ways, Nava's logic is hard to fathom. Stock raiding by Apaches at peace was nothing new, and, in the years prior, El Compá and other influential peaceful Apache leaders and auxiliaries had been doing a good job of limiting ties between independent Apaches and those at peace and policing their people and punishing them for transgressions.¹⁵ By definition, permitting Apaches to live farther from the presidios meant that Spaniards would have had more difficulty monitoring their movements and controlling their behavior.

By this time, however, Nava was convinced "that the Apaches will never be our true friends because they know their strength and the weakness of our civilians." His shift in attitude was likely prompted by the recent Mescalero revolts at San Elizario in March and at El Paso in July and the rapid escalation of violence that ensued. In that four-month span alone, renegade Mescaleros and their independent kinsmen had killed at least seventy-four Spanish pursuers, including the San Elizario post commander.¹⁶

Nava's policy change was significant because it transformed at least some presidios from Indian agencies for administering reservation-dwelling Apaches back into trading posts. With his hands tied by lack of funds from Madrid on the one hand and a burgeoning Apache population adept at running up costs on the other, Nava scaled back his ambitious plans, presumably to fall more in line with Bernardo de Gálvez's more modest 1786 policy. Following Lieutenant Colonel Antonio Cordero's recommendations, Spaniards requested that Mescaleros at San Elizario and Presidio del Norte now inhabit the mountains on the north side of the Rio Grande closest to their frontier, rather than those nearest the presidio line.¹⁷ Any Apaches living inside of the thirty-league limit would be treated as enemies, except for those Indians who came to the presidios to make their "exchanges," which could not include stolen livestock. To avoid having trading parties double as raiding parties, Nava further stipulated that only those groups numbering four Indians or fewer be permitted to trade. In this way, he hoped, only the most faithful Apaches would receive rations at the posts. Nava claimed that rather than making lots of loyal Apaches leave, he instead intended for the policy change to keep the least faithful or suspicious ones away. In short, it was a way to punish those Apaches at peace who continued to raid by denying them resources.¹⁸

In practice, Nava's policy influenced Apaches de paz to revert from a semisedentary mode of subsistence to a seminomadic one on at least four reservations in Nueva Vizcaya. Nearly seven weeks after Nava's order of October 10, 1794, only "a small number" of Apaches de paz "of confirmed loyalty and very subordinate" remained at the posts as scouts and auxiliaries. Nava specifically ordered Cordero not to admit any new groups to peace, and he wanted to keep those bands that had opted to return to their homeland from coming back to disrupt those who remained. The only exception to this was that Nava granted post commanders permission to assist Apaches however they could whenever the Indians "suffer scarcity because of poor harvests." On November 26 Nava authorized Cordero to distribute copies of his orders from October 10 and 28 to the commanders of El Norte, San Elizario, Carrizal, and Janos. He advised that commanders permit neither independent Apaches nor former Apaches de paz living outside the thirty-league limit to settle at those posts in the future.[19]

When Apaches tested Nava's new policy by seeking peace, the commander-in-chief initially held firm. In late December 1794 the well-known peaceful Chokonen leader Nac-coge, whom Spaniards called El Guero or "the light-haired one," sought permission for his relative Tadiyá's band to live at Janos. Nava permitted them to make peace but insisted that they remain thirty leagues away. As of December 22, Nava and Cordero were still in the process of resettling the Apaches de paz and, ironically, providing them with Spanish horses and military escorts to move away from the reservations to the sierras of the Apachería. Nava permitted the Apaches to move back to the Sierra del Corral de Quinteros in today's Chihuahua and the Alamo Hueco, Hacha (Hatchet), and Florida ranges of modern southwestern New Mexico, but he banned them from settling in the more proximate Sierras de Corral de Piedra, Capulín, Escondida, and Malpais. He also allowed them to farm on the western slopes of the Sierra del Corral de Quinteros but banned them from doing so around the Laguna de Guzman, Janos, and San Buenaventura.[20]

At first, Nava's policy of Apache removal did not radically alter the status quo at Janos. By April 1795, only Ojos Colorados's and Manta Negra the Elder's Chihene Mimbres bands had moved from the outskirts of Janos back to the Apachería. Since these two leaders were notorious for frequently moving between posts and raiding while at peace, in many ways their removal was a sign of improvement rather than decline. Nava was worried that they would simply keep raiding, however, by targeting the vulnerable frontier communities between the Rio Grande and the presidios. Whatever the case, by the summer of 1796 conditions had drastically changed at Janos, for Apache numbers had dropped by 70 percent.[21]

Nava's policy change, in combination with newly appointed Governor Fernando Chacón's profound mistrust of Apaches, also seriously affected the Chihenes at Sabinal. Although scholars have suggested that Apaches never returned to Sabinal after December 1794, that is not the case.²² In May 1795 sixteen Apache families remained at peace near the pueblo, and throughout the spring Chacón, following Commander-in-Chief Nava's orders much more closely than Concha usually did, repeatedly rebuffed Apache emissaries requesting to return there. When an Apache woman carrying a cross requested peace at Sabinal in late July and complained of Spanish attacks on her people, who had done nothing wrong, Sandia Pueblo auxiliaries seized her and tried to bring her to Santa Fe. After she escaped near the Sandía Mountains, the auxiliaries hunted her down, killed her, and presented her severed ears to Governor Chacón. Meanwhile, former Apaches de paz from Sabinal, most likely in concert with their independent kinsmen, responded to the Spanish policy of removal and escalation of violence toward them by defiantly camping inside Nava's thirty-league limit and boldly striking settlements in the Laguna, Albuquerque, and Tomé districts of New Mexico.²³

On the heels of his order to remove Apaches at peace from the presidios, Nava implemented a third policy change. In January 1795 he made a major effort to scale back rations and gifts to Apaches at Janos. Again, although problems in Spain's imperial economy undoubtedly influenced his decision, he was responding principally to changing conditions on the frontier, namely the rising annual expenses for Apaches at Janos. According to Nava there were two reasons for this. First, as we have seen, Apaches at Janos were not attempting to supplement their subsistence by farming, as Article 18 of his 1791 policy stipulated. Second, and more importantly in Nava's view, officers at Janos were dispensing rations far too liberally, especially cigars and *piloncillo* (conical cakes of brown sugar), which Nava did not think Apaches truly needed to survive. In response, Nava ordered Janos acting commander Dionisio Valle to issue no more than two cases of cigars to each Apache head of family and stipulated that they only dispense piloncillo to the most trusted chiefs. Furthermore, because of the increased Apache expenses at Janos in 1794, Nava advised Lieutenant Valle to only give Apaches those items specifically mentioned in his 1791 Instructions and his subsequent resolutions. He specifically forbade officers from issuing Apaches "money, *adargas* [leather shields], deer skins, sheep, and other gifts," and he asked that Spaniards stop abandoning their horses and mules for the Apaches to slaughter and consume.²⁴

This last request was not new and indicated a wider problem within the program. Two years earlier, Nava had ordered post commanders to stop issuing Apaches horses as rations because it was reducing the effectiveness of Spanish operations against the Indians. The only exceptions to this were horses that were lame, maimed, or too old for service. Otherwise meat rations should be issued. If cattle were lacking, then the companies should purchase them from other presidios, purchase them from their outskirts, or receive them on loan and then pay them back with crown-issued cattle from Chihuahua once it arrived.[25]

In spite of Nava's repeated directives, however, Apache expenses at Janos continued to rise dramatically in 1795. The following January Nava was amazed to find out that the Janos garrison spent 2,000 pesos more on Apaches in 1795 than it had in 1794. In fact, in the first six months of 1795 alone, Janos spent 1,000 pesos more supporting Apaches than the crown spent on all of the Indians at peace in New Mexico combined for the entire year. Although Bernardo de Gálvez had warned that costs of gifts would rise the first few years after any Indian group made peace, Nava believed that it should not still be happening at this stage and that Apaches were simply taking advantage of Spanish hospitality. He noted that officers were continuing to issue Apaches an inordinate number of "superfluous and excessive items," including "muskets, deerskins, packs of cards, calves, sheep, horses, mules, saddle blankets, bridles, musket cases, hats, silk ribbons, [and] flannel cloth."[26]

This time Nava responded with a laundry list of ways for Janos officers to scale back rations and gifts to Apaches. He required them to record every Apache's name on the weekly ration lists, economize the meat rations so that the largest head of cattle would feed more people, and stop issuing Apaches supplies and provisions when they left to hunt or to visit their relatives at other posts. In short, Apaches should only receive rations from a post when they were actually living near it, and, as Nava had stipulated in his order of October 8, 1793, when Apaches visited a presidio with passports, they should only receive corn and some cigars. Finally, and most significantly, Nava resolved that Janos officers distribute rations every week and that they only distribute them from inside the presidio.[27]

Nava also held specific officers responsible for negligence. He ordered Lieutenant José María de la Riva "not to give the Indians anything except their ration" and fined him 250 pesos for his excessive gift giving. The commander-in-chief was also displeased with acting commander Dionisio Valle's "carelessness, condescension, and lack of activity" but did not fine him in hope that he would finally reduce the Apache expenses in the coming year. Nava expected Valle to cut Janos's expenses by a third in the first six months of 1796 and to ensure this happened without angering the Apaches at peace.[28]

That spring Valle made a concerted effort to carry out Nava's requests. He had been giving the Apaches ten steers per week. But, in response to the commander-in-chief's continuous pressure, he began issuing them fourteen to fifteen animals every two weeks instead. That meant he saved ten to twelve head of cattle per month. Nava, however, remained displeased and wanted him to bring the costs down even further in the next two months. Valle, for his part, remained equally upset with Nava's policy changes. Although he agreed that he administered an excessive number of Apaches during the previous year, he disliked Nava's resolutions to the problem. Apaches would be disgusted with such diminished rations, Valle argued, and, as a result of Spaniards' lack of support and their greater distance from the presidios, they would increase their raids.[29]

In the past, some scholars have been so mesmerized by Janos's careful record keeping that they have failed to see the extent of corruption at the post. While it is true that Janos officers kept diligent and copious records, the more important point is what those records reveal, namely that their officers were "giving away the store" to the Apaches. As Nava himself noted, no other post spent as many royal funds on Apaches as Janos or dispensed rations and gifts to them in such a disorderly fashion.[30] This situation has important implications for any scholar interested in patterns of colonial incorporation and Indian adaptation. While it seems fair to say that Apaches de paz had become partially "dependent" on the Spanish military for their daily survival, Spanish officials were completely unhappy with the status quo and did not believe that officers at Janos were moving any closer to meaningfully incorporating Apaches into Spanish society.

Major cracks in the system thus appeared prior to 1800. A decline in strong leadership among Spaniards, their Comanche and Navajo allies, and Apaches reduced Spanish control over other Indian groups, including Apaches. The sharpest decline occurred in eastern Nueva Vizcaya, as Mescaleros deserted their reservations in 1794 and returned to their homeland. In response to that and Spain's war with France, Pedro de Nava decided to turn Apaches away from Chihuahua, remove them from the presidios, and reduce their rations. His decision damaged the system by confusing and angering the most loyal Apaches at peace and clearly hastened Sabinal's collapse. Finally, by driving up costs to such exorbitant levels, presidial officers and Apaches put a major financial strain on the overextended Spanish crown. As the crown continued to divert money and resources away from the frontier during the first two decades of the 1800s, the reservations would face further challenges.

THE DECLINE IN PRESIDIO SUPPLY

Spain's series of costly foreign wars from 1793 to 1808 and from 1810 to 1821 caused a shortage of consumer goods in New Spain that affected frontier Spaniards and Apaches alike. The war against France from 1793 to 1795 was followed by two disastrous wars against Great Britain from 1796 to 1802 and from 1804 to 1808. After experiencing growth from 1770 to 1795, New Spain's economy subsequently stagnated and inflation set in until 1810. Finally, during the Mexican War of Independence from 1810 to 1821, the Spanish military began neglecting the Apaches at peace, as it diverted much of its men, money, and resources away from the frontier to fight insurgent *mexicanos* in the interior. As civil war disrupted trade and transportation networks from Mexico City to Santa Fe during the 1810s, peaceful Apaches and presidial soldiers received fewer rations and supplies and increasingly turned to contraband trade to obtain the products they needed. Whenever droughts and floods struck, they wreaked further havoc on regional food suppliers.[31]

Shortly after assuming office in November 1802, Commander-in-Chief Nemesio Salcedo made a creative and generous attempt to help offset the gun shortage by using his own funds to construct an arms factory in Chihuahua. At the end of 1802, the royal treasuries had only 200 muskets and 180 pistols on hand to supply New Spain's 3,150 presidial troops and their thousands of Indian allies. But the supply deficits were too great to overcome. The factory produced up to fifty muskets per month, which, Salcedo argued, benefited soldiers more than having no weapons at all. Each weapon, however, cost more than twice as much to produce as those imported from Spain, and they were probably not as well constructed. If Comanches "expressed disgust over the difference in quality" in the regionally produced trade goods they received in San Antonio in the first decade of the 1800s, Spanish soldiers and Apache auxiliaries probably did as well.[32]

In response to regional supply shortages, Apaches and *norteño* settlers had engaged in contraband trade since at least the early nineteenth century. In late July 1804 Commander-in-Chief Nemesio Salcedo learned that "some warring Indians" had acquired "gunpowder, cigars, and broad knives" and suspected that they came from either Apaches at peace or vecinos living near the presidios. In an effort to crack down on these illicit exchanges, Salcedo ordered post commanders to make sure that troops and settlers do not sell or exchange gunpowder or broad knives with Apaches de paz. He also banned their sale in stores and houses and asked that officers only issue gunpowder to troops when they actually needed it, rather than giving it to them as a reward.³³

Just as Pedro de Nava had in the 1790s, Spanish officials suspected that Janos officers were not always giving Apaches all of the rations and gifts they recorded. Although it is very difficult to prove, some post commanders may have charged for items that they never issued the Apaches. Janos commander José María de Tovar alleged this was the case with his predecessor, Captain José Ochoa, in 1803. But when Tovar went over a bill with several Apaches de paz they claimed that they received every item on the list. Six years later Salcedo complained of unaccounted-for discrepancies in numbers of horses and mules in Janos' monthly reports, which also suggests corruption.³⁴

As of 1810, New Spain's frontier economy was in trouble but still solvent. Commander-in-Chief Salcedo reported that the royal treasury had to rely on "the contributions of a million pesos in payments and loans," to cover the expenses of military hospitals, missions, and the Apaches at peace. Sonora and Nueva Vizcaya's mining productivity and burgeoning population, however, ensured that "the total value of the products of the royal treasury exceed the enunciated expenses."³⁵

By 1813, the escalation of the Mexican War of Independence put the royal treasury in deeper trouble. With Spanish imports already in short supply because of the wars against France and England, the ensuing civil war simply made things worse. Without imported goods to tax, Spanish officials had no money and frontier settlers turned to contraband trade to obtain the products they wanted.³⁶

Whatever the precise level of contraband trade on the Spanish frontier in the first decade of the nineteenth century, then, it clearly increased during the chaotic decade of the 1810s. In July 1812, in a direct violation of Salcedo's 1804 order, one of the inhabitants of the Santa Rita del Cobre mining settlement sold gunpowder to a peaceful Apache named Insacé from San Elizario.³⁷ In May 1816 Commander-in-Chief of the Western Interior Provinces Bernardo de Bonavía lamented the excessive contraband tobacco trade across Nueva Vizcaya and took specific measures to try to reduce it at the establecimientos. Bonavía held presidial officers, especially the commanders and paymasters, responsible for the problem. He accused them of ordering more tobacco than they really needed. To resolve the issue he wanted officers to dispense cigars as part of troops' weekly rations rather than giving them out separately and charging the bill to soldiers' personal accounts.³⁸

One of the biggest problems presidial commanders faced in the 1810s was a regional currency shortage. Some resourceful Spanish officers responded to the crisis by using cigars as a substitute for coins or paper money. This practice may shed even more light on why Janos commander Alberto Maynez so desperately wanted more cigars sent to Janos in the fall and winter of 1818. In late November 1817 three priests complained that Maynez had nothing to pay them with because "the few cigars that exist he keeps to sustain the peaceful [Apaches'] rations." Maynez corroborated the priests' contention the following day, noting "their need is equal to mine."[39]

The cigar and currency shortage were emblematic of the overall shortage of food and supplies presidial garrisons experienced in these years. In the summer of 1817, as a result of the "total scarcity ... of provisions to sustain the troops and families of this company and the Indians at peace," Janos commander Maynez suggested that the fifteen troops garrisoned at San Buenaventura be supplied from Chihuahua rather than from Janos.[40]

Political and economic instability in interior Mexico were not the sole causes of the supply shortages. Environmental changes on the frontier, such as floods and droughts, damaged crops and reduced the supply of rations for presidial troops and Apaches at peace. Flooding in June 1816, for example, ruined corn crops in northwestern Nueva Vizcaya and diminished the available supply of corn for feeding troops and Apaches at peace. One hard-working vecino in the San Buenaventura Valley, Gregorio de la Peña, could only supply the Janos company with 50 fanegas of wheat and no corn, instead of his customary 150 fanegas, because his fields and unthreshed grain piles were so damaged from the rains. "Until now," he wrote, "I have not sown one seed" of corn.[41] Although Janos commander José Ronquillo eventually acquired the crops the garrison needed from other farmers in the valley, de la Peña's experience still demonstrates that farming was a risky enterprise in the borderlands and that a presidio's annual food supply was never guaranteed.

Droughts also caused supply shortages and compounded the economic problems Spaniards already faced. The year 1817, for instance, was an especially dry year. Because of the scant rainfall, the farmers at Janos "raised very little corn" and the company tried to purchase most of it from Casas Grandes and the San Buenaventura Valley. But because of the lack of money in circulation on the frontier, the Janos garrison had no money to pay these suppliers up front. So the farmers in those areas preferred to sell their crops in the urban center of Chihuahua instead, where they could get compensated immediately.⁴² The survival of the troops at Janos and other posts thus depended on the timely receipt of royal funds to pay farmers for food.

Starvation was a problem *all* people faced on the frontier, not simply Apaches and other Native groups. In fact, at Janos at least one Apache helped supply the company with food. In 1814, the Chihene headman Chirimi, who resided at San Buenaventura and Janos for more than a decade, sold "some fanegas of corn for the subsistence of the troops" for 35 pesos, and, four years later, he still had not received fair payment from the Janos commander. In this case, then, Janos officers were not exaggerating their plight to cover up corruption. They truly did lack money and resources. As a result, in the fall of 1818 the Janos commander ceased issuing Apaches cigar rations and temporarily stopped issuing them salt and beef rations, which meant they received only corn. This was a major change from the early years at Janos when ordinary Apaches routinely received corn, beans, cigars, salt, soap, and piloncillo and chiefs were issued steers, sheep, mules, or horses and occasionally even sugar, flour, chocolate, and suits of clothes.⁴³

Janos experienced another shortage of corn rations in late December 1821. Acting commander José de Medina reported that the vecinos at the post "have not taken the step of supplying this company with the corn that it needs for sustaining the troops and the Apaches at peace of this establecimiento." Medina tried to convince them that he would pay for half of the cost at the current price of two pesos per fanega to no avail and lamented the extreme scarcity of grain at the post.⁴⁴

The total value of Apache rations issued at Janos actually increased in 1822 to their highest known level in the Mexican period. Part of the reason for this may have been because Apaches from Carrizal were visiting and that Chihenes from the Mogollon range, whom Spaniards called Mogolloneros, came for the first time. In any event, the numbers are misleading and conceal a sharp drop in supplies over the second half of the year. Apaches received 87 percent of their rations from January 1 to June 14. The Janos commander distributed no cigar rations for the entire year, and issued only eleven more rations totaling a mere 393 pesos from June 14 through December. Other signs of supply shortages in the latter half of the year include issuing Apaches a mere eighteen pesos in hard currency on September 16, giving them only corn in certain weeks, and restricting meat rations to the most-favored chiefs.⁴⁵

By 1823 the Janos garrison had an enormous shortage of manpower, money, and supplies. In March it was reduced to a mere 111 men from

TABLE 5.1 *Janos Presidio Average Garrison Strength, 1791–1834 (Selected Years)*

Year	Total # of men	% of Full Strength*
1791	142 (8)	99
1792	142 (1)	99
1793	139 (12)	97
1794	143 (8)	99
1795	144 (5)	100
1796	144 (2)	100
1797	144 (3)	100
1798	141 (10)	98
1799	143 (7)	99
1800	143 (1)	99
1801	142 (5)	99
1804	139 (2)	97
1807	143 (12)	99
1812	138 (7)	96
1813	140 (1)	97
1814	128 (2)	89
1815	116 (6)	81
1817	133 (12)	92
1818	135 (12)	94
1819	133 (4)	92
1820	132 (2)	92
1821	118 (1)	82
1823	111 (7)	77
1824	55 (3)	38
1825	55 (9)	38
1826	90 (8)	63
1827	93 (3)	65
1828	87 (1)	60
1829	83 (6)	58
1832	84 (4)	58
1834	58 (3)	40

*Full strength=144 men: 116 troops, 28 officers
( ) = number of monthly reports per year
Source: Monthly inspection reports of the Janos garrison from 1791–1834: "Extracto de la revista," "Estado de la revista," and "Estado de fuerza," JPR, JHA, and JA.

144 at full strength (see Table 5.1). With less than 25 percent of the required number of horses and mules, only 26 saddles, a mere 72 muskets, and a pittance of uniforms that were all "in awful shape," the men were in no position to defend their own post, let alone launch any

military offensives into the Apachería. To make matters worse, the company had been without a commander since Colonel Gaspar de Ochoa left the previous June. Although the garrison could report a positive balance of close to 2,000 pesos for the previous year, it had no money in savings because of the large sum the Hacienda Pública (public treasury) owed them, and the Bank of Chihuahua failed to deposit the necessary funds "because of the circumstances of the current era."[46]

Given that the garrison itself was so weakened and impoverished, it is hardly surprising that Janos officers offered Apaches a smaller variety of rations in ensuing years. In the winter months, when Apaches most needed food, they received no rations at all. Officials administered the first ration on March 22. Only 169 Apaches came to receive them. Many of the most well-known leaders, including Juan Diego Compá, failed to accompany their people. Those who did show up received no beef, cigars, or salt. Some were issued horses and others merely corn. In 1830, and probably for several years before this, Janos officers issued Apaches only corn.[47]

A decline in Apache rations at Janos presidio is thus clearly evident between the 1790s and the 1820s. After receiving a little more than 13,000 pesos worth of rations in 1796, Apaches only obtained rations valuing approximately 4,000 pesos in 1801 and 1804. By the 1810s, Spanish annual ration expenditures at the post dropped even further, averaging only slightly under 2,000 pesos between 1816 and 1820. Things did not immediately fall apart at Janos after Mexican independence, however. Mexican officers maintained this same average through 1825. Only after that, from 1826 to 1832, did ration expenditures finally hit an all-time low, averaging less than 500 pesos annually (see Table 5.2).[48]

Not surprisingly, the number of peaceful Apaches camped near Janos directly correlated with the available supply of rations. When rations were at their known height in 1796, 738 Apaches resided at the post. As rations dropped to a third of that level, from 1800 to 1803, an average of 269 Apaches camped there. In the 1810s, as rations continued to plummet, Apache numbers at Janos further dropped to an average of 201. Apache numbers then rose to an average of 261 from 1821 to 1825 before falling to their lowest average of less than 90 from 1826 to 1831.[49]

APACHE AND COMANCHE RAIDING

Despite the monetary and supply problems plaguing the establecimientos before and after Mexican independence, the system remained intact. In December 1821, 1,423 Apaches resided near six presidios in Nueva

TABLE 5.2 *Annual Expenditures for the* Apaches de paz *at Janos Presidio, 1791–1843 (Selected years)*

Date	Amount*	Source
1791	9,493	1
1796	13,011	2
1799	3,244	3
1800	2,222***	4
1801	3,993	5
1802	4,704	6
1803	6,109	7
1804	4,647	8
1805	1,997**	9
1806	2,761**	10
1808	2,105***	11
1815	1,356**	12
1816	1,132	13
1817	2,446	14
1818	2,499	14, 15
1819	1,619	15
1820	2,244	15
1821	2,844	15
1822	3,107	15
1823	1,437	15
1824	487	15
1825	2,024	15
1826	331	15
1827	571	15
1828	661	15
1829	547	15
1830	325	15
1832	527	16
1843	4,894**	17

*rounded to the nearest peso.
**total for first six months of year.
***total for last six months of year.

[1] Total is through August 21 only. Capt. Manuel de Casanova and Lt. José María de la Riva, "Cuenta general de cargo, y data formada ... hasta fin de Junio de 1791," Janos, August 23, 1791; Casanova and Riva, "Razón de lo subministrado ... desde 1.0 de Julio de 91 hasta 21 de Agosto," Janos, August 23, 1791, F7, S2, JPR-UTA.
[2] Sgt. José Tapia, "Compañia de Janos: Distribución del primer medio situado ... corresponde al presente año de 1796," Chihuahua, January 17, 1796; Tapia, "Compañia de Janos: distribución del medio situado del 2.0 semestre de este año [1796]," Chihuahua, July 11, 1796, Roll 10, JHA-UTEP.
[3] Capt. José Manuel de Ochoa, "Cuenta general que manifiesta los gastos que se han originado en los apaches establecidos de paz en este presidio en los seis primeros meses del corriente año," Janos, June 13, 1799; Ochoa, "Cuenta seguida a los Apaches de paz en los 6

últimos meses del corriente año," Joseph Manuel de Ochoa, Janos, December 31, 1799, F15, S2, JPR-UTA.

[4]Total is for last six months of 1800 only. Lt. Dionisio Valle and Ensign Francis Quintanilla, "Cuenta seguida a los Apaches establecidos de paz en el real presidio de Janos en los seis últimos meses de dicho año," Janos, December 31, 1800, Roll 14, JHA-UTEP.

[5]Lt. Mariano Varela and Ensign Ignacio Sotelo, "Cuenta general de entrega que ha de la habilitación de esta compañía ... de los caudales que manejó el primer semestre de ... 1801," Janos, September 2, 1801, F16, S1; "Cuenta general de entrega que hace de la habilitación de compañía de Janos ... de los caudales que manejó el segundo semestre del presente año," Janos, December 31, 1801, F18, S1, JPR-UTA.

[6]Quintanilla, "Cuenta seguida a los Apaches de paz establecidos en el real presidio de Janos [Jan. 1-June 30]," Janos, June 30, 1802; Quintanilla, "Cuenta seguida a los Apaches de paz establecidos en el real presidio de Janos [July 1–December 31]," Janos, December 31, 1802, Roll 14, JHA-UTEP.

[7]Capt. Joseph Manuel Ochoa and Sotelo, "Cuenta seguida a los Apaches establecidos en este real presidio de Janos de las suministraciones hechas desde 1.o de enero del corriente año hasta la fecha," Janos, June 30, 1803, Roll 15, JA-UA; Sotelo and Lt. Col. José María de Tovar, "Cuenta que manifiesta las suministraciones hechas a los Apaches establecidos de paz en este real presidio de Janos en los seis últimos meses del corriente año de 1803," Janos, December 31, 1803, F17, S1, JPR-UTA.

[8]Sgt. Baltasar Acosta, "Distribucion del medio situado perteneciente a los seis últimos meses del corriente año," Chihuahua, July 22, 1804, F17, S2, JPR-UTA; Acosta, "Cuenta seguida a los apaches establecidos de paz en este presidio de Janos de las suministraciones hechas en los últimos seis meses de este año," Janos, December 31, 1804, Roll 15, JA-UA.

[9]Total is only through June 30. Lt. Joseph María Do Porto, "Cuenta de las suminstracion hechas a los Apaches establecidos de paz en el presidio de Janos desde 1.o de enero de 1805 hasta la fecha," Janos, June 30, 1805, Roll 15, JA-UA.

[10]Total is only through June 30. [Accountant] Manuel José de Zuloaga, "Ampliación a la cuenta seguida a los Apaches establecidos de paz, de las subministraciones heachas en los primeros seis meses del año de 1806," Chihuahua, January 14, 1807, F18, S3, JPR-UTA.

[11]Total is for last six months of 1808. Sgt. Baltasar Acosta, "Distribución que rinde el habilitado de dicha compañía ... del primer medio situado correspondiente al corriente año," Chihuahua, Janury 28, 1809, F19, S3, JPR-UTA.

[12]Total is only through June 30. Emsign José Ignacio Ronquillo, "Cuenta general de las suministraciones que se han hecho a los Apaches de paz de este establecimiento en los seis 1.os meses del presente año," Janos, June 30, 1815, F21, S3, JPR-UTA.

[13]Capt. José Ramón Ronquillo and Ensign José María Ronquillo, "Cuenta general de las suministraciones que se han hecho a los Apaches de paz de este establecimiento en los seis primeros meses del presente año," Janos, June 30, 1816, F22, S1; Pedro Ruiz de Larramendi to the Janos commander, March 4, 1817, F22, S3, JPR-UTA.

[14]Ensign Domingo Martinez, "Corte cuenta general formado ... de los intereses de dicha compañía en fin de diciembre de 1818," Janos, December 31, 1818, F23, S2, JPR-UTA.

[15]Lt. Juan José de Bustamante and Ensign Rafael Carbajal, "Corte cuenta y entrega de habilitación que hace el teniente de esta compañía ... por fin de diciembre de 1830," Janos, December 31, 1830, F32, S2, JPR-UTA.

[16]Carbajal and Sec. José García, "Cuenta de gastos de indios gentiles de paz establecidos en dicho presidio en los primeros seis meses de 1832," Janos, June 30, 1832, F34, S2; Carbajal and García, "Cuenta de gastos de indios gentiles de paz establecidos en este presidio en los segundos seis meses de 1832," Janos, December 31, 1832, F34, S2, JPR-UTA.

[17]Total is only through June 30. Lt. Gervacio Montes and Ensign Francisco Arzate, "Cuenta de gastos de indios gentiles de paz establecidos en dicho presidio en los primeros seis meses de 1843," Janos, 30 June 1843, F43, S2, JPR-UTA.

Vizcaya alone. This figure is nearly a 60 percent increase from 1804 and is nearly equivalent to the 1,525 Apaches settled in the province at the height of Spanish control in the spring of 1793. The only comprehensive numbers for all of the Apaches at peace after 1804, most likely from the year 1822, indicate that 2,496 Apaches still resided near ten presidios. Of these, 2,125 (85 percent) were in Nueva Vizcaya, which represents a 67 percent increase from 1821 and the highest known total of Apaches at peace ever recorded in the province. The 1,202 Mescaleros at San Elizario comprised more than half of the total. The 371 Apaches at Bacoachi, Bavispe, and Tucson in Sonora is also the highest known total of Apaches at peace recorded in that province, representing a slight increase from the 334 Apaches who lived there in 1804.[50]

The last question to consider, then, is the effect of Indian raiding on the reservations. When, where, and why did Indian raids increase from 1791 to 1832; what role, if any, did peaceful and independent Apaches have in them; and how did the Spanish and Mexican military respond? Given the possibility that more Mescaleros, Chihenes, Chokonens, and Western Apaches may have been at peace in Nueva Vizcaya and Sonora than ever before in 1825, does it make sense to say that the system collapsed in that year, as have scholars who have relied on Ignacio Zuñiga?

Ironically, the Mescalero Apaches, who were the first Apaches to settle near Spanish presidios in eastern Nueva Vizcaya 1779, proved the most difficult group to retain there. Numerous specialists have overlooked the breakdown in the system prompted by the desertion of all but three Mescalero rancherías at peace at San Elizario in February 1794. Most likely, the Mescaleros returned to their homeland to avenge the loss of independent kinsmen whom Spaniards targeted in their repeated punitive expeditions. Spaniards launched these expeditions to punish those independent Mescaleros who were allegedly living off of the supplies of the Apaches at peace and pilfering Spanish livestock. Yet, eight of the Apaches whom Spanish troops killed in July 1793 were returning from a buffalo hunt.[51]

As a result of this and several other attacks, independent Lipan and Mescalero chiefs made repeated calls throughout 1793 for all Apaches to join them in making war on the Spaniards. Two thirds of the Mescaleros at Presidio del Norte followed suit in July 1795. Reuniting with their independent kinsmen in the Apachería, the Mescaleros launched frequent revenge raids on Spanish frontier settlements. The violence continued to escalate, as Spaniards sought to avenge their own losses by launching coordinated campaigns into the eastern Apachería through at least 1799.[52]

Throughout the ongoing hostilities, however, some Mescaleros kept the peace faithfully at San Elizario and Presidio del Norte. The fighting might have ended sooner had Pedro de Nava not ordered all Apache prisoners of war deported southward to Chihuahua at the same time that several Mescalero chiefs were negotiating the resettlement of their people at San Elizario. One can only imagine the pain and rage that Mescalero Apache leaders such as Barrio and Mayá must have felt, when, instead of reciprocally exchanging war captives as the customary first step in treaty negotiations, Spaniards shipped off sixty of their kinsmen in chains. Little wonder that on the anniversary of Nava's order, Spanish troops found twenty-seven Spanish corpses slain by Apaches in the mountains near San Elizario, including two soldiers from the post.[53]

From Nava's perspective, however, his actions were completely justified. In November 1798, New Mexico Governor Fernando de Chacón reported that more than a hundred Apaches stole 224 horses from Laguna Pueblo. Citing the fact that the Indians left behind boxes of cigars, Chacón alleged that the perpetrators were Mescaleros de paz from San Elizario. Although this very well may have been the case, the governor might have considered that independent Mescaleros needing resources in their ongoing war with Spanish troops could have obtained those same items in exchanges with Apaches at San Elizario or former San Elizario Apaches. Whatever the precise identity of these Apache raiders, in March 1799, Nava responded to Governor Chacón's report by instructing San Elizario commander Manuel Merino to cease harboring any Apaches at San Elizario who were suspected of raiding in other jurisdictions.[54]

If Nava contributed to the escalation of violence by intensifying military offensives, deporting Mescalero prisoners southward, and adopting a zero-tolerance policy on stock raiding, he also helped restore peaceful relations between the two groups in the fall of 1799, when he ordered the San Elizario commander to cease harboring Mescaleros at that post who were conducting raids in other jurisdictions. Although Spanish troops continued to launch monthly campaigns against independent Mescaleros through at least August 1807, the provisions of Bernardo de Gálvez's "bad peace" had been restored and would remain intact, even along the volatile eastern Apache frontier, for close to a decade. Spanish officers believed their combined carrot and stick approach was bringing the Apache wars to a close. As Manuel Merino wrote in approximately 1804, "We have managed to lower the level of hostilities to a large degree, and to reduce the number of our enemies, as much by those we have killed in expeditions made into their territories to prevent them from invading our own, as through those who are now settled in peace."⁵⁵

An encroaching U.S. Army officer, Captain Zebulon Montgomery Pike, offered a different perspective on the Apaches at peace in these years. After Spanish officials arrested Pike at the headwaters of the Rio Grande north of Santa Fe for trespassing in the spring of 1807, he spent several days at San Elizario en route to Chihuahua and had the chance to observe the independent spirit of the Mescaleros at peace firsthand. "Around this fort were a great number of Appaches [sic]," Pike wrote, who "appeared to be perfectly independent in their manners, and were the only savages I saw in the Spanish dominions, whose spirit was not humbled, whose necks were not bowed to the yokes of their invaders."⁵⁶

So what accounts for the discrepancy between Merino's emphasis on Spanish control over Apaches and Pike's emphasis on their independent spirit? One factor may be Pike's willingness to acknowledge that former Mescaleros at peace raided south of the presidial line. As Pike observed, those Mescaleros "who have been for some time around the forts and villages, become by far the most dangerous enemies the Spaniards have, when hostile, as they acquire the Spanish language, manners, and habits, and passing through the populated parts under the disguise of the civilized and friendly Indians, commit murders and robberies that are not suspected." One such Apache, named Rafael or Rafaelillo, disguised himself as a peasant and bought provisions, gambled, and even attended mass in Coahuila. But as Rafael, his brother Antonio, and their wives pushed farther south into Durango from 1805 to 1809, and perhaps joined forces with renegade mission Indians, deserting soldiers, and bandits, they left such a trail of destruction – allegedly killing more than eight hundred persons – that the Spanish government placed a thousand-dollar reward on Rafael's head.⁵⁷

Independent Ndé raiding escalated further during the Mexican War of Independence. Writing in approximately 1810, Commander-in-Chief Nemesio Salcedo explained that Apaches, whom he called "gileños, faraones and mezcaleros," were adapting to coordinated Spanish offensives departing from Sonora, Nueva Vizcaya, and New Mexico by forging alliances and launching their own joint raids on Spanish settlements from Sonora to Coahuila in the troops' absence. As money and manpower for fighting Indians diminished at the presidios during the 1810s, Tucson-born Ignacio Zúñiga argued in 1835, independent Apaches took advantage by increasing the frequency of their raids.⁵⁸

From El Paso eastward, Indian raiding became more intensive and widespread than in the past as independent Mescaleros, Lipans, and Comanches forged new relationships and intensified their raids on Spanish livestock during the 1810s. According to one Spanish officer, the change came about in 1811. Prior to that, "the Comanches were not so well armed, nor so war-like, nor had they penetrated into places where they are now seen." Commander-in-Chief Nemesio Salcedo claimed the Comanches remained compliant until November 1812, when they intensified their raids on Spanish livestock, while Spanish forces were preoccupied fighting the filibusters in a siege at La Bahía (Goliad).[59]

Although Salcedo is correct that the diversion of Spanish troops to combat the invaders from Louisiana made it easier for Comanches to raid farther southward, their reasons for doing so were more complicated than that. While many Comanche chiefs still tried to honor their long-standing alliance with Spaniards in Texas, beginning at least as early as October 1810, groups of young Comanche men led by Chief El Sordo ("The Deaf One") joined Taovayas, Tawakonis, and Skidi Pawnees to raid for Spanish horses across Texas and Coahuila – from the San Sabá Valley as far south as Monclova – to trade to Anglo-Americans. As El Sordo explained to Texas Governor Manuel de Salcedo (Nemesio's cousin) in October 1810, Spaniards "were not friends" of his people because they "wouldn't give them guns, nor permit trade with the Americans." The influx of Anglo-American traders across the southern plains, then, in combination with Spanish military and political instability in Texas during the disruptive Mexican War of Independence, was changing the balance of power in New Spain's northeastern borderlands. Clearly, whoever retained power in San Antonio would have to up the ante to meet the Anglo-American challenge if they hoped to keep Indian allies on their side. This was nearly an impossible task as long as long as royalists and mexicanos continued to fight one another. The Mexican War of Independence had so disrupted trade and communication that the garrison at San Antonio de Béxar had no more gifts to offer Comanches. As Salcedo himself wrote elsewhere in his 1810 report, the lack of trade goods at Béxar "has had an influence on the discontent" of the Comanches.[60]

To make matters worse, Spaniards themselves inadvertently encouraged Comanche raiding by treacherously arresting and deporting a Comanche trading party in San Antonio in the fall of 1811. In a clear demonstration of peaceful intent, the very same Comanche chief El Sordo returned to San Antonio completely unarmed with buffalo hides to trade and accompanied by one other man, two women, and a child. This time, El Sordo was unable to reconnect with Governor Salcedo because revolutionaries had captured the official the previous January. Instead, the Comanche spoke with acting governor Lieutenant Colonel Simón de Herrera. Less tolerant of El Sordo's stock raiding than Salcedo and evidently less seasoned in Indian diplomacy, Herrera arrested all five members of the chief's envoy and allowed a *junta* of military and civil authorities to decide their fate. After this council determined that El Sordo's entire party, even the women and child, constituted a military threat to Texas, Herrera sent them to the jail at La Bahía (Goliad) for four months and then moved them farther south to a prison in Coahuila.[61]

Not surprisingly, Herrera's action outraged the easternmost Comanche groups. In 1814 a Comanche delegation in Santa Fe explained that eastern bands made war on Coahuila because of the Comanche prisoners that Spaniards held there. Spanish treachery, then, in combination with Anglo-American firearms and encouragement lay behind the increased Comanche raiding that Commander-in-Chief Nemesio Salcedo described in November 1812. The unfortunate result for both Comanches and Spaniards is that San Antonio stopped being a regional epicenter for Indian trade and diplomacy for many years. In the wake of the El Sordo affair and Governor Salcedo's assassination by the Magee-Gutiérrez filibusterers in 1813, Comanches ceased going there altogether through 1820.[62]

Those Comanche leaders most loyal to Spaniards, however, attempted to revive the same kind of relationship that had served them well for so many years in San Antonio at points farther south. At the easternmost Apache establecimientos of San Elizario and Presidio del Norte, for example, Spanish officers issued Comanches provisions and gifts to pursue Mescaleros and other Apaches in 1811. Although Spaniards asked the Comanche chiefs to remain north of the Rio Grande when pursuing Apaches, they, of course, could not prevent them from crossing the river. Comanches pursuing Apaches, then, had the perfect alibi for raiding Spanish livestock. If Spanish troops stopped them, they could simply claim that they recovered the animals from Apache raiding parties and planned on returning them. This was not a new development. For decades Comanches had been helping themselves to Spanish livestock under the pretext of campaigning against Apaches. As early as 1795, Spanish officials were aware that Comanches were doing this around San Antonio and between the Nueces and Rio Grande.[63]

Although Spaniards supported Comanche pursuit of Mescaleros and Lipans, Tejano revolutionaries, such as José Francisco Ruíz, who sought refuge among the Comanches once royalists recaptured San Antonio in August 1813, encouraged Comanches and other Texas tribes to weaken Spanish control over the northeastern frontier by waging war on Texas and Coahuila from 1813 to 1820. Surprisingly, Lipan Apaches, who had been long-time Comanche enemies, launched joint attacks with eastern Comanches in Texas, Coahuila, Nuevo Santander, and Nuevo León, stealing "cattle, horses, and other property of the inhabitants" and killing and capturing men, women, and children. Lipans and Comanches would continue to work together as allies until at least 1823 (see Map 5.1).[64]

The most intensive year of Comanche and Lipan raiding during the last decade of Spanish rule was 1819. With good reason, Spanish officials believed it was the easternmost Comanches who still led these violent attacks. As Ceuta-born Commander-in-Chief of the Western Interior Provinces Alejo García Conde pointed out in the spring of 1819, the westernmost Comanche divisions still "are observing the peace" in New Mexico and only the eastern Comanche divisions of Texas "threaten us with raids." According to Juan Antonio Padilla, the destruction was "due entirely to the encouragement given them by foreigners and certain perverse Spaniards because of their covetousness." The Spaniards Padilla referred to were soldiers around Natchitoches, who, like Anglo-Americans, sold Eastern Comanches munitions and other goods in exchange for stolen animals, encouraged them to kill and burn the countryside, and even guided them southward to new lands.[65]

As a result of these rapid developments, the state of affairs with Mescaleros de paz in the 1810s seems to have grown increasingly unstable. What little scholars know of Mescalero activities in these years indicates some of them negotiated a treaty with Spaniards in Chihuahua in 1810 and agreed to receive rations at San Elizario and obtained the legal right to settle in their home territory from San Elizario to the Sacramento Mountains. As of 1814 an untold number were still at peace but had received little or no rations to sustain themselves. In July 1815, a smallpox epidemic ravaged the Indians. Many sick and hungry groups of Mescaleros left the reservation and temporarily camped farther up the Rio Grande near Belén, New Mexico.[66]

In the face of numerous setbacks, Mescaleros continued to settle near posts in eastern Nueva Vizcaya until at least 1822. Even though Comanches attacked San Elizario in December 1819, Mescaleros at San Elizario and Presidio del Norte still managed to go on their customary buffalo hunt without incident. In December 1821, 350 Mescaleros remained at San Elizario and 74 others camped farther east near El Príncipe and

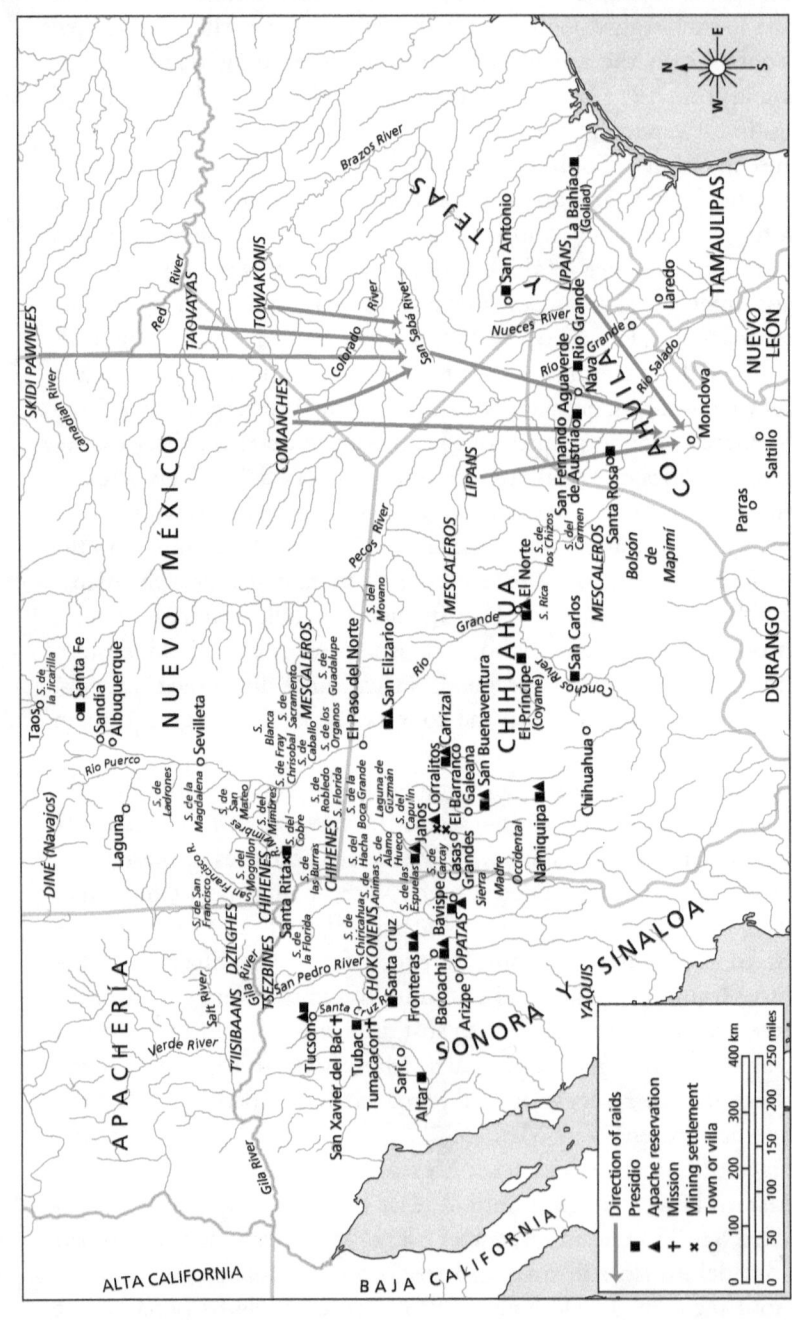

MAP 5.1 The Apache–Mexican frontier, 1821–1832.
Source: Adapted from José Agustín de Escudero, ed., "De las naciones bárbaras que habitan las fronteras del estado de Chihuahua" in *Noticias estadísticas de Chihuahua*, 233–234; *Mapa de los Estados Unidos de Méjico*, New York: White, Gallagher, and White, 1828; and sources from Maps I.2 and 6.1.

Presidio del Norte. The following spring, 1,202 Mescaleros camped near San Elizario and 69 others resided outside the other two posts.[67] Pending further research, the available data indicate that Mescaleros not only maintained a continuous presence at San Elizario but increased their numbers to the highest recorded level on any reservation in the Spanish or Mexican period.

Ignacio Zúñiga maintained that Apache raids helped cause the establecimientos to decline in this period. Such a broad statement needs qualification. As we have seen, Lipan Apaches, Comanches, and their Norteño allies launched raids from Texas during the 1810s. It is less clear what independent Mescaleros were doing. The little information available, however, suggests that neither Apache nor Comanche raiding caused Mescaleros to leave their reservations. Zúñiga was probably focusing his statement on the region of western Nueva Vizcaya and Sonora that he knew best, but even there his statement rings hollow. Spaniards managed to maintain peace with Southern Apaches at Janos and Western Apaches at Tucson through the 1810s. As we have seen, after negotiating peace in 1816, Chihene Mogollons received rations at Janos from 1818 until at least 1822, and Nantan Chilitipagé and more than two hundred T'iisibaan (Pinals) joined the Tsézhinés (Aravaipas) at Tucson in 1819.[68]

When Apaches de paz disrupted the peace in Sonora during the 1810s, Spaniards retained enough power to control them. In the fall of 1814 a peaceful Apache at Tucson named José María fled to the independent Apaches and "caused quite a lot of damage," and the presidial commander, following Commander-in-Chief of the Western Provinces Bernardo Bonavía's orders, had him deported southward to Chihuahua in chains.[69] In one sense, this action must have seemed unduly harsh to most Ndé people. It showed them, however, that, in spite of the diminished strength of the Spanish military, those Apaches who broke their peace agreement would be punished in a way that stopped short of outright killing. By the late 1820s this would no longer be the case.

Since American traders and trappers had not yet reached Southern and Western Apache territory, these groups did not yet have a plentiful source of firearms, nor a burgeoning market for stolen livestock. As a result, Apache raiding west of the Rio Grande was less intense than in Spanish Texas. From Janos to Tucson, independent Southern and Western Apache groups targeted Spanish livestock but generally confined their raids to the most exposed rural areas. More populated areas, such as Tubac and Tucson, remained largely unaffected. Sonoran sacramental registers confirm that, overall, Apaches took plenty of livestock but killed few people between 1812 and 1820. Even though Ndé groups stepped up their raids in these years, then, they were less violent and intense than their attacks prior to 1786. These were clearly resource raids rather than acts of war and probably reflected the same status quo that had existed since the 1790s.[70]

Southern and Western Apaches did not declare an all-out war on Mexicans until the 1830s. Nevertheless, they increased the frequency of their livestock raids in western Nueva Vizcaya and Sonora, especially in the winter months when food was scarce, beginning in 1825 for several reasons. First, as a cost-cutting measure, Mexican officials banned post commanders from issuing rations *in absentia* in 1824. Since individuals could no longer pick up rations for family members who were away nor so easily exchange surplus rations with independent Apaches, this reduction in food opened the door for more raiding. Second, the already diminished and poorly supplied Mexican presidial troops were called away from their posts yet again to put down a Yaqui revolt in Sonora, which erupted in November 1825 and continued through 1827, and independent Ndé groups responded by stepping up their raids. Third, Chokonens and Western Apaches in modern Arizona may have increased their raids in response to the occupation of Spanish land grants issued in their territory. Hostilities remained low as Mexicans settled on the first four land grants in today's southern Arizona between 1821 and 1825, known as the San Ignacio de la Canoa, San José de Sonoita, San Bernadino, and San Rafael de la Zanja grants. But by the late 1820s, Apaches were raiding more frequently and intensely across the Sonoran frontier, especially in the Altar Valley, where Mexicans abandoned Sáric in the spring of 1828.[71]

Most importantly, by at least 1830 Southern and Western Apaches had acquired a new market for stolen livestock and a reliable source for rifles and ammunition. The first American traders and trappers pushed into the Apachería in 1825 and reached Tucson via the Gila River watershed and the Santa Rita mines in 1826. As a result, the T'iisibaan may have had Anglo-American guns by 1830, and by at least 1834, Southern Apaches were acquiring American-made rifles from James Kirker. Kirker obtained them in central Chihuahua from Comanches, either directly or indirectly via Mexican citizens. Comanches, in turn, had exchanged horses for the weapons in Texas and the Indian Territory, which they received from American traders and relocated eastern Indians. Although their numbers paled in comparison to the numbers of those who passed through the Comanchería, Kirker and other Anglo-American merchants along the Santa Fe–Chihuahua Trail helped shift the balance of power between Apaches and Mexicans in the region.[72]

The first clear signs of Apaches at peace raiding in Sonora occurred in 1826. In probable response to the reduction in rations and military defense, they began butchering cattle. In March of that year, Tucson *Alcalde de Policía* (Chief of Police) Ignacio Pacheco stressed that independent Apaches were not solely responsible for the frequent livestock raids transpiring in and around Tucson. Apaches at peace "are causing the greatest damages," Pacheco wrote, by "carrying off the livestock of this community and killing them almost in the presence of everyone." Even more distressing, the Tucson presidial commander was not punishing them for their transgressions. In July, peaceful Apaches struck again, taking the horse herd from Aribac and butchering the animals in their rancherías.[73]

The fact that Apaches at peace could now raid for livestock, slaughter it in plain view of Mexicans, and not be punished for it was a marked contrast from the 1790s and early 1800s. When troublesome peaceful Apaches, such as Ojos Colorados, raided in those years, Spanish officials responded by sending troops and Apache auxiliaries to their camps to recover the animals. They removed repeat offenders to the most remote posts, such as Janos, and placed them in leg irons in the presidio jail. Spanish officials still ordered recalcitrant Apaches de paz to be deported to Chihuahua as late as the fall of 1814, and they still held Apache prisoners at San Buenaventura in October 1818. If that did not work, deportation was another harsher option. There is no evidence that Mexicans continued these practices after independence, however. When it came to Apaches who stole horses, Janos commander José Medina wrote, "those savages don't recognize any other authority except that of the military," and he placed little faith in the ability of local mayors to punish them through the legal system.[74]

Once Mexicans defeated the Yaquis in 1827, they gained a little hope, when a combined force of 1,000 O'odham (Pimas and Papagos) drove the Apaches northward in November. But independent Apache raids continued. Indeed, on November 1 – the same day that the O'odham defeated the Apaches – a Mexican official reported that Tohono O'odham (Papagos) and independent Apaches were stealing horses and illicitly trading them to Mexican thieves along the Colorado River. Apache raiding in Sonora continued to escalate in the 1830s. According to one Tucson resident, in 1831 sheep could no longer be raised at Tucson because Apaches killed them, and it was too dangerous to exploit gold deposits near the Salt River.[75]

Between 1791 and 1832, then, three distinct periods of intensive Indian raiding are evident. The first occurred from 1794 until at least 1799, when peaceful Mescaleros at San Elizario and El Paso deserted their reservation. After temporarily reasserting their cultural independence, a significant portion of Mescaleros – more than a thousand as late as 1825 – apparently resettled at San Elizario and other presidios in eastern Nueva Vizcaya. The second wave of raids transpired during the Mexican War of Independence from 1811 through at least 1820. Eastern Comanches severed their alliance with Spaniards in San Antonio and began raiding with Lipan Apaches and their other Indian allies across Texas, eastern Nueva Vizcaya, Coahuila, Nuevo León, and Nuevo Santander. The fact that peaceful Mescaleros were frequent targets of these raids might explain why they again sought shelter at the presidios. Finally, independent and peaceful Apaches increased their raids in Sonora in 1826 and Southern and Western Apache raids continued to escalate across Nueva Vizcaya and Sonora in the 1830s, as peaceful Apaches deserted their reservations and reunited with their kinsmen in the Apachería. The major factors driving these three increases in raiding were Spanish punitive expeditions in the first case and the reduced supply of rations, supplies, and soldiers in combination with new markets offered by U.S. traders in the other two.

THE FINAL COLLAPSE

On top of the sustained problems of presidio supply, alternative markets for goods, and Indian raiding, at least three other factors came together to cripple the reservation system by the early 1830s. Land dispossession, a smallpox outbreak, and, most importantly, the cessation of all Apache rations at the presidios by 1832 helped end four decades of uneasy peace in northern Mexico.

By the fall of 1828, Janos vecinos were taking land from the Apaches rather than selling it to them. In a complete disregard of Mexican law, the vecino Zeferino Calderón dispossessed the Chihenes Bocón, Pisago, and Chirimi of their farmlands and maguey crops in the rugged Alamo Hueco Mountains (in today's southwestern New Mexico), calling them "baldíos" or "barren." As a result, the Indians protested to the Janos commander and a court case ensued. Interestingly, the governor of Chihuahua supported the Apaches. He required Calderón to document his claim to the land, and he tried to make sure that "necessity, politics, the character of the Indians, and our actual circumstances" never disturb "the peace that [the Apaches] maintain with us." He promised that the state government would make every effort to cooperate with local judges and protect Apache interests. Apparently, the Apaches had faith in the governor's promise because they filed similar suits against other encroaching settlers, including José Manuel Zamaniego.[76]

Apaches at peace sometimes voluntarily sold their tracts. In the same year, Nantans Antuna, Benito, and other peaceful Apache leaders at Tucson offered to sell a tract of land that Adjutant Inspector Roque de Medina had issued to them in 1796 to Teodoro Ramírez, the brother-in-law of Tucson commander Lieutenant Antonio Comadurán. After meeting with these headman on January 18, 1828, and learning that no coercion was involved, Comadurán and Mayor Ignacio Sardina approved it. In exchange for the tract, which included much of what would become Barrio Anita in the 1870s, the Indians received a hundred pesos worth of goods, including two muskets, four serapes, a horse, tobacco, and ten pesos for purchasing powder.[77]

Northern Mexico's state and local officials' support for peaceful Apaches' legal rights to their lands in the 1820s, even in the face of deteriorating relations with frontier settlers, suggests that, with respect to Apaches at least, the Spanish and Mexican legal systems may have been more similar than specialists have realized. This stood in marked contrast to the general trend across most of independent Mexico in the 1820s, where state officials authorized the privatization of Indian lands and dissolved courts providing Indians with legal protection.[78] Regardless of the quality of legal protection Apaches at peace received, however, the fact that they had to rely on it so frequently signified serious instability and decline within the system.

A second factor that helped cripple the reservation system was a smallpox outbreak. Apaches had left their reservations to protect themselves from disease outbreaks since the system's inception (see Chapter 4). Economic decline, then, was not the sole reason for the collapse of the system. When disease struck, Apaches left their reservations regardless of how many gifts and rations Spaniards and Mexicans had to offer. This was just as true in Spanish colonial times, when rations and gifts were more plentiful, as in the Mexican period. When smallpox spread across western Nueva Vizcaya and eastern Sonora in 1797 and again from 1799 to 1800, Apaches left their reservations.[79]

Janos presidio experienced a heightened period of disease-induced fatalities from 1827 to 1831, which culminated in Apaches deserting their reservation. Between 1819 and 1826, Janos chaplain Antonio Carrasco buried less than ten residents annually on average (77 people total). In 1827, when a measles epidemic struck, he buried 79 vecinos (60 children and 19 adults). After a typical year in 1828 (10 burials), his successor, Rafael Echevarría buried 58 people from 1829 to 1830, including one Apache, José Quide, whom he baptized before death. The most prevalent causes of death were *dolor de costado* ("pain in the side"), or pleurisy, and typhus. In 1831 Echevarría buried another 55 people in a smallpox epidemic, including one "Apachito" who was baptized before death. According to one Janos officer, the five remaining peaceful Apache bands left the Janos area in July 1831 "because of fear of smallpox."[80]

The leading scholar on the establecimientos in the Mexican period contends that the system collapsed because Sonora and Chihuahua state officials determined that Apaches were costing the government too much and ordered their rations discontinued prior to May 1831, when smallpox struck Janos and the peaceful Apaches supposedly left. No primary source proves state officials did this at that time, however, and the Mexican reports that this scholar relies on were written after the fact and are vague and conflicting on this point. Regardless of what Mexican writers say state officials ordered, the documents indicate that Apaches remained at Janos until July 1831, and even then, officials did not immediately consider their desertion permanent. After all, Apaches were simply doing what they had always done. In fact, an undisclosed number of them continued to receive small amounts of rations at Janos, even after returning to their homeland, from October 1831 through June 1832. Not until July 1832 does the tone of Janos officers seem to change toward the former Apaches at peace, when one officer wrote, "they have revolted and we don't know where they are."[81]

Apaches, then, do not appear to have left their reservations in 1831 because Mexican officials ordered rations to be ceased. At Janos, at least, they left because of a smallpox outbreak. By October 16, 1831, Chihuahua governor José Joaquín Calvo had declared war on Apaches. The meager evidence indicates he was probably responding to Juan José Compá's departure from San Buenaventura presidio (at Galeana, thirty miles south of Janos) in the fall of 1831 and the fear that renegade Apaches from Janos and San Buenaventura would attack them. Yet, in early 1832, peaceful Apaches still camped in the vicinity of Presidio del Norte, San Elizario, Carrizal, and, most assuredly, Tucson. Not until January 1832, in the midst of diplomatic negotiations, does documentary evidence indicate that Mexicans refused to issue rations to these former

Apaches de paz. Only then, without any reliable winter food source and in the face of attacks from the Mexican military, did the majority of Apaches apparently collectively desert their reservations and escalate their raiding and warfare.[82] The motivations and underlying responsibility for this reciprocal violence and the efforts of former Apaches de paz and Mexican officers to mitigate it through negotiation and exchange are the subject of the next chapter.

Notes

1 Lt. Col. Alberto Maynez to the Ayudante Inspector [draft], Janos, January 26, 1818, F23, S1, JPR-UTA).
2 See, for example, Weber, *Mexican Frontier*, ch. 6, especially 107.
3 Scholars mistakenly conflating Gálvez's policy with practice include Bancroft, *History of the North Mexican States and Texas*, 682–684; Park, "Spanish Indian Policy," 342, and reprinted in Weber, *New Spain's Northern Frontier*, 230. For the lack of alcohol issued to Apaches de paz in this period, see Weber, *Bárbaros*, 185; Griffen, *Apaches at War and Peace*, 132; Hendricks and Timmons, *San Elizario*, 40.
4 Commander-in-Chief Pedro de Nava to the Conde de Revillagigedo [Viceroy Juan Vicente de Güemes], no. 313, Chihuahua, November 25, 1791, f. 358, 360, AGN, PI, 61, BL-microfilm. The first three quotations are from fol. 358. For "strong drink," see Henrique de Grimarest to Commander-in-Chief Jacobo Ugarte, Arizpe, June 14, 1791, f. 362, AGN, PI, 61, BL-microfilm.
5 Lt. Manuel de Echeagaray to Nava, no. 136, Arizpe, November 7, 1791, f. 366, AGN, PI, 61, BL-microfilm.
6 Echeagaray to Nava, no. 136, Arizpe, November 7, 1791, and Nava to the Conde de Revillagigedo, no. 313, Chihuahua, November 25, 1791, ff. 367–8, AGN, PI, 61, BL-microfilm.
7 For the alleged Comanche destruction of Sabinal, see Hämäläinen, *Comanche Empire*, 139; Brooks, *Captives and Cousins*, 451. For a theory of gradual decay because of lack of Spanish encouragement, see Simmons, *Coronado's Land*, 60.
8 For Navajo attacks on Apaches, see Concha to the Conde de Revillagigedo, Santa Fe, July 12, 1791, fr. 559, roll 12, SANM-HL. For "Dinétah," see Peter Iverson, *Diné: A History of the Navajo People* (Albuquerque: University of New Mexico Press, 2002), 4, 19–20. For the death of Antonio El Pinto, see [Concha] to Nava, Santa Fe, November 19, 1793, fr. 426–427, roll 13, SANM-HL; Benes, "Anza and Concha," 70; John, *Storms Brewed*, 763.
9 Simmons, *Coronado's Land*, 60; August, "Balance-of-Power Diplomacy in New Mexico," 156.
10 For the original documents on Ecueracapa's death and Encaguané's election, see Nava to Concha, no. 1247, Chihuahua, August 8, 1793, and Nava to Concha, no. 1272, December 31, 1793, roll 13, SANM-HL. See also Concha to Nava, no. 458, Santa Fe, December 4, 1793, AGS, GM, 7023, Exp. 1. For English translations of the first two documents, see Simmons, *Border*

Comanches: Seven Spanish Colonial Documents, 1785–1819, 29–31. For Antonio El Pinto's death, see n8. For the short-lived 1795 Comanche–Pawnee peace, see John, *Storms Brewed*, 763–764; Stanley Noyes, *Los Comanches: The Horse People, 1751–1845* (Albuquerque: University of New Mexico Press, 1993), 159. On Comanche political instability in the 1790s, see Thomas W. Kavanagh, *The Comanches: A History, 1706–1875* (Lincoln: University of Nebraska Press, 1999), 189–190.

11 Nava to the Governor of New Mexico [Fernando Chacón], Chihuahua, December 21, 1796, fr. 1025, roll 13, SANM-HL; Frank D. Reeve, "Navaho Foreign Affairs, 1795–1846," *New Mexico Historical Review* 46 (April 1971): 107.

12 Griffen, *Apaches at War and Peace*, 103; Lt. Col. Antonio Cordero, "Papel que manifiesta los puntos tratados por los Capitanes Mimbreños," Chihuahua, January 17, 1791, Article 5, roll 14, microfilm, JHA-UTEP. For El Guero and Juan Diego, respectively, see Nava to the Janos commander [Confidential], Chihuahua, August 8, 1795, F11, S1, and Tovar to the Commander-in-Chief, no. 9 [copy], Janos, July 20, 1803, F17, S3, JPR-UTA.

13 Cordero to the Janos commander, El Paso, August 12, 1791, F7, S1, JPR-UTA; Marcel Mauss, *The Gift: The Form and Reason for Exchange in Archaic Societies*, trans. W. D. Halls (1967; reprint, New York: W. W. Norton, 1990), 13; Navarro García, *Don José de Gálvez*, 493.

14 Nava to [Cordero], Chihuahua, December 22, 1794, F11, S2, JPR-UTA. For an overview of this policy change and the mistaken notion that cutting costs was the main cause, see Griffen, *Apaches at War and Peace*, 81. For the quotation and the 1791 policy, see Nava, "Instructions," 105, para. 18. For inflation, see Dobyns, *Spanish Colonial Tucson*, 41. On France's war with Spain from 1793 to 1795, see Charles J. Esdaile, *The Spanish Army in the Peninsular War* (Manchester and New York: Manchester University Press, 1988), 37–40; John Lynch, *Bourbon Spain, 1700–1808* (Oxford: Basil Blackwell, 1989), 37–40; Griffen, *Apaches at War and Peace*, 81; Navarro García, *Don José de Gálvez*, 501; and the King of Spain to Sec. of War Manuel de Negrete y de la Torre, Aranjuez, March 25, 1793, F9, S1, JPR-UTA. For the first quotation, see Nava to Lt. Dionisio Valle, Chihuahua, February 6, 1796, F13, S1, JPR-UTA. For the remaining quotations, see Nava to Capt. Manuel de Casanova, Chihuahua, October 10, 1794, F10, S1, JPR-UTA.

15 For Nava's reasoning behind the policy, see Nava to [Antonio Cordero], Chihuahua, December 22, 1794 (filed in 1795), F11, S2, JPR-UTA. For effective policing by Apaches de paz, see, for example, Nava to Casanova, Chihuahua, November 26 1791, F7, S1, JPR-UTA.

16 For the quotation, see Nava to [Cordero], Chihuahua, December 22, 1794, F11, S2, JPR-UTA. For the 1794 Mescalero revolts, see Chapter 4.

17 Nava to Cordero, Chihuahua, October 28, 1794, F10, S2, JPR-UTA.

18 For the quotation, see Nava to Casanova, Chihuahua, October 10, 1794, F10, S1, JPR-UTA; Nava to Cordero, Chihuahua, October 28, 1794, F10, S2, JPR-UTA.

19 For the respective quotations, see Nava to [Cordero], [Confidential], Chihuahua, November 26, 1794 and Nava to [Cordero], Chihuahua, December 22, 1794, F11, S2, JPR-UTA.

20 Nava to [Cordero], Chihuahua, November 26, 1794, and Nava to [the Janos commander], Chihuahua, December 22, 1794, F11, S2, JPR-UTA.
21 Nava to the Janos commander, Chihuahua, April 9, 1795, F11, S1, JPR-UTA; Griffen, *Apaches at War and Peace*, 71–72. For proof of Ojos Colorados's raids at Carrizal, see Lt. Marcos Reaño to Nava, Carrizal, July 8, 1792, F8, S1, JPR-UTA. For the 70 percent drop, see Griffen, "Chiricahua Apache Population," 160.
22 See, for example, Benes, "Anza and Concha," 73; John, *Storms Brewed*, 752; August, "Balance-of-Power Diplomacy in New Mexico," 156.
23 Nava to the Governor of New Mexico [Fernando Chacón], Chihuahua, June 26, 1795, fr. 708–711, and [Chacón] to Nava, Santa Fe, July 15, 1795, fr. 735–736, roll 13, SANM-HL.
24 Nava to [the Janos commander], Chihuahua, January 18, 1796, and Nava to Valle, Chihuahua, February 6, 1796, F13, S1, JPR-UTA. The quotation is from the second document.
25 Lt. Col. Diego de Borica to the Janos commander, Chihuahua, July 23, 1792, F8, S1, JPR-UTA.
26 Nava to Valle, Chihuahua, February 6, 1796, F13, S1, JPR-UTA; Gálvez, *Instructions*, para. 79.
27 Nava to [the Janos commander], Chihuahua, January 18, 1796, F13, S1, JPR-UTA.
28 Nava to Valle, Chihuahua, February 6, 1796, and Nava to [the Janos commander], Chihuahua, January 18, 1796, F13, S1, JPR-UTA. The quotations are from the first document.
29 Nava to the Janos commander, Chihuahua, March 9, 1796, F13, S1, JPR-UTA; Valle to Nava, Janos, March 1, 1796; and Valle to Nava, no. 112 [draft], [Janos], February 26, 1796, roll 10, JHA-UTEP. The quotations are from the final document.
30 Nava to Valle, Chihuahua, February 6, 1796, F13, S1, JPR-UTA.
31 Lynch, *Bourbon Spain, 1700–1808*, 360, 367, 371, 395, 414; J. H. Elliott, *Empires of the Atlantic World: Britain and Spain in America, 1492–1830* (New Haven, CT: Yale University Press, 2006), 373; Park, "Spanish Indian Policy," 343–344; Eric Van Young, *The Other Rebellion: Popular Violence, Ideology, and the Mexican Struggle for Indpendence, 1810–1821* (Stanford, CA: Stanford University Press, 2001), 71–86.
32 Don Nemesio Salcedo y Salcedo Salcedo, *Instrucción reservada de don Nemesio Salcedo y Salcedo, Comandante General de Provincias Internas a su sucesor [June 16, 1813]*, ed. Isidro Vizcaya Canales (Chihuahua, Mexico: Centro de Información del Estado de Chihuahua, 1990), 34–36, 46, paras. 8, 10, 11, 26.
33 Commander-in-Chief Nemesio Salcedo to the Janos commander, Chihuahua, July 23, 1804, F17, S2, JPR-UTA.
34 Tovar to the Commander-in-Chief [N. Salcedo], no. 8 [copy], Janos, July 19, 1803, F17, S3; Salcedo to the Janos commander, Chihuahua, January 6, 1809, F19, S2, JPR-UTA.
35 Salcedo, Instrucción reservada, 66, para. 64.
36 Salcedo, Instrucción reservada, 66–67, para. 66.

37 Salcedo to the Janos commander, Chihuahua, July 24, 1812, F20, S3; [The Janos commander?] to [Commander-in-Chief] Alejo García Conde, Janos, [no date], F19, S4, JPR-UTA.
38 Capt. Antonio García de Texada to the Janos commander, Chihuahua, May 13, 1816, F22, S1, JPR-UTA.
39 Sgt. Juan Lombán to the Janos commander, Chihuahua, October 2, 1818, F23, S1, JPR-UTA; Fray Antonio Carrasco et al. to García Conde, Janos, November 30, 1817, and Maynez to García Conde, Janos, December 1, 1817, F22, S3, JPR-UTA. The quotations are from the second and third documents, respectively
40 The Janos commander to [Commander-in-Chief] Bernardo Bonavía [draft], no. 42, Janos, July 1, 1817, F22, S3, JPR-UTA.
41 [Vecino] Don Gregorio de la Peña y Arze to Ensign Paymaster José María Ronquillo, San Buenaventura, June 19, 1816, F22, S1, JPR-UTA.
42 The Janos commander to the Ayudante Inspector [draft], Janos, December 1, 1817, F22, S3, JPR-UTA.
43 García Conde to the Janos commander, Durango, August 25, 1818, F23, S1; the Janos commander to García Conde, no. 88, Janos, October 1, 1818, F23, S1; Juan Lombán to the Janos commander, Chihuahua, October 2, 1818, F23, S1; Casanova and Josef María de la Riva, "Razón de lo subministrado por el Don Jose Ignacio Escageda," Janos, August 23, 1791, F7, S2, JPR-UTA. The quotation is from the first document.
44 The Janos commander to García Conde [copy], Janos, December [28], 1821, F24A, S2, JPR-UTA.
45 Lt. Col. José Antonio Vizcarra et al., "Ración dada a los indios de paz," no. 1, Janos, January 1, 1822, roll 14, JHA-UTEP and subsequent weekly rations from that year.
46 Lt. Ignacio Pérez, "Estado de la fuerza," Janos, March 1, 1823, F25, S3, JPR-UTA. See also Table 5.1.
47 Sgt. Manuel Aguilar, Capt. José Medina, "Ración dada a los indios de paz," no. 1, Janos, March 22, 1824, F25B, S2; Capt. Ramón Zúñiga, "Ración dada a los indios de paz hoy," no. 1, Janos, July 5, 1830, F32, S2, JPR-UTA.
48 See Table 5.2. This point was missed by anthropologist William Griffen, who apparently did not consult treasury records. See Griffen, *Apaches at War and Peace*, 119–138.
49 For data, see Griffen, *Apaches at War and Peace*, 269–270.
50 For the 1822 numbers, see Carlos Bustamente, ed., "Indios Apaches," *Voz de la Patria*, Saturday, May 21, 1831, 22–23; Escudero, "De las naciones bárbaras," 233–234. I date these numbers to the year 1822, rather than the ca. 1825 date that anthropologist William B. Griffen has given, because, as Griffen himself notes elsewhere, Mano Mocha was only present at Janos for "a short interlude in early 1822." See Griffen, *Apaches at War and Peace*, 94. For the 1804 figures, see Manuel Merino, "Noticia de las tribus de yndios gentiles que havitan en la frontera de las provincias del reyno de Nueva España, ca. 1804," Huntington Manuscript 543. For an English translation, see John and Wheat, "Views from a Desk in Chihuahua," 166. For a

combined look at the 1793, 1821, and 1822 figures, see Griffen, *Apaches at War and Peace*, 267–268.
51 Hendricks and Timmons, *San Elizario*, 33–35.
52 Moorhead, *Presidio*, 259.
53 Hendricks and Timmons, *San Elizario*, 36.
54 Hendricks and Timmons, *San Elizario*, 37–39. Although the authors do not make the connection, this is almost certainly the same Manuel Merino who served as secretary of the General Command from 1787 to 1804. For a brief biography of Merino, see John and Wheat, "Views from a Desk in Chihuahua," 139–147.
55 Hendricks and Timmons, *San Elizario*, 37–39. For the quotation, see John and Wheat, "Views from a Desk in Chihuahua," 157; Merino, "Noticia de las tribus de yndios gentiles," p. 17.
56 Zebulon Pike, "Journal of the Western Expedition, Part II: From the Conejos River to Natchitoches," San Elizario, March 23, 1807, in Donald Jackson, ed., *The Journals of Zebulon Montgomery Pike with Letters and Related Documents*, vol. 1 (Norman: University of Oklahoma Press, 1966), 410.
57 Jackson, *Journals of Zebulon Montgomery Pike*, 56; Miguel Vallebueno G., "Apaches y comanches en Durango durante los siglos XVIII y XIX," in *Nómadas y sedentarios en el norte de México: Homenaje a Beatriz Braniff* (México: Universidad Nacional Autónoma de México, 2000), 673.
58 Salcedo, *Instrucción reservada*, 38–39, paras. 16–17. Although the official year of Salcedo's report is 1813, he had sought retirement for many years and probably wrote all but the marginal annotations of his report in 1810. See Vizcaya Canales, "Introducción," in Salcedo, *Instrucción reservada*, 23, 29; Zúñiga, *Rápida ojeada al estado de Sonora*, 71f.
59 Juan Antonio Padilla, "Report on the Barbarous Indians of the Province of Texas," Villa de Mier, December 27, 1819 in Mattie Austin Hatcher, trans., "Texas in 1820," *Southwestern Historical Quarterly* 23 (July 1919): 55; Salcedo, *Instrucción reservada*, 36, para. 12. The quotation is from Padilla.
60 Elizabeth A. H. John, "Nurturing the Peace: Spanish and Comanche Cooperation in the Early Nineteenth Century," *New Mexico Historical Review* 59 (October 1984): 361–362; Kavanagh, *Comanches*, 156; Salcedo, *Instrucción reservada*, 46, para. 26. The first quotation is from Kavanagh, quoted from Manuel de Salcedo, Bernardo Bonavía, and Símon de Herrera, "Council of War," October 1810, Bexar Archives 47: 123, and the second is from Salcedo.
61 John, "Nurturing the Peace," 362–363; Kavanagh, *The Comanches*, 157.
62 Kavanagh, *Comanches*, 161, 158.
63 Kavanagh, *The Comanches*, 158; Mañuel Muñoz to Nava, no. 265, San Antonio de Béxar, February 15, 1795, AGS-Simancas, GM, 7025, Exp. 1; Félix Calleja, *Informe sobre la colonia del Nuevo Santander y Nuevo Reino de Leon-1795*, ed. José Porrúa (México: José Porrúa, 1949), 51.
64 John, "Nurturing the Peace," 365; José Francisco Ruíz, *Report on the Indian Tribes of Texas in 1828*, ed. John C. Ewers and trans. Georgette Dunn (New Haven, CT: Yale University Press, 1972), 7; Jean Louis Berlandier, *The Indians of*

Texas in 1830, ed. John C. Ewers and trans. Patricia Reading LeClercq (Washington, DC: Smithsonian Institution Press, 1969), 119; "Instructions which the Constitutional Ayuntamiento of the city of San Fernando de Bexar draws up," November 15, 1820, in Hatcher, "Texas in 1820," 61–62. The quotation comes from Hatcher. Although Ruíz and Berlandier claimed this alliance began in 1816, historian Elizabeth A. H. John dates the alliance to 1813, which Spanish documents support. See José Francisco de la Barreda y Cos et al. to Gaspar López, San Juan Bautista del Río Grande, August 20, 1821, Archivo General del Estado de Coahuila, Fondo Colonial, Caja 47, Expediente 108, Folio 4.

65 For the first two quotations, see García Conde to the Interim Governor of New Mexico [Facundo Melgares], Durango, May 11, 1819 in Simmons, *Border Comanches, 1785–1819*, 35–36; Dobyns, *Spanish Colonial Tucson*, 127–128. For a brief biography of Alejo García Conde, see Dobyns, *Spanish Colonial Tucson*, 127–128. For the third quotation, see Padilla, "Report on the Barbarous Indians of the Province of Texas," Villa de Mier, December 27, 1819, in Hatcher, "Texas in 1820," 55.

66 Alfred Barnaby Thomas, "The Mescalero Apache, 1653–1874," in *Apache Indians XI* (New York: Garland Publishing, 1974), 15; Hendricks and Timmons, *San Elizario*, 44. Although Hendricks and Timmons do not make the connections, this was likely the same devastating smallpox epidemic that killed approximately four thousand Comanches – one fifth of their tribe – from 1815 to 1816 and struck Tumácacori in November 1816. See Berlandier, *Indians of Texas*, 84n86; Officer, *Hispanic Arizona*, 87.

67 For the Comanche attack, see Hendricks and Timmons, *San Elizario*, 44. For the buffalo hunt, see Corp. Antonio Torres to Capt. José Ramón Ronquillo, Presidio del Norte, January 29, 1820, roll 14, JHA-UTEP. For the 1822 figure, see Bustamente, "Indios Apaches," 22–23; Escudero, "De las naciones bárbaras," 233–234; Griffen, *Apaches at War and Peace*, 267.

68 Zúñiga, *Rápida ojeada al estado de Sonora*, 71f. For the Mogollon peace at Janos, which Griffen omits, see Capt. Laureano de Murga to Capt. José Ronquillo, Namiquipa, July 27, 1816, F22, S1; Capt. Miguel Ortiz to the Janos commander, Carrizal, August 27, 1816; Maynez to Bonavía, no. 6, Janos, October 3, 1816; Maynez to the Commander-in-Chief, no. 7, Janos October 9, 1816, F22, S1, JPR-UTA. For the Pinal peace at Tucson, see Capt. José Romero to Col. Antonio Narbona, Tucson, May 21, 1819, facsimile, in Brinckerhoff and Faulk, *Lancers for the King*, 116; Dobyns, *Spanish Colonial Tucson*, 102–103; Officer, *Hispanic Arizona*, 87; Jacoby, *Shadows at Dawn*, 159.

69 Bonavía to the Janos commander, Chihuahua, October 11, 1814, F21, S2, JPR-UTA.

70 For the level of violence in Texas, Nueva Vizcaya, and Sonora from 1800 to 1821, see Alejo García [Conde], Review of trial of Francisco Xavier Díaz, November 16, 1813, in McCarty, *Desert Documentary*, 109; Griffen, *Apaches at War and Peace*, 91; Officer, *Hispanic Arizona*, 86–87.

71 For the 1824 ration ban, see Griffen, *Apaches at War and Peace*, 125. For increased Apache raiding in Sonora in conjunction with the Yaqui revolt and

the northward expansion of Mexican ranching, see Officer, *Hispanic Arizona*, 102, 112, 108.

72 For Americans trapping along the Gila in 1826, see David J. Weber, *The Taos Trappers: The Fur Trade in the Far Southwest, 1540–1846* (Norman: University of Oklahoma Press, 1971), 121; Weber, *Mexican Frontier*, 132. For Apache acquisition of American-made firearms, see Henry F. Dobyns, *From Fire to Flood: Historic Human Destruction of Sonoran Desert Riverine Oases* (Anthropological Papers no. 20, Socorro: Ballena Press, 1981), 25; Ralph Adam Smith, *Borderlander: The Life of James Kirker, 1793–1852* (Norman: University of Oklahoma Press, 1999), 48. For a contrary argument that Anglo-American traders merely engaged in "incidental commerce" with Comanches and other Plains Indians along the Santa Fe Trail in this era and that "Mexican observers exaggerated" the trade's extent and significance, see DeLay, *War of a Thousand Deserts*, 101, 104.

73 Mayor Ignacio Pacheco to Gov. Nicolás María Gaxiola, Tucson, March 6, 1826, Archivo General del Estado de Sonora, Ramo Apaches, Expediente 3, f. 63, (hereafter, AGES, RA, Exp. Number, fol. number); [the Tucson commander] to Pacheco, Tucson, July 4, 1826, AGES, RA, Exp. 3, f. 72, both courtesy of Karl Jacoby. The quotations come from the first document.

74 For examples of raids by Apaches at peace in the 1790s and Spanish punishments, see the correspondence between Nava and Casanova during fall 1791, F7, S1; Sgt. Marcos Reaño to Nava, Carrizal, July 8, 1792, F8, S1; and Nava to the Janos commander, Chihuahua, August 16, 1793, F9, S2, JPR-UTA; Griffen, *Apaches at War and Peace*, 75–79. For leg irons and jail as a punishment, see Salcedo to the Janos commander, Chihuahua, May 3, 1804, F17, S2, JPR-UTA. For Apache deportation, see Bonavía to the Janos commander, Chihuahua, October 11, 1814, F21, S2; Maynez et al., "Ración dada a los indios de paz," no. 17, October 19, 1818, F23, S3, JPR-UTA. For the quotations, see the Janos commander to the Commander-in-Chief, Janos, no. 23, June 30, 1827, F28, S2, JPR-UTA.

75 Mariano Tisnado to the Governor of Occidente, Altar, November 1, 1827, AGES, RA, Exp. 3, fol. 88; Diego Moreno to [no recipient: the Governor of Occidente?], Altar, November 1, 1827, RA, Exp. 3, ff. 89–90, both courtesy of Karl Jacoby; Officer, *Hispanic Arizona*, 122.

76 Commander-in-Chief Simón Elias to the Janos commander, no. 9, Chihuahua, January 10, 1829, F29, S2, JPR-UTA.

77 Officer, *Hispanic Arizona*, 114–115.

78 For the general trend, see Weber, *Bárbaros*, 265.

79 Nava to the Janos commander, Chihuahua, October 7, 1797, F14, S1, JPR-UTA; Griffen, *Apaches at War and Peace*, 81, 89, 106; [Bavispe commander?] Francisco Fernández to Capt. Manuel Rengel and Capt. José Manuel de Ochoa, Bavispe, September 19, 1799; Ochoa, "Padrón que manifiesta el número de Apaches de paz establecidos en este puesto y su inmediación," January 1, 1800, roll 14, JHA-UTEP.

80 "Libro de disfunciones, 1819–1835," Fray Antonio Carrasco and Fray Rafael Echevarria, Janos, F24, S3, JPR-UTA. For *dolor de costado* as pleurisy, see David Noble Cook, *Born to Die: Disease and New World Conquest*,

1492–1650 (New York: Cambridge University Press, 1998), 102. For the quotation, see Sgt. Ramón Nuñez, "Estado de fuerza," Janos, February 1, 1832, F34, S2, JPR-UTA.

81 Griffen, *Utmost Good Faith*, 28; Griffen, *Apaches at War and Peace*, 133. For the ongoing Apache presence at Janos, see Sgt. Rafael Carbajal and Sgt. José García, "Cuenta de gastos de indios gentiles de paz establecidos en dicho presidio en los primeros seis meses de 1832," Janos, June 30, 1832, F34, S2, JPR-UTA. For the quotation, see Carbabjal, "Estado de la fuerza," Janos, July 1, 1832, F34, S2, JPR-UTA.

82 Carbajal to Commander-in-Chief Ramón Zuñiga, Janos, January 22, 1832, roll 25, microfilm, JA-UA; Griffen, *Utmost Good Faith*, 29–30; Griffen, *Apaches at War and Peace*, 139.

6

Resilience and Survival

From their hastily constructed ranchería on the southeastern slope of the Animas Mountains (eighty miles northwest of Janos in today's Hidalgo County, NM) Juan José and Juan Diego Compá's mixed group of Southern Apaches watched an Anglo-American pack train move up the broken cattle trail in late April 1837. Numbering approximately three hundred men, women, and children and boasting eighty armed men, the Apaches, who included many former Apaches de paz from Janos and Galeana, held an impressive numerical advantage over the group of eighteen Anglo-American traders and five Mexican mule drivers who pursued them. Nonetheless, Juan José and Juan Diego had been suspicious of the merchants' intentions since witnessing their kinsmen's first smoke signal warning in the surrounding hills. Why were these Americans coming to trade in such a remote area, especially on the heels of recent Apache revenge raids in Sonora? (see Map 6.1.)[1]

The leader of the party, Kentucky native and recently naturalized Mexican citizen John J. Johnson, approached the Apache camp. After explaining that they were on their way from Sonora to the Santa Rita del Cobre mine (near present-day Silver City, NM), Johnson told the Compás that, in exchange for a guide and safe passage, he could offer them flour, sugar, and gunpowder the following morning. Upon hearing this, Juan José felt reassured, for he had bought arms and ammunition from American traders many times since the opening of the Santa Fe Trail without incident.[2]

Two days later, on the morning of April 22, Johnson finally seemed ready to make good on his promise. As the Apaches gathered to receive

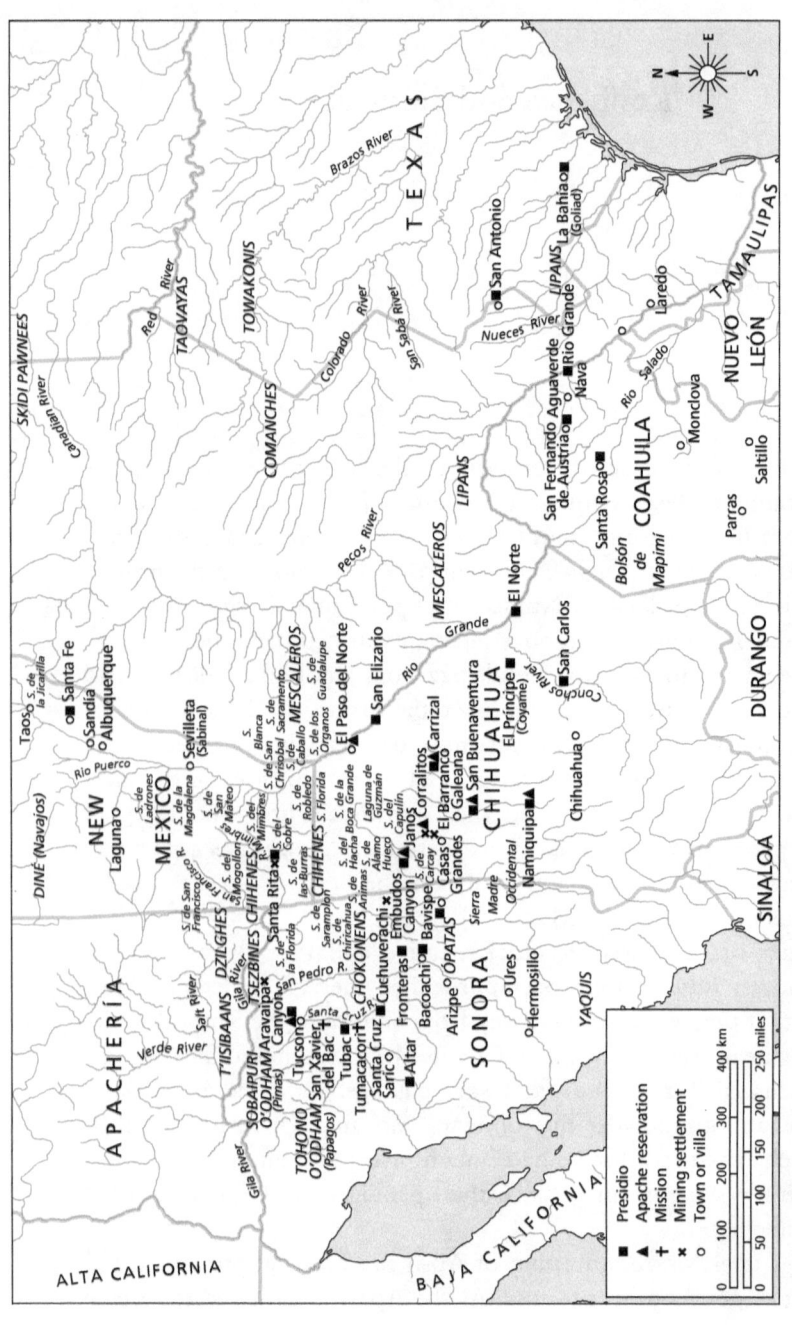

MAP 6.1 The Apache–Mexican frontier and the revived *establecimientos*, 1842–1845.
Source: Adapted from Ralph Adam Smith, *Borderlander: The Life of James Kirker, 1793–1852* (Norman: University of Oklahoma Press, 1999), 31; William B. Griffen, *Utmost Good Faith: Patterns of Apache-Mexican Hostilities in Northern Chihuahua Border Warfare, 1821–1848* (Albuquerque: University of New Mexico Press, 1988), xi–xii; Griffen, *Apaches at War and Peace*, 20; Karl Jacoby, *Shadows at Dawn: A Borderlands Massacre and the Violence of History* (New York: Penguin, 2008), 12, 47, 142; Kieran McCarty, ed. and trans., *A Frontier Documentary: Sonora and Tucson, 1821–1848* (Tucson: University of Arizona Press, 1997), viii–ix; Robert M. Utley, *Geronimo* (New Haven, CT: Yale University Press, 2012), 170.

bags of *pinole* (corn meal) and *panocha* (brown sugar), however, Johnson's men opened fire on them, using a mounted swivel gun that probably came from Fronteras presidio. In less than five minutes, nearly all of the principal headmen, including Juan José, his brother Juan Diego, and Marcelo, lay dead. Only the Chihene leader Antonio Vívora, a long-time Janos resident, managed to escape. After more than two hours of fighting, Johnson's men suffered no losses other than a third of the pack train containing clothing and expense money. Nineteen Ndé men, women, and children died and another twenty were wounded.[3]

More fluent in Spanish and politically savvy than any other Ndé leaders of the 1830s, the Compá brothers had risen to prominence in an era when trading and diplomacy trumped raiding and warfare as the dominant forms of Hispanic and Apache interaction. On the heels of the establecimiento system's collapse, however, that pattern reversed. Mexican presidios and towns, which were previously zones for reciprocal diplomacy and exchange, disintegrated into arenas of treacherous violence. Desperate to curtail Apache raiding and killing, officials in underfunded and undermanned northern Mexican states implemented an Apache scalp bounty, and money-hungry soldiers, citizens, and contract killers gunned down unsuspecting and unarmed Ndé men, women, and children, which simply escalated the reciprocal violence. A minority of Mexican military officers and Ndé leaders, however, still valued peace and trusted one another enough to try to renegotiate, and small groups of Apaches temporarily resettled at presidios in Chihuahua and Sonora.

Although one historian has called Johnson's killing of Apaches "a comparatively minor affair," in fact his treacherous attack helped encourage Mexico's transition to mercenary warfare against Apaches, which seriously exacerbated the violent nature of Mexican–Apache relations in the region. Johnson did not show up in the Animas Mountains merely to trade for mules. Before leaving the battle site, he took the scalps of the three dead Ndé leaders, the Chihenes Juan José and Juan Diego and the Chokonen Marcelo, and subsequently presented them to Janos commander Francisco Parea in hopes of receiving a reward. No Mexican state officially offered a bounty on Apache scalps at this time and there is no evidence that any Mexican official ever compensated Johnson for his scalps. What is clear, however, is that Sonora's military commander, Ignacio de Inclán, gave Johnson permission to keep half of the spoils he took from hostile Apaches.[4]

VIOLENT ESCALATION

Johnson's success directly influenced Chihuahua to become the first Mexican state to offer a reward for Indian scalps on July 29, 1837. Chihuahua officials offered bounties of 100 pesos for the scalp of each male Indian, 50 pesos for each female Indian, and 25 pesos for each child under twelve whom they captured.[5] Under the provisions of the law, James Kirker and his mixed band of Delaware, Shawnee, Mexican, and American mercenaries, with plenty of help from Mexican vecinos, took the scalps of an estimated 487 Apaches. But that does not tell the whole story. Attempting to clarify the law, Chihuahuan presidial commanders implored Kirker and his contract killers not to attack peace-seeking Apache rancherías and reservation-dwelling Apaches de paz. But they repeatedly ignored the warnings, and routinely captured, scalped, imprisoned, and killed peace-abiding Apaches. This began with their imprisoning and killing of 53 peaceful Apaches near Janos in January and March 1840, including the abduction and deportation of Chihene Mimbres leader Pisago Cabezón's son Marcelo to Chihuahua, and culminated in the slaughter of 148 Apaches de paz at Galeana and the San Buenaventura Valley in July 1846.[6] Little wonder, then, that Apaches were distrustful and fearful of coming into presidios and towns to negotiate and trade in this era.

Relations between Apaches and Mexicans had already worsened before the Johnson Massacre and the initiation of scalp bounty warfare. In April 1833 from his camp in the Carcay Mountains Juan José Compá wrote to his Mexican godfather, Janos Mayor Mariano Varela, of the Mexican military's treachery toward Apaches. His principal target was former Janos commander José Ignacio Ronquillo. Captain Ronquillo led a rare Chihuahuan military offensive along the upper Gila River of the northern Apachería the previous May, surprising and soundly defeating three hundred Apaches, killing twenty-two, wounding more than fifty, and taking two captives. Compá discussed none of this, however. Instead, in an apparent attempt to undermine Mexican honor, Juan José told Varela that he had heard reports of Ronquillo attacking Apaches de paz at Janos and killing others in their own homes in Agua Nueva and on the road to Chihuahua. As if Apaches had not experienced enough damage from Ronquillo, at the conclusion of peace negotiations with Apache leaders at El Paso del Norte in October 1834 he had the Chihene Mimbres leader Jasquedegá's delegation seized and held in the guardhouse as leverage for compliance for seven months.[7]

A further blow to the prospect of Apache–Mexican reconciliation occurred in the same month after Sonora's adventurous governor, Manuel Escalante y Arvizu, led a mixed force of more than three hundred Mexican troops and Indian auxiliaries into the foothills of the Mogollons. There they captured the allegedly "treacherous" Apache leader Tutijé, who supposedly commanded the *Janeros* (former Janos-dwelling Apaches de paz) and "all the rebel warriors" and was just returning with long-time Janos resident Vívora from a livestock raid in Chihuahua. Following Ronquillo's successful Mogollon offensive two and a half years earlier from the State of Chihuahua, Governor Escalante tried to assert Sonora's dominance over Apaches by having his troops drag the humiliated war leader through the streets of Arizpe and hanging him in the town square. Instead, however, it made the Ndé more angry than fearful, and they responded with intensified retaliatory raids across the state.[8]

Mexican citizens were also active participants in the escalation of violence. Residents at the mining settlement of Santa Rita del Cobre butchered Apaches twice during peaceful negotiations. They did so first in the late 1820s and again in October 1836, when they knifed and lanced two unarmed Apache men and a woman from the respected Chihene leader Pisago Cabezón's peace delegation a mere six months before Johnson's disgraceful act.[9]

It was the treachery of Johnson in 1837 and Kirker in 1846 that Apaches most remembered, and, in contrast to many contemporary scholars, they remembered them as Mexicans rather than Americans and found nothing exceptional about them other than their brutality. As the prolific Chihene Mogollon nantan Mangas Coloradas recalled decades later, "a trader was sent among us from Chihuahua. While innocently engaged in trading, often leading to words of anger, a cannon concealed behind the goods was fired upon my people and quite a number were killed." Moving on to events at Galeana, Mangas continued: "Some time ago my people were invited to a feast: *aguardiente* or whiskey was there; my people drank and become intoxicated, and were lying asleep, when a party of Mexicans came in and beat out their brains with clubs." Not surprisingly, the primary result of these treacherous acts of violence and Chihuahua's ongoing scalp bounty policy was that most Apaches refused to negotiate peace agreements with Mexicans after 1830 and the few that did generally failed to make lasting ones.[10]

Of course, Mexicans do not deserve all of the blame for the escalation in violence across the Southwest during these years. If Mexican officials helped to amplify the intensity of Apache raiding and warfare by failing to issue adequate rations and gifts to peace-seeking Apaches and by sanctioning the contract killing of independent groups, Americans and Apaches also bore responsibility for the mayhem. Anglo-American trappers and traders helped to intensify violence in this era by illicitly supplying Apaches with alcohol, guns, and ammunition in exchange for stolen Mexican horses and mules in frequent rendezvous along the Gila River and around the Santa Rita copper mines. And Apaches, after maintaining peace with Spaniards and Mexicans for more than forty years, chose to abandon their reservations and attack northern Mexican settlements more intensely than at any time since the 1770s. In January 1834, Juan José Compá freely admitted to Mexican authorities that although Mexicans had harmed Apaches, Apaches themselves "had caused many evils."[11]

Armed with American firearms and ammunition, Apaches gradually picked up the intensity of their raiding in the early 1830s in Chihuahua and Sonora by forming large inter-band raiding parties, brazenly targeting livestock and troops at Mexican presidios where they were formerly at peace, and expanding their stock raiding southward. In late September 1834, for example, more than two hundred "Gileño" warriors, who probably consisted of Chihenes based in the Mogollon and Mimbres (today's Black Range) Mountains, attacked Janos directly, running off the horse herd and killing two soldiers. And at Fronteras, where John Johnson obtained his infamous swivel gun, Chokonen and Chihene Mogollon Apaches killed an estimated two hundred people from 1832 to 1849. In August 1835 Mescalero nantan Gómez led a joint Mescalero and Chihene raiding party into central and southern Chihuahua, and by 1841 these so-called "Gileños" had pushed even farther southward into Durango. At the same time in Sonora, Ndé groups traveled as far southward as Ures and the outskirts of Hermosillo in the central part of the state. Mexicans knew many of these Apaches because they were former Apaches de paz, and some, like Gómez, still entered into periodic negotiations with presidial officers.[12]

These attacks are an underexplored part of what one historian has called "The War of a Thousand Deserts." Apaches were central players in this conflict, which extended beyond Comanches and their indigenous allies of the southern plains. In 1842 Chihuahua's governor and military commander Francisco García Conde, son of the last Spanish Commander-in-Chief of the Western Interior Provinces, Alejo García Conde, wrote, the Apaches had "dismantled the frontier" and "sacked the countryside," in a conflict so intense that it was "a thousand times worse than a foreign war" and "more disastrous than civil war." Together, Apaches,

Navajos, Comanches, and Kiowas pushed the Mexican frontier backward during these years, making the American conquest of Mexico much easier than it would have been otherwise. Between 1820 and 1835, Indians killed more than five thousand Mexicans across the northern frontier and forced the evacuation of four thousand others, and from 1831 to 1848 in Chihuahua alone Indians killed three times more Mexicans than the number of Indians Mexicans killed.[13]

Operating from vast and impenetrable mountain strongholds that stretched from the Rio Grande in the east to the Rio Gila in the west, Ndé raiding parties avoided Mexico's meager military force and began reasserting control over the southern reaches of their territory, which encompassed large portions of northern Mexico. After prompting Mexicans to abandon their river valley settlements, Apaches wisely utilized the well-watered grazing lands of the ghost towns that remained to feed their burgeoning herds of stolen, semiwild, and wild livestock. The notoriously impotent Mexican troops had an even greater challenge following the departure of the Apaches de paz in 1832 as Comanches, who often bore passports stating they were Mexican allies, pushed southwestward into interior Chihuahua. In 1833 they captured livestock within a league of Chihuahua City and took an estimated 2,000 animals over a nine-day period in January 1835, which made it even more difficult for authorities to distinguish them from Apaches.[14]

PERSISTENT PEACE

What, though, is the legacy of the establecimientos? In the midst of this prolonged cycle of reciprocal violence, it is tempting to conclude that the reciprocal benefits that Spaniards and Apaches had once achieved through political negotiation and peaceful exchange were a forgotten memory. True enough, the vast majority of Mexicans and Apaches chose war over peace in this period and forgot the lessons they had previously learned from one another. Yet vestiges of that era still remained. During the 1830s, Mexican officials distinguished Chihene and Mescalero bands formerly at peace at Janos and Carrizal during these years by calling them Janeros and Carrizaleños in their reports, and a minority of Mexican military officers and Apache leaders still valued peace and trusted one another enough to try to renegotiate. Small groups of Apaches temporarily resettled at presidios in Chihuahua and Sonora, and they would repeat this pattern with Mexican officers in those states and with Americans in New Mexico in ensuing decades.[15]

Apache and Mexican leaders frequently tried to quell the rampant violence during the 1830s by negotiating peace treaties. As early as late January 1832 from his camp at the summit of the highest peak in the Sierra Escondida southeast of Janos Juan José Compá solicited "peace and tranquility" in writing with Mayor Mariano Varela and by sending envoys Maria Antonia and Perrona to negotiate on his behalf at Janos. Even though the former Apaches de paz had allied and united to make war against Mexico, Juan José promised that if Mexicans granted them peace, "each one of them will withdraw to their *establecimiento*."[16]

The first agreement transpired in late August 1832 at Santa Rita del Cobre between Colonel Cayetano Justiniani and twenty-nine unnamed Ndé leaders, who were compelled to make peace as a result of unprecedented back-to-back successful Mexican military offensives into the Apachería. In late May Captain José Ignacio Ronquillo's troops attacked Southern Apache groups along the upper Gila River, killing twenty men, wounding fifty, and taking two captives and 140 horses, and in early June commander Joaquín Vicente Elías's Sonoran "citizen volunteers" ambushed T'iisibaan (Pinal) leader Chiquito's former Apaches de paz from Tucson and Santa Cruz presidios at Aravaipa Canyon, killing seventy-one men, capturing thirteen children, and recovering 116 horses and mules. As a result, Ndé leaders negotiated for several weeks. They included Juan Diego Compá and seven former Apaches de paz from Janos, Francisco from San Buenaventura, and others from Namiquipa and the establecimientos in Sonora. Apaches agreed to stop raiding Mexican livestock, return all branded Mexican livestock, and to stay out of the State of Chihuahua unless they received permission to enter it.[17]

In exchange, Justiniani naively tried to bestow supreme political authority on three Apache leaders and confine Apache groups to four bordering territories, based on a prior treaty with Mescaleros and Gileños in 1810. He named Juan José Compá General of the former Apaches de paz from Janos, San Buenaventura (Galeana), and Carrizal (Agua Nueva). This region stretched from Galeana in the south to Santa Lucía Springs (modern Mangas Springs, NM) in the north, and Juan José would be headquartered at Janos. Fuerte was named General of the second group of Apaches, whom Mexicans called Gileños, and the Ndé recognize as Chihene Mimbres and Mogollons, whose territory stretched across the Mimbres, Black, and Mogollon Mountains. The T'iisibaan General Aquién, who was Chihene Mogollon by birth, was to govern the third region, which stretched across the middle Gila region. Mescaleros were not assigned a General, but agreed to remain at peace in the region stretching from San Elizario and Presidio del Norte in the south to the Sacramento Mountains in the North.[18]

Because the treaty was fraught with problems, most specialists have emphasized its shortcomings. True enough, it only succeeded in reducing hostilities with Southern Apaches and Mescaleros until the spring of 1833 and granted too much political power to Spanish-speaking Apache diplomats such as Juan José, who commanded only limited influence in a time of war. By temporarily reducing violence across the frontier, however, it benefited both parties. Generals Juan José and Matías both visited Janos in October 1832, and presidial officers occasionally issued livestock or money to purchase food to other loyal Apache male leaders, such as the Chihene leader Cigarrito. Other important benefits Apaches received from this agreement included Mexican medical assistance for those suffering from illness and the freedom to farm in their territory without being attacked. Mayor Varela was undoubtedly pleased to learn that the Chihene Mimbres headmen Chirimi and Caballo Ligero and the Chihene Mogollons Mano Mocha and Antonio Pluma and their wives, all former Apaches de paz at Janos and San Buenaventura, were preparing lands for cultivation along the banks of the Mimbres River near Santa Rita in May 1833, while many of their children were working in the El Cobre mine.[19]

More broadly, this treaty stood in the face of Mexican military officers' rampant ethnocentric descriptions of Apaches as landless, roving *enemigos* (enemies) and *gandules* (loafers) in their reports. Despite underestimating Apaches' overall land base, the agreement nevertheless placed the State of Chihuahua on record as recognizing an extensive Mescalero, Mimbreño, and Gileño Apache home territory that extended from Presidio del Norte, San Elizario, and Galeana in Chihuahua northward through the Hatchet and Burro Mountains to the Sacramento, Black, and Mogollon ranges of modern New Mexico. By October Chihuahua would also recognize other unspecified Apache groups along the middle Gila River drainage in modern Arizona.[20]

The next treaty, negotiated by the Chihene Mimbres nantan Jasquedegá in November 1834 at El Paso del Norte, produced more immediately damaging results. Ndé leaders never adhered to the treaty's provisions because of Captain José Ignacio Ronquillo's unjust seizure and imprisonment of Jasquedegá and his family. The agreement is still significant, however, for identifying prominent Southern Apache leaders and their band affiliations at the time. Twenty-six Ndé leaders, whom Mexicans called Gileños, Mimbreños, and Mescaleros, including Juan José and Juan Diego Compá, signed the agreement. Interestingly, in this treaty

Juan José self-identified as a Gileño and identified his brother Juan Diego as a Mimbreño. This suggests that Juan José and Juan Diego, whose father, El Compá, is identified as Chiricagui (Chiricahua) in Spanish documents, subsequently married into two distinct Chihene subgroups. Other prominent Apache leaders signing the document included Pisago Cabezón, who is listed as a Mimbreño, and the recently named General Fuerte who is listed as a Gileño, which suggests he could be the same person as the famous Chihene Mogollon nantan Mangas Coloradas, whose name does not surface in Mexican documents until 1842. In the wake of this agreement, despite the treachery shown by Ronquillo in November, Juan José Compá continued to correspond with Captain Ronquillo in writing from the safety of his camp in the Sierra de la Negrita (between today's San Mateo and Black ranges), and he helped heal deep wounds between Apaches and Mexicans by returning to Santa Rita twice for talks with Mexican military officers, civil authorities, and mine operator Robert McKnight in late January and early February 1835.[21]

Encouraged by Juan José's diplomacy and the prospect for renewing a broader Apache peace, Chihuahua officials reissued Pedro de Nava's 1791 regulations in late January, and Governor Calvo added five new articles to reflect current realities. First, military officers would not issue weekly rations to Apaches, and Chihuahuan residents were not to sell Apaches food in place of the old rations. State residents and foreign fur traders were also prohibited from selling or trading ammunition and firearms to Apaches, even in "Apache territory." Any resident caught doing so would receive fifteen to twenty years of imprisonment, and any foreign fur trader convicted of dealing firearms to Apaches would be put to death. Finally, Apaches de paz traveling through the interior of Chihuahua were required to receive prior permission of the state's military commander-in-chief or risk being treated as hostiles.[22]

As with most Spanish and Mexican decrees, Governor Calvo's prohibitions said far more about Chihuahua's impoverishment and lack of control over frontier inhabitants and their own state than anything else. Calvo refused to reinstitute the ration program not only because he suspected most Apache men would continue to raid for livestock as they had done in the past but also because the state could not afford it. The subsequent prohibitions demonstrate that Chihuahuan residents and American merchants such as James Kirker and Robert McKnight were doing precisely what the governor did not want – selling and trading food, ammunition, and firearms to Apaches who were then raiding for livestock and captives across the states of Chihuahua and Sonora. As Governor

Calvo himself acknowledged the following spring, the "small number" of "permanent troops" were so busy "protecting the frontiers" of northern Mexico that "they cannot attend with timeliness to the defense of the interior." According to an Apache woman at Tucson in July 1834, only about half of the former Apaches de paz were raiding for livestock in interior Mexico. Approximately half of them were living and sowing crops in the Mogollon Mountains, while the other half "came south with their families to gather agave in the Chiricahua Mountains, which they also used "as a base camp for their raids" into Mexican territory. Armed with ammunition obtained from residents at Santa Rita del Cobre in exchange for stolen mules, Apache men also sent stolen Mexican "horses, mules, cattle, and sheep" northward to their kinsmen in the Mogollons.[23]

Despite the ongoing violence raging across Chihuahua and Sonora as Southern Apaches sought to avenge Jasquedegá's unjust imprisonment at El Paso del Norte and Tutijé's brutal murder in Arizpe, Juan José Compá and sixteen other unidentified Apache headmen managed to contain their emotions long enough to sign a twelve-point treaty at Santa Rita del Cobre on March 31, 1835. In this treaty, Juan José agreed to try to persuade the rancherías of twelve other, more militant Southern Apache leaders – Pisago Cabezón, Fuerte, Mano Mocha, Tebuca, Costilla, Tucileto, Torres, Cristóbal, Cigarrito, Manuel, Chirimi, and Antonio Vívora – to make peace. Of these twelve, only Antonio Vívora was physically present, and he refused to enter the room Colonel Justiniani was in, which suggests the Chihene leader feared that the officer would imprison him just as Captain Ronquillo had done to Jasquedegá at El Paso. After lengthy negotiations with the other headmen who signed the treaty, Juan José agreed that if he failed to convince the other headmen to sign the agreement, his people would "make war on any of their fathers, brothers, sons, or brothers who should refuse to accept the good that is offered them," which they never carried out. To seal the agreement, each side exchanged captives in the classic manner with the Apaches turning over three young children in exchange for a male and female Apache held prisoner by Justiniani. As additional signs of the Mexican military's sincere intentions to make a just peace, Justiniani requested that Governor Calvo order the release and return of all of Jasquedegá's relatives held prisoner in El Paso, and Calvo sent Justiniani a suit, hat, and cane for Juan José Compá and arranged for suits to be sent subsequently to the other headmen.[24]

In the spring and summer of 1836 Apache leaders sought peace again at Santa Rita del Cobre and at Tucson and Arizpe in Sonora. The

T'iisibaans and Chokonens enjoyed more success in their negotiations in Sonora than Chihene leaders did at Santa Rita. This would be the final rounds of talks between Chihene headmen and Mexican military officials at Santa Rita prior to the mine's abandonment in 1838 because of declining productivity. Proceedings began in mid-April when the four leaders Francisquillo, Itán, Ronquillo, and Muchacho negotiated with Robert McKnight for six hours. Camped with their families at El Carrizo and the Ojo del Berrendo (between the Rio Grande and Rio Mimbres), the Chihenes agreed "to try to plant crops" at El Berrendo and along the Mimbres River. Although initially optimistic, Lieutenant Mariano Rodríguez Rey questioned the veracity of their request upon discovering that they held Mexican captives and were selling stolen sheep to Santa Ritan residents. He suspected these Apaches and any others that might seek peace were doing so to gain temporary protection and avoid being attacked by Mexican troops, which, in his view, reflected "their hypocrisy, inconstancy, and perfidy." Yet he also acknowledged that the "fatal condition" of the Mexican Republic was a major factor preventing the negotiation of a lasting peace. Apaches did not take Mexicans seriously either because they had little of value to offer them and frequently killed them during peaceful exchanges.[25]

On May 10, eleven months before his violent murder, the Chihene "ambassador" Juan José Compá arrived outside of Santa Rita with his kinsman Pisago Cabezon. Tellingly, neither trusted Mexican officials enough to risk entering the town, and Pisago, who exercised more influence among the Ndé than Juan José at this point, merely agreed to hold talks with those Apaches and former Apaches de paz living in the Mogollon Mountains and in the San Francisco and Gila River Valleys. Following a violent captive exchange at Santa Rita on June 1 in which Mexican troops nearly killed Juan José's brother Juan Diego with an artillery piece, Juan José made a final attempt to negotiate with Lieutenant Rodríguez Rey's successor, Captain Mariano Ponce de León, at Santa Rita on June 21. Once again, the Chihene leader wisely refused to enter the town out of fear of being killed or held prisoner. Given that soldiers were training cannons on him from either side of the *fortín* (small fort), however, Juan José's decision to bear a white flag and negotiate on horseback with a Mexican officer on the town's outskirts was already potentially life-threatening. Despite the danger and his understandable suspicion of Mexican intent, Juan José still sent a message to De León with "an image of the Virgin of Guadalupe" as a sign of the Apaches' good faith.

The following day, Juan José, Pisago Cabezón, Itán, Caballo Ligero, and several other Chihene leaders entered the fort and met with De León and their well-behaved kinsman Chato, who had recently attended mass, and whom De León was holding as a bargaining chip. Juan Jose confessed that "war had brought" the Chihenes "many damages" and "hard times." Although he "was not innocent," he and his people would "celebrate a solid and true peace" with the entire state of Chihuahua, not just Santa Rita. If the commander issued him rations and gifts and granted his delegation the opportunity to solidify the agreement before Governor Calvo in Chihuahua City, then Juan José and his family would agree to live at Santa Rita. What Juan José and the other Ndé leaders most wanted, however, was for De León to return Chato and San Juan, another Apache captive he held, to their families. But the Santa Rita commander refused to do so until Apaches turned over two more of their leaders, Santana and El Adivino ("The Soothsayer") in exchange for them. De León accused Santana of taking a Mexican as captive, and El Adivino of rustling horses from Robert McKnight.[26]

Unfortunately, neither side complied with these initial terms. Instead, recognizing that Pisago Cabezón held more prestige than Juan José among the Chihenes, Captain De León commenced a final round of talks outside of town with Pisago, two of his sons, and the Chihene leader Tapila on September 28. Pisago explained that the Ndé were divided on their Mexican policy. He had stayed away and "never entered in any treaties" previously because none of the Ndé leaders negotiating with Mexican officers legitimately wanted peace, and he did not want Mexicans to consider Chihenes "a ridiculous and scornful people." In contrast to his prior experience with Juan José, the Santa Rita commander came away from this discussion encouraged about the prospects for a viable peace with the Chihene Mimbres and Mogollons. De León even granted Pisago a license to sell stolen livestock from Sonora, provided he did not enter Santa Rita.

Several days later five women and three men from the families of Chihene leaders Pisago Cabezón and Sidé showed up to trade livestock with Santa Rita residents. De León, seeking to avoid trouble, invited only the women, who included two of Pisago Cabezón's wives, into town. But vecinos lured the men in too. As soon as the trading concluded, a Santa Rita citizen killed one of the Apache men on the orders of acting mayor Manuel Ruedas, while other townspeople, backed by Mexican soldiers, closed in to massacre the entire group, knifing and lancing an Apache woman and two men to death. As Captain Ponce de León acknowledged,

Mexican treachery had given Pisago Cabezon just cause for what Mexicans feared the most – a full-scale Apache war of revenge.[27] Thus, it was ultimately Mexican citizens, soldiers, and their elected civil officials, more than Mexican military officers or Apaches, who killed any hope for peace at Santa Rita in the 1830s.

In spite of the fact that they typically targeted Sonora in their raids, T'iisibaans and Chokonens had much better luck in their dealings with military officers at Tucson and Arizpe than the Chihene Mimbres and Mogollons did at Santa Rita. On March 3, 1836, the T'iisibaan headmen Navicaje and Quiquiyatle, accompanied by twelve warriors and two "Tonto" observers, met with Colonel José María Elías González, commander-in-chief of Sonora's northern line, at his temporary residence in Tucson. Navicaje and Quijuiyatle told Elías González they had come to Tucson "for the sole purpose of seeking a stable and enduring peace," and they spoke the truth. Janeros were furious that Mexican officers had chosen Antuna's Apaches de paz from Tucson to guard and escort Tutijé and two other former Janos-dwelling Apache leaders from the Mogollon Mountains to Fronteras for imprisonment. Thus, the T'iisibaans sought protection at Tucson from revenge raids that Janeros threatened to carry out against them and Sonorans alike.[28]

The terms of the treaty Navicaje and Quijuiyatle negotiated with Sonora's governor, Rafael Elías González, consisted of ten articles. Perhaps most importantly, given the rampant treachery of the era, Governor Elías González assured the T'iisibaan headmen that "no Mexican troop[s] will attack them," and Navicaje and Quijuyatle promised "not to harm any Mexican citizen." They also agreed to a mutual exchange of captives, with the governor promising to return two captured Apaches in exchange for any female Mexican captives of the T'iisibaans. In a move reminiscent of past Spanish treaties with Apaches de paz, Elías González gave permission for the T'iisibaans to settle at a place they knew as Lee Ndlii ("Flows Together") at the confluence of Aravaipa Arroyo and the San Pedro River and, upon their compliance, would issue them food rations and tools and oxen to farm. In exchange for these concessions, the T'iisibaan leaders agreed to "submit themselves to the government of the Mexican nation" and "to observe its laws"; to settle and farm in the designated area; and that their men would serve "as allies" to Tucson's presidial troops against all enemies, including Tonto and White Mountain Apaches. In addition, they pledged to seek Mexico's consent before allying with other native nations, especially the Janeros; to obtain a passport from Tucson's commander whenever they traveled south of that post in a group of no more than five; and to brief him on the plans and movements of independent native peoples in the region every two weeks.²⁹ Although Sonorans were asking more of the T'iisibaans than the T'iisibaans were asking of them, the terms that Navicaje and Quijuiyatle received were more favorable than the more restrictive ones Chihuahuans were offering the Chihenes at Santa Rita in this period – rations, tools, and oxen were hard to come by in the Mexican era.

Unfortunately, the T'iisibaans were unable to fulfill their principal aim of averting violence by making peace. Although the treaty stated that no Mexican troops would attack the T'iisibaans, it said nothing about other allied Indians. In the late summer of 1837 Chief Azul of the Akimel O'odham ("river people" or Gila River Pimas) presented "fifteen pairs of Apache ears" that his people allegedly severed from the Apaches de paz residing at Lee Ndlii to interim Tucson commander José María Martínez in hopes of a reward. Prior to the 1836 T'iisibaan treaty, Martínez had promised to give Azul a suit of clothes for every campaign he led against "hostile" Ndé. Confronted with the choice of maintaining loyalty to the Akimel O'odham or the T'iisibaans, Martínez wisely chose the T'iisibaans and refused to compensate Azul. Determined to be rewarded somehow, Azul went to the prominent local merchant Teodoro Ramírez. The brother-in-law of Tucson commander Antonio Comadurán, Ramírez had successfully bartered for a parcel of land from the T'iisibaan leader Antuna's Apaches de paz at Tucson a decade earlier. Ramírez issued Azul clothing, handkerchiefs, knives, a bottle of liquor, and fifteen rifle cartridges to go out and kill more Apaches.

Once again, the actions of local Mexican citizens were threatening to undermine peace between Apaches and Mexican military leaders. It appears that the possibility of being attacked by Akimel and Tohono O'odham ("desert people" or Papagos) armed with Mexican rifles and ammunition proved too much for most T'iisibaans to take. The majority of T'iisibaans who made peace in March 1836 returned to their Pinal Mountain homeland north of Aravaipa Canyon and the Gila River Valley (south of today's Globe, AZ) and sought revenge against Mexicans and their Indian allies by driving them off their lands.³⁰

The third treaty Apaches negotiated in 1836 was also with Commander-in-Chief Elías González with preliminary talks taking place at his home in Arizpe. Five Chokonen headmen, Reyes, Matías, Marcelo, Eugenio, and Miguel (possibly Miguel Narbona) tentatively accepted a fifteen-point peace treaty and promised to return to sign it at Fronteras in October. Just as with the T'iisibaans at Tucson, Elías González tried to issue the Chokonens rations in an effort to prevent Apaches from raiding for livestock. But, much like neighboring Chihuahua, Sonora lacked sufficient funds to pay for them, and this obligation was excluded from the terms of the final treaty. When Elías González went to Fronteras in late October, he was surprised to be meeting with Chihene leaders Pisago Cabezón, Caballo Ligero, and Boca Matada in addition to Chokonen leaders. Pisago Cabezón was apparently so incensed over the murder of his family members at Santa Rita that he decided to negotiate with Sonora instead of Chihuahua. Elías González appointed Matías as General of the Chokonens and assigned them to settle at Cuchuverachi (part of modern Agua Prieta). He named Boca Matada General of the Chihenes and granted them the territory from Santa Lucía Springs to the Gila River in modern New Mexico, which they already occupied anyway because it was their homeland.[31]

That winter Chokonen groups, including a number of rancherías formerly at peace at Fronteras, began moving south and reoccupying their former territory along the modern Arizona–Sonora border. Reyes and Matías camped at Dziltilcil (Black Mountain) in the Sierra del Sarampión (today's Piloncillo Mountains), and Marcelo camped southeast of Cuchuverachi at Embudos Canyon, where Geronimo would famously negotiate with General George Crook fifty years later. But without being issued rations, the Chokonens soon violated the terms of the peace agreement, raiding for livestock in Chihuahua and Sonora alike.[32]

The next group of Apaches to solicit peace with Mexicans in the 1830s were the Chihene Mimbres leaders Antonio Mancisco, Yescas, Cristóbal, and Cigarrito the younger, who began negotiations at El Paso del Norte with Colonel José Ignacio Ronquillo on behalf of 939 of their war-weary men, women, and children in mid-1838. Yescas was formerly at peace at San Elizario, and Cigarrito's father was a long-time Carrizal resident. After turning over more than thirty horses and mules to Chihuahua state officials, the Chihene nantans signed a twelve-point peace treaty on November 15 "with the goal of ending the grave ills which necessarily come from the war of extermination which we have endured" in the hope of "enjoy[ing] the good which results from a firm and lasting peace."[33]

The treaty was significant for identifying the territorial boundaries of both parties. In contrast to previous treaties, Colonel Ronquillo, who was standing in for an ill frontier commander, represented "the Mexican nation" or, more specifically, the northern Mexican states of New Mexico, Chihuahua, Sonora, Durango, Coahuila, and Texas. But the Chihene Mimbres were simply one Apache group and would be hard pressed to prevent their own people from committing future acts of violence, let alone those from other Ndé bands. Denoting an area consistent with the Chihene nantan Sanaba's kingdom of Chi'laa of 1630, Ronquillo designated Chihene territory as "the country and mountains" surrounding "the river Gila, that of the Mimbres, the Florida and the plains of" the Rio Grande from El Paso del Norte to the San Mateo Mountains from south to north. They were thus free to settle anywhere within their own territory, provided that "each tribal Chief" specified their people's precise location and number of men, women, and children.[34]

Because of limited resources and the large number of Chihenes seeking peace, Ronquillo had to be less liberal in distributing rations than Spaniards once were. Many of his terms, however, mirrored those of prior Spanish agreements. This makes sense, given that he was a thirty-seven year veteran, the son of former Janos presidial captain José Ramón Ronquillo, and had personally ratified the 1816 peace treaty at that post with the Chihene Mogollons. Colonel Ronquillo would only issue rations to those Chihenes who "should suffer some disease or another urgent calamity." But in exchange for Chihene auxiliary assistance against Comanches and other indigenous enemies, including other Chihene rancherías "that have yet to make peace," Ronquillo *would* issue provisions to Chihene auxiliaries. They would be distinguished from other Apaches by "the use of a white handkerchief, belt or chamois worn around the head," which, apparently, Chihenes were obliged to supply.[35]

The care with which both parties addressed trading practices and Apache movement in the treaty also suggests a desire to hammer out a workable and mutually beneficial pact. Ronquillo permitted Chihene trading without passports in the Rio Grande communities of El Paso, San Elizario el Viejo, Presidio del Norte, Vado de Piedra (twenty-four miles southeast of Presidio del Norte), and Colonia de San Carlos in northeastern Chihuahua, but required them to request passports from post commanders at these locations if they intended to visit groups of Apaches de paz or to travel farther south into interior Mexico for any reason. Ronquillo banned the sale of arms and munitions to "any individual who is in a state of war with the Mexicans," which suggests that one of the Chihenes' prior motives for peace was to obtain these items and redistribute them to their independent kinsmen. In a departure from prior practice, however, he permitted them to "sell all beasts of burden" currently in their possession, which by definition included stolen livestock. The only conditions were that they had to make an effort to resell branded animals to their rightful owners and that all sales be conducted in the presence of a civil or military official.

The majority of the remaining points reflected the Mexican military's desire to control Apache behavior and utilize their labor. Ronquillo requested that within forty days each Chihene headman present all of the farming tools from his ranchería to the appropriate military officer for branding, and that these same leaders return any criminals, delinquents, or Mexican captives in their villages without seeking compensation.[36] The fact that Chihenes could remain in their own territory, sell any stolen livestock currently in their possession, and continue to trade freely in five Rio Grande communities, however, suggests these headmen extracted some important concessions from Ronquillo during their negotiations.

The last Apache treaty of the 1830s, which scholars have not closely examined, was negotiated by Mescalero nantan Barela and six other Mescalero headmen with Lieutenant Damasio Salazar at San Miguel del Vado, New Mexico, on March 1, 1839. In exchange for turning over a Mexican captive in their possession and promising "to surrender other Apaches under their control," Salazar named Barela "General" of the Mescalero tribe and issued him a staff and a reward before the six leaders and thirty-six others.[37]

Throughout the 1830s, Ndé people faced escalating violence against them from Mexican soldiers, settlers, and their indigenous allies as the states of Sonora and Chihuahua transitioned from a policy predicated on partial peace to one emphasizing offensive war and contract killing. At El Paso del Norte and Santa Rita del Cobre, which, ironically, lay within the heart of their own Chi'laa homeland, Chihene emissaries found their lives increasingly at risk. In spite of these obstacles, Ndé leaders from Juan José Compá to Barela demonstrated a persistent desire to reconcile relations with Mexican military officers at frontier presidios and towns.

Overall, these agreements show that Ndé leaders sought peace with Mexicans for many of the same reasons that they had with Spanish officers, including protection from unprovoked attacks, recovering captured kinsmen, exchanging goods, and obtaining food and supplies. Some of their reasons, such as obtaining medical assistance for those suffering illness, however, were new solutions to recurring problems that they may have learned about during their prior experience at the establecimientos. Because Mexican officials lacked the financial resources to follow through on their treaty obligations, however, Apaches were more likely to go to Americans to fulfill their needs or simply appropriate them from the largest Mexican ranchos and haciendas themselves.

The Mexican military strategy of reducing Apache violence by granting individual Southern Apache leaders the power to govern distinct zones of the Apachería proved no more successful in 1832 than the original Spanish attempt in 1810. This treaty and the 1838 agreement with Colonel Ronquillo are still significant, however, for helping to clarify the approximate territorial boundaries of distinct Southern Apache groups and demonstrating that not all Mexican military officers sought to eradicate Apaches. The fact that numerous Chihene Mimbres and Mogollon families formerly at peace at presidios in Chihuahua were farming along the Mimbres River in the spring of 1833, while their children labored in the Santa Rita mines, is also revealing, given the prevalent assumption that Apaches were simply raiding the Mexican frontier in this era.

RISKING RESETTLEMENT

Perhaps because it seemed so impossible, given Mexico's underfunded and undermanned frontier military and the extreme violence that bookended it on either side, most scholars have paid little attention to the three-year uneasy peace between the Ndé and Mexicans from 1842 to 1845.[38] According to Mexican documents, the diplomacy of Chihuahua and New Mexico civil and military officials, rather than Mexican military force, was responsible for the reduction in violence. Frustrated with the escalation in Apache raiding across Chihuahua that Mexican military force had helped encourage, Chihuahua political and business leader José Cordero, perhaps a descendant of former Spanish officer and Texas governor Antonio Cordero, repeatedly advised New Mexico governor Manuel Armijo to seek peace with Apache leaders. In early 1842 Armijo appointed Lieutenant Vicente Sánchez Vergara and Captain Damasio Salazar to negotiate terms for peace in Santa Fe with nantans representing 28 Ndé headmen, including the Chihene Pisago Cabezón, from groups Mexicans called Mescaleros and Gileños, which both groups accepted. At the conclusion of the initial agreements, these leaders subsequently appointed emissaries, most notably the Chihene Mimbres leader Vicente, to be escorted by Sánchez Vergara and Salazar to Chihuahua City to seal the treaties.[39]

Ndé headmen were likely more receptive to Armijo's overtures than those of presidial commanders in Chihuahua or Sonora for three main reasons. Santa Fe civilians and military personnel had not acted treacherously toward them; Mescaleros had previously worked with Salazar in 1838; and Ndé leaders were able to negotiate favorable terms that may have included gaining access to Mexican firearms and gunpowder.[40]

Governor Francisco García Conde's decision to employ a more conciliatory Apache policy in Chihuahua was an interrelated important factor. Echoing the sound logic of Spanish viceroy Bernardo de Gálvez, Governor García Conde believed that even if a peace treaty produced a mere "truce" it was still worth it because it reduced hostilities, was far cheaper than war, and allowed Mexicans and Apaches to make friendships and better understand each other. "Exterminating their race," García Conde wrote, "is neither convenient, nor just, nor possible."[41]

Despite the governor's compelling rhetoric, Mexican officers failed to even properly identify the band affiliation of the Ndé leaders with whom they were negotiating. In February 1842 the Chihene Ojo Caliente nantan Ponce, whom Mexicans mistakenly deemed a Mescalero chief and misnamed José María, reviewed a set of three Mexican-imposed preliminary treaty terms with Captain Salazar in Santa Fe. These stated that the Ndé wanted to make peace with the State of Chihuahua in exchange for an annual allotment of 5,000 pesos for rations, the acquisition of a unique brand for their livestock, the rights to sell their branded livestock and ransom their Mexican captives to anyone, and the freedom to retain those Mexican captives who had joined their ranks voluntarily.[42]

Ndé leaders accepted Salazar's terms and also issued him five demands of their own. These were clear-cut attempts to avoid being subjected to senseless, treacherous Mexican- and American-initiated violence, which Governor Donaciano Vigil recorded in Santa Fe in late February 1842. Thus, they demanded that only Apaches occupy Santa Rita del Cobre and that James Kirker and Robert McKnight not be permitted in New Mexico, and that Shawnees be banned from the State of Chihuahua. In addition, they asked that those "Apaches who might not wish peace" receive "a mountain" to reside in "while being pursued and reduced to order." Rather than risk being slaughtered while at peace in Chihuahua, they requested "lands within New Mexico" and specifically asked that the sons of the leader Saguestequi receive the Laguna de Guzmán (south of the Florida Mountains and northwest of Janos at the mouth of the Casas Grandes River in today's northwestern Chihuahua), La Boca Grande (probably the Boca Grande Mountains of today's northwestern Chihuahua), Alamo Grueso (possibly the Alamo Hueco Mountains of southwestern New Mexico), and Cusán or Las Ánimas (probably the Animas Mountains eighty miles northwest of Janos in today's Hidalgo County, NM, and site of the Johnson Massacre) as establecimientos for their people. More important than whether these lands lay within the imagined state boundaries of New Mexico or Chihuahua is the fact that all of these lands were part of the Chihene homeland of Chi'laa, where Ponce's people had been residing for centuries.[43]

Following negotiations in Santa Fe, Ponce sent two envoys to Chihuahua City in mid-April. There they renegotiated terms with state officials to correspond with previously successful Spanish policy, and Chihuahua officials imposed false authority on Ponce by naming him Mescalero "General." After sending his approval of the renegotiated terms to the San Elizario presidial commander, Ponce and his people, who, based on the locations of the lands they requested alone, were clearly Chihenes rather than Mescaleros, peacefully settled on the outskirts of El Paso in June.[44]

On the heels of Ponce's success, Mescalero leaders initiated their own negotiations with Governor García Conde in Chihuahua City and El Paso. While Nantan Espejo met with the governor in the capital in May, Chihuahuans stopped to observe his Mescalero delegation in the streets. Impressed by their skillful blending of the latest Mexican and Apache fashion trends, the citizens noted "the new use of moustaches by the men," "the delicate features of some of" the women, and "the uniqueness of their adornments and ... designs painted on their faces." On June 12 a second Mescalero leader, Gómez, representing all of the Ndé bands from the area of Agua Nueva (70 miles southeast of Carrizal), including that of the Chihene Mimbres headman Cigarrito, met with Governor Francisco García Conde at El Paso del Norte to sign a treaty enabling them to resettle near Carrizal presidio under terms identical to those signed by Ponce's emissaries in Chihuahua.[45]

Mescaleros and Mimbreños de paz near El Paso remained compliant through at least October 1842. They received biweekly rations and interacted with Mexican residents routinely and without incident, despite frequently getting drunk. Those few Apache men who were still conducting livestock raids, were members of independent bands.[46]

Peace proceedings with Chihene Gila groups farther west proved more volatile given the escalating reciprocal treachery that had transpired over the past decade. They were still smarting from James Kirker's unauthorized ambush of Pisago Cabezón's ranchería in January 1840, while the nantan was negotiating at Janos to recover his son Marcelo, whom Mexicans had imprisoned in Chihuahua as a bargaining chip. It was not until late April 1842, after a meeting of twenty-eight Ndé headmen along the banks of the Gila River, that Lieutenant Antonio Sánchez Vergara escorted the Chihene Mimbres leader Vicente to Chihuahua City, where, like previous Ndé groups, they renegotiated the terms of their agreement. After the emissaries returned to the Apachería to seek the approval of Pisago Cabezón, Manuel, and the rest of their people, the Chihenes named Manuel "General" in place of Pisago Cabezón, who was apparently now too old to travel much.⁴⁷

On July 4 General Manuel and three Chihene delegates from the rancherías of Jasquedegá and Jasquiatil – Anaya, Vicente, and Ponce – returned to Janos presidio to ratify the ten-point treaty with Governor García Conde on behalf of their people. The governor authorized the post commander to assign them to designated "unowned wilderness areas" near the presidio and issue them rations "under the same terms as those that the Government of the King of Spain used to give." Chihenes also retained the rights to "freely exchange their goods" at Janos and to retain all horses in their possession. In return, General Manuel agreed to brand each Chihene horse, cease all hostilities against Mexico, report "all hostile movements" his people observed among their native neighbors, and inform the post commander of any alliances or war declarations the Chihenes made with them. Manuel would also appoint a chieftain to remain at the post with his family and several other men to help the troops maintain peace, provided that they received rations and "the clothing which is available." Like Juan José Compá in the treaty at Santa Rita in March 1835, Manuel agreed to use his authority to influence other hostile Chihene bands to make peace, after which time he would authorize reservation-dwelling Chihene men to serve as Mexican auxiliaries against them and independent Mescaleros. Upon ratification of the treaty, both parties agreed to exchange all "captives in their custody" as a sign of their friendship.⁴⁸

Almost immediately, independent Ndé men tested the strength of the new Janos peace by raiding for the presidio's livestock. Faithfully complying with their agreement, General Manuel and Nantan López had Apaches de paz track down the guilty parties. The Chihene scouts identified one group as members of Mangas Coloradas's ranchería, and the others were likely also Chihene holdouts, including members of the rancherías of Sargento, Chinito, Itán, and Nagúe, who was closely associated with Pisago Cabezón.⁴⁹

Now, for the longest period since the eve of the dissolution of the establecimientos in 1832, peaceful accommodation prevailed over violence on the Apache–Chihuahua frontier. On July 13 the Chihene headmen Torres, Francisco, Antonio, Negrito, Vívora, Francisquillo, Vicente, Rosario, and El Rapado agreed to settle in the San Joaquín Mountains near San Buenaventura presidio under terms similar to those of their kinsmen at Janos, based in part on Commander-in-chief Pedro de Nava's 1791 Instructions. All recognized Manuel as their "General," and by August at least five Chihene Gila rancherías, under the leadership of Manuel, Pisago Cabezón, Anaya, Coyante, and Cristóbal, were residing peacefully around Janos.[50]

Picking up where Governor García Conde left off, the recently appointed Governor and Commander-in-Chief José Mariano Monterde concluded treaties with two more Apache groups in northern Chihuahua during the month of April. Meeting first with the Chihene headmen Mangas Coloradas, Fusilito (Little Musket), and Itán at Janos on April 1, 1843, whom Mexicans collectively deemed Mogolloneros, he surprisingly secured peace under the same terms his predecessor had with Chihene General Manuel. With the leaders Manuel, Anaya, and Torres serving as witnesses, Monterde named Mangas Coloradas "General." After initially voicing their mistrust of Monterde based on more than a decade of Mexican treachery, Mangas and the Chihene Mogollons "publically declared their absolute agreement" with the terms of the treaty and proclaimed "the true and good faith with which they embrace peace." Monterde then traveled to El Paso and concluded an agreement with Chihene Mimbres leaders Sargento and Chinito, who, just as Mangas's people had, had remained independent and at war with Chihuahua.[51]

According to one scholar, the reason that the Chihene Mogollons trusted Chihuahuans enough to come to Janos to negotiate peace in the first place is that Lieutenant Antonio Sánchez Vergara had previously met with Chihene leaders, including Mangas Coloradas and Itán, in the Mogollon Mountains in late January. Governors García Conde and Monterde's willingness to issue rations to Apaches and return captives was also critical to maintaining peace and minimizing Apache raiding. Finally, Monterde also deserves credit for openly admitting that Mexicans had helped escalate war with Apaches by committing treacherous acts of violence from the Johnson Massacre to Kirker's ambush of Pisago Cabezón's ranchería.[52]

More broadly, this peace may represent the desire of a new generation of Mexicans and Apaches to reforge the bonds of kinship once enjoyed by their parents. If you compare the last names of the Mexican leaders pushing for peace in this decade, they sound quite familiar. Antonio Sánchez Vergara was meeting with Southern Apache rancherías in their own camps, just as Domingo Vergara had done in 1786. José Cordero, an early advocate for peace with Apaches in 1842 and future Governor of Chihuahua, may have been related to former Janos commander and Commander-in-Chief Antonio Cordero, and Chihuahua's governor Francisco

García Conde was one of three sons of Sonora's former governor and Commander in Chief of the Western Interior Provinces Alejo García Conde. Similarly, Chihenes believe that Mangas Coloradas is the grandson of Ojos Colorados, which may help explain why Mangas Coloradas, like his grandfather fifty-three years earlier, was able to dispel enough of his distrust of Chihuahuenses to make peace at Janos.[53] However strong the factor of kinship may have been, after a decade of intensive warfare interspersed with sporadic and chaotic peace agreements with individual Mexican communities and states, many Mexican and Southern Apache leaders were ready for a change.

With the Mogollons now at peace, enough Apache and Mexican leaders were cooperating with one another that they could potentially manage the reciprocal acts of violence still being carried out by Apaches and Mexicans. Their first test came in Sonora. On May 26 a Western Apache (Coyotero) raiding party ran off the presidial horse herd at Fronteras, wounding a soldier and killing two citizens. After closely pursuing the Indians, a posse of seven Apache auxiliaries and Sonoran troops managed to recover many of the horses. However, one of the Apaches knew the attackers and ran off with them. At that point, instead of continuing to pursue their adversaries, the Sonorans instead treacherously killed the remaining six Apaches de paz. In the 1830s a violent incident such as this would have completely ruptured any chance at reconciliation. But, now, with influential Mexican and Apache political leaders working together, diplomacy prevailed. Rather than initiate a reciprocal raid on Sonora, five Ndé leaders – Mangas Coloradas, Manuel, Torres, and Anaya from Janos and Zozaya from Carrizal – voiced their displeasure with Janos Captain Madrigal by calling for Mexican authorities to punish the Sonoran troops for their treachery.[54]

As a result of their efforts, Governor Monterde of Chihuahua issued a formal complaint to Sonora's governor José Urrea on the Apaches' behalf, and an Ndé delegation traveled to Guaymas to meet with him. With the assistance of Lieutenant Sánchez Vergara, on June 4, 1843, the Chihene Mogollon leader Negrito and Chokonen emissaries Matías and Marcelo concluded a four-point peace treaty with Governor Urrea. In exchange for the governor's "friendship" and offer to issue them "some supplies when they need them," the headmen promised that the Chihenes and Chokonens "will make no hostile movement" in Sonora, to seek permission of Colonel Antonio Narbona prior to approaching any Sonoran town or presidio, and to accompany Sonoran troops on campaigns against independent Indians "who have not adopted peace."[55]

From at least January 1843 through June 1844, officers at Janos and the nearby mining town of Corralitos issued Apaches de paz weekly rations of beef, corn, piloncillo, and cigars, when they had sufficient quantities. Not surprisingly, given the political instability and compromised economic resources of the Mexican state, quantities were limited. Making frequent complaints of corn, piloncillo, and cigar shortages, Janos officers sometimes supplemented such meager rations by issuing Apaches money to purchase additional items, such as salt, chili, and bread, and their "vices," which almost certainly included liquor. During the first week of January at Janos 245 Chihenes de paz (38 men, 66 women, and 141 children), including General Manuel and the nantan José María Ponce and their families, received a little over 112 pesos worth of beef drawn from a single steer, nearly 17 bushels of corn, and 1,165 cigars. At Corralitos during the same week, 130 Chihenes de paz (22 men, 30 women, and 78 children), including Nantans Anaya and Francisquillo and their families, accepted just under 44 pesos worth of beef, 9 bushels of corn, and 98 cigars. Although the provisions were inadequate in both locations, Apaches at Janos fared better than those at Corralitos, and the Janos garrison would spend an average of 816 pesos per month on rations at both locations from January through June. Also telling are the high percentage of widows among reservation-dwelling women at Janos (21 percent), suggesting that prolonged warfare was taking a heavy toll on the Chihene adult male population in this era.[56]

Apaches at Janos and Corralitos, for their part, were dissatisfied not only with the small quantities of food they were receiving but also with the Mexican military's efforts to protect them. In late June Captain Pedro Madrigal observed that rations were so insufficient that Apache women at Janos needed to supplement their families' subsistence by harvesting mescal, and during the same month the leader Reyes expressed concern that Mexican officers issued provisions to Apaches at the same time that armed troops were gathering. On November 1, Captain Madrigal reported some of "the principal men" of Janos presidio had been giving Apaches their own meat, panocha, cigars, salt, soap, and money in order to give the Indians something, but that corn was now all that was left to give, and the Apaches were unwilling to accept that alone. Despite the officers' efforts to honor their end of the bargain, the unfortunate reality is that the Chihenes remained upset with the frequent ration shortages, outright ration omissions, and the paltry garrison's inability to protect and regulate them.[57]

In spite of these obstacles, just as they had done previously with Spaniards, some Apache leaders expressed an interest in farming. After meeting with Governor Monterde in late March 1843, twelve citizens in the Galeana District donated parcels of arable land for Apaches to farm, including one to Nantan Charro in the San Buenaventura Valley. Although Apaches de paz still periodically raided for livestock, they generally confined their most intense activities to Sonora, reducing the frequency and intensity of their raiding in Chihuahua for a two-and-a-half-year period from July 1842 to February 1845. When Apaches de paz did target Chihuahuan livestock, it was typically an individual Apache male butchering an animal to supplement his family's meager rations or, in an increasingly prevalent pattern, stealing one to trade for alcohol.[58]

Once again, half a century after they had done so the first time, a minority of Ndé headmen and Mexican officers relied on diplomacy to garner reciprocal benefits and reduce violence. With Chihene Generals Manuel and Mangas Coloradas leading the way, Ndé leaders were quite busy, conducting negotiations with Mexican officials on the northern and southern frontiers of their vast homeland, from Santa Fe to Chihuahua City, and resettling in establecimientos at Janos, Corralitos, and Carrizal. Although rations and gifts were meager and protection uncertain, these peace agreements still demonstrated the soundness of Spanish Bourbon Indian policy in relying on localized peace to foster cross-cultural and material exchange. Apaches and Mexicans still possessed reciprocally desirable resources. Both groups had valuable information and employed captives as bargaining chips. Some Ndé men still offered Mexicans their services as scouts or farmed on plots of arable land. Most frequently, however, Apaches attempted to trade wild, semiwild, and appropriated Mexican livestock for gunpowder, firearms, and liquor, which they increasingly demanded.

DEATH AND DISSOLUTION

Unfortunately, disease and Sonoran-initiated violence, which posed an unexpected new threat to peaceful relations between Apaches and Chihuahuans, were the primary causes of the breakdown in peace. Just as in 1831, Apaches de paz initially left their reservations because of a smallpox outbreak, and those at Janos led the exodus. In February 1844 they began departing the presidio. Although only five Apaches had been infected with the illness, three of them had died, and Apaches believed that Chihuahuenses intentionally contaminated their rations with the disease. By June 1844 only forty Apaches remained at peace at Janos. By early 1845 a majority of Apaches de paz in Chihuahua had vacated their posts as well. Just as in 1831, Apaches de paz were also dissatisfied with the insufficient rations. Consequently, they immediately escalated their raiding in interior Chihuahua in 1845.[59]

That said, the unauthorized ambush of Apaches de paz at Corralitos and Janos by Sonoran officers José María Elías González and Antonio Narbona in the summer of 1844 was a devastating blow to Apaches de paz already suffering from disease and hunger and helped undermine the peace. In response to the decimation of a Sonoran force near Santa Cruz by unidentified Apaches in July 1844, Colonels Elías Gonzalez and Narbona decided to punish the most accessible Apache groups they find. Although it was common knowledge that some male Apaches de paz raided for Sonoran livestock and traded it in Chihuahua, González and Narbona had no prior proof that any of those Indians participated in the July attack on Sonoran troops. Instead, in violation of Governor Monterde's warning for Sonoran troops not to track Apaches into Chihuahua and without notifying Chihuahuan officers ahead of time, in late August Elías González and Narbona killed eighty and captured thirty unsuspecting Apaches – the vast majority women and children.[60]

These attacks fueled mistrust between Apaches de paz and Chihuahuan presidial officers and violence between Apaches and Mexicans throughout the region; however, peace and diplomacy were still not completely dead. As in 1832, a small group of Apaches de paz remained at some posts. In February 1845, Mescaleros still resided at Agua Nueva under Nantan Gómez and at the Colonia de San Carlos, and at Janos about a dozen Apaches under the Chokonen leader Reyes and the Chihene headman Torres continued to help presidial troops capture raiding Apaches. Ndé and Mexican leaders made reciprocal visits to try to ease tensions and retain peace. In early 1845 Apaches de paz traveled to Chihuahua City; in late June three female emissaries tried to negotiate peace at Janos on behalf of Chihene General Manuel and former Janos residents Matías, Nagué, and Irigoyen; and in August Lieutenant Sánchez Vergara made a return trip to the Mogollon Mountains, where he met with the Chihene Ojo Caliente leader Ponce, who led the former Apaches de paz.[61]

But it was not long before the treacherous violence of Chihuahua's own citizens and bounty hunters would make it unsafe for Apaches to remain at peace. In late December 1845 Southern Apache leaders Ramón, Zozaya, Ponce, and Anselmo had settled at Carrizal and were receiving biweekly rations. One night while visiting and drinking with Carrizaleños, the vecino Luis Rodríguez ambushed and knifed the Apaches to death. Similarly, as another group of Southern Apaches was attempting to resettle at Galeana and Namiquipa in July 1846, James Kirker's indigenous and Mexican contract killers slaughtered 148 of them, including the Chihene leader Torres and the Chokonen Reyes, at Galeana and in the San Buenaventura Valley. Given the reescalation of treacherous violence in northern Chihuahua towns, it is not surprising that by January 1846 Apaches had completely vacated Carrizal and Janos, and that, following Kirker's attack, Apaches made no further attempts to make peace with Mexicans until after the U.S.–Mexican War. Subsistence, survival, and keeping encroaching Mexicans and Americans out of the Apachería were the main challenges all Ndé groups faced during these years, but the very same conflict also provided them, especially those west of the Rio Grande, unexpected relief.[62]

Notes

1 Sweeney, *Mangas Coloradas*, 71; Rex W. Strickland, "The Birth and Death of a Legend: The Johnson 'Massacre' of 1837," *Arizona and the West* 18 (Autumn 1976): 270–271. For the most reliable primary source on this event, see John J. Johnson to José Joaquín Calvo, Janos, April 24, 1837, translated in Strickland, "The Birth and Death of a Legend," 277–278.

2 Strickland, "The Birth and Death of a Legend," 265, 268, 272.

3 Strickland, "The Birth and Death of a Legend," 271, 273–274. For Antonio Vívora's survival and his father Vívora as Mimbreño, see Griffen, *Apaches at War and Peace*, 72, 174. Former Chihene Ndé Nation of New Mexico Historical Record Keeper Lorraine García confirms that Antonio Vívora was Chihene (personal communication).

4 Smith, *Borderlander*, 269n11, 270n17; Strickland, "The Birth and Death of a Legend," 260n4, 275–277. The quotation is from p. 276. For the argument that Johnson's primary motive was to obtain mules rather than collect Apache scalps, see Officer, *Hispanic Arizona*, 150. I thank Michael Paul Hill for confirming the Chihene affiliation of Juan José and Juan Diego Compá (personal communication). For Juan José and Juan Diego as Gileño and Mimbreño, respectively, see Griffen, *Apaches at War and Peace*, 149–150. For the misidentification of Juan José and Juan Diego Compá as Nednhi, see Sweeney, *Mangas Coloradas*, 5. For Marcelo, who is distinct from the son of Pisago Cabezón with the same name, as either Chokonen or Nednhi, see Sweeney, *Mangas Coloradas*, 66, 69.

5 Smith, *Borderlander*, 70–71. Prior to 1976, numerous writers, from John Russell Bartlett to Ralph A. Smith, erroneously reported that a Sonoran decree of September 7, 1835, authorized scalp bounty warfare. Rex. W. Strickland corrected this error. See Strickland, "The Birth and Death of a Legend," 260n4. At least two well-respected historians have subsequently repeated the error. See Sweeney, *Mangas Coloradas*, 45, 65; Jacoby, *Shadows at Dawn*, 61.

6 Ralph A. Smith, "Indians in American–Mexican Relations Before the War of 1846," *Hispanic American Historical Review* 43 (February 1963): 45–46, 62–63; Smith, *Borderlander*, 103, 170; Griffen, *Apaches at War and Peace*, 187, 216; Sweeney, *Mangas Coloradas*, 83–86, 134–136. The scalp estimate comes from Smith, 170. According to Lorraine García, Pisago Cabezón the younger was a Chihene leader from the middle Gila River Valley region, who succeeded his father as leader, following Pisago Cabezón the elder's passing in the late 1830s (personal communication). For Pisago Cabezón the younger as a Mimbreño and as a likely son of Pisago Cabezón the elder, who died in the 1790s, see Griffen, *Apaches at War and Peace*, 127, 149; Smith, *Borderlander*, 48. For an alternative view that Pisago the younger was Chokonen (Chiricahua), see Sweeney, *Mangas Coloradas*, 7. For the same leader as a Bedonkohe, see Dan L. Thrapp, *Encyclopedia of Frontier Biography*, vol. II, (1988; reprint, Lincoln: University of Nebraska Press, 1991), 413. In an 1842 treaty at Janos he is called a Gileño, which supports all prior interpretations except Sweeney's. See Antonio Sánchez Vergara, "Treaty with the Gila Apache," Janos, July 4, 1842, translated in Deloria and DeMallie, *Documents of Indian Diplomacy*, 167–168. He also camped in the Mogollon Mountains during the winter months, which points against him being a Chokonen. See for example, Griffen, *Apaches at War and Peace*, 187; [Unsigned draft] to the Commander-in-Chief, no. 3, Janos, February 11, 1840, F4, S1, JPR-UTA.
7 Juan José Compá to Mariano Barela, Cacai, April 25, 1833, roll 25, JA-UA; Rafael Carbajal, "Filiación" for Matias Villalobos, Janos, May 27, 1832, F34, S2, JPR-UTA; Griffen, *Apaches at War and Peace*, 144; Joseph C. Jastrzembski, "Treacherous Towns in Mexico: Chiricahua Personal Narratives of Horrors," *Western Folklore* 54 (July 1995): 172. For Ronquillo's actions at El Paso del Norte, see Sweeney, *Mangas Coloradas*, 58, 64. Although historian Edwin R. Sweeney identifies Jasquedegá (Jasquidega, Jasquiedegá) as a Nednhi, he was Chihene Mimbres and a relative of Vívora. See Griffen, *Apaches at War and Peace*, 90, 127.
8 Sweeney, *Mangas Coloradas*, 58–60; Smith, *Borderlander*, 50–51; DeLay, *War of a Thousand Deserts*, 156. For the quotation, see Manuel Escalante, Hacienda de San Pedro, November 2, 1834, translated in McCarty, *Frontier Documentary*, 46. In reality, Tutijé was probably a Bedonkohe Apache from the Mogollon range. See Thrapp, *Encyclopedia of Frontier Biography*, vol. III, 1042.
9 Jastrzembski, "Treacherous Towns in Mexico," 177–178; Griffen, *Utmost Good Faith*, 171–172; [Unsigned draft] to the Commander-in-Chief of the State of Chihuahua, no. 94, [El Cobre], October 3, 1836, F38, S2, JPR-UTA.
10 United States Congress, *Condition of the Indian Tribes: Report of the Joint Special Committee, Appointed under Joint Resolution of March 3, 1865.* (Washington, DC: Government Printing Office, 1867), 328. The Ndé people and scholars disagree about Mangas Coloradas' band affiliation by birth and as a leader. According to Lorraine Garcia, Mangas Coloradas was a Chihene Mogollon leader from the Big Burro Mountains of the lower Gila River Valley in modern Grant County, NM (personal communication). For support of Mangas Coloradas as Chihene Mogollon by birth and as a leader, see Griffen,

Utmost Good Faith, 74; Griffen, *Apaches at War and Peace*, 90, 94, 192. For a contrary view that Mangas Coloradas was Chihene Mimbres by birth, see Jason Betzinez, *I Fought With Geronimo* (Harrisburg, PA: Stackpole Company, 1959), 4, 43; Christopher J. Huggard and Terrence M. Humble, *Santa Rita del Cobre: A Copper Mining Community in New Mexico* (Boulder: University Press of Colorado, 2012), 18. For a third perspective that Mangas Coloradas was a Bedonkohe (Mogollonero) by birth who married into a mixed Mimbreño-Bedonkohe group, see Sweeney, *Mangas Coloradas*, 9–10, 30–31.

11 For Anglo-American trappers and traders, see Smith, *Borderlander*, 42–53; Griffen, *Apaches at War and Peace*, 187; the Commander of the Western Frontier [Capt. Mariano Ponce de León] to the Commander-in-chief, [El Cobre], January 12, 1836, F38, S2; [Unsigned draft] to the Commander-in-chief, no. 3, Janos, February 11, 1840, F4, S1, JPR-UTA. For the quotation, see Juan José Compá, January 6, 1834, roll 26, JHA-UTEP, quoted in Jastrzembski, "Treacherous Towns in Mexico," 177 (my translation).

12 For Apache raiding in Chihuahua and Durango during these years, see Griffen, *Utmost Good Faith*, 35, 46, 58, 71. For Apache raiding in Sonora, see Robert C. Stevens, "The Apache Menace in Sonora, 1831–1849," *Arizona and the West* 6 no. 3 (Autumn 1964): 211, 215–221; Spicer, *Cycles of Conquest*, 240; McCarty, *Desert Documentary*, 119. For general syntheses, see Ralph A. Smith, "Apache Plunder Trails Southward, 1831–1840," *New Mexico Historical Review* 37 (January 1962): esp. 20–32; Smith, "Indians in American-Mexican Relations," esp. 35–40; Ralph A. Smith, "Apache 'Ranching' Below the Gila, 1841–1845," *Arizoniana* 3 (Winter 1962): 1–17; Weber, *Mexican Frontier*, 83–121; Brian DeLay, "Independent Indians and the U.S.–Mexico War," *American Historical Review* 112 (February 2007): esp. 35–37, 40–42, 51, 60. For Mexican recognition of Apaches, see Griffen, *Utmost Good Faith*, 102; Sweeney, *Mangas Coloradas*, 70.

13 For the first quotation, see DeLay, *War of a Thousand Deserts*, xv. Although DeLay includes Apache, Navajo, and Kiowa raiding in northern Mexico in his analysis, he is more focused on Comanches, as is historian Pekka Hämäläinen. See Hämäläinen, *Comanche Empire*, 193–238. For the remaining quotations, see Francisco García Conde, "Manifiesto que dirige á los habitantes del departamento de Chihuahua ... explicando los motivos de su visita á las fronteras del Paso y Janos, los resultados de ella y todo lo concerniente á los tratados de paz que acaba de celebrar con los apaches," Chihuahua, September 23, 1842, in Jorge Chávez Chávez, "Construcción de una cultura regional en el norte de México" (Ph.D. diss., Universidad Nacional Autónoma de México, 2007), 252–253. For indigenous equestrians pushing back the northern Mexican frontier after 1820, see DeLay, *War of a Thousand Deserts*, 303; Reséndez, *Changing National Identities at the Frontier*, 45–51; Spicer, *Cycles of Conquest*, 240; Stevens, "Apache Menace," 220–221; Escudero, *Noticias estadísticas*, 78; Zúñiga, *Rápida ojeada al estado de Sonora*, 15; Griffen, *Utmost Good Faith*, 235. The statistics for northern Mexico come from Escudero and for Chihuahua from Griffen.

14 Samuel Truett, "The Ghosts of Frontiers Past: Making and Unmaking Space in the Borderlands," *Journal of the Southwest* 46 (Summer 2004): 312, 315, 317,

322–323; Griffen, *Utmost Good Faith*, 49; Dobyns, *From Fire to Flood*, 87. For Comanche raiding in interior Chihuahua during the 1830s, see "Discurso: Pronouncement of the Vice Governor of Chihuahua," [no day or year – 1833], roll 25, JA-UA; Gov. Jose Joaquín Calvo, Chihuahua, October 20, 1834, roll 6, JA-UA; Calvo to the Commander of the Western Frontier, Chihuahua, April 20, 1836, F38, S1, JPR-UTA; *El Fanal de Chihuahua*, January 25, 1835, 67, microfilm, UTEP; and Matthew Babcock, "Transnational Trade Routes and Diplomacy: Comanche Expansion, 1760–1846" (M.A. thesis, University of New Mexico, 2001), 102–104. For "the notorious impotence of the presidial troops," see the first document.

15 Griffen, *Apaches at War and Peace*, 140–142, 145–151, 158–160, 162, 168–169, 172, 176, 186–187, 248–249, 254–255; Sweeney, *Mangas Coloradas*, 5, 312, 50–52, 56–58, 61–62, 66–69, 85–87, 92–107, 110–112, 133–134, 166–170, 185–189, 191–196, 198–205, 217–218, 226, 284–293, 303–314, 318, 322–323, 331–341, 351–352, 358–359, 364, 370–387.

16 Ramón Zuñiga to the Commander-in-Chief of the State of Chihuahua [draft], Janos, January 22, 1832, roll 25, JA-UA. For the Sierra Escondida's location, see Griffen, *Apaches at War and Peace*, 139. For a rare, preliminary analysis of Native treaties with Mexicans in this period, see Ralph A. Smith, "Many Mini Treaties with West Texas Indians," *West Texas Historical Association Year Book* 47 (1971): 62–77.

17 Capt. José Ignacio Ronquillo, "Lista de la gente que asistió a la campaña que se hallo en ... el rio de Gila," Janos, June 4, 1832, roll 24, JA-UA; Griffen, *Apaches at War and Peace*, 141; Sweeney, *Mangas Coloradas*, 48; Edwin R. Sweeney, *Cochise: Chiricahua Apache Chief* (Norman: University of Oklahoma Press, 1991), 20; Smith, *Borderlander*, 43–45. For the Sonoran attack on the T'iisibaan (Pinals), see Sonora Governor Manuel Escalante y Arvizu to Chihuahua Governor José Isidro Madero, Arizpe, June 27, 1832, translated in McCarty, *Frontier Documentary*, 36; Jacoby, *Shadows at Dawn*, 161.

18 Commander-in-Chief of the State of Chihuahua and Territory of New Mexico José Joaquín Calvo, "Bases principales para conceder la paz, a los Apaches sublevados en el estado de Chihuahua," Encinillas, July 28, 1832, roll 5, JA-UA; Griffen, *Apaches at War and Peace*, 141–142; Sweeney, *Mangas Coloradas*, 50–51. For the location of Santa Lucía Springs, see Robert Hixson Julyan, *The Place Names of New Mexico*, 2nd ed. (1996; reprint, Albuquerque: University of New Mexico Press, 1998), 219. General Aquién's band affiliations are courtesy of Lorraine Garcia (personal communication). Historian Edwin R. Sweeney makes several claims that are not supported by Griffen or the documents that I have consulted, maintaining that José Joaquín Calvo personally conferred with the Mescalero and "Chiricahua" leaders at Santa Rita del Cobre and that "Chokonens and Nednhis" correspond to the former *Apaches de paz* at Janos, San Buenaventura, and Carrizal. See Sweeney, *Mangas Coloradas*, 51.

19 For the treaty's shortcomings, see Sweeney, *Mangas Coloradas*, 60. For a more balanced assessment that also includes the treaty's benefits and the proper band affiliations of all the Ndé leaders, see Griffen, *Apaches at War and Peace*, 90, 126–127, 142. For Pluma as Chihene and Bedonkohe, see

Sweeney, *Mangas Coloradas*, 7, 58. For Apache farming, see José Victor Saenz to the Alcalde Constitucional of Janos [Mariano Varela], Real de Cobre, May 10, 1833, roll 6, JA-UA.
20 For the Apache territorial boundaries, which excluded Lipans in Texas and Coahuila and Western Apache groups north of the Gila River, see Calvo, "Bases principales para conceder la paz, a los Apaches sublevados," Encinillas, July 28, 1832; Griffen, *Apaches at War and Peace*, 141–142.
21 Griffen, *Apaches at War and Peace*, 148–150, 157–158; Sweeney, *Mangas Coloradas*, 57–58, 61. For the argument that Fuerte may have later been called Mangas Coloradas, see Griffen, *Apaches at War and Peace*, 94, 192; Sweeney, *Mangas Coloradas*, 7, 27–28. My own research supports Sweeney's statements that Fuerte is last mentioned in Mexican documents in 1837 and that they contain no references to Mangas Coloradas prior to 1842. See Calvo to the Commander of the Segunda Sección y Frontera Occidental, Chihuahua, February 28, 1837, F40, S1; Commander-in-Chief Francisco García Conde to the Janos commander, Chihuahua, August 18, 1842, F42, S1, JPR-UTA. That said, an equally valid conclusion from the evidence is that Fuerte died in 1837 and Mangas Coloradas succeeded him as nantan. For Fuerte as a "Mogollonero" or Chihene Mogollon, see Griffen, *Apaches at War and Peace*, 90. While at peace at Janos, El Fuerte's ranchería frequently camped together with the Chihene Mogollon Pluma's ranchería, which supports El Fuerte's kinship ties to the Mogollons, and in January 1832, he was camped seventy leagues north of Janos on the Mimbres River, which suggests he may have also had Mimbres kinship ties. See [no signature], "Estado de Fuerza," Janos, October 1 and November 1, 1820, F24, S3, JPR-UTA; Sgt. Rafael Carbajal, "Estado de fuerza," Janos, January 1, 1832, roll 5, JA-UA. For Mangas Coloradas (Fuerte) as a Mogollonero by birth who had allegedly intermarried into a mixed Chihene–Bedonkohe (Mimbres–Mogollon) band near Santa Lucía Springs around 1810 and became a leader of both groups by 1820, see Sweeney, *Mangas Coloradas*, 10, 30–31.
22 Gov. Jose Joaquín Calvo, Circular, Chihuahua, February 25, 1835, roll 6, JA-UA; Griffen, *Apaches at War and Peace*, 158–159.
23 For the quotations, see Gov. Jose Joaquín Calvo, Circular, Chihuahua, March 29, 1836, roll 25, JA-UA; Ensign Loreto Ramírez to Adjutant Inspector of the Northern Line José María González, Tucson, July 3, 1834, translated in McCarty, *Frontier Documentary*, 40. See also Griffen, *Apaches at War and Peace*, 157–159; Sweeney, *Mangas Coloradas*, 64–65; Helen J. Lundwall and Terrence M. Humble, *Copper Mining in Santa Rita, New Mexico, 1801–1838* (Santa Fe, NM: Sunstone Press, 2012), 85; Smith, *Borderlander*, 54–58; DeLay, *War of a Thousand Deserts*, 147–148, 150.
24 For a description of the treaty without the original articles, see "Treaty with the Apache," March 31, 1835, translated in Deloria and DeMallie, *Documents of Indian Diplomacy*, 158–159. For the original document, see Col. Cayetano Justiniani to the General Commander of Chihuahua, April 3, 1835, Sonora Archives, microfilm, roll 13, University of Arizona Library, Tucson. See also [El Cobre commander Justiniani] to the Commander-in-Chief of the State of Chihuahua [Calvo], El Cobre, April 28, 1835, F37, S1, JPR-UTA;

Griffen, *Apaches at War and Peace*, 158–160; Sweeney, *Mangas Coloradas*, 61–62; Sweeney, *Cochise*, 25–26.

25 For the quotations, see Lt. Mariano Rodriguez Rey to the Commander of the Western Line, El Cobre, April 20, 1836, F38, S1, JPR-UTA; Griffen, *Apaches at War and Peace*, 149–150, 166–167, 173; Sweeney, *Mangas Coloradas*, 66. Mexicans identified Muchacho as a Mescalero in the treaty, but Griffen states he lived along the Mimbres River, which suggests he was Chihene Mimbres. According to Lorraine García, Itán was a co-leader of the Chihene Coppermine and Mimbres groups (personal communication). Mexicans identified Itán as a Gileño in the treaty and historian Edwin R. Sweeney argues he is Chihene, both of which support her statement. Mexicans identified Ronquillo as a Gileño in the treaty, but Sweeney argues that he was Nednhi. Documents place Ronquillo's ranchería on the Mimbres River during treaty negotiations at Santa Rita in mid-April 1836 and in the Florida Mountains in July, which are both within Chihene Mimbres territory. See above document and Western Frontier Commander [Capt. Mariano Ponce de León] to the San Buenaventura Commander [José Rodriguez], [El Cobre], July 23, 1836, F38, S1, JPR-UTA.

26 [Draft – Western Frontier Commander] to the Commander-in-Chief, nos. 52 and 54, [El Cobre], June 2, 1836; [Western Frontier Commander] to the Commander-in-Chief, June 21, 1836; [Unsigned draft – El Cobre commander] to the Commander-in-Chief, no. 83, [El Cobre], August 22, 1836, F38, S2, JPR-UTA; Griffen, *Apaches at War and Peace*, 166–169; Lundwall and Humble, *Copper Mining*, 108–109. For "ambassador," see the June 2 document. All other quotations are from the June 21 document.

27 [Unsigned draft] to the Commander-in-chief, no. 90, [El Cobre], September 28, 1836, and [Unsigned draft] to the Commander-in-chief, no. 94, [El Cobre], October 3, 1836, F38, S2, JPR-UTA; Griffen, *Apaches at War and Peace*, 150, 169, 171–172. Quotations are from the September 28 document.

28 "Tucson Makes Peace with the Pinal Apaches," Presidio de San Agustín del Tucson, March 5, 1836, and Lt. Col. José María Martínez to Col. José María Elías González, Tucson, February 6, 1837, translated in McCarty, *A Frontier Documentary*, 51, 54; Officer, *Hispanic Arizona*, 136–137, 141, 158; Jacoby, *Shadows at Dawn*, 161. The quotation comes from p. 54.

29 "Tucson Makes Peace with the Pinal Apaches," translated in McCarty, *Frontier Documentary*, 51–52; Jacoby, *Shadows at Dawn*, 161. The Pinal place name comes from Jacoby.

30 Teodoro Ramírez to Interim Governor of Sonora Rafael Elías González, Tucson, September 6, 1837, translated in McCarty, *Frontier Documentary*, 53, 55–56; Officer, *Hispanic Arizona*, 114–115, 123, 141–142. For "Akimel O'odham" and "Tohono O'odham," see Jacoby, *Shadows at Dawn*, 285, 289, 159. For the T'iisibaan (Pinal) homeland, see Jacoby, *Shadows at Dawn*, 159; Goodwin, *Social Organization*, 3–4. Their territory was entirely distinct from the often-confused Pinaleño range to the southeast, which Western Apache groups may not have even inhabited except when pursued. See Averam B. Bender and Homer Aschmann, *Apache Indians V* (New York: Garland Publishing, 1974), 16.

31 Sweeney, *Mangas Coloradas*, 66–67; Sweeney, *Cochise*, 69.
32 Sweeney, *Mangas Coloradas*, 69; Sweeney, *Cochise*, 30.
33 "Treaty with the Mimbres Band of Apache," November 15, 1838, in Deloria and DeMallie, *Documents of Indian Diplomacy*, 161–163; Griffen, *Apaches at War and Peace*, 176. For a copy of the original document, see *El Noticioso*, no. 197, Chihuahua, January 11, 1839, Periódico oficial del gobierno del estado de Chihuahua, University of Texas at El Paso Library (hereafter, UTEP). All quotations are from p. 162. For Crístobal as Nednhi and the argument that this group actually consisted of Nedhnis and "most of the Mescaleros," see Sweeney, *Mangas Coloradas*, 5, 80.
34 "Treaty with the Mimbres Band of Apache," November 15, 1838, in Deloria and DeMallie, *Documents of Indian Diplomacy*, 161–163; Griffen, *Apaches at War and Peace*, 176. All quotations are from Deloria and DeMallie, *Documents of Indian Diplomacy*, 162.
35 José Ignacio Ronquillo, "Hoja de Servicio," December 31, 1821, F24A, S2, JPR-UTA; "Treaty with the Mimbres Band of Apache," November 15, 1838, in Deloria and DeMallie, *Documents of Indian Diplomacy*, 161–163; Griffen, *Apaches at War and Peace*, 176. All quotations are from Deloria and DeMallie, Documents of Indian Diplomacy, 162.
36 "Treaty with the Mimbres Band of Apache," November 15, 1838, in Deloria and DeMallie, *Documents of Indian Diplomacy*, 161–163; Griffen, *Apaches at War and Peace*, 176. All quotations are from Deloria and DeMallie, *Documents of Indian Diplomacy*, 162.
37 Second Lt. and Justice of the Peace Damasio Salazar, "Treaty with the Mescalero Apache," San Miguel del Vado, March 1, 1839, translated in Deloria and DeMallie, *Documents of Indian Diplomacy*, 163–164. For the original document, see Sub-Prefect José María Ortiz to Gov. Manuel Armijo, San Miguel del Vado, March 1, 1839, Sender Collection, New Mexico State Records Center and Archives, Santa Fe, roll 2, fr. 251.
38 The well-respected historian Brian DeLay, for example, devotes a single sentence to these treaties and historian Donald E. Worcester devotes three. See DeLay, *War of a Thousand Deserts*, 214; Worcester, *The Apaches*, 42. For complete omissions, see Sonnichsen, *The Mescalero Apaches*, 62; Haley, *Apaches*, 52. For notable exceptions, see Griffen, *Utmost Good Faith*, 69–84; Griffen, *Apaches at War and Peace*, 189–211; Sweeney, *Mangas Coloradas*, 92–107; Smith, *Borderlander*, 125–128.
39 Griffen, *Utmost Good Faith*, 69; Griffen, *Apaches at War and Peace*, 189; Smith, *Borderlander*, 125. For Vicente as a Mimbreño, see Griffen, *Apaches at War and Peace*, 150. For Vicente as Chokonen, see Sweeney, *Mangas Coloradas*, 94.
40 Griffen, *Utmost Good Faith*, 85n1.
41 García Conde, "Manifiesto que dirige á los habitantes del departamento de Chihuahua," Chihuahua, September 23, 1842, in Chávez, "Construcción de una cultura regional," 269–270.
42 Griffen, *Utmost Good Faith*, 70–71; Smith, *Borderlander*, 125–126. The first three quotations are from Smith, *Borderlander*, 126, and the last two are from

125. According to Lorraine García, Ponce was a Chihene Ojo Caliente leader (personal communication). For Ponce, also known as José María Ponce, as an important Chihene leader who was the same person as José María, see Sweeney, *Mangas Coloradas*, 131, 485n21. For Ponce as a Gileño, see Griffen, *Apaches at War and Peace*, 191.
43 Gov. Donaciano Vigil, "Propositions on which the Apaches have agreed to make peace with the Department of Chihuahua," Santa Fe, February 28, 1842, translated in Smith, *Borderlander*, 125–126. For the original document, see Mexican Archives of New Mexico, microfilm, Huntington Library, roll 27, fr. 27.
44 Griffen, *Utmost Good Faith*, 70–71.
45 For the Mescalero treaty in Chihuahua City, see *La Luna*, vol. II, no. 50, May 6, 1842, Almada Collection, translated in Griffen, *Utmost Good Faith*, 71. For Espejo as a Mescalero leader, see Sonnichsen, *The Mescalero Apaches*, 102. For the Mimbres treaty in El Paso, see Secretary of the District Juan N. de Urquidi, "Treaty with the Mimbres Apache," El Paso del Norte, June 13, 1842, translated in Deloria and DeMallie, *Documents of Indian Diplomacy*, 166–167. For a copy of the original document, see *La Luna*, no. 57, Chihuahua, June 21, 1842, Periódico oficial del gobierno del estado de Chihuahua, UTEP. See also, Griffen, *Utmost Good Faith*, 75.
46 Griffen, *Utmost Good Faith*, 71–72, 75–76.
47 Griffen, *Utmost Good Faith*, 73; Griffen, *Apaches at War and Peace*, 190–191; Sweeney, *Mangas Coloradas*, 84–85, 94; [Draft – Janos commander] to Commander-in-chief [Francisco García Conde], no. 7, Janos, April 10, 1842, F42, S1; Capt. Mariano Rodríguez Rey, "Diario de las nobedades ocurridas en todo el mes en junio anterior," Janos, July 1, 1842, F42, S2, JPR-UTA. For Manuel (Manuelito) as "capitan" of "la Nación Gileña" and then "Gileño General," see [Draft – Janos commander] to Commander-in-chief [Francisco García Conde], no. 9, Janos, June 4, 1842; Commander-in-chief Francisco García Conde to the Janos commander, Chihuahua, August 18, 1842, F42, S1, JPR-UTA.
48 Antonio Sánchez Vergara, "Treaty with the Gila Apache," Janos, July 4, 1842, translated in Deloria and DeMallie, *Documents of Indian Diplomacy*, 167–168; Griffen, *Utmost Good Faith*, 73; Griffen, *Apaches at War and Peace*, 191. All quotations are from Deloria and Demallie, *Documents of Indian Diplomacy*, 167. For a copy of the original document, see *Suplemento á la Luna*, no. 60, Chihuahua, July 15, 1842, Periódico oficial del estado de Chihuahua, UTEP. For "Vicente de Namiquipa" as Mimbreño, see Griffen, *Apaches at War and Peace*, 150. Historian Edwin R. Sweeney mistakenly calls Pisago Cabezón, Manuelito, and Vicente Chokonens (Chiricahuas), which neither the treaty itself, other Mexican documents, nor Chihene oral history support. See Sweeney, *Mangas Coloradas*, 94.
49 Griffen, *Utmost Good Faith*, 74, 79.
50 Capt. Antonio Rey, et al., "Treaty with the Gila Apache," July 23, 1842. For a copy of the original document, see *Suplemento á la Luna*, no. 63, Chihuahua, August 2, 1842, Periódico oficial del estado de Chihuahua, UTEP; Griffen, *Utmost Good Faith*, 74–75.

51 Jesus M. Armendariz, "Treaty with the Mogoyonero Apache," Janos, April 1, 1843, translated in Deloria and DeMallie, *Documents of Indian Diplomacy*, 169–170; Griffen, *Utmost Good Faith*, 78–80; Griffen, *Apaches at War and Peace*, 196. For a copy of the original document, see *Revista Oficial*, vol. 1, no. 18, Chihuahua, April, 18, 1843, Periódico oficial del gobierno de Chihuahua, UTEP.

52 Sweeney, *Mangas Coloradas*, 101, 103–104.

53 For the Corderos and García Condes, see Francisco R. Almada, *Diccionario de historia, geografía y biografía chihuahuenses* (Ciudad Juárez: Impresora de Juárez, 1968), 116–177, 215–216; Francisco R. Almada, *Diccionario de historia, geografía y biografía sonoronses* (Chihuahua: Impresora Ruíz Sandoval, 1952), 294–295. The Ojos Colorados–Mangas Coloradas connection is from Chihene Ndé Nation of New Mexico Chairman Manuel P. Sanchez and Lorraine García (personal communication).

54 [Draft] Capt. Pedro Madrigal to the Comandante General [Mariano Monterde], no. 21, Janos, May 31, 1843, F43, S1, JPR-UTA; Griffen, *Apaches at War and Peace*, 198–199; Sweeney, *Mangas Coloradas*, 106.

55 Lt. Antonio Sánchez Vergara, "Treaty Between the Mogoyonero and Gileno Apache and the Department of Sonora," Guaymas, June 4, 1843, translated in Deloria and DeMallie, *Documents of Indian Diplomacy*, 171; Griffen, *Utmost Good Faith*, 80. For a copy of the original document, see *Revista Oficial*, vol. 1, no. 28, Chihuahua, June 27, 1843, Periódico oficial del gobierno del estado de Chihuahua, UTEP. I thank Lorraine García for clarifying the proper band affiliations of these leaders (personal communication).

56 Lt. Gervacio Montes and Francisco Arzate, "Cuenta de Apaches: "Ración repartida a los Apaches establecidos de paz en la fecha," no. 1, Janos, January 2, 1843; Prudencio Galindo, "Cuenta de Apaches: "Ración repartida a los indios establecidos en Corralitos," no. 2, Corralitos, January 2, 1843, F43, S2; [Draft] Capt. Pedro Madrigal to [Gov. José Mariano Monterde], no. 17, Janos, February 18, 1843; [Draft] Capt. Pedro Madrigal to the Commander-in-Chief and Governor [Monterde], no. 3, Janos, July 24, 1843, F43, S1, JPR-UTA. For the duration of ration issuing, see Griffen, *Apaches at War and Peace*, 207–209. For quotation, see [Draft] Capt. Pedro Madrigal to [Monterde], no. 13, Janos, April 21, 1843, F43, S1, JPR-UTA. For the 816 peso figure, see Lt. Gervacio Montes and Francisco Arzate, "Cuenta de gastos de Indios gentiles de paz establecidos en dicho presidio en los primeros seis meses de 1843," Janos, June 30, 1843, F43, S2, JPR-UTA.

57 [Draft] Capt. Pedro Madrigal to [Gov. José Mariano Monterde], no. 25, Janos, June 24, 1843; [Draft] Capt. Pedro Madrigal to the Commander-in-Chief and Governor [Monterde], no. 19, Janos, November 1, 1843, F43, S1, JPR-UTA.

58 Griffen, *Utmost Good Faith*, 74–75, 78, 80. For the Apache rancherías around Janos presidio as "Gileños" – not Chokonens (Chiricahuas) – see, Commander-in-Chief Francisco García Conde to the Janos commander, Chihuahua, August 18, 1842, F42, S1, JPR-UTA.

59 Griffen, *Apaches at War and Peace*, 208–209; Griffen, *Utmost Good Faith*, 85.

60 For the most complete treatments of these events, see Sweeney, *Mangas Coloradas*, 118–127; McCarty, *Frontier Documentary*, 101–106. See also [The Janos commander] to the Commander-in-Chief [Monterde], September 1, 1844, F44, S1, JPR-UTA; Griffen, *Apaches at War and Peace*, 211–214; Officer, *Hispanic Arizona*, 179–180; Joseph F. Park, "The Apaches in Mexican-American Relations, 1848–1861: A Footnote to the Gadsden Treaty," *Arizona and the West* 3 (Summer 1961): 135; Smith, "Indians in American-Mexican Relations," 53–54. For subsequent evidence of male "Janos Apaches" participating in raiding and war parties in Sonora and selling Sonoran livestock in Chihuahua, see Capt. Teodoro Aros to Col. José María Elías González, Fronteras, November 2, 1844, translated in McCarty, *Frontier Documentary*, 102–103.

61 Griffen, *Utmost Good Faith*, 93–96, 100–102; Griffen, *Apaches at War and Peace*, 209–210.

62 Griffen, *Utmost Good Faith*, 101, 105; Griffen, *Apaches at War and Peace*, 216; Sweeney, *Mangas Coloradas*, 134–136; Smith, *Borderlander*, 163–164. For these Apaches as Chihenes, whose location and date are misidentified as Ramos pueblo in the summer of 1850, see Betzinez, *I Fought With Geronimo*, 3. For these Apaches as Chokonens and Nednhis, see Sweeney, *Mangas Coloradas*, 135. For Torres as a Gileño and brother of General Manuel, see Griffen, *Apaches at War and Peace*, 191. For Reyes (Relles) as Chokonen (Chiricahua), see Griffen, *Apaches at War and Peace*, 173; Sweeney, *Mangas Coloradas*, 45, 56.

Epilogue

The U.S.–Mexican War presented Apaches with new opportunities. Taking advantage of the Mexican military's preoccupation with the U.S. invasion of Chihuahua in February 1847 and blockade of the Sonoran port of Guaymas the following fall, militant and moderate Ndé groups united and, together with Navajos and Comanches, pummeled northern Mexico with renewed vigor. Although fewer Mexican officers meant fewer chances for Ndé leaders to negotiate peace and trade agreements, their absence also meant fewer Mexican military offensives to contend with. If the U.S. military's entry in the Southwest posed a potential obstacle for the Apaches, Ndé leaders appreciated that these soldiers were also fighting Mexicans and could help them police the most unruly traders, miners, and settlers. Offering higher quality goods, including firearms and ammunition, the increasing number of American traders west of the Rio Grande after 1846 offset the immediate need for many Ndé groups to renegotiate peace in northern Mexico in the first place.[1]

Although scholars routinely claim that the United States acquired nearly half of Mexico's national territory in the Treaty of Guadalupe Hidalgo in 1848, that perspective ignores the fact that American Indians, including Apaches, who were not consulted in the treaty controlled the majority of that land. The influential Chihene Mogollon Nantan Mangas Coloradas demonstrates this well. By following a combined strategy of peace, neutrality, and war, his Chihenes retained control of virtually all of Chi'laa, and, together with allied Chokonens and Nednhis, helped former Apaches de paz extract revenge on Chihuahua and Sonora by punishing the communities that had wronged them.[2]

After three years of intensified warfare with Mexico, a minority of Southern Apache political leaders continued to negotiate treaties with Mexican officers at the presidios where they formally settled at peace. War-weary headmen such as Vívora, Francisquillo, and Coleto Amarillo, whose people had formerly settled near Mexican presidios and served as auxiliaries, tried to reestablish the old pattern at Galeana and Janos in February and March 1849. They failed to settle permanently, however, most likely because they were afraid of being held as prisoners by Mexican officers or killed by Mexican and American *Apacheros* (Apache scalp hunters). One exception was the Chihene El Negrito de Carretas (brother of Ronquillo), who resided at Janos presidio and advised the post commander on Apache affairs.[3]

A Chokonen faction was the first Southern Apache group to negotiate a peace treaty in 1850. The process began when a small delegation of their emissaries traveled to Bacoachi on February 7 to meet with Captain Manuel Martínez. A primary Chokonen goal was securing the release of Spanish-held captives. Valtasar el Chino and several men and women made this clear by returning three weeks later and offering to exchange all of the captive Mexicans they held for the nine (one man and eight women and children) taken by officer José Terán y Tato's troops in an attack on the Chokonen leader San Juan's ranchería the previous May. The Chokonen leaders Posito Moraga, Demos, and Yrigóllen continued negotiations with Sonora military commander José María Elías González at Bacoachi in March and turned over eight Mexicans in exchange for Demos's wife and mother-in-law, whom Elías González had held in Arizpe. After concluding a preliminary peace treaty in March that excluded rations based on his own doubts of Chokonen sincerity, Elías González drew up new terms in April that met this important Chokonen demand.[4] As the commander recognized, "without supplying them with what they need to exist," including plots of fertile land, tools, and enough grain to sustain themselves until the first harvest, "it is not possible to oblige them to live in fixed places."[5]

After another round of talks at Bacoachi, the Chokonen emissary Valtasar el Chino and five others ratified the new six-article agreement with Elías González in Arizpe on April 23, 1850, on behalf of Chokonen headmen Yrigollen and Posito Moraga. In exchange for rations of grain, which Sonora could not afford to issue until July 1, and fertile plots of land near Bacoachi, Bavispe, and Santa Cruz presidios, the Chokonens agreed to "assume the responsibilities they had under the Spanish government," which consisted of ceasing hostilities, obeying Mexican authorities, helping Mexican troops pursue Apaches at war, and "cooperat[ing] in getting the youth to go to work." Elías González remained suspicious of a long-term peace, however, pessimistically concluding that "the outcome cannot be foreseen with complete certainty, due to the audacity, double-crossing, and unreliability of the Indians," a feeling Chokonen leaders no doubt echoed, given Mexico's propensity for killing unarmed Apaches; imprisoning Apache men, women, and children; and skimping and defaulting on rations.[6]

The Chihenes and Nednhis acted next. After conducting preliminary negotiations in May, on June 24, 1850, six Southern Apache headmen – Itán, Delgadito, and Ponce representing the Chihenes and Coleto Amarillo, Arvizo, and Placer for the Nednhis – negotiated a nine-point treaty at Janos with Chihuahua military and civil officials, including Political Chief of the Janos District Juan Zozaya, José Barela, and Alejo García Conde, the brother of the recently deceased Chihuahua governor Francisco García Conde.[7] Like the Chokonens, their primary goal was to secure the release of the sixteen Apache men, women, and children whom Chihuahua military officers held as prisoners, which they achieved, despite selling off the majority of their own captives in New Mexican towns and exchanging only two captive Mexicans in return. As in past treaties, the Chihenes and Nednhis agreed to cease all hostilities in the state of Chihuahua, to settle in designated locations near Janos and Carrizal presidios, to present their horses for branding, to obtain passports before traveling to interior Mexico, and that their men would assist Mexican troops in pursuing independent Apache groups still waging war. In return, Chihuahua officials named Coleto Amarillo "General" of the reservation-dwelling Apaches at Janos and Carrizal, whom Mexicans called Janeros and Carrizaleños, and promised to issue rations at both locations according to Pedro de Nava's 1791 terms.[8]

In late June Delgadito, Ponce, Coleto Amarillo, and Arvizo settled their people near Janos presidio, and by February 1851 five Chihene and Nednhi rancherías, consisting of 180 families, were receiving rations at the post before Colonel José María Carrasco's four-hundred-man Sonoran force treacherously ambushed them in early March. According to Carrasco, his volunteers killed twenty-one Apaches – sixteen men and five women – and captured sixty-two men, women, and children. This was almost certainly an undercount, as the Chihene Mogollon war leader Geronimo (Goyahkla or "The One Who Yawns") claimed that his mother, wife, and three children were slain by Carrasco's men. Carrasco's volunteers also mowed down the faithful Nednhi leader Arvizo while he was unarmed in the street and the recently relocated Chokonen leader Yrigollen as he tried to parley with them west of Janos. Incredibly, roughly two-thirds of the Apaches at peace at Janos (ninety-five families) prior to Carrasco's attack returned to receive their rations in April.[9]

Carrasco's actions and his subsequent trial at Janos highlight the differing perspectives on livestock rustling between Sonorans, Chihuahuans, and Apaches and another recurring legacy of the establecimientos that extends back at least as far as Juan de Ugalde: misplaced violence. According to Carrasco, all Apaches de paz in Chihuahua were treacherous and deserved to be killed because they were stealing Sonoran livestock, killing innocent civilians in the process, and then selling the stolen stock to Chihuahuans. Chihuahuan state officials, on the other hand, claimed that Carrasco's attack was a criminal act because he had crossed state boundaries and killed Apaches de paz who had not participated in any raids or sales of stolen stock and remained peacefully settled on their reservations. Apaches, for their part, recognized that the reality was somewhere in between. Most Apaches de paz, including the vast majority of the elderly, women, and children, were faithfully following the terms of their treaty. But some of the men, such as Delgadito's and Ponce's Chihenes at Janos and Yrigollen's Chokonens at Fronteras, did participate in joint livestock raids with Mangas Coloradas's independent Apaches in Sonora. These same Apaches often sold their stolen livestock in Janos to local merchants who would then sell them at higher prices in El Paso or in other Chihuahuan towns.[10] The problem in their mind was that Carrasco's response was excessively violent, callous, and age- and gender-blind. Even if his men targeted the right individual, why should the act of stealing someone's horse warrant death? Even if Apaches were to accept Carrasco's rationalization that his force was simply carrying out his recently announced policy of unrelenting warfare on all Apache men, the killing and captive-taking still should have been restricted to specific Apache males identified in raids in Sonora. From the Ndé perspective, Carrasco's attack was treacherous, and they needed to avenge the deaths and capturing of their kinsmen with a revenge raid of their own.[11]

Despite the risk of treachery, a small contingent of loyal Apache men continued serving Mexican interests as scouts, and a minority of Apache families continued to settle at presidios in Chihuahua and Sonora as they had since Spanish times. During the early 1850s the Nednhis Josécito and Gervacio Compá, a son of Juan José, guided Mexican troops on Apache campaigns from Janos, and at Tucson Pinal auxiliaries kept fighting for Captain Antonio Comadurán.[12] After conducting preliminary talks at

Janos and Chihuahua in January 1857, in February the Nednhi leaders Láceres and Poncito (brother of the recently deceased Chihene chief Ponce) and 182 of their people settled six miles south of Janos presidio along the Casas Grandes River and received rations. They were joined by fifty Chihenes under Delgadito and ninety-seven Nednhis under Felipe in April and 258 more Chihenes under Mangas Coloradas, Victorio, Riñon, El Sargento, and Veinte Reales in June. Comprising more than 600 individuals overall, these were the last Apache families to reside near Janos prior to its closing in 1858. They remained faithfully at peace until the fall when families began fleeing because their people were suddenly dying from illness. Apparently, the retired captain and prominent political leader José María Zuloaga deliberately issued them poisoned rations. In spite of the danger, some groups remained at peace until March 1858.[13]

Perhaps the most important and least recognized legacy of the establecimientos is that they helped familiarize Apaches with a system remarkably similar to the reservations the U.S. military established for Apaches at military posts in New Mexico in the 1850s.[14] Specialists have long known of the peaceful relations between Apaches and Anglo Americans in the decades preceding the discovery of gold at Pinos Altos, New Mexico, in 1860.[15] That Apaches initially sought peace with U.S. officials should not be surprising considering the material resources American traders had been supplying to Apaches since the 1830s. The United States, too, had a vested interest in making peace with Apaches not only to facilitate settlement in New Mexico after victory in the U.S.–Mexican War but also to uphold Article XI of the Treaty of Guadalupe Hidalgo. Under its provisions, the U.S. Government had an obligation to prevent Apaches and other independent Indians living north of the U.S.–Mexico border from raiding into Mexico, capturing Mexicans, and ransoming them to either nation – a commitment that was impossible for the undermanned American troops to uphold.[16]

Knowing that the first group of Apaches who agreed to settle on U.S.-run reservations were Chihenes, who had previously resided on Hispanic reservations, helps us better understand the political dynamics of this period from a Native perspective.[17] Although U.S. military historians have made much of Colonel Edwin Vose Sumner's allegedly innovative and cost-cutting policy of relocating garrisons from civilian settlements to the Apache frontier, to Chihenes this simply looked like a revival of previous Spanish and Mexican policy. Thus, it should not be surprising that within twenty-four hours of Captain Israel Bush Richardson's reoccupation of the refurbished Mexican fort at Santa Rita del Cobre on January 23, 1852, which was renamed Fort Webster, Chihene headmen Delgadito and Ponce and a hundred of their people met with the commanding officer to try to negotiate peace. Despite Richardson's unprovoked order for his troops to fire their muskets and a howitzer at the delegation following the talks, Ponce and three other Chihene leaders – Cuchillo Negro (Baishan), Itán, and Josécitio – still courageously renewed their peace request at the fort on June 15 in a meeting with Major Gouvernor Morris.[18]

After Fort Webster was moved fourteen miles northeastward to the Mimbres River Valley in early September, Ponce, Negrito, Delgadito, and virtually all other Chihene leaders except Mangas Coloradas renewed talks with new post commander Captain Enoch Steen in January and February 1853. In a proposal that sounded very much like the old Spanish Apache policy, Steen suggested to a receptive Governor William Carr Lane that the U.S. Army should temporarily issue rations to the Chihenes until they could be taught how to farm and breed livestock.[19] In early April Cuchillo Negro, accompanied by more than three hundred Chihenes, met with Governor Lane for three days of talks at Fort Webster and agreed to a thirteen-point treaty. Although fraught with problematic assumptions of Chihene culture on the part of Governor Lane and never ratified by the U.S. government, the agreement is still important because it was negotiated with Chihenes who included former Apaches de paz and for its similarities to prior Spanish and Mexican treaties with Apaches. Like Spanish and Mexican officers, Lane proposed that the Chihenes "locate themselves, in permanent camps," which in this case were in the heart of their homeland along the Mimbres River, that they elect a captain for each band, and that they be issued rations "of corn & Beef, with salt," and that "an experienced Farmer teach them how to till the Earth." Although it was a short-lived experiment, in late April Captain Steen reported that approximately three hundred Chihenes, including the rancherías of Cuchillo Negro and Ponce, had planted fifty acres of corn, pumpkins, and melons. Despite the lack of promised rations, the Chihenes continued to comply faithfully with virtually every article of the problematic treaty's provisions – warts and all – until the U.S. Army evacuated the post on December 20, 1853, and relocated to the future site of Fort Thorn on the west bank of the Rio Grande (in the abandoned town of Santa Barbara near modern Hatch, NM).[20]

When U.S. Indian agent Michael Steck met with Mangas Coloradas and other Chihene leaders at the Apache agency near Fort Thorn in the fall of 1854, the peace terms Steck offered them must have seemed strangely familiar. Much like Spaniards, Steck wanted to turn Apache raiders into farmers and issue their families monthly rations of corn, mutton, and beef. Just as they had with Spaniards and Mexicans, Apaches helped shape the terms of peace. Whenever possible Apaches employed male and female interpreters fluent in Spanish. In this case, two Chihene women, Monica and Refugia, participated in the negotiations, and Monica was fully literate in Spanish.[21] Although Congress never ratified this treaty either, Chihenes and Americans still reached an accommodation at the local level that reflected both of their interests.

One of the Southern Apaches' most notable accomplishments at Fort Thorn was that they convinced Steck to issue them rations farther west at the first site of Fort Webster at Santa Rita del Cobre. This was a more convenient and meaningful location for most Apaches to receive them, given the site's history as a place of diplomacy and exchange with Spaniards, Mexicans, and Americans.[22] Much like Mexicans, however, Americans failed to supply the beef rations they promised, and issued corn rations only once a month rather than weekly or biweekly as Spaniards and Mexicans had. Just as they did with Spaniards and Mexicans, Apaches responded in mixed ways to this problem. The majority resumed raiding into Chihuahua and Sonora, especially in the winter when food was most scarce.[23] Others, however, sought peace at their former establecimientos at Janos and Fronteras in an effort to redeem Apache prisoners, whom Mexicans held as bargaining chips, and in hopes of receiving more rations than Americans were furnishing them.[24]

The principal achievement of the Apaches who made peace at Fort Thorn was their farming, but historians have not properly understood it. Chihene families, including that of Mangas Coloradas and numerous others who had previously settled in establecimientos, raised hundreds of acres of corn along the Mimbres and Gila Rivers in 1855–56 and 1858–59.[25] If we recognize that the Apaches were doing this in their own territory, where they had farmed for centuries prior to being subjected to monthly coordinated military offensives by Spaniards, this accomplishment looks much more like a "return to normalcy" than a "rise of civilization." Chihene Mimbres and Gila Apaches did not need Steck or U.S. soldiers to teach them how to farm, but they did appreciate the protection Americans offered them from Mexican troops and Apacheros.

During the 1860s Ndé people would face many of the same problems they had been wrestling with for centuries. If subsistence, survival, and retention of their homeland remained their primary concerns during this decade, some familiar problems took on new urgency. U.S. and Mexican soldiers, miners, ranchers, and settlers continued to have difficulty distinguishing between peaceful and hostile Apaches when they encountered them in the field, and rustlers posing as Apaches only made matters worse. As U.S. Apache policy hardened under Colonel James Carleton and soldiers carried on the Spanish and Mexican legacy of misplaced violence by treacherously killing a sleeping Mangas Coloradas in cold blood at Fort McLane in 1863, the declining number of healthy Ndé men created a crisis in leadership, which encouraged factionalism among Ndé groups. Although Chihenes viewed the killing of their nantan as "incomprehensible," they were even more angered by "the mutilation of his body." "Most objectionable," however, were "the prospectors and miners" who disturbed the earth and "invoked the wrath of the Mountain Gods by seeking gold," a metal that symbolizes the sun and is sacred to their Creator Ussen, Giver of Life. More broadly, mutual mistrust posed an ongoing threat to peaceful negotiations between Apaches, Mexicans, and Americans, which would become increasingly common as Apache groups began resettling on U.S. reservations, where Indian agents and U.S. Army officers routinely mistreated them.[26]

Demonstrating a final long-lasting legacy of the establecimientos, some Ndé men adapted to these challenges by serving U.S. interests at military posts across the Southwest. In some cases, these scouts themselves were former Apache auxiliaries in northern Mexico. For example, during the 1860s T'iisibaan auxiliaries at Tucson become scouts at Fort Goodwin. In other exceptional instances, they were former prisoners of war. Bilingual Apaches chose this path over warfare because they believed they could best serve their people by doing so, for, in contrast to those interpreters representing U.S. interests, they would not twist the meaning of the messages their leaders conveyed to U.S. Army officers.[27] More knowledgeable of Southwestern terrain and more effective at tracking Apache raiding and war parties than most U.S. troops, scouts such as the Chokonen leader Chihuahua were instrumental in enabling U.S. troops to track down the Chihene headmen Victorio in 1880 and Nana in 1881. Some Apache men continued to serve effectively as scouts for the U.S. military as late as the 1940s. During the 1890s the U.S. Army briefly employed Apache men as formally integrated soldiers in three infantry regiments in Arizona at San Carlos Reservation, Fort Bowie, and Fort Apache and a fourth made up of Southern Apache prisoners of war at Mount Vernon Barracks, Alabama.[28]

Accommodation, then, not just conflict, characterized Apache relations with Anglo Americans in these years. Although reciprocal treachery frequently disrupted efforts to seek common ground, negotiating, translating, settling, trading, scouting, and soldiering remained important if poorly understood legacies of the establecimientos in the pre- and post–Civil War eras. Chihene descendants of Apaches de paz have continued to loyally serve the United States throughout the twentieth and twenty-first centuries as soldiers, sailors, pilots, archivists, and federal agents in higher percentages than most other Americans.[29]

Notes

1 Sweeney, *Mangas Coloradas*, 137–138, 152, 212; Smith, *Borderlander*, 218; Park, "Apaches in Mexican–American Relations," 129, 137, 139; DeLay, "Independent Indians and the U.S.–Mexico War," 35–40, 58, 60.
2 For examples of scholars making this claim, see Richard Griswold del Castillo, *The Treaty of Guadalupe Hidalgo: A Legacy of Conflict* (Norman: University of Oklahoma Press, 1990), xii; DeLay, *War of a Thousand Deserts*, xx; Michael Scott Van Wagenen, *Remembering the Forgotten War: The Enduring Legacies of the U.S.–Mexican War* (Amherst: University of Massachusetts Press, 2012), 1. For Mangas Coloradas, see Sweeney, *Mangas Coloradas*, 118–119, 138, 147, 212, 215, 291, 296.
3 Griffen, *Apaches at War and Peace*, 224–226, 228, 220n19. I thank Lorraine Garcia for clarifying Negrito's band affiliation (personal communication).
4 Sweeney, *Mangas Coloradas*, 191–197, 165–166.
5 José María Elías González to the Governor of Sonora, April 15, 1850, Archivo Histórico del Estado de Sonora, translated in Sweeney, *Mangas Coloradas*, 197.
6 José María González to the Minister of War and the Navy, April 30, 1830, folder 221, *Ramo Militar*, Archivo Histórico del Estado de Sonora, translated in Deloria and DeMallie, *Documents of Indian Diplomacy*, 172–174.
7 Sweeney, *Mangas Coloradas*, 202. Governor García Conde died from cholera in 1849. For brief biographies of both brothers see Francisco R. Almada, *Diccionario de historia, geografía y biografía chihuahuenses* (Ciudad Juárez: Impresora de Juárez, 1968), 216.
8 Juan José de Zozaya, "Treaty between the Chihenne and Nahni Bands of Chiricahua Apache and Chihuahua," Janos, June 25, 1850, folder 221, *Ramo Militar*, Archivo Historíco del Estado de Sonora, Hermosillo, Mexico, translated in Deloria and DeMallie, *Documents of Indian Diplomacy*, 174–175; Griffen, *Apaches at War and Peace*, 235; Sweeney, *Mangas Coloradas*, 204.
9 Griffen, *Apaches at War and Peace*, 235, 237–238; Sweeney, *Mangas Coloradas*, 216, 219, 222; Edwin R. Sweeney, "'I Had Lost All': Geronimo and the Carrasco Massacre of 1851," *Journal of Arizona History* 27 (Spring 1986): esp. 43–46. On Geronimo's name and band affiliation, see Robert M. Utley, *Geronimo* (New Haven, CT: Yale University Press, 2012), 6.
10 Sweeney, "'I Had Lost All,'" esp. 35, 42, 46.
11 On Apache revenge raids and warfare, see Opler, *An Apache Life-Way*, 336–349; Goodwin, *Western Apache Raiding and Warfare*, 16–18.

12 For Gervacio Compá, see Griffen, *Apaches at War and Peace*, 226, 232–233, 242–243; Sweeney, *Mangas Coloradas*, 171, 252, 279. For Tucson, see Officer, *Hispanic Arizona*, 177, 190, 206, 264; John L. Kessell, Friars, Soldiers, and Reformers: Hispanic Arizona and the Sonora mission Frontier, 1767–1856 *(Tucson: University of Arizona Press, 1976)*, 313. For Fronteras, see José Francisco Velasco, Noticias Estádisticas del Estado de Sonora (1850) *(Hermosillo: Gobierno del Estado de Sonora, 1985)*, 229.
13 Griffen, *Apaches at War and Peace*, 253–257; Sweeney, *Mangas Coloradas*, 357–358, 485, 490.
14 Moorhead, *Presidio*, 243.
15 Numerous scholars have treated U.S.–Apache relations in these years. See, for example, Dan L. Thrapp, *The Conquest of Apachería* (Norman: University of Oklahoma Press, 1967), 6–14; Haley, *Apaches*, 191–230; Griffen, *Apaches at War and Peace*, 248–249; Sweeney, *Cochise*, 137–158, 220–390; Sweeney, *Mangas Coloradas*, 137–158, 220–390; William S. Kiser, *Dragoons in Apacheland: Conquest and Resistance in Southern New Mexico, 1846–1861* (Norman: University of Oklahoma Press, 2012), 50-283.
16 DeLay, *War of a Thousand Deserts*, xiii, 301–302; Park, "Apaches in Mexican–American Relations," 129.
17 Brian DeLay has noted the lack of scholarly understanding of Indian politics in the Southwest in the 1830s and 1840s. See DeLay, *War of a Thousand Deserts*, xix.
18 Sweeney, *Mangas Coloradas*, 243–245, 253, 255; Utley, *Geronimo*, 31; William S. Kiser, *Turmoil on the Rio Grande: History of the Mesilla Valley, 1846–1865* (College Station: Texs A&M Press, 2011), 109.
19 Robert W. Frazer, "Army agriculture in New Mexico," *New Mexico Historical Review* 50 (October 1975): esp. 323, 332n49; Sweeney, *Mangas Coloradas*, 263, 269–270.
20 William Carr Lane, "Treaty with the Rio Mimbres and Rio Gila Apache," Fort Webster, April 7, 1853 in Vine Deloria, Jr., and Raymond J. DeMallie, eds., *Documents of Indian Diplomacy: Treaties, Agreements, and Conventions, 1775–1979*, vol. 2 (Norman: University of Oklahoma Press, 1999), 1298–1299; Sweeney, *Mangas Coloradas*, 272–274, 278–279, 284, 287, 292–293.
21 Sweeney, *Mangas Coloradas*, 307, 309, 312. Seventy years old at the time, Monica's mother had given her to Catholic nuns, who taught her to read and write in Spanish. When her mother died, her father brought her back to her Apache kinsmen. See David Meriwether, *My Life in the Mountains and on the Plains*, ed. Robert A. Griffen (Norman: University of Oklahoma Press, 1965), 217.
22 Sweeney, *Mangas Coloradas*, 309.
23 Sweeney, *Mangas Coloradas*, 348–349, 364.
24 Griffen, *Apaches at War and Peace*, 252–257; Sweeney, *Mangas Coloradas*, 317–318, 336–337, 352–359.
25 Griffen, *Apaches at War and Peace*, 250; Sweeney, *Mangas Coloradas*, 328, 331, 362–364, 380; Kiser, *Dragoons in Apacheland*, 277–278.
26 Sweeney, *Mangas Coloradas*, 286, 305–306, 318–319, 334–335, 381–385, 391–398, 426, 458–459; Ball, *In the Days of Victorio*, 46, 48; Ball, *Indeh*,

19–20; Kiser, *Dragoons in Apacheland*, 250, 259, 282–283. All quotations are from Ball, *In the Days of Victorio*.

27 Goodwin, *Western Apache Raiding and Warfare*, 192; Ball, *In the Days of Victorio*, 165, 187, 190.

28 Kiser, *Dragoons in Apacheland*, 52–53; Michael L. Tate, "Soldiers of the Line: Apache Companies in the U.S. Army: 1891–1897," *Arizona and the West* 16 no. 4 (Winter 1974): esp. 343, 349–350, 355–356; Janne Lahti, "Colonized Labor: Apaches and Pawnees as Army Workers," *Western Historical Quarterly* 39 no. 3 (Autumn 2008): 301; Douglas C. McChristian, *Fort Bowie, Arizona: Combat Post of the Southwest, 1858–1894* (Norman: University of Oklahoma Press, 2005), 331; Utley, *Geronimo*, 104, 158, 185, 230–231, 243; Angie Debo, *Geronimo: The Man, His Time, His Place*, The Civilization of the American Indian Series (Norman: University of Oklahoma Press, 1976), 226–228.

29 The final statement is drawn from my personal observations at family gatherings of Chihene descendants in 2013–14. For the high enlistment rates of American Indians in the U.S military during the twentieth century, see Bruce White, "Ethnicity and Race in the Military," in *The Oxford Companion to American Military History*, ed. John Whiteclay Chambers II (New York: Oxford University Press, 1999), 254.

Appendix

Ndé Groups and Their Homelands (c. 1800)

I. "EASTERN APACHES"

A. Lipan

Rio Grande Valley and southern plains between Pecos and Colorado Rivers[1]

Spanish name: Ypande (before 1760), Lipan (after 1760)

1. Túédine Ndé ("No Water People")
Upper Rio Grande Valley and southern plains between Pecos and Colorado Rivers

Spanish name: Lipanes de arriba (Upper Lipans)

2. Túsís or Kúnetsa Ndé ("Big Water People")
Lower Rio Grande Valley and Gulf Coast

Spanish name: Lipanes de abajo (Lower Lipans)

B. Mescalero

Sierra Blanca and Siete Rios ranges, southern plains east of Organ Mountains, Santa Rosa Mountains, and Bolsón de Mapimí

Spanish names: Mescalero, Faraon, Llanero, Lipiyan, Natagé

1. Nitahen Ndé ("Earth Crevice People")
Mountains along western and southwestern periphery of southern plains

Spanish name: Mescalero, Faraon

2. Cúelcahén Ndé ("People of the Tall Grass")
Southern plains east of Organ Mountains

Spanish name: Llanero, Lipiyan, Natagé

C. Jicarilla

Sangre de Cristo Mountains, Taos Valley, and southern plains

Spanish name: Jicarilla, Ollero, Llanero

1. Sait Ndé ("Sand People")
Western slope of Sangre de Cristo Mountains and Taos Valley

Spanish name: Ollero ("Potter") or Hoyero ("Mountain-dwelling People")

2. Gulgahén ("People of the Plains")
Eastern slope of Sangre de Cristo Mountains and southern plains

Spanish name: Llanero

II. "SOUTHERN APACHES" (SO-CALLED CHIRICAHUAS)

A. Chihene ("Red Paint People")

San Mateo Mountains, Black Range, Mimbres and upper Gila River valleys, and Mogollon Mountains

Spanish names: Gila, Mogollon, Mimbres

B. Chokonen ("Juniper People")

Chiricahua and Dragoon Mountains

Spanish name: Chiricagui

C. Nednhi ("Enemy People")

Western Sierra Madre Mountains

III. "WESTERN APACHES"

Spanish name: Tonto, Coyotero

A. *Dzilghą'é* ("On Top of the Mountain People")

White Mountains and San Francisco River Valley

Spanish name: Sierra Blanca (White Mountain), Coyotero (1830s)

B. *T'iisibaan* ("Cottonwood in Grey Wedge Shape People")

Pinal Mountains and ranges near the confluence of the Gila and San Pedro Rivers

Spanish name: Pinal

C. *Tsézhiné* ("Black Rocks People")

Aravaipa Canyon and Creek

Spanish name: Aravaipa

Notes

1 Matson and Schroeder, "Cordero's Description," 336, 350–355; The Marqués de Rubí, "Dicatmen," Tacubaya, April 10, 1768, translated by Ned F. Brierly, in Jackson and Foster, eds., *Imaginary Kingdom*, Articles 14–16, 173–175, 179–180; Lafora, *Frontiers of New Spain*, 76–79, 85–86, 144, 155; Bourke, "Notes," 115; Robinson, *I Fought a Good Fight*, 103, 113, 387–388; Maestas, "Culture and History of Native American Peoples," 313, 350; Morris E. Opler, "Lipan Apache," in *Handbook of North American Indians: Vol. 13 Plains Pt. 2*, ed. Raymond J. DeMallie (Washington, DC: Smithsonian Institution, 2001), 952; Gunnerson, *Jicarilla Apaches*, 160–162, 164; Eiselt, *Becoming White Clay*, 134n20, 146–147; Tiller, "Jicarilla Apache," 441, 460; Opler, "Summary of Jicarilla," 202–203; Griffen, *Apaches at War and Peace*, xiv, 3, 5; Schroeder, *Apache Indians IV*, 117, 134–135; Nentvig, *Rudo Ensayo*, 21n3; Opler, *An Apache Life-Way*, 1; Bender and Aschmann, *Apache Indians V*, 18–20, 23; Jacoby, *Shadows at Dawn*, 158–159, 286, 289–290; Reuse, *Practical Grammar*, 195; Ives Goddard, "Synonmy" in Basso, "Western Apache," 487–488.

Bibliography

UNPUBLISHED MANUSCRIPT COLLECTIONS

Archivo General de Indias. Seville, Spain. Audiencia de Guadalajara.
  Legajos 267–268, 270–271, 276–279, 282, 284, 287, 289–290, 390, 416.
  Max Leon Moorhead Collection. Western History Collections, University of Oklahoma, Norman. Legajos 278, 282, 286, 287, 520.
Archivo General de la Nación. Mexico City, Mexico. Provincias Internas.
  Max Leon Moorhead Collection. Western History Collections, University of Oklahoma, Norman. Legajo 128.
  Microfilm collection. Bancroft Library, University of California, Berkeley. Legajos 61, 66, 76, 128, 159.
  Microfilm collection. Center for Southwest Research, Zimmerman Library, University of New Mexico. Legajo 65.
  Microfilm roll. Legajo 193, courtesy of Brian DeLay.
Archivo General de Simancas. Simancas, Spain. Guerra Moderna.
  Legajos 7020, 7022–7029, 7031, 7042, 7278.
Archivo Parroquial de San Felipe el Real de Chihuahua.
  Data, courtesy of Chantal Cramaussel.
Colección Archivo Franciscano. Biblioteca Nacional de México, Fondo Reservado, available online.
Janos Archives. Main Library, University of Arizona, Tucson.
  Rolls 5, 6, 15, 24, 25.
Janos Historical Archives. Microfilm Collection. University of Texas at El Paso.
  Rolls 9, 10, 14.
Janos Presidio Records. Benson Latin American Collection, University of Texas at Austin.
  Years 1778, 1787, 1790–1844.
Merino, Manuel. "Noticia de las tribus de indios gentiles que havitan en la frontera de las provincias del reino de Nueva España," Huntington Manuscript 543, Huntington Library, San Marino, California.

Spanish Archives of New Mexico. Microfilm collection. Huntington Library, San Marino, CA.
Rolls 11–13.

PUBLISHED WORKS

Aboites Aguilar, Luis. *Norte precario: poblamiento y colonización en México, 1760–1940*. Mexico: Colegio de México, Centro de Estudios Históricos: Centro de Investigaciones y Estudios Superiores en Antropología Social, 1995.
Almada, Francisco R. *Diccionario de historia, geografía y biografía sonoronses*. Chihuahua, México: Impresora Ruíz Sandoval, 1952.
  Diccionario de historia, geografía y biografía chihuahuenses. Ciudad Juárez, México: Impresora de Juárez, 1968.
Anderson, Gary Clayton. *The Indian Southwest, 1580–1830: Ethnogenesis and Reinvention*. Norman: University of Oklahoma Press, 1999.
Archer, Christon I. "The Deportation of Barbarian Indians from the Internal Provinces of New Spain, 1789–1810." *The Americas* 29 (January 1973): 376–385.
Arques, Enrique and Narciso Gibert. *Los mogataces: los primitivos soldados moros de España en Africa*. Málaga, Spain: Editorial Algazara, 1992.
August, Jack. "Balance-of-Power Diplomacy in New Mexico: Governor Fernando de la Concha and the Indian Policy of Conciliation." *New Mexico Historical Review* 56 (April 1981): 141–160.
Babcock, Matthew. *Transnational Trade Routes and Diplomacy: Comanche Expansion, 1760–1846*. M.A. thesis, University of New Mexico, 2001.
  Turning Apaches into Spaniards: North America's Forgotten Indian Reservations. Ph.D. diss., Southern Methodist University, 2008.
  "Rethinking the Establecimientos: Why Apaches Settled on Spanish-Run Reservations, 1786–1793." *New Mexico Historical Review* 84 (Summer 2009): 363–397.
Ball, Eve. *In the Days of Victorio: Recollections of a Warm Springs Apache*. Tucson: University of Arizona Press, 1970.
  Indeh: An Apache Odyssey. 1980; reprint, Norman: University of Oklahoma Press, 1988.
Bancroft, Hubert Howe. *History of the North Mexican States and Texas*. 2 vols. San Francisco, CA: The History Company, 1884–9.
  History of Arizona and New Mexico, 1530–1888. San Francisco, CA: The History Company, 1889.
Barr, Juliana. *Peace Came in the Form of a Woman: Indians and Spaniards in the Texas Borderlands*. Chapel Hill, NC: University of North Carolina Press, 2007.
Barr, Juliana and Edward Countryman. "Introduction: Maps and Spaces, Paths to Connect, and Lines to Divide." In *Contested Spaces of Early America*. Edited by Juliana Barr and Edward Countryman. Philadelphia: University of Pennsylvania Press, 2014, 1–28.
Barrett, S. M. *Geronimo, His Own Story: The Autobiography of a Great Patriot Warrior*. New edition. 1906, reprint; New York: Penguin, 1996.

Basehart, Harry W. "Mescalero Apache Band Organization and Leadership." In *Apachean Culture History and Ethnology*. Edited by Keith H. Basso and Morris E. Opler. Tucson: University of Arizona Press, 1971, 35–49.
Basso, Keith H. "Western Apache." In *Handbook of North American Indians: Southwest*. Vol. 10. Edited by Alfonso Ortiz. Washington, DC: Smithsonian Institution, 1983, 462–488.
  Wisdom Sits in Places: Landscape and Language among the Western Apache. Albuquerque: University of New Mexico Press, 1996.
Bellah, Robert N. *Apache Kinship Systems*. Cambridge, MA: Harvard University Press, 1952.
Benavides, Alonso de. *Fray Alonso de Benavides' Revised Memorial of 1634*. Edited and translated by Frederick Webb Hodge, George P. Hammond, and Agapito Rey. Albuquerque: University of New Mexico Press, 1945.
  Benavides' Memorial of 1630. Edited by Cyprian J. Lynch and translated by Peter P. Forrestal. Washington, DC: Academy of Franciscan History, 1954.
  The Memorial of Fray Alonso de Benavides, 1630. Edited by Frederick Webb Hodge and Charles Fletcher Lummis. Translated by Mrs. Edward E. Ayer. Albuquerque, NM: Horan and Wallace, 1965.
Bender, Averam B. and Homer Aschmann. *Apache Indians V*. New York: Garland Publishing, 1974.
Benes, Ronald. "Anza and Concha in New Mexico, 1787–1793: A Study in New Colonial Techniques." *Journal of the West* 4 (January 1965): 63–76.
Bense, Judith A. "Introduction: Presidios of the North American Spanish Borderlands." *Historical Archaeology* 38 (2004): 1–5.
Berlandier, Jean Louis. *The Indians of Texas in 1830*. Edited by John C. Ewers and translated by Patricia Reading LeClercq. Washington, DC: Smithsonian Institution Press, 1969.
Betzinez, Jason. *I Fought with Geronimo*. Harrisburg, PA: Stackpole Company, 1959.
Blackhawk, Ned. *Violence over the Land: Indians and Empires in the Early American West*. Cambridge, MA: Harvard University Press, 2006.
  "Toward an Indigenous Art History of the West: The Segesser Hide Paintings." In *Contested Spaces of Early America*. Edited by Juliana Barr and Edward Countryman. Philadelphia: University of Pennsylvania Press, 2014, 276–299.
Blyth, Lance R. "The Presidio of Janos: Ethnicity, Society, Masculinity, and Ecology in Far Northern Mexico, 1685–1858." Ph.D. diss., Northern Arizona University, 2005.
  Chiricahua and Janos: Communities of Violence in the Southwestern Borderlands, 1680–1880. Borderlands and Transcultural Series. Lincoln: University of Nebraska Press, 2012.
Bolt, Christine. *American Indian Policy and American Reform: Case Studies of the Campaign to Assimilate the American Indian*. London: Allen and Unwin, 1987.
Bolton, Herbert Eugene, ed. and trans. *Athanase de Mézières and the Louisiana-Texas Frontier, 1768–1780*. 2 vols. Cleveland: Arthur H. Clark Co., 1914.
  Texas in the Middle Eighteenth Century. Berkeley: University of California Press, 1915.

ed. *Spanish Exploration in the Southwest, 1542–1706*. Original Narratives of Early American History Series. New York: Charles Scribner's Sons, 1916.

"The Mission as a Frontier Institution." *American Historical Review* 22 (1917): 42–61.

Rim of Christendom: A Biography of Eusebio Francisco Kino, Pacific Coast Pioneer. New York: MacMillan, 1936.

Bourke, John G. "Notes Upon the Gentile Organization of the Apaches of Arizona." *Journal of American Folklore* 3 (April–June 1890): 111–126.

Braatz, Timothy. *Surviving Conquest: A History of the Yavapai Peoples*. Lincoln: University of Nebraska Press, 2003.

Braudel, Fernand. *The Mediterranean and the Mediterranean World in the Age of Philip II*. Vol. II. New York: Harper & Row, 1973.

Brinckerhoff, Sidney B. "The Last Years of Spanish Arizona, 1786–1821." *Arizona and the West* 9 (Spring 1967): 5–20.

Brinckerhoff, Sidney B. and Odie B. Faulk, eds. and trans. *Lancers for the King: A Study of the Frontier Military System of Northern New Spain, with a Translation of the Royal Regulations of 1772*. Phoenix: Arizona Historical Foundation, 1965.

Bringas, Father Diego. *Friar Bringas Reports to the King: Methods and Indoctrination on the Frontier of New Spain 1796–97*. Edited by Daniel S. Matson and translated by Bernard L. Fontana. Tucson: University of Arizona Press, 1977.

Britten, Thomas A. *The Lipan Apaches: People of Wind and Lightning*. Albuquerque: University of New Mexico Press, 2009.

Brooks, James F. *Captives and Cousins: Slavery, Kinship, and Community in the Southwest Borderlands*. Chapel Hill: University of North Carolina Press, 2002.

Brugge, David M. "Navajo Prehistory and History to 1850." In *Handbook of North American Indians: Southwest*. Vol. 10. Edited by Alfonso Ortiz. Washington, DC: Smithsonian Institution, 1983, 489–501.

Buskirk, Winfred. *The Western Apache: Living with the Land Before 1950*. Norman: University of Oklahoma Press, 1986.

Bustamente, Carlos, ed. "Indios Apaches." *Voz de la Patria*, Saturday, May 21, 1831, 1–24.

Calleja, Félix. *Informe sobre la colonia del Nuevo Santander y Nuevo Reino de Leon-1795*. Mexico: José Porrúa, 1949.

Calvo Berber, Laureano. *Nociones de Historia de Sonora*. Mexico: Librería de Manuel Porrúa, 1958.

Cameron, Catherine M. "Introduction: Captives in Prehistory." In *Invisible Citizens: Captives and Their Consequences*. Edited by Catherine M. Cameron. Salt Lake City: University of Utah Press, 2008.

Carlson, Phil. *Across the Northern Frontier: Spanish Explorations in Colorado*. Boulder, CO: Johnson Books, 1998.

Carter, William B. *Indian Alliances and the Spanish in the Southwest, 750–1750*. Norman: University of Oklahoma Press, 2009.

Castañeda, Carlos E. *Our Catholic Heritage in Texas, 1519–1936*. The Chicano Heritage Series. 1936; reprint, New York: Arno Press, 1976.

Castetter, Edward F. and Morris E. Opler. *The Ethnobiology of the Chiricahua and Mescalero Apache*. University of New Mexico Bulletin, Biological Series. Albuquerque: University of New Mexico Press, 1936.

Catlos, Brian. *Muslims of Medieval Latin Christendom, c. 1050–1614*. New York: Cambridge University Press, 2014.

Chávez, Jorge Chávez. "Construcción de una cultura regional en el norte de México." Ph.D. diss., Universidad Nacional Autónoma de México, 2007.

Chipman, Donald E. *Spanish Texas, 1519–1821*. Austin: University of Texas Press, 1992.

Clark, Laverne Herrell. "Early Horse Trappings of the Navajo and Apache Indians." *Arizona and the West* 5 (Autumn 1963): 233–248.

Clastres, Pierre. "Society against the State." In *Society against the State: Essays in Political Anthropology*. Edited by Pierre Clastres. 1977; reprint, New York Zone Books, 1987, 189–218.

Concha, Fernando de la. "Advice on Governing New Mexico, 1794." *New Mexico Historical Review* 24 (July 1949): 236–254.

Conrad, Paul. "Captive Fates: Displaced American Indians in the Southwest Borderlands, Mexico, and Cuba, 1500–1800." Ph.D. diss., University of Texas at Austin, 2011.

Cook, David Noble. *Born to Die: Disease and New World Conquest, 1492–1650*. New York: Cambridge University Press, 1998.

Cordero y Bustamante, Antonio. "Noticias relativas a la nación apache, que en el año de 1796 extendió en el Paso del Norte, el Teniente Coronel D. Antonio Cordero, por encargo del Sr. Comandante general Mariscal de Campo D. Pedro Nava." In *Geografía de las lenguas y carta etnográfica de México*. Edited by Manuel Orozco y Berra. Mexico: Impr. de J. M. Andrade y F. Escalante, 1864, 369–383.

Corripio, Fernando. *Gran diccionario de sinónimos: voces afines e incorrecciones*. Barcelona: Ediciones B, S.A., 2000.

Cortés, José. *Views from the Apache Frontier: Report on the Northern Provinces of New Spain by José Cortés, Lieutenant in the Royal Corps of Engineers, 1799*. Edited by Elizabeth A. H. John and translated by John Wheat. Norman: University of Oklahoma Press, 1989.

Cramaussel, Chantal. *Poblar la frontera: la provincia de Santa Bárbara en Nueva Vizcaya durante los siglos XVI y XVII*. Zamora: El Colegio de Michoacán, 2006.

"The Forced Transfer of Indians in Nueva Vizcaya and Sinaloa: A Hispanic Method of Colonization." In *Contested Spaces of Early America*. Edited by Juliana Barr and Edward Countryman. Philadelphia: University of Pennsylvania Press, 2014, 184–207.

Curtin, Philip D. *The Atlantic Slave Trade: A Census*. Madison: University of Wisconsin, 1969.

De la Teja, Jesús F., ed. and John Wheat, trans. "Ramón De Murillo's Plan for the Reform of New Spain's Frontier Defenses." *Southwestern Historical Quarterly* 7 (April 2004): 500–533.

Debo, Angie. *Geronimo: The Man, His Time, His Place*. The Civilization of the American Indian Series. Norman: University of Oklahoma Press, 1976.

Deeds, Susan M. *Defiance and Deference in Mexico's Colonial North: Indians under Spanish Rule in Nueva Vizcaya*. Austin: University of Texas Press, 2003.

DeLay, Brian. "Independent Indians and the U.S.–Mexico War." *American Historical Review* 112 (February 2007): 35–68.

War of a Thousand Deserts: Indian Raids and the U.S.–Mexican War. New Haven, CT: Yale University Press, 2008.

"Blood Talk: Violence and Belonging in the Navajo-New Mexico Borderland." In *Contested Spaces of Early America*. Edited by Juliana Barr and Edward Countryman. Philadelphia: University of Pennsylvania Press, 2014, 229–256.

Deloria, Vine, Jr. and Raymond J. DeMallie, eds. *Documents of Indian Diplomacy: Treaties, Agreements, and Conventions, 1775–1979*. 2 vols. Norman: University of Oklahoma Press, 1999.

Di Peso, Charles C. *Casas Grandes: A Fallen Trading Center of the Gran Chichimeca*. 3 vols. Dragoon, AZ: Amerind Foundation, 1974.

Dobyns, Henry F. *Spanish Colonial Tucson: A Demographic History*. Tucson: University of Arizona Press, 1976.

From Fire to Flood: Historic Human Destruction of Sonoran Desert Riverine Oases. Anthropological Papers no. 20. Socorro, NM: Ballena Press, 1981.

Doolittle, William E. *Cultivated Landscapes of Native North America*. New York: Oxford University Press, 2000.

Driessen, Henk. "The Politics of Religion on the Hispano-African Frontier: An Historical-Anthropological View." In *Religious Regimes and State Formation: Perspectives from European Ethnology*. Edited by Eric R. Wolf. Albany: State University of New York Press, 1991.

Dunlay, Thomas Wm. "Indian Allies in the Armies of New Spain and the United States: A Comparative Study." *New Mexico Historical Review* 56 (July 1981): 239–258.

Dunn, William E. "Apache Relations in Texas, 1718–1750." *Southwestern Historical Quarterly* 14 (January 1911): 198–274.

"Missionary Activities among the Eastern Apaches Previous to the Founding of the San Sabá Mission." *Southwestern Historical Quarterly* 15 (January 1912): 186–200.

"The Apache Mission on the San Sabá River: Its Founding and Failure." *Southwestern Historical Quarterly* 17 (April 1914): 379–414.

Edmunds, R. David and Joseph F. Peyser. *The Fox Wars: The Mesquakie Challenge to New France*. Norman: University of Oklahoma Press, 1993.

Eiselt, B. Sunday. *Becoming White Clay: A History and Archaeology of Jicarilla Apache Enclavement*. Salt Lake City: University of Utah Press, 2012.

Elliott, J. H. *Empires of the Atlantic World: Britain and Spain in America, 1492–1830*. New Haven, CT: Yale University Press, 2006.

Endfield, Georgina H. *Climate and Society in Colonial Mexico: A Study in Vulnerability*. Malden, MA: Blackwell, 2008.

Escudero, José Agustín de, ed. "De las naciones bárbaras que habitan las fronteras del estado de Chihuahua." In *Noticias estadísticas del estado de Chihuahua*. Mexico: Juan Ojeda, 1834, 211–234.

Noticias estadísticas de Sonora y Sinaloa (1849). Edited by Héctor Cuauhtémoc Hernández Silva. Hermosillo, Mexico: Universidad de Sonora, 1997.

Esdaile, Charles J. *The Spanish Army in the Peninsular War.* Manchester and New York: Manchester University Press, 1988.

Espinosa, José Manuel. "The Legend of Sierra Azul." *New Mexico Historical Review* 9 (April 1934): 113–158.

"The Recapture of Santa Fé, New Mexico, by the Spaniards, December 29–30, 1693." *Hispanic American Historical Review* 19 (1939): 443–463.

Faulk, Odie B. *The Last Years of Spanish Texas, 1778–1821.* The Hague: Mouton, 1964.

"The Presidio: Fortress or Farce?" *Journal of the West* 8 (January 1969): 22–28.

Feather, Adlai, ed. "Colonel Don Fernando de la Concha Diary, 1788." *New Mexico Historical Review* 34 (October 1959): 285–304.

Fenn, Elizabeth A. *Pox Americana: The Great Smallpox Epidemic of 1775–82.* New York: Hill and Wang, 2001.

Fernández de Santa Ana, Benito. *Letters and Memorials of the Father Presidente Fray Benito Fernández de Santa Ana, 1736–1754: Documents on the Missions of Texas from the Archives of the College of Querétaro.* Edited and translated by Fr. Benedict Leutenegger, O. F. M. San Antonio, Our Lady of the Lake University, 1981.

Fey, Henri-Léon. *Historia de Orán. Antes, durante y después de la dominación española.* Málaga: Editorial Agazara, 1999.

Flint, Richard and Shirley Cushing Flint, eds. *Documents of the Coronado Expedition, 1539–1542.* Dallas, TX: Southern Methodist University Press, 2005.

Forbes, Jack D. "The Janos, Jocomes, Mansos and Sumas Indians." *New Mexico Historical Review* 32 (October 1957): 319–334.

"The Appearance of the Mounted Indian in Northern Mexico and the Southwest, to 1680." *Southwestern Journal of Anthropology* 15 (Summer 1959): 189–212.

Apache, Navaho, and Spaniard. 2nd ed. 1960; reprint, Norman: University of Oklahoma Press, 1994.

Foster, William C. *Spanish Expeditions into Texas, 1689–1768.* Austin: University of Texas Press, 1995.

Frank, Ross. *From Settler to Citizen: New Mexican Economic Development and the Creation of Vecino Society, 1750–1820.* Berkeley: University of California Press, 2000.

Frazer, Robert W. "Army Agriculture in New Mexico." *New Mexico Historical Review* 50 (October 1975): 313–334.

Gálvez, Bernardo de. *Instructions for Governing the Interior Provinces of New Spain, 1786.* Edited and translated by Donald E. Worcester. Berkeley, CA: Quivira Society, 1951.

Garate, Donald T. *Juan Bautista de Anza: Basque Explorer in the New World.* Reno: University of Nevada Press, 2003.

García, Luis Alberto. *Guerra y frontera: el ejército del norte entre 1855 y 1858.* Monterrey, Mexico: Fondo Editorial de Nuevo León, 2007.

Gerhard, Peter. *The North Frontier of New Spain.* 1982; reprint, Norman: University of Oklahoma Press, 1993.

Getty, Harry T. "Changes in Land Use among the Western Apaches." In *Indian and Spanish American Adjustments to Arid and Semiarid Environments*. Edited by Clark S. Knowlton. Lubbock: Texas Technological College, 1964.

Gleach, Frederic W. *Powhatan's World and Colonial Virginia: A Conflict of Cultures*. Lincoln: University of Nebraska Press, 1997.

Goodwin, Grenville. "The Social Divisions and Economic Life of the Western Apache." *American Anthropologist* 37 (1935): 55–64.

"The Southern Athapascans." *The Kiva* 4 (1938): 5–10.

Western Apache Raiding and Warfare. Edited by Keith H. Basso. Tucson: University of Arizona Press, 1971.

Gradie, Charlotte M. "Discovering the Chichimecas." *The Americas* 51 (July 1994): 67–88.

The Tepehuan Revolt of 1616: Militarism, Evangelism, and Colonialism in Seventeenth-Century Nueva Vizcaya. Salt Lake City: University of Utah Press, 2000.

Griffen, William B. *Culture Change and Shifting Populations in Central Northern Mexico*. Anthropological Papers of the University of Arizona. Tucson: University of Arizona Press, 1969.

Indian Assimilation in the Franciscan Area of Nueva Vizcaya. Tucson: University of Arizona Press, 1979.

"The Compás: A Chiricahua Family of the late 18th and Early 19th Centuries." *American Indian Quarterly* 7 (1983): 21–49.

"Southern Periphery: East." In *Handbook of North American Indians: Southwest*. Vol. 10. Edited by Alfonso Ortiz. Washington, DC: Smithsonian Institution, 1983, 329–342.

"Apache Indians and the Northern Mexican Peace Establishments." In *Southwestern Culture History: Collected Papers in Honor of Albert H. Schroeder*. Papers of the Archaeological Society of New Mexico, no. 10. Santa Fe, NM: Ancient City Press, 1985, 183–195.

Utmost Good Faith: Patterns of Apache-Mexican Hostilities in Northern Chihuahua Border Warfare, 1821–1848. Albuquerque: University of New Mexico Press, 1988.

"The Chiricahua Apache Population Resident at the Janos Presidio, 1792 to 1858." *Journal of the Southwest* 33 (Summer 1991): 151–199.

Apaches at War and Peace: The Janos Presidio, 1750–1858. 1988; reprint, Norman: University of Oklahoma Press, 1998.

Griswold del Castillo, Richard. *The Treaty of Guadalupe Hidalgo: A Legacy of Conflict*. Norman: University of Oklahoma Press, 1990.

Guest, Francis F. "Mission Colonization and Political Control in Spanish California." *Journal of San Diego History* 24 (Winter 1978): 97–116.

Gunnerson, Dolores A. *The Jicarilla Apaches: A Study in Survival*. DeKalb: Northern Illinois University Press, 1974.

Gunnerson, James H. and Dolores A. Gunnerson. "Apachean Culture: A Study in Unity and Diversity." In *Apachean Culture History and Ethnology*. Edited by Keith H. Basso and Morris E. Opler. Tucson: University of Arizona Press, 1971, 7–27.

Gutiérrez, Ramón A. and Elliott Young. "Transnationalizing Borderlands History." *Western Historical Quarterly* 41 (Spring 2010): 27–53.

Hackett, Charles Wilson, ed. *Historical Documents Relating to New Mexico, Nueva Vizcaya, and Approaches Thereto, to 1773*. 3 vols. Washington, DC: Carnegie Institution of Washington, 1923–37.

Hadley, Diana, Thomas H. Naylor, and Mardith Schuetz-Miller, eds. *The Presidio and Militia on the Northern Frontier of New Spain, Vol. 2, Part 2: The Central Corridor and the Texas Corridor*. Tucson: University of Arizona Press, 1997.

Hagan, William T. "How the West Was Lost." In *Indians in American History: An Introduction*, edited by Frederick E. Hoxie and Peter Iverson. Wheeling, IL: Harlan Davidson, 1998, 156–176.

Hagle, Paul. "Military Life on New Spain's Northern Frontier." M.A. thesis, University of Texas at Austin, 1962.

Haines, Francis. "The Northward Spread of Horses among the Plains Indians." *American Anthropologist* 40 (March–April 1938): 112–117.

  "Where did the Plains Indians Get Their Horses?" *American Anthropologist* 40 (January–March 1938): 429–437.

Haley, James L. *Apaches: A History and Culture Portrait*. Garden City, NY: Doubleday, 1981.

Hall, Thomas D. "Incorporation in the World System: Toward a Critique." *American Sociological Review* 51 (1986): 390–402.

  Social Change in the Southwest, 1350–1880. Lawrence: University Press of Kansas, 1989.

  "Frontiers, Ethnogenesis, and World-Systems: Rethinking the Theories." In *A World-Systems Reader: New Perspectives on Gender, Urbanism, Cultures, Indigenous Peoples, and Ecology*. Edited by Thomas D. Hall. Lanham, MD: Rowman and Littlefield, 2000.

Hämäläinen, Pekka. "The Rise and Fall of Plains Indian Horse Cultures." *Journal of American History* 90 (2003): 833–862.

  The Comanche Empire. Lamar Series in Western History. New Haven, CT: Yale University Press, 2008.

Hämäläinen, Pekka and Samuel Truett. "On Borderlands." *Journal of American History* 98, no. 2 (September 2011): 338–361.

Hart, E. Richard, ed. *Zuni and the Courts: A Struggle for Sovereign Land Rights*. Lawrence: University Press of Kansas, 1995.

Hatcher, Mattie Austin, trans. "Texas in 1820." *Southwestern Historical Quarterly* 23 (July 1919): 47–68.

Hendricks, Rick. "Massacre in the Organ Mountains: The Death of Manuel Vidal de Lorca." *Password* 39 (Winter 1994): 169–177.

Hendricks, Rick and Gerald Mandell. "The Apache Slave Trade in Parral, 1637–1679." *Journal of Big Bend Studies* 16 (2004): 59–81.

Hendricks, Rick and W. H. Timmons. *San Elizario: Spanish Presidio to Texas County Seat*. El Paso: Texas Western Press, 1998.

Hickerson, Nancy Parrott. *The Jumanos: Hunters and Traders of the South Plains*. Austin: University of Texas Press, 1994.

"The War for the South Plains, 1500–1700." In *The Coronado Expedition: From the Distance of 460 Years*. Edited by Richard Flint and Shirley Cushing Flint. Albuquerque: University of New Mexico Press, 2003.

Hodge, Frederick Webb, ed. *Handbook of American Indians North of Mexico*. Smithsonian Institution, Bureau of American Ethnology, Bulletin 30. Washington, DC: Government Printing Office, 1907.

Hodgson, Wendy C. *Food Plants of the Sonoran Desert*. Tucson: University of Arizona Press, 2001.

Hoig, Stan. *Came Men on Horses: The Conquistador Expeditions of Francisco Vásquez de Coronado and Don Juan de Oñate*. Boulder: University Press of Colorado, 2013.

Hoijer, Harry. *Chiricahua and Mescalero Apache Texts*. Chicago, IL: University of Chicago Press, 1942.

Huggard, Christopher J. and Terrence M. Humble. *Santa Rita Del Cobre: A Copper Mining Community in New Mexico*. Boulder: University Press of Colorado, 2012.

Hurt, R. Douglas. *The Indian Frontier, 1763–1846: Histories of the American Frontier Series*. Albuquerque: University of New Mexico Press, 2002.

Iverson, Peter. *Diné: A History of the Navajo People*. Albuquerque: University of New Mexico Press, 2002.

Izquierdo, José Juan. "El problema de los indios bárbaros a la terminación de la guerra con los estados unidos." *Memorias de la academia mexicana de la historia* 7 (1948): 5–14.

Jackson, Donald, ed. *The Journals of Zebulon Montgomery Pike with Letters and Related Documents*. Vol. 1. Norman: University of Oklahoma Press, 1966.

Jackson, Jack and William C. Foster, eds. *Imaginary Kingdom: Texas as Seen by the Rivera and Rubí Military Expeditions, 1727–1767*. Austin: Texas State Historical Association, 1995.

Jacoby, Karl. *Shadows at Dawn: A Borderlands Massacre and the Violence of History*. New York: Penguin, 2008.

Jastrzembski, Joseph C. "Treacherous Towns in Mexico: Chiricahua Personal Narratives of Horrors." *Western Folklore* 54 (July 1995): 169–196.

John, Elizabeth A. H. *Storms Brewed in Other Men's Worlds: The Confrontation of Indians, Spanish, and French in the Southwest, 1540—1795*. College Station: Texas A&M University Press, 1975.

"Nurturing the Peace: Spanish and Comanche Cooperation in the Early Nineteenth Century." *New Mexico Historical Review* 59 (October 1984): 345–369.

John, Elizabeth A. H., ed., and John Wheat, trans. "Views from a Desk in Chihuahua: Manuel Merino's Report on Apaches and Neighboring Nations, ca. 1804." *Southwestern Historical Quarterly* 95 (October 1991): 139–176.

Johnson, Benjamin H. and Andrew R. Graybill. "Introduction: Borders and Their Historians in North America." In *Bridging National Borders in North America: Transnational and Comparative Histories*. Edited by Benjamin H.

Johnson and Andrew R. Graybill. Durham, NC: Duke University Press, 2010.

Johnson, Troy R. *The Occupation of Alcatraz Island: Indian Self-Determination and the Rise of Indian Activism*. Urbana: University of Illinois Press, 1996.

Jones, Oakah L., Jr. "Pueblo Indian Auxiliaries in New Mexico, 1763–1821." *New Mexico Historical Review* 80 (April 1962): 81–109.

"Pueblo Indian Auxiliaries and the Reconquest of New Mexico, 1692–1704." *Journal of the West* 2 (July 1963): 257–280.

Pueblo Warriors and Spanish Conquest. Norman: University of Oklahoma Press, 1966.

Julyan, Robert Hixson. *The Place Names of New Mexico*. 2nd ed. 1996; reprint, Albuquerque: University of New Mexico Press, 1998.

Kavanagh, Thomas W. *The Comanches: A History, 1706–1875*. Lincoln: University of Nebraska Press, 1999.

Kawashima, Yasu. "Legal Origins of the Indian Reservation in Colonial Massachusetts." *American Journal of Legal History* 13 (January 1969): 42–56.

Keeley, Lawrence H. *War before Civilization*. New York: Oxford University Press, 1996.

Kenner, Charles L. *A History of New Mexican-Plains Indian Relations*. Norman: University of Oklahoma Press, 1969.

Kessell, John L. *Friars, Soldiers, and Reformers: Hispanic Arizona and the Sonora Mission Frontier, 1767–1856*. Tucson: University of Arizona Press, 1976.

Spain in the Southwest: A Narrative History of Colonial New Mexico, Arizona, Texas, and California. Norman: University of Oklahoma Press, 2002.

Kino, Father Eusebio Francisco. *Kino's Historical Memoir of Pimeria Alta: A Contemporary Account of the Beginnings of California, Sonora, and Arizona, 1683–1711*. Edited and translated by Herbert Eugene Bolton. 1st ed., 1919; reprint, Berkeley: University of California Press, 1948.

Kiser, William S. *Turmoil on the Rio Grande: History of the Mesilla Valley, 1846–1865*. College Station: Texas A&M Press, 2011.

Dragoons in Apacheland: Conquest and Resistance in Southern New Mexico, 1846–1861. Norman: University of Oklahoma Press, 2012.

Knaut, Andrew L. *The Pueblo Revolt of 1680: Conquest and Resistance in Seventeenth-Century New Mexico*. Norman: University of Oklahoma Press, 1995.

La Vere, David. *The Texas Indians*. College Station: Texas A&M Press, 2004.

Lafora, Nicolás de. *The Frontiers of New Spain: Nicolás de Lafora's Description, 1766–68*. Edited by George P. Hammond. Berkeley: Quivira Society, 1958.

Lahti, Janne. "Colonized Labor: Apaches and Pawnees as Army Workers." *Western Historical Quarterly* 39 (Autumn 2008): 283–302.

Lee, Wayne E. "Projecting Power in the Early Modern World: The Spanish Model?" In *Empires and Indigenes: Intercultural Alliance, Imperial Expansion, and Warfare in the Early Modern World*. Edited by Wayne E. Lee. New York: New York University Press, 2011, 1–16.

Liebmann, Matthew. *Revolt: An Archaeological History of Pueblo Resistance and Revitalization in 17th Century New Mexico*. The Archaeology of Colonialism in Native North America Series. Tucson: University of Arizona Press, 2012.

Limerick, Patricia Nelson. *The Legacy of Conquest: The Unbroken Past of the American West*. New York: W.W. Norton, 1987.

Lockwood, Frank C. *The Apache Indians*. New York: Macmillan, 1938.

Lundwall, Helen J. and Terrence M. Humble. *Copper Mining in Santa Rita, New Mexico, 1801–1838*. Santa Fe, NM: Sunstone Press, 2012.

Lynch, John. *Bourbon Spain, 1700–1808*. Oxford: Basil Blackwell, 1989.

Maestas, Enrique Gilbert-Michael. "Culture and History of Native American Peoples of South Texas." Ph.D. diss., University of Texas at Austin, 2003.

Mails, Thomas E. *Secret Native American Pathways: A Guide to Inner Peace*. 1st ed., 1988; reprint, Tulsa, OK: Council Oak Books, 2003.

Mandell, Daniel R. *King Philip's War: Colonial Expansion, Native Resistance, and the End of Indian Sovereignty*. Baltimore, MD: Johns Hopkins University Press, 2010.

Mandrini, Raúl José. "Transformations: The Rio de la Plata During the Bourbon Era." In *Contested Spaces of Early America*. Edited by Juliana Barr and Edward Countryman. Philadelphia: University of Pennsylvania Press, 2014, 142–160.

Manje, Juan Mateo. *Unknown Arizona and Sonora, 1693–1721: From the Francisco Fernández del Castillo version of Luz de Tierra Incógnita*. Edited and translated by Harry J. Karns. Arizona Silhouettes: Tucson, 1954.

Matson, Daniel S. and Albert H. Schroeder, eds. and trans. "Cordero's Description of the Apache – 1796." *New Mexico Historical Review* 32 (October 1957): 335–356.

Matson, Daniel S. and Bernard L. Fontana, eds. *Friar Bringas Reports to the King: Methods and Indoctrination on the Frontier of New Spain 1796–97*. Tucson: University of Arizona Press, 1977.

Mattison, Ray H. "Early Spanish and Mexican Settlements in Arizona." *New Mexico Historical Review* 21 (October 1946): 273–327.

Mauss, Marcel. *The Gift: The Form and Reason for Exchange in Archaic Societies*. Translated by W. D. Halls. 1967; reprint, New York: W. W. Norton, 1990.

McCarty, Kieran, ed. and trans. *Desert Documentary: The Spanish Years, 1767–1821*. Tucson: Arizona Historical Society, 1976.

"Bernardo de Gálvez on the Apache Frontier: The Education of a Future Viceroy." *Journal of the Southwest* 36 (Summer 1994): 103–30.

A Frontier Documentary: Sonora and Tucson, 1821–1848. Tucson: University of Arizona Press, 1997.

McChristian, Douglas C. *Fort Bowie, Arizona: Combat Post of the Southwest, 1858–1894*. Norman: University of Oklahoma Press, 2005.

Meriwether, David. *My Life in the Mountains and on the Plains*. Edited by Robert A. Griffen. Norman: University of Oklahoma Press, 1965.

Merrell, James H. *The Indians' New World: Catawbas and Their Neighbors from European Contact through the Era of Removal*. Chapel Hill: University of North Carolina Press, 1989.

Merrill, William L. "Cultural Creativity and Raiding Bands in Eighteenth-Century Northern New Spain." In *Violence, Resistance, and Survival in the Americas: Native Americans and the Legacy of Conquest.* Edited by William B. Taylor and Franklin Pease. Washington, DC: Smithsonian Institution Press, 1994, 124–152.

"La economía política de las correrías: Nueva Vizcaya al final de la época colonial." In *Nómadas y sedentarios en el norte de México: homenaje a Beatriz Braniff.* Edited by Marie-Areti Hers, et al. Mexico: UNAM, 2000, 623–668.

Mirafuentes Galván, José Luis. "Los dos mundos de José Reyes Pozo y el alzamiento de los Apaches Chiricahuis (Bacoachi, Sonora, 1790)." *Estudios de Historia Novohispana* 21 (2000): 67–105.

Moore, Mary Lu and Delmar L. Beene, trans. and ed. "The Interior Provinces of New Spain: The Report of Hugo O'Conor, January 30, 1776." *Arizona and the West* 13 (Autumn 1971): 265–282.

Moorhead, Max L. *The Apache Frontier: Jacobo Ugarte and Spanish-Indian Relations in Northern New Spain, 1769–1791.* Civilization of the American Indian Series. Norman: University of Oklahoma, 1968.

The Presidio: Bastion of the Spanish Borderlands. Norman: University of Oklahoma Press, 1975.

"Spanish Deportation of Hostile Apaches: The Policy and the Practice." *Arizona and the West* 17 (Autumn 1975): 205–220.

Morfi, Fray Juan Agustín. *History of Texas, 1673–1779.* Edited by Carlos Eduardo Castañeda. Albuquerque, NM: Quivira Society, 1935.

Morgenthaler, Jefferson. *La Junta De Los Rios: The Life, Death and Resurrection of an Ancient Desert Community in the Big Bend Region of Texas.* Boerne, TX: Mockingbird Books, 2007.

Morrison, Kenneth W. *The Solidarity of Kin: Ethnohistory, Religious Studies, and the Algonkian–French Religious Encounter.* Albany: State University of New York Press, 2002.

Nava, Pedro de. "Instructions for Dealing with Apaches at Peace in Nueva Vizcaya, Chihuahua, October 14, 1791." In *San Elizario: Spanish Presidio to Texas County Seat.* Edited by Rick Hendricks and W. H. Timmons. El Paso: Texas Western Press, 1998.

Navarro García, Luis. *Don José de Gálvez y la Comandancia General de las Provincias Internas del norte de Nueva España.* Sevilla: Escuela de Estudios Hispano-Americanos, 1964.

Naylor, Thomas H. and Charles W. Polzer, eds. *The Presidio and Militia on the Northern Frontier of New Spain, 1570–1700.* University of Arizona Press: Tucson, 1986.

eds. *Pedro de Rivera and the Military Regulations for Northern New Spain, 1724–1729: A Documentary History of His Frontier Inspection and the Reglamento de 1729.* Tucson: University of Arizona Press, 1988.

Nelson, Al B. "Campaigning in the Big Bend of the Río Grande in 1787." *Southwestern Historical Quarterly* 39 (January 1936): 200–227.

Nentvig, Juan, S. J. *Rudo ensayo: tentativa de una prevencional descripción geográphica de la provincia de Sonora, sus terminos, y confines.* St. Augustine: [Albany, Munsell, printer], 1863.

Rudo Ensayo: Arizona and Sonora in 1763. 1st edition, 1894; Tucson: Arizona Silhoutees, 1951.

Rudo Ensayo: A Description of Sonora and Arizona in 1764. Edited and translated by Alberto Francisco Pradeau and Robert R. Rasmussen. Tucson: University of Arizona Press, 1980.

Noyes, Stanley. *Los Comanches: The Horse People, 1751–1845*. Albuquerque: University of New Mexico Press, 1993.

O'Brien, Jean M. *Dispossession by Degrees: Indian Land and Identity in Natick, Massachusetts*. New York: Cambridge University Press, 1997.

O'Conor, Hugo. *The Defenses of Northern New Spain: Hugo O'Conor's Report to Teodoro de Croix, July 22, 1777*. Edited and translated by Donald C. Cutter. Dallas, TX: Southern Methodist University Press/DeGolyer Library, 1994.

Officer, James E. *Hispanic Arizona, 1530–1856*. Tucson: University of Arizona Press, 1987.

Opler, Morris E. "A Summary of Jicarilla Apache Culture." *American Anthropologist* 38 (April–June 1936): 202–223.

Myths and Tales of the Chiricahua Apache Indians. 1942; reprint, Lincoln: University of Nebraska Press, 1994.

An Apache Life-Way: The Economic, Social, and Religious Institutions of the Chiricahua Indians. 1941; reprint, New York: Cooper Square Publishers, 1965.

"Cause and Effect in Apachean Agriculture, Division of Labor, Residence Patterns, and Girls' Puberty Rites." *American Anthropologist* 74 (October 1972): 1133–1146.

"The Apachean Culture Pattern and Its Origins." In *Handbook of North American Indians: Southwest*. Vol. 10. Edited by Alfonso Ortiz. Washington, DC: Smithsonian Institution, 1983, 10, 368–92.

"Chiricahua Apache." In *Handbook of North American Indians: Southwest*. Vol. 10. Edited by Alfonso Ortiz. Washington, DC: Smithsonian Institution, 1983, 401–418.

"Mescalero Apache." In *Handbook of North American Indians: Southwest*. Vol. 10. Edited by Alfonso Ortiz. Washington, DC: Smithsonian Institution, 1983, 419–439.

"Lipan Apache." In *Handbook of North American Indians: Plains*. Vol. 13, Pt. 2. Edited by Raymond J. DeMallie. Washington, DC: Smithsonian Institution, 2001.

Ortelli, Sara. "Crisis de subsistencia y robo de ganado en el septentrión novohispano: San José de Parral (1770–1790)." *Relaciones* 121, 31 (2004): 21–56.

"Enemigos internos y súbditos desleales: La infidencia en Nueva Vizcaya en tiempos de los Borbones." *Anuario de Estudios Americanos* 61 (2004): 467–489.

Trama de una guerra conveniente: Nueva Vizcaya y la sombra de los Apaches (1748–1790). Mexico City: El Colegio de México, 2007.

Osborn, Alan J. "Ecological Aspects of Equestrian Adaptations in Aboriginal North America." *American Anthropologist* 85 (September 1983): 563–591.

Park, Joseph F. "The Apaches in Mexican-American Relations, 1848–1861: A Footnote to the Gadsden Treaty." *Arizona and the West* 3 (Summer 1961): 129–146.
  "Spanish Indian Policy in Northern Mexico, 1765–1810." *Arizona and the West* 4 (Winter 1962): 325–344.
  "Spanish Indian Policy in Northern Mexico, 1765–1810." In *New Spain's Northern Frontier: Essays on Spain in the American West, 1540–1821*. Edited by David J. Weber. Albuqurque: University of New Mexico Press, 1979, 219–234.
Parker, Geoffrey. *The Military Revolution: Military Innovation and the Rise of the West, 1500–1800*. 2nd ed. New York: Cambridge University Press, 1996.
Patterson, Orlando. *Slavery and Social Death*. Cambridge, MA: Harvard University Press, 1982.
Perry, Richard J. *Apache Reservation: Indigenous Peoples and the American State*. Austin: University of Texas Press, 1993.
Pichardo, José Antonio de. *Pichardo's Treatise on the Limits of Louisiana and Texas*. 2 vols. Edited by Charles Wilson Hackett. Austin: University of Texas Press, 1931–4.
Polzer, Charles W. and Thomas E. Sheridan. *The Presidio and Militia on the Northern Frontier of New Spain: A Documentary History. Volume Two, Part One: The Californias and Sinaloa-Sonora, 1700–1765*. Tucson: University of Arizona Press, 1997.
Posada, Alonso de. *Alonso de Posada Report, 1686: A Description of the Area of the Present Southern United States in the Seventeenth Century*. Spanish Borderlands Series. Edited and translated by Alfred B. Thomas. Pensacola: Perdido Bay Press, 1982.
Powell, Philip Wayne. "The Chichimecas: Scourge of the Silver Frontier in Sixteenth-Century Mexico." *Hispanic American Historical Review* 25 (August 1945): 315–338.
  Soldiers, Indians, and Silver: The Northward Advance of New Spain, 1550–1600 Berkeley: University of California Press, 1952.
  "Peacemaking on North America's First Frontier." *Americas* 16 (January 1960): 221–250.
  Mexico's Miguel Caldera: The Taming of America's First Frontier, 1548–1597. Tucson: University of Arizona Press, 1977.
  "Genesis of the Frontier Presidio in North America." *Western Historical Quarterly* 13 (April 1982): 124–141.
Radding, Cynthia. *Wandering Peoples: Colonialism, Ethnic Spaces, and Ecological Frontiers in Northwestern Mexico, 1700–1850*. Durham, NC: Duke University Press, 1997.
  Landscapes of Power and Identity: Comparative Histories in the Sonoran Desert and the Forests of Amazonia from Colony to Republic. Durham, NC: Duke University Press, 2005.
  "Agaves, Human Cultures, and Desert Landscapes in Northern Mexico." *Environmental History* 17 (January 2012): 84–115.

Reeve, Frank D. "Early Navaho Geography." *New Mexico Historical Review* 31 (October 1956): 290–309.

"Navaho Foreign Affairs, 1795–1846." *New Mexico Historical Review* 46 (April 1971): 101–32.

Reséndez, Andrés. *Changing National Identities at the Frontier: Texas and New Mexico, 1800–1850.* New York: Cambridge University Press, 2005.

Reuse, Willem J. de. *A Practical Grammar of the San Carlos Apache Language.* Munich, Germany: Lincom Europa, 2006.

Reuse, Willem J. "Apache Names in Spanish and Early Mexican Documents: What They Can Tell Us about the Early Contact Apache Dialect Situation." In *From the Land of Ever Winter to the American Southwest: Athapaskan Migrations, Mobility, and Ethnogenesis.* Edited by Deni J. Seymour. Salt Lake City: University of Utah Press, 2012.

Richter, Daniel K. *The Ordeal of the Longhouse: The Peoples of the Iroquois League in the Era of European Colonization.* Chapel Hill, NC: University of North Carolina Press, 1992.

Riley, Carroll L. *The Kachina and the Cross: Indians and Spaniards in the Early Southwest.* Salt Lake City: University of Utah Press, 1999.

Rivaya-Martínez, Joaquín. "San Carlos de los Jupes: une tentative avortée de sédentarisation des bárbaros dans les territoires frontaliers du nord de la Nouvelle-Espagne en 1787–1788." *Recherches amérindiennes au québec* 41, 2–3 (2011): 29–59.

Robert, Paul. *Le petit Robert 2: dictionnarie universel des noms propres alphabétique et analogique.* Paris: Le Robert, 1991.

Robinson, Sherry. *I Fought a Good Fight: The History of the Lipan Apaches.* Denton: University of North Texas Press, 2013.

Rodríguez, Martha. *La guerra entre bárbaros y civilizados: El exterminio del nómada en Coahuila, 1840–1880.* Saltillo, Mexico: Centro de Estudios Sociales y Humanísticos, A.C., 1998.

Roseberry, William. *Anthropologies and Histories: Essays in Culture, History, and Political Economy.* New Brunswick, NJ: Rutgers University Press, 1989.

Ruíz, José Francisco. *Report on the Indian Tribes of Texas in 1828.* Edited by John C. Ewers and translated by Georgette Dunn. New Haven, CT: Yale University Press, 1972.

Ruiz Medrano, Ethelia and Susan Kellogg, eds. *Negotiation within Domination: New Spain's Indian Pueblos Confront the Spanish State.* Mesoamerican Worlds Series. Boulder: University Press of Colorado, 2010.

Rushforth, Brett. *Bonds of Alliance: Indigenous and Atlantic Slaveries in New France.* Chapel Hill: University of North Carolina Press, 2012.

Salcedo, Don Nemesio Salcedo y Salcedo. *Instrucción reservada de don Nemesio Salcedo y Salcedo, Comandante General de Provincias Internas a su sucesor [June 16, 1813].* Edited by Isidro Vizcaya Canales. Chihuahua, Mexico: Centro de Información del Estado de Chihuahua, 1990.

Santiago, Mark. *The Jar of Severed Hands: Spanish Deportation of Apache Prisoners of War, 1770–1810.* Norman: University of Oklahoma Press, 2011.

Sauer, Carl. *The Distribution of Aboriginal Tribes and Languages in Northwestern Mexico.* Berkeley: University of California Press, 1934.

Schaafsma, Curtis F. and Carroll R. Riley. "The Casas Grandes World: Analysis and Conclusion." In *The Casas Grandes World*, edited by Curtis F. Schaafsma and Carroll R. Riley. Salt Lake City: University of Utah Press, 1999.

Schilz, Thomas Frank and Donald E. Worcester. "The Spread of Firearms among the Indian Tribes on the Northern Frontier of New Spain." *American Indian Quarterly* 11 (Winter 1987): 1–10.

Scholes, France V. Church and State in New Mexico, 1610–1650. *New Mexico Historical Society Publications in History*. Albuquerque: University of New Mexico Press, 1937.

Schroeder, Albert H. "Documentary Evidence Pertaining to the Early Historic Period of Southern Arizona." *New Mexico Historical Review* 27 (April 1952): 137–167.

"Shifting for Survival in the Spanish Southwest." *New Mexico Historical Review* 43 (October 1968): 291–310.

A Study of the Apache Indians. Vols. 1, 4. American Indian Ethnohistory: Indians of the Southwest Series. New York: Garland, 1974.

Scott, James C. *The Art of Not Being Governed: An Anarchist History of Upland Southeast Asia*. Yale Agrarian Studies Series. New Haven, CT: Yale University Press, 2009.

Secoy, Frank Raymond. *Changing Military Patterns on the Great Plains (17th Century through Early 19th Century)*. Monographs of the American Ethnological Society Series. Locust Valley, NY: J.J. Augustin, 1953.

Sedelmayr, Jacobo. *Sedelmayr's Relacion of 1746*. Bureau of American Ethnology, Bulletin 23. Edited and translated by Ronald L. Ives. Washington, DC: Smithsonian Institution, 1939.

Seymour, Deni J., ed. *From the Land of Ever Winter to the American Southwest: Athapaskan Migrations, Mobility, and Ethnogenesis*. Salt Lake City: University of Utah Press, 2012.

A Fateful Day in 1698: The Remarkable Sobaipuri-O'odham Victory over the Apaches and Their Allies. Salt Lake City: University of Utah Press, 2014.

Simmons, Marc. "New Mexico's Smallpox Epidemic of 1780–1781." *New Mexico Historical Review* 41 (October 1966): 319–326.

trans. and ed. *Border Comanches: Seven Spanish Colonial Documents, 1785–1819*. Santa Fe, NM: Stagecoach Press, 1967.

Coronado's Land: Essays on Daily Life in Colonial New Mexico. Albuquerque: University of New Mexico Press, 1991.

Simpson, Lesley B., ed., and Paul D. Nathan, trans. *The San Sabá Papers: A Documentary Account of the Founding and Destruction of San Sabá Mission*. San Francisco, CA: Josh Howell Books, 1959; reprint, Dallas, TX: Southern Methodist University Press, 2000.

Sjoberg, Andrée F. "Lipan Apache Culture in Historical Perspective." *Southwestern Journal of Anthropology* 9 (Spring 1953): 76–98.

Smith, Fay Jackson, John L. Kessell, and Francis J. Fox, S.J. *Father Kino in Arizona*. Arizona Historical Foundation: Phoenix, 1966.

Smith, Ralph A. "Apache Plunder Trails Southward, 1831–1840." *New Mexico Historical Review* 37 (January 1962): 20–42.

"Apache 'Ranching' Below the Gila, 1841–1845." *Arizoniana* 3 (Winter 1962): 1–17.

"Indians in American-Mexican Relations before the War of 1846." *Hispanic American Historical Review* 43 (February 1963): 34–64.

"Many Mini Treaties with West Texas Indians." *West Texas Historical Association Year Book* 47 (1971): 62–77.

Borderlander: The Life of James Kirker, 1793–1852. Norman: University of Oklahoma Press, 1999.

Smith, Sherry L. *The View from Officers' Row: Army Perceptions of Western Indians*. Tucson: University of Arizona Press, 1990.

Sonnichsen, C. L. *The Mescalero Apaches*. 2nd ed. Norman: University of Oklahoma Press, 1973.

Spicer, Edward H. *Cycles of Conquest: The Impact of Spain, Mexico, and the United States on the Indians of the Southwest, 1533–1960*. 1962; reprint, Tucson: University of Arizona Press, 1997.

Stevens, Robert C. "The Apache Menace in Sonora, 1831–1849." *Arizona and the West* 6 (Autumn 1964): 211–222.

Stockel, H. Henrietta. *On the Bloody Road to Jesus: Christianity and the Chiricahua Apaches*. Albuquerque: University of New Mexico Press, 2004.

Salvation through Slavery: Chiricahua Apaches and Priests on the Spanish Colonial Frontier. Albuquerque: University of New Mexico Press, 2008.

Stodder, Ann L.W. and Debra L. Martin. "Health and Disease in the Southwest before and after Spanish Contact." In *Disease and Demography in the Americas*. Edited by John W. Verano and Douglas H. Ubelaker. Washington, DC: Smithsonian Institution Press, 1992.

Strickland, Rex W. "The Birth and Death of a Legend: The Johnson "Massacre" of 1837." *Arizona and the West* 18 (Autumn 1976): 257–286.

Sweeney, Edwin R. "'I Had Lost All': Geronimo and the Carrasco Massacre of 1851." *Journal of Arizona History* 27 (Spring 1986): 35–52.

Cochise: Chiricahua Apache Chief. Norman: University of Oklahoma Press, 1991.

Mangas Coloradas: Chief of the Chiricahua Apaches. Norman: University of Oklahoma Press, 1998.

Tamez, Margo. "The Texas-Mexico Border Wall and Ndé Memory." In *Beyond Walls and Cages: Prisons, Borders, and Global Crisis*. Edited by Jenna M. Loyd, Matt Mitchelson, and Andrew Burridge. Athens: University of Georgia Press, 2012.

Tate, Michael L. "Soldiers of the Line: Apache Companies in the U.S. Army: 1891–1897." *Arizona and the West* 16 (Winter 1974): 343–364.

Taylor, Alan. *The Divided Ground: Indians, Settlers, and the Northern Borderland of the American Revolution*. New York: Alfred A. Knopf, 2006.

Thomas, Alfred B. "San Carlos: A Comanche Pueblo on the Arkansas River, 1787." *Colorado Magazine* 6, (May 1929): 79–91.

"The Mescalero Apache, 1653–1874." In *Apache Indians XI*. New York: Garland Publishing, 1974, 13–60.

Thomas, Alfred Barnaby, ed. and trans. *Forgotten Frontiers: A Study of the Spanish Indian Policy of Don Juan Bautista de Anza, Governor of New Mexico, 1777–1787*. Norman: University of Oklahoma Press, 1932.

ed. and trans. *After Coronado: Spanish Exploration Northeast of New Mexico, 1696–1727*. Norman: University of Oklahoma Press, 1935.

ed. and trans. *The Plains Indians and New Mexico, 1751–1778: A Collection of Documents Illustrative of the History of the Eastern Frontier of New Mexico*. Albuquerque: University of New Mexico Press, 1940.

ed. and trans. *Teodoro de Croix and the Northern Frontier of New Spain, 1776–1783: From the Original Document in the Archives of the Indies, Seville*. Norman: University of Oklahoma Press, 1941.

Thrapp, Dan L. *The Conquest of Apachería*. Norman: University of Oklahoma Press, 1967.

Encyclopedia of Frontier Biography. 3 Vols. 1988; reprint, Lincoln: University of Nebraska Press, 1991.

Tiller, Veronica E. "Jicarilla Apache." In *Handbook of North American Indians: Southwest*. Vol 10. Edited by Alfonso Ortiz. Washington, DC: Smithsonian Institution, 1983, 440–461.

Torre Curiel, José Refugio de la. *Twilight of the Mission Frontier: Shifting Interethnic Alliances and Social Organization in Sonora, 1768–1855*. Stanford and Berkeley, CA: Stanford University Press and Academy of American Franciscan History, 2012.

Trasviña Retis, Juan Antonio de. *The Founding of Missions at La Junta de Los Rios*. Supplementary Studies of the Texas Catholic Historical Society. Edited by Reginald C. Reindorp. Austin: Texas Catholic Historical Society, 1938.

Truett, Samuel. "The Ghosts of Frontiers Past: Making and Unmaking Space in the Borderlands." *Journal of the Southwest* 46 (Summer 2004): 309–350.

Tunnell, Curtis D. and W. W. Newcomb, Jr. *A Lipan Apache Mission: San Lorenzo de La Santa Cruz, 1762–1771*. Vol. 14. Bulletin of the Texas Memorial Museum. Austin: Texas Memorial Museum, July 1969.

Twitchell, Ralph Emerson. *The Spanish Archives of New Mexico*. Vol. 2. Cedar Rapids, IA: Torch Press, 1914.

United States Joint Special Committee to Inquire into the Condition of Indian Tribes, Thirty-ninth Congress, first session and Thirty-eighth Congress, second session. *Condition of the Indian Tribes: Report of the Joint Special Committee, Appointed under Joint Resolution of March 3, 1865*. Washington, DC: Government Printing Office, 1867.

Usner, Daniel H., Jr. "Iroquois Livelihood and Jeffersonian Agrarianism: Reaching behind the Models and Metaphors." In *Native Americans in the Early Republic*. Edited by Ronald Hoffman, Frederick E. Hoxie, and Peter J. Albert. Charlottesville: University Press of Virginia, 1999, 220–225.

Utley, Robert M. *Geronimo*. New Haven, CT: Yale University Press, 2012.

Vallebueno G., Miguel. "Apaches y comanches en Durango durante los siglos XVIII y XIX." In *Nómadas y sedentarios en el norte de México: Homenaje a Beatriz Braniff*. Edited by Marie-Areti Hers, et. al. México: UNAM, 2000, 669–681.

Van Wagenen, Michael Scott. *Remembering the Forgotten War: The Enduring Legacies of the U.S.–Mexican War*. Amherst: University of Massachusetts Press, 2012.

Van Young, Eric. *The Other Rebellion: Popular Violence, Ideology, and the Mexican Struggle for Indpendence, 1810–1821*. Stanford, CA: Stanford University Press, 2001.

Vargas, Diego de. *By Force of Arms: The Journals of Don Diego de Vargas, New Mexico, 1691–93*. Edited by John L. Kessell and Rick Hendricks. Albuquerque: University of New Mexico Press, 1992.

  Blood on the Boulders: The Journals of Don Diego de Vargas, New Mexico, 1694–97. Edited by John L. Kessell, Rick Hendricks, and Meredith D. Dodge. Albuquerque: University of New Mexico Press, 1998.

Velasco, José Francisco. *Noticias estádisticas del estado de Sonora (1850)*. Hermosillo: Gobierno del Estado de Sonora, 1985.

Velasco Ávila, Cuauhtémoc. "Negociaciones con los lipanes a fines del siglo xviii: avances y retrocesos." In *52nd Congreso de las Americanistas*. Universidad de Sevilla, Spain, 2006.

Velásquez, María del Carmen, ed. *La frontera norte y la experiencia colonial*. Mexico: Secretaría de Relaciones Exteriores, 1982.

Vetancurt, Fray Agustín de. *Teatro Mexicano: descripción breve de los sucesos exemplares de la Nueva-España en el Nuevo Mundo Occidental de las Indias*. Vol. III: Chronica de la provincia del santo evangelico. 4 vols. Coleccion Chimalistac de libros y documentos acerca de la Nueva España. 1st ed., Mexico, 1698 [1697]; Madrid: José Porrua Turanzas, 1961.

Vizcaya Canales, Isidro, ed. *La invasión de los indios bárbaros al noreste de México en los años de 1840 y 1841*. Monterrey, Mexico: Publicaciones del Instituto Tecnológico y de Estudios Superiores de Monterrey, 1968.

  Incursiones de indios al noreste en el México independiente (1821–1855). Monterrey, Mexico: Archivo General del Estado de Nuevo León, 1995.

Wayland, Virginia, Harold Wayland, and Alan Ferg. *Playing Cards of the Apaches: A Study in Cultural Adaptation*. Tucson, AZ: Screenfold Press, 2006.

Weber, David J. *The Taos Trappers: The Fur Trade in the Far Southwest, 1540–1846*. Norman: University of Oklahoma Press, 1971.

  The Mexican Frontier, 1821–1846: The American Southwest under Mexico. Albuquerque: University of New Mexico Press, 1982.

  The Spanish Frontier in North America. New Haven, CT: Yale University Press, 1992.

  "Bourbons and Bárbaros: Center and Periphery in the Reshaping of Spanish Indian Policy." In *Negotiated Empires: Centers and Peripheries in the Americas, 1500–1820*, edited by Christine Daniels and Michael V. Kennedy. New York: Routledge, 2002, 79–103.

  Bárbaros: Spaniards and Their Savages in the Age of Enlightenment. New Haven, CT: Yale University Press, 2005.

Weddle, Robert S. *The San Sabá Mission: Spanish Pivot in Texas*. Austin: University of Texas Press, 1964.

White, Bruce. "Ethnicity and Race in the Military." In *The Oxford Companion to American Military History*. Edited by John Whiteclay Chambers II. New York: Oxford University Press, 1999, 252–254.

Williams, Jack S. "The Evolution of the Presidio in Northern New Spain." *Historical Archaeology* 38 (2004): 6–23.

Williams, Jack S. and Robert L. Hoover. *Arms of the Apachería: A Comparison of Apachean and Spanish Fighting Techniques in the Later Eighteenth Century.* Greeley, CO: Museum of Anthropology, University of Northern Colorado, 1983.

Worcester, Donald E. "The Beginnings of the Apache Menace of the Southwest." *New Mexico Historical Review* 41 (January 1941): 1–14.

"The Use of Saddles by American Indians." *New Mexico Historical Review* 20 (April 1945): 139–143.

"The Weapons of American Indians." *New Mexico Historical Review* 20 (July 1945): 227–238.

"The Navajo During the Spanish Regime in New Mexico." *New Mexico Historical Review* 26 (April 1951): 101–118.

The Apaches: Eagles of the Southwest. Norman: University of Oklahoma Press, 1979.

Wyllys, Rufus Kay, ed. and trans. "Padre Luís Velarde's Relación of Pimería Alta, 1716." *New Mexico Historical Review* 6 (April 1931): 111–151.

Zúñiga, Ignacio. *Rápida ojeada al estado de Sonora: dirigida y dedicada al supremo gobierno de la nación.* Mexico: Juan Ojeda, 1835.

Index

accommodation, 257–258
acculturation, 106, 154
adaptation
  of auxiliary troops, 155–156
  cultural, 5, 23
  mutual, 154
  to peace, 154–160
  to rations, 155–156
  reservations and, 2–5, 158–159
  to Spanish colonialism, 9
  to vices, Spanish, 156–157
adopted Apache, 148
agaves, 50–51
Agua Nueva, 216, 220–221, 233, 239. *See also* Carrizal
Akimel O'odham, 227
alcohol, 25–26, 174–175, 217–218, 237–238
allies, Apache, 144. *See also specific tribes*
Alonso, Dajunné (Mescalero), 63–64
Americans. *See* United States-Apache relations
ammunition
  American, 200–201, 213, 217–218, 222–223, 250
  French, 30–31, 70–71
  Mexican, 217–218, 222–223, 227, 231, 238
  Spanish, 66, 114–115, 172
Anaya (Chihene), 234–235, 237
Animas Mountains, 213, 215, 232–233
Anza, Juan Bautista de, 76–79, 112–113
Apachería (Apache Country), 5–6, 84–86

dispossession of, 202–203
expansion of, 47–48, 65–68
legal protection of, 203
New Spain expansion into, 151
sale of, 203
Treaty of Guadalupe Hidalgo and, 250
Apaches (Ndé), 1–5. *See also specific groups and topics*
  origins, 23–28
  roles of, 5
  social structure of, 24–25
Apaches de paz (peaceful Apaches), 2–5
  horse raids by, 159–160
  independent Apache relations with, 158
  at Janos presidio, annual expenditures for, 190–191
  Mexican-Apache relations and, 216, 253
  raiding by, 178–179
  Spanish and, 116–117, 160, 199
  Spanish military and, 6–8, 183
  supply problems affecting, 172–173
  threat of, 159
Aravaipa Apaches. *See* Tsézhiné Apaches
Aravaipa Canyon, 38, 220, 227
Arizona
  as part of Apachería, 5–6, 24, 26–27, 38, 200, 228
  as site of U.S. reservations for Apaches, 257
  Spanish and Mexican expansion into, 152–153, 200, 221 (*See also* Sonora; Tucson)
Arizpe, 154–155, 177–178, 217, 223, 226–228, 251

287

auxiliary troops, Apache, 89–90, 155
  adaptation of, 155–156
  Mexico's use of, 253–254
  Spanish use of, 79–80, 111–112

Bacoachi pueblo, 105
  Chokonen at, 143–144, 158
  Denojeant, Antonio, at, 174
  rations issued at, 119–120
baptisms, Apache, 147–148, 165
  of children, 147–148
  for illness, 147–148
Barela (Mescalero), 230
Bavispe presidio, 111–112, 125–126, 144–145, 158, 189–192, 251–252
Benavides, Alonso de, 19–23, 65
Benites, Antonio Rafael, 147–148
Berroterán, José de, 79–80
Bigotes (Mescalero), 61, 71, 88, 90, 92
Biñolas, Pedro de Mata, 174–175
bison, 27
Black Range. *See* Mimbres Mountains
Bolsón de Mapimi, 5–6, 79–80, 90–92, 117–118, 261
borderlands, comparative, 5–6, 8–9. *See also* frontiers
Bringas, Diego, 159–160
Buena Esperanza
  Mescalero at, 63–65, 87–93
  peace negotiations, 89–91
  peace treaty, 63–64
  rations at, 89–91

Caddoans, 84–86, 127–128
Caddos, 27, 68–69
Calderón, Zeferino, 202–203
Calvo, José Joaquín, 204–205, 222–223, 225
capitulations, 106–107
captive Apaches, 68–69, 129–130, 142
  as allies, 144
  extradition of, 148–149
  military service by, 145
  negotiating release of, 154–155
  peace and retrieving, 129, 225, 251–252
  recovering, 121–122
captive Spaniards, 129–130
Carrasco, José María, 252–253
Carrizal presidio, 2, 121–122, 150, 204–205, 236, 239–240, 252
Carrizaleño Apaches, 239–240, 252

Casas Grandes, 32–35, 152–153, 186–187
Catholicism, 9, 19–23, 65–68
  baptisms and, 147–148
  "civilizing" and, 74–75
  as cultural adaptation, 23
  reasons for, 71–73
  Spanish military force and, 69–70
  Vaquero Apaches and, 21–22
  Xila Apaches and, 19–21
Chacón, Fernando de, 175–176, 180–181, 192–193
Chafalote (Chihene), 122–123
Cherokees, 8
Chichimecas, 62–63
Chiganstegé (El Chiquito, Chokonen), 158
Chihene Apaches, 1
  allies, 35–36, 126, 159
  Catholicism and, 19–21
  farming, 146–147
  Great Southwestern Revolt peace agreement and, 36–38
  lands, 231–233
  Mexican peace negotiations with, 232–233, 252–253
  mining exploration by, 151–152
  Navajo and, 113, 175
  peace negotiations, 46–47, 80, 82–84, 105–106
  raids, 32–33, 127
  resettlement post-Great Southwestern Revolt, 46–47
  at Sabinal pueblo, 180–181
  Spanish military punitive campaigns against, 113–114
  in Spanish military-run reservations, 2
  U.S. peace negotiations with, 255–256
  on U.S.-run reservations, 254–255
Chihene Gila Apaches, 233–234
Chihene Mimbres Apaches
  Mexican peace treaty with, 221–222, 228–230
  peace negotiations, 118–119, 121–122, 126–127
  territory, 228–229
Chihene Mogollon Apaches, 151–152, 235
Chihuahua, province of
  Mexican-Apache relations in, 220–221, 231–234
  violence in, 239–240
Chihuahua, villa of
  Apaches at, 177–178

arms factory in, 184
Chi'laa, 19–21, 26–27, 36–37, 46, 228–230, 232–233, 250
Chilitipagé (T'iisibaan), 154–155
Chilpain Apaches, 39–40
Chinarras, 41
Chiricahua Mountains (Sierra de Chiricagui), 38, 41, 105, 223
Chiricahuas (Chiricagui) Apaches, 38. *See also* Chokonen Apaches
Chirimi (Chihene), 202–203, 221, 223
Chokonen Apaches, 1, 38
  at Bacoachi pueblo, 143–144, 158
  Hispanicization of, 143–144
  Mexican peace treaty with, 227–228, 251–252
  peace negotiations, 105, 118–119
  Spanish military punitive campaigns against, 113–114
  in Spanish military-run reservations, 2
  weaponry, 25
Chokonens de paz, 116–117
Christianization, 154. *See also* Catholicism; spiritual power
Cigarrito (Chihene), 221, 223, 228, 233
"civilized," 5, 7–8, 106
  Catholic conversion and, 74–75
  farming and, 8
Coahuila, 122–123
Cochise, 7–8
colonialism, Spanish
  Apache adaptations to, 9
  horse raids and preventing, 32–33
  reservation policy and, 9–10
colonized groups, 5
colonizing powers, 5–6
Comanchería (Comanche Country), 5–6, 73, 113, 117, 143, 200–201
Comanches, 5–6
  alliance with Spanish, 112–114
  Apaches and, 71–73, 84–86, 112–114, 141–142
  attacks on Apaches, 117, 127–128
  Lipans and, 196–197
  Mescaleros and, 117, 128–129, 141, 196–197
  Navajo alliance with, 153
  Pawnees and, 176
  peace with, 153
  political instability of, 176
  raids, 189–202

Compá, Juan Diego (Nayulchi, Chihene), 1–2, 146, 154
  Johnson massacre and, 213–215
  mining exploration by, 151–152
Compá, Juan José (Chihene), 1–2, 146
  Johnson massacre and, 213–215
  Mexican-Chihene Mimbres peace treaty and, 221–222
  Mexican-Ndé peace treaty and, 220–221
  Santa Rita del Cobre peace treaty and, 223–225
Concha, Fernando de la
  Jasquenelté and, 146
  Sabinal pueblo and, 175–176
  Spanish military punitive campaigns, 110–111
Conchos, 35–36
Cordero, Antonio, 105–106, 149–151, 160
corn. *See* maize
Coronado, Francisco Vásquez de, 28
Corralitos, 152, 237–238
Coyotero Apaches, 236, 263. *See also* Western Apaches
Croix, Teodoro de, 61–62
  Apache pueblo settlements and, 84–87, 103
  auxiliary troops used by, 111–112
  Buena Esperanza and, 63–65
  Chihene peace negotiations, 82–84
  Mescaleros and, 89–93
  military tactics of, 108–110
  peace negotiations and, 81–82, 93–94
  war councils, 80–84
Cuartelejo Apaches, 47–48, 66–68. *See also* El Cuartelejo
Cuba, 142, 148–149
Cubero, Pedro Rodríguez, 44–45
Cuchillo Negro (Chihene), 254–255
currency shortage, 186

deerskins, 19–21, 27, 45–46, 79, 156, 182
Delgadito (Chihene), 252, 254–255
Denojeant, Antonio, 174–175
deporation, 142, 201, 216
Díaz, Domingo, 105–106, 117, 119–120
Diné (Navajo), 27–28
  agricultural practices, 26–27
  Chihene and, 113, 175
  Comanche alliance with, 153
  political instability in, 176
  Spanish alliance with, 113–115
disease, 158. *See also* smallpox

Domingo Alegre, 63, 87
Domínguez, Atanasio, 147
drought, 27
  farming and, 119–120
  raiding and, 29–30
  rations and, 119–120
  supply shortages and, 186–187
drunkenness, 174
Durango, province of, 2, 91, 194, 218, 228–229
Durango, villa of, 93–94, 151
Dzilghą́'é (White Mountain) Apaches, 26–27, 153–154, 226–227, 263

Eastern Apaches, 27, 65–68. *See also* Jicarilla Apaches; Lipan Apaches; Mescalero Apaches
Echeagaray, Manuel de, 121–122
economics, 29
  of Comanche-Navajo alliance, 153
  of *establecimientos*, 6–7, 150
  of missions, 71
  Nava's policy changes and, 177–183
  of peace and war, 93–94
  of rations, 156, 161
  of reservations, 10
  of Spain, 161, 184–185
  supply shortages and, 184–186
El Chilmo (Chihene), 29–30, 43–44
El Compá (Chokonen), 1–2, 158
  captive Apaches' release and, 121–122, 154–155
  political authority of, 145–146
  Spanish and, 145–146
El Cuartelejo, 28–29, 43–44
El Guero (Nac-cogé, Chokonen), 1, 177, 180
El Ligero, 79–80
El Padre (Tadiya, Chokonen), 149–150
El Paso del Norte, 105–106
El Quemado (Mescalero), 117, 120–121
El Tabobo, 41–42
El Zurdo (Inclán, Chihene), 82, 105–106, 115, 118
Elías González, José María
  Apache ambush by, 239
  Chokonen peace treaty with, 227–228, 251–252
  T'iisibaan peace treaty with, 226–227
environment, 27, 129–131, 186–187. *See also* drought

equestrian natives, 32–33, 47–48
establecimientos (establishments or settlements), 2, 142–143
  Buena Esperanza, 63–65
  collapse of, 6–7, 10, 202–205
  de paz, 8
  decline of, 173–183
  drunkenness and, 174
  economics of, 6–7, 150
  leadership and, 174–175, 177
  Lipan in, 6–7
  material benefits of, 119–120
  Mescaleros in, 6–7
  in Nueva Vizcaya, 150
  peace and legacy of, 219
  policy changes and, 177–183
  precedents, 62–63
  precursors to, 61–62
  prelude to, 63–65
  presidio supply decline and, 184–189
  protection and, 143, 176
  raiding and, 189–202
  relocation to, 142–143
  Sabinal pueblo and, 175–176
  to Spanish, 142–143
  territory expansion resulting from, 150
Eugenio (Chokonen), 227–228
exiled Apaches, 148–149

Faraon (Faraón) Apaches, 39, 44, 48, 112, 131, 194, 261–262
farming, 26–27
  Chihene, 146–147
  "civilized" and, 8
  drought and, 119–120
  in Mexican-Apache relations, 237–238
  peace negotiations and, 81–82
  Spanish military's targeting of Apache crops and, 115–116
  in U.S.-Apache relations, 255–256
Fernández de la Fuente, Juan, 40–43, 45–46
firearms
  Apaches' use of, 30–31, 159
  French, 30–31, 73
  Indians' use of, 41, 73
  Mexican, 222, 231, 238
  Spanish, 30–31, 196
  U.S., 199–200, 218, 250
flooding, 91
Flores, Nicolás, 69–70

Florida Mountains (Sierra Florida), 36, 38, 115, 180, 232
Fort Thorn, 255–256
Fort Webster, 255
Franciscan priests, 65, 68–69
Francisquillo (Chihene), 224, 234–235, 237, 251
Fronteras presidio
  Apache prisoners at, 154–155, 226, 256
  Apache raiding at, 76, 235
  Apaches de paz at, 158, 174, 177, 227
  Apaches negotiating peace at, 75–76, 105, 120–121, 227, 256
  source of firearms, 213, 217–218
frontiers, comparative, 5, 8–9, 94, 141–142. *See also* borderlands, comparative
Fuerte (Chihene), 220–223

Galeana (San Buenaventura), 216, 239–240, 251
Gálvez, Bernardo de, 8–10
  on Apache raids, 123
  on Chihene-Tarahumara alliance, 126
  Indian policy of, 106–107, 133
  "Instructions for Governing the Interior Provinces of New Spain," 105–107, 123, 133
Gálvez, José de, 86–87, 106–107, 110
gambling, 156–157
gangs. *See quadrillas*
García Conde, Alejo, 197, 218, 235–236, 252
García Conde, Francisco, 232–234
Geronimo (Goyahkla, Chihene), 7–8, 252–253
Gervacio (son of Juan José Compá), 253
gift giving, 120–121
  at Janos presidio, 181–183
  Nava's policy change, 181–183
Gila (Gileño) Apaches, 38. *See also* Chihene Gila Apaches; Xila Apaches
Gila River
  American trappers and traders on, 200–201, 217–218
  Apaches living along, 36–37, 42–43, 220–221, 233–234, 256
  as part of Apachería, 220–221, 228–229
Gómez (Mescalero), 218, 239
González, José María, 145
González, Joseph, 69–70
Great Southwestern Revolt, 65
  Apaches in, 31–45
  missions and, 33–35
  native allies in, 32–36
  near Parral, 33
  O'odham uprising in, 41–42
  peace agreement, 36–38
  peace negotiations, 41–43, 45–48
  raiding in, 35, 40–41
  resettlement post-, 46–47
  Spanish punitive expeditions, 36–38
Gutiérrez, Joaquín, 144

Hispanicization, 10, 145–146, 154
  of Chokonen, 143–144
  morals and, 156–157
  on reservations, 143–144
Hopis, 26–27
horses, 28–30. *See also* livestock
  as gifts, 120–121
  raiding, 32–33, 159–160
  as rations, 181–182
  trading, 32–33
  wild, 127
hostilities
  Apache, 38–41, 129–130
  Spanish, 129–130
hunting, 25, 159–160

Indian policy, 8–9
  establecimiento precedents, 62–63
  extradition of Apaches, 148–149
  gender and, 8
  "Instructions for Governing the Interior Provinces of New Spain," 106–107, 133
  inter-tribal wars and, 106–107
  Mescaleros and, 92–93
  military and, 74–75
  Nava's changes to, 177–183
  on peace, 81–82, 106–107
  on presidio settlements, 77–79
  royal order of 1779, 86–87
  of Spain, 28–31
  Spanish-indigenous alliances and, 112–116
  U.S., 256–257
  violence and, 62–63
  warfare and, 80–84, 106–107
indigenous military pressure, 84–86, 128–129
"Instructions for Governing the Interior Provinces of New Spain" (Gálvez, B.), 105–107, 123, 133

intermarriage, 24–25, 33–36, 42, 71, 105,
    153–154, 222
intertribal alliances, 126–127. *See also*
    specific tribes
    quadrillas, 125
    raiding and, 126–127
    threat of, 159
intertribal relations, 141–142. *See also*
    specific tribes
intertribal wars, 47–48
    Apache pueblo settlements and, 84–86
    Indian policy and, 106–107
    Mexican-Apache relations and, 227
Iroquois, 8
Itán (Chihene), 223, 233–234, 251,
    253–254

Janero Apaches, 217, 219, 226–227,
    252
Janos
    Chihene alliance with, 35–36
    in Great Southwestern Revolt, 33–35, 41
    peace negotiations, 45–46
    resettlement post-Great Southwestern
        Revolt, 46–47
Janos presidio, Nueva Vizcaya, 1–2, 189
    Apaches de paz annual expenditures at,
        190–191
    baptisms in, 165
    corruption at, 183, 185, 187
    demographic expansion of, 152–153
    expenses at, 182
    garrison strength of, 187–189
    gift giving at, 181–183
    land dispossession and, 202–203
    leadership at, 177
    officer negligence at, 182–183
    policy of removal at, 180
    rations at, 181–183, 185, 187, 189
    reservation near, 1
    shortages at, 186–189
    smallpox outbreak at, 238–239
    supply problems, 172–173
    supply shortages at, 186–187
Jasquedegá (Chihene), 216
Jasquenelté (Chihene), 146
Jesuits, 46–47
Jicarilla Apaches, 21–22, 29
    Catholic conversion of, 65–68
    Spanish relations with, 39–40, 113
Jirónza, Domingo, 40–42
Jocomes, 42–43

    in Great Southwestern Revolt, 41
    peace negotiations, 45–46
    resettlement post-Great Southwestern
        Revolt, 46–47
Johnson, John J., 213–215
Johnson Massacre, 10–11, 213–215
Juan Tuerto (Mescalero), 63–64, 88–89
Jumanos, 27, 29
Justiniani, Cayetano, 220–221, 223

Kino, Eusebio, 38, 41–42, 46–47
Kirker, James, 232–234, 239–240

La Junta de los Rios, 61–63, 65–66, 79,
    105–106
Lafora, Nicolás de, 127
Lane, William Carr, 255
leadership
    in *establecimientos*, 174–175, 177
    at Sabinal pueblo, 175
Lipan (Ypande) Apaches, 29
    Caddoans and, 84–86
    Catholicism and, 21–22
    Comanches and, 196–197
    in *establecimientos*, 6–7
    Mescalero fighting with, 85–86, 106–107
    missions, 68–69
    peace negotiations, 70
    peace with, 122–123, 160–161
    Santa Cruz de San Sabá mission, 71–73
    in Spanish military-run reservations, 2
    Spanish relations with, 39–40, 192–193
liquor, 145–146, 174, 227, 237–238. *See
    also* alcohol
livestock
    rations of, 155
    stolen, 129–130
livestock raids, 201–202, 253
    Apaches de paz, 159–160
    Chihene, 32–33
    Comanche, 196
    coordinated, 126–127
    in Great Southwestern Revolt, 35, 40–41
    in Nueva Vizcaya, 127
    retaliatory, 127
    wild horse herds from, 127

maize, 19, 26–28, 39, 62, 71, 147, 187
Mangas Coloradas (Chihene), 244, 250,
    256–257
    U.S.-Chihene peace negotiations and,
        255–256

Mansos
  Chihene alliance with, 35–36
  in Great Southwestern Revolt, 33–35, 41
  peace negotiations, 45–46
Manuel (Chihene), 233–234
Manuel Cabeza (Mescalero), 91–93
Marcelo (Chokonen), 227–228, 236
Martínez, José María, 227
Matías (Chokonen), 227–228, 236
McKnight, Robert, 232–233
men, 25
  Indian policy with, 8
  peace negotiations and, 81–82
Merino, Manuel, 193–194
mescal, 25–26, 50–51, 116
Mescalero Apaches, 29, 159
  at Buena Esperanza, 63–65, 87–93
  Caddoans and, 84–86
  Catholicism and, 21–22
  Comanches and, 117, 128–129, 141, 196–197
  in *establecimientos*, 2, 6–7
  Lipan fighting with, 85–86, 106–107
  livestock raids by, 127
  Mexican peace negotiations with, 233
  Mexican peace treaty with, 230
  Muñoz and, 88–89
  Nava and, 192–193
  peace negotiations, 79–80, 89–91, 105–106, 117–118
  peace with, 160–161
  at Presidio del Norte, 117–118
  presidio settlements and, 192
  "pueblos formales," 61–62
  raiding by, 91–92
  revolts, 179
  Spanish relations with, 9–10, 39–40, 192–193
Mescaleros de paz, 91–92, 159, 193–194, 197–199
Mexican military, 218–219
Mexican War of Independence, 6, 184–185
  Apache raiding and, 151, 194
  raiding during, 194–195
  reservation supply problems and, 172–173
Mexican-Apache relations, 200–202. *See also specific tribes*
  Apache raids in, 218
  Apaches de paz and, 216, 253
  in Chihuahua, 231–234
  death and dissolution in, 238–240
  farming in, 237–238
  inter-tribal wars and, 227
  Johnson Massacre and, 213–215
  kinship in, 235–236
  livestock raids and, 253
  peace treaties and, 220–222, 251–252
  rations and, 222–223, 237
  resettlement and, 231–238
  Santa Fe peace negotiations and, 231–233
  Santa Rita del Cobre massacre, 224–226
  Santa Rita del Cobre peace treaty and, 223–226
  treachery in, 217, 239–240, 252–253
  U.S. and, 217–218
  U.S.–Mexican War and, 250
  violence in, 216–219, 236, 252–253
  "War of a Thousand Deserts," 217–219
Mexico. *See also* Sonora, Mexico
  Apaches and, 200
  exiled Apaches in, 148–149
  territory, 228–229
  U.S. war with, 250
Miguel (Chokonen), 227–228
military-run reservations
  Spanish, 2, 131
  U.S., 131, 254–255
Mimbres Mountains (Sierra de las Mimbres), 1, 110–111, 146, 218, 220–221, 228–229, 262
Mimbres River, 221, 224, 231, 255
mining, 151–152
misplaced violence, 253
missionized tribes, 63–64
missions, 65–75, 151. *See also specific missions*
  economics of, 71
  Great Southwestern Revolt and, 33–35
  Lipan, 68–69
  locations of, 71, 73
  peace negotiations and, 68–69
  reservations compared with, 106
Mogollon Mountains
  Apaches living in, 32, 39, 223–224, 235
  Mexican mining and military in, 151–152, 217, 235, 239
  as part of Apachería, 5–6, 220–221, 262
Monterde, José Mariano, 235–236
morals, Hispanicization and, 156–157
moros de paz, 9–10, 62–63, 94, 142–143
Muñoz, Manuel, 63–64, 88–89, 151

Namiquipa, 122, 128, 150, 220, 239–240
nantan, 1–2, 24–25. *See also specific nantans*
Napachuli (Chihene), 175
Narbona, Antonio, 151, 239
Natagé Apaches, 79–80. *See also* Mescalero Apaches
Nations of the North (Norteños), 72–74, 81, 83–85, 184–185, 199. *See also* Caddoans; Caddos; Wichitas
Nava, Pedro de, 8
  on baptisms, 147
  "confidential order," 177–178
  El Compá and, 154–155
  Mescaleros and, 192–193
  policy changes implemented by, 177–183
  policy of removal, 178–181
  on relocation program, 142–143
Navajos. *See* Diné
Navicaje (T'iisibaan), 226–227
Ndé. *See* Apaches
Nednhi (Apaches), 252–253
Negrito (Chihene), 236
New Mexico. *See also geographical features; individual towns*
  Catholic conversion of Apaches in, 19–23, 65–66
  Mexican-Apache relations in, 230–231
  as part of Apachería, 1, 5–6, 19–21, 38, 221, 228, 231
  Spanish-Indian relations in, 111–114, 141–142, 153, 175–176, 197
New Spain
  demographic expansion of, 152–153, 161
  frontier, 151, 160–161
  "Instructions for Governing the Interior Provinces of New Spain," 105–107, 123, 133
  Spain's economy and, 184–185
North Africa, Spanish in, 62–63, 142–143
Nuestra Señora de la Candelaria mission, 73–74
Nueva Vizcaya, 10. *See also* Janos presidio, Nueva Vizcaya
  establecimientos in, 150
  in Great Southwestern Revolt, 35–36
  livestock raids in, 127
  "pueblos formales" in, 61–62
  quadrillas in, 125

O'Conor, Hugo, 80, 110–111
Ojos Colorados (Yangongli, Chihene), 116, 129–131, 155–156, 180, 201, 236

O'odham
  as auxiliary troops, 111–112
  peace negotiations with, 46–47
  Spanish alliance with, 47
  uprising, 41–42, 46–47
Ópatas, 47, 111–112
Organ Mountains, 80, 117, 158–159, 261–262

Parral, 33–35, 40, 79, 125–126
Parrilla, Diego Ortiz, 63, 71–73
Pascual (ancestral Mescalero), 79–80
Patule (Mescalero), 63–64, 90, 92–93
Pawnees, 176
peace, 105, 122–123
  adaptation to, 154–160
  captive Apaches and, 121–122, 129
  Comanches and, 153
  by deceit, 123
  in eastern New Spain, 160–161
  economics of, 93–94
  environment and, 129–131
  establecimientos and, 219
  fruits of, 119–122
  gift giving and, 120–121
  "Golden Age" of, 160
  Indian policy and, 81–82, 106–107
  indigenous military pressure and, 128–129
  information and, acquiring, 122–123
  with Lipans, 160–161
  material benefits of, 131
  with Mescaleros, 117–118, 160–161
  in Mexican-Apache relations, 231–238
  motives for, 117, 122–131, 230
  partial, legacy of, 160–162
  persistent, 219–231
  policy of removal and, 179–180
  protection and, 107–119
  by purchase, 94
  rations and, 119–120
  semisedentary Apaches and, 131
  Spanish and, 39–40, 128–129, 144–154, 193–194
  Spanish military pressure and, 117–118, 128–129
  in Spanish military-run reservations, 131
  Spanish-Apache relations and, 142
  trade passports and, 121

U.S.-Apache relations and, 254
warfare and, 107–111, 142
peace negotiations, 45–46, 81–82
  with Anza, 76–79
  at Buena Esperanza, 89–91
  Chihene, 46–47, 80, 82–84, 105–106
  Chihene Mimbres, 118–119, 126–127
  Chokonen, 105, 118–119
  farming and, 81–82
  Great Southwestern Revolt, 41–43, 45–48
  Mexican-Apache, at Santa Fe, 231–233
  Mexican-Chihene, 232–233, 252–253
  Mexican-Chihene Gila, 233–234
  Mexican-Mescalero, 233
  with O'odham, 46–47
  U.S.-Chihene, 255–256
peace treaties
  Buena Esperanza, 63–64
  Mexican-Apache, 220–222, 251–252
  Mexican-Chihene Mimbres, 221–222, 228–230
  Mexican-Chokonen, 227–228, 251–252
  Mexican-Mescalero, 230
  Mexican-T'iisibaan, 226–227
  presidio, 75–80
  Santa Rita del Cobre, 223–226
peaceful Apaches. *See* Apaches de paz
Pima Rebellion, 65
Pimas. *See* Akimel O'odham; O'odham; Sobaipuri O'odham
Pinal Apaches. *See* T'iisibaan; Western Apaches
Pinaleño Mountains (Sierra Santa Rosa de la Florida), 38–39, 43
Pisago Cabezón (Chihene), 224–225, 233–234
Plains Apaches, 28–30, 32, 39, 69, 81
poblaciones, 75–76
political instability
  Comanche, 176
  Navajo, 176
  in reservations, 158
  in Spanish-native alliances, 176
  supply shortages and, 184–186
Ponce (Chihene), 232–233, 237, 239–240, 252–255
Ponce de León, Mariano, 224–225, 232–233, 239–240, 246–247
Presidio del Norte, 9–10
  benefits of, 88–89

Mescaleros at, 105–106, 117–118
rations issued at, 119–120
presidios. *See also specific presidios*
  Apache peace pacts at, 75–80
  Apache raiding routes and, 123
  Apache removal from, policy of, 178–181
  Apaches settled near, 75–76, 189–192
  Indian policy and settlements near, 77–79
  Mescaleros and, 192
  military defense of, 6–7
  reservations and, 7–8
  supply, decline in, 184–189
protection, 107–119, 143, 176
Pueblo Revolt, 31–45, 65
pueblos, 80–84, 95. *See also specific pueblos*
  Croix and, 103
  Indigenous and Spanish military pressure, 84–86
  royal order of 1779 and, 86–87
Pueblos, 27
  agricultural practices, 26–27
  Apaches and, 31–32, 43–44
  as auxiliary troops, 111–112
  Spanish and, 28–29, 47

quadrillas (gangs), 125–127
Quijuiyatle (T'iisibaan), 226–227

raids, 6–8, 29–30, 76. *See also* livestock raids
  coordinated, 126–127
  drought and, 29–30
  establecimientos and, 189–202
  exaggeration of, 123
  in Great Southwestern Revolt, 35, 40–41
  livestock, 201–202
  Mescalero, 91–92
  Mexican War of Independence and, 151, 194–195
  Mexican-Apache relations and, 218
  missions and, 68–69
  on Ópatas, 47
  peace and continuing, 123
  periods of, 202
  policy of removal and, 178–179
  presidio locations and, 123
  resource, 199–200
  revenge, 47
  seasonal, 44–45, 47
  in Sonora, 200
  Spanish-Apache relations and, 69

raids (cont.)
  strategies, 40–41
  Tarahumara, 125–126
Ramírez, Andrés, 65–68
rancheros, 151
rations, 1–2
  adaptation to, 155–156
  at Bacoachi pueblo, 119–120
  of breeding animals, 155
  at Buena Esperanza, 89–91
  corruption in dispensing, 185
  discontinuation of, 204
  drought and, 119–120
  economics of, 156, 161
  flooding and, 91
  horses as, 181–182
  at Janos presidio, 181–183, 185, 187, 189
  Mexican-Apache relations and, 222–223, 237
  in Mexican-Chihene Mimbres peace treaty, 229
  Nava's policy change, 181–183
  at Presidio del Norte, 119–120
  reasons for seeking, 119–120
  scaling back of, 181–183
  shortages, 155–156, 159–160, 172–173
  value of, 187
religion. See Catholicism; Christianization; spiritual power
relocation
  to *establecimientos*, 142–143
  to reservations, 10
  Spanish military pressure and, 10
removal, policy of, 178–181
  Apache raids and, 178–179
  at Janos presidio, 180
  peace and, 179–180
  at Sabinal, 180–181
  trading and, 179
Rengel, José Antonio, 117
reservations. See also *establecimientos*
  adaptations to, 2–5
  benefits of, 143–144
  commanders at, 151
  complications of, 161–162
  diplomacy on, 162
  economics of, 10
  infectious disease outbreaks on, 158, 203–204
  Janos presidio, 1
  leadership at, 177

Mexican War of Independence and, 172–173
  missions compared with, 106
  moving off, 158–159
  politics on, 158
  presidios and, 7–8
  relocation/resettlement to, 10
  Spain's economy and, 161
  Spanish policy towards, 9–10
  system, 10
  U.S.-run, 254–255
resettlement
  Mexican-Apache relations and, 231–238
  policy of removal and, 179–180
  post-Great Southwestern Revolt, 46–47
  reasons for voluntary Apache, 106
  to reservations, 10
revenge raids, 47
Reyes, 227–228, 239–240
Rio Grande
  Apache resettlement along, 61, 66, 71, 80, 117, 131, 146–149
  Apache-Mexican trading along, 228–229
  Apaches living along, 84–85, 179, 197, 261
Ronquillo, José Ignacio, 216, 228–230, 245
rumors, 154

Sabinal pueblo, 146–147
  collapse of, 175–176
  leadership crisis at, 175
  policy of removal at, 180–181
Sacramento Mountains, 85, 117, 197, 220–221
Saeta, Francisco Xavier, 41–42
Salazar, Damasio, 231–233
Salcedo, Nemesio, 184–185, 195
San Antonio, villa of
  Mexican-Indian relations at, 195–197, 202
  Spanish-Indian relations at, 68–71, 79–80, 112–113, 184
  war councils at, 80–81
San Antonio de Béxar presidio, 68–69, 195
San Antonio de Valero (mission), 68–72
San Buenaventura presidio (Galeana)
  Apaches de paz at, 105–106, 150, 186, 204–205, 216, 220–221, 234–235, 237–238
  Apaches negotiating peace at, 82, 118–119, 126
San Carlos presidio, 89, 92–93, 117–118

San Elizario presidio, 192–193, 197–199
San Lorenzo de la Santa Cruz mission, 73–74
San Mateo Mountains, 146, 175, 222, 228–229, 262
San Xavier del Bac mission, 41–42, 44–45, 151
Sanaba (Chihene), 19–21
Sánchez Vergara, Antonio, 233–236, 239
Santa Cruz de San Sabá mission, 71–73
Santa Fe, villa of
  Mexican-Indian relations at, 231–233, 238
  Spanish reoccupation of, 44
  Spanish-Indian relations at, 21–22, 39, 111, 146, 181, 196
Santa Fe presidio, 82, 113
Santa Lucia Springs, 220–221, 228
Santa Rita del Cobre
  massacre at, 224–226
  mining community, 151–152
  peace treaty at, 223–226
Santa Rita mines, 200–201, 221–222, 231
Sargento (Chihene), 234–235, 254
scalp bounty, 10–11, 216
scouts, Apache, 144–145, 257
semisedentary Apaches, 2–5, 75–76
  agricultural practices of, 26–27
  independence of, 131
  peace and, 131
Senecú Pueblo, 19–22, 29–30
settlements. *See establecimientos*
shortages
  cigar, 186
  corn, 187
  currency, 186
  environmental changes and, 186–187
  at Janos presidio, 186–189
  political and economic instability causing, 184–186
  rations, 155–156, 159–160, 172–173
  starvation and, 187
  supply, 184–189
Shoshones, 27
Sierra Blanca, 66, 82, 84–85, 113–114, 261
Sierra del Alamo Hueco, 80, 180, 202–203, 232
Sierra del Hacha, 80, 110–111, 180
Sierra Madre, 5–6, 62, 105–108, 116, 125–127, 262
Siete Rios Apaches, 35–36
slave trade, 28

slaves, 33, 68–69, 149–150
smallpox, 87–88, 210
  at Janos presidio, 238–239
  on reservations, 158, 203–204
Sobaipuri O'odham, 38, 44–45
Solis, Antonio, 41–42
Sonora, 160, 200
Sotelo Osorio, Felipe de, 21–22
Southern Apaches, 2, 24. *See also* Chihene; Chokonen; Nednhi
Spain
  economics of, 161, 184–185
  Indian policy of, 8–9, 28–31
Spaniards
  El Compá and, 145–146
  establecimientos and, 142–143, 150
  intertribal relations and, 141–142
  in North Africa, 62–63
  peace and, 39–40, 144–154, 193–194
  Pueblo contact with, 28–29
  in Pueblo Revolt, 31–32
  territory expansion resulting from *establecimientos*, 150
  vices, 156–157
Spanish empire, 2–5, 9–10, 150
Spanish military
  Apaches and, 28, 84–86, 115–116
  Apaches as scouts for, 144–145
  Apaches de paz and, 6–8, 183
  Apaches in, 145
  auxiliary troops used by, 79–80, 111–112
  Catholicism and, 69–70
  commanders, 151
  drunkenness in, 174
  establecimientos and, 6–7
  Indian policy and, 74–75
  livestock raids and, retaliatory, 127
  peace and, 117–118, 128–129
  presidios and, 6–7
  pressure from, 10, 117–118, 128–129
  in Spanish-Apache relations, 74–75
  tactics, 107–111, 133
Spanish military punitive campaigns, 69–70, 110–111, 142
  Apache raids and retaliatory, 69–70
  Apache revenge for, 158–159
  against Chihene, 113–114
  against Chokonen, 113–114
  Great Southwestern Revolt and, 36–38
  peace and, 128–129

Spanish military-run reservations, 2, 131
Spanish-Apache relations, 7–10, 28. *See also specific tribes*
   Apache attacks and, 128
   Apaches de paz and, 199
   distrust in, 117–118
   military's role in, 74–75
   missions and, 68–69
   Nava's policy changes and, 177–183
   peace and, 119–122, 142
   raiding and, 29–30, 69
   reservation policy and, 9–10
   violence in, 9–11
   warfare and, 107–111
Spanish-native alliances, 44–45, 112–116
   Apaches de paz and, 116–117
   Comanche and, 112–114
   Jicarilla and, 113
   Mescalero and, 88–89
   Navajo and, 113–115
   political instability among, 176
   success of, 115–116
   Tarahumara and, 47
   Ute and, 113
Spanish-native relations, 47, 62–63, 75–76
spiritual power, 21, 30, 65, 68–69, 148, 156–158
spoils from battle, as material benefit, 121
starvation, 187
Steck, Michael, 255–256
stereotypes, Apache, 7–8
Sumas
   Chihene alliance with, 35–36
   in Great Southwestern Revolt, 33–35, 41
   peace negotiations, 45–46
   resettlement post-Great Southwestern Revolt, 46–47

Tarahumara Rebellion, 65
Tarahumaras (Rarámuri)
   Chihene alliance with, 126
   in Great Southwestern Revolt, 35–36
   in *quadrillas*, 125
   raids, 125–126
   Spanish alliance with, 47
Tepehuan Revolt, 65
Tepehuanes, 35–36, 125
Terán de los Rios, Domingo, 41
Terreros, Alonso Giraldo de, 71–73
Texas
   Apache missions in, 65–68

Apache raiding in, 69, 73–74
   Apaches de paz in, 61, 131
   as part of Apachería, 5–6, 48, 127–128
Teyas, 27
T'iisibaan (Pinal) Apaches, 226–227
Topios, 125
Torres (Chihene), 239–240
trade, 27
   contraband, 184–185
   in horses, 32–33
   Mexican-Chihene Mimbres peace treaty and, 229–230
   passports, 121
   policy of removal and, 179
   slave, 28
   of Spanish horses, 28–30
Treaty of Guadalupe Hidalgo, 250, 254
Tsézhiné (Aravaipa) Apaches, 2
Tubac, 111, 153–154, 199–200
Tucson, 153–154, 226–227
Tuerto, Juan, 63–64, 88–89
Tumacácori mission, 151
Tupatú, Luis, 32
Tuscon, 153–154, 226–227
Tutijé (Southern Apache), 217, 226

Ugalde, Juan de, 92–94, 108–110, 117–118, 144
Ugarte, Jacobo, 117, 125–126
   auxiliary troops led by, 155
   captive Apaches and, 121–122
   peace and, 122–123
   peace negotiations, 118–119
   on punitive expeditions, 128–129
   Sabinal pueblo and, 175
United States
   Indian policy of, 8–9, 256–257
   weaponry, 200–201
Urrea, José, 236
U.S. military, Apache scouts in, 257
U.S. military-run reservations, 131, 254–255
U.S.-Apache relations, 7–8, 254–258
   accommodation of Apaches in, 257–258
   Chihene peace negotiations and, 255–256
   farming in, 255–256
   Mexican-Apache relations and, 217–218
   peace and, 254
   traders and trappers, 200–201
   U.S.-run reservations and, 254–255

U.S.-Mexican War, 250
Utes, 27, 113

Valle, Dionisio, 182–183
Valtasar el Chino (Chokonen), 251–252
Vaquero Apaches, 21–22, 25, 28
Varela, Mariano, 216, 220–221
Vargas, Diego de, 28, 36–39, 43–44
Velarde, Luis, 46–47
Velasco, José Ortiz de, 65–68
Vergara, Domingo de, 105, 118–119
Vergara, Gabriel de, 68–69
vices, Apache adaptation to Spanish, 156–157
violence, 27–28
   Apache-Pueblo, 31–32
   in Chihuahua, 239–240
   Indian policy and, 62–63
   Johnson Massacre, 213–215
   in Mexican-Apache relations, 216–219, 236, 252–253
   misplaced, 253
   in Pueblo Revolt, 31–32
   raiding, 29–30
   Santa Rita del Cobre massacre, 224–226
   in Spanish-Apache relations, 9–11
Vívora (Antonio Vivora, Chihene), 1, 128, 215, 217, 223, 234–235, 251
Volante (Mescalero), 141

"War of a Thousand Deserts", 217–219
warfare, 27–28. *See also* intertribal wars; specific wars
   economics of, 93–94
   Indian policy and, 80–84, 106–107
   peace and, 142
   scalp bounty, 216
   Spanish military tactics, 107–111, 133
weaponry, 25, 30–31
   American-made, 200–201
   Apache (Ndé), 25, 30–31, 40–41, 126
   Chihuahua arms factory, 184
Western Apaches, 2, 24, 38. *See also* T'iisibaan; Tsézhiné
Wichitas, 29
wild horses, 127
women, 25–26
   Indian policy with, 8
   peace negotiations and, 81–82
   as scouts for Spanish military, 144–145

Xila Apaches, 19–21. *See also* Chihene Gila Apaches; Gila Apaches

Yrigollen (Chokonen), 251–253

Zapato Tuerto (Quijiequsyá, Mescalero), 92–93, 117–118

For EU product safety concerns, contact us at Calle de José Abascal, 56–1°,
28003 Madrid, Spain or eugpsr@cambridge.org.

www.ingramcontent.com/pod-product-compliance
Lightning Source LLC
LaVergne TN
LVHW091530060526
838200LV00036B/554